Further Acclaim for
Canada: A New Tax Haven
by Alain Deneault

Essential reading … Deneault illuminates the blowback
effect of Caribbean tax havens becoming, in the hands of
big banks and transnational business, a powerful lever for
dismantling a century of social progress and democracy
itself at home – in this case, in Canada.

—HAROLD CROOKS
DIRECTOR, *THE PRICE WE PAY*

Rigorously decrypts the mechanisms that have led Canada
to adopt "laws of convenience" that are nothing more than
criminogenic legal tools enabling their users to circumvent
the obligations and rules that underpin the law states.

—CHANTAL CUTAJAR
EUROPEAN COLLEGE OF FINANCIAL INVESTIGATIONS
AND ANALYSIS OF FINANCIAL CRIMES (CEIFAC)

Deneault shows that the tax-haven problem is not simply
a problem of illegal tax evasion or money laundering by
the underground economy or criminal gangs but a much
larger issue of how the Canadian state has legalized the use
of tax havens by large corporations so that they can evade
paying their fair share of taxes.

—DENNIS HOWLETT
CANADIANS FOR TAX FAIRNESS

D1547824

CANADA

A NEW TAX HAVEN

■ ALSO BY ALAIN DENEAULT

Imperial Canada Inc.: Legal Haven of Choice for the World's Mining Industries, with William Sacher. Vancouver: Talonbooks, 2012.

Offshore: Tax Havens and the Rule of Global Crime. New York and London: The New Press, 2011.

Paul Martin & Companies: Sixty Theses on the Alegal Nature of Tax Havens. Vancouver: Talonbooks, 2006.

■ IN FRENCH

"Gouvernance": Le management totalitaire. Montreal: Lux, 2013.

Faire l'économie de la haine. Douze essais pour une pensée critique. Montreal: Écosociété, 2011.

Noir Canada. Pillage, corruption, et criminalité en Afrique, with Delphine Abadie and William Sacher. Montreal: Écosociété, 2008.

CANADA
A NEW TAX HAVEN

How the Country That Shaped Caribbean
Offshore Jurisdictions Is Becoming One Itself

ALAIN DENEAULT

with the assistance of
Aaron Barcant, Catherine Browne, Pierre-Antoine Cardinal, Mathieu Denis,
Normand Doutre, Gabriel Monette, Stéphane Plourde, Ghislaine Raymond,
Pierre Roy, William Sacher, Alexandre Sheldon, and Aline Tremblay

OF RÉSEAU POUR LA JUSTICE FISCALE

TRANSLATED BY CATHERINE BROWNE

TALONBOOKS

Talonbooks
278 East First Avenue, Vancouver, British Columbia, Canada V5T 1A6
www.talonbooks.com

First printing: 2015

Typeset in Minion
Printed and bound in Canada on 100% post-consumer recycled paper

Interior and cover design by Typesmith

Talonbooks acknowledges the financial support of the Canada Council for the Arts, the Government of Canada through the Canada Book Fund, and the Province of British Columbia through the British Columbia Arts Council and the Book Publishing Tax Credit.

This work was originally published in French as *Paradis fiscaux: la filière canadienne. Barbade, Caïmans, Bahamas, Nouvelle-Écosse, Ontario…* by Éditions Écosocieté, Montreal, Quebec, in 2014. We acknowledge the financial support of the Government of Canada, through the National Translation Program, for our translation activities.

LIBRARY AND ARCHIVES CANADA CATALOGUING IN PUBLICATION

Deneault, Alain, 1970–, author
     Canada : a new tax haven : how the country that shaped Caribbean tax havens is becoming one itself / Alain Deneault ; translated by Catherine Browne.

Translation of: Paradis fiscaux : la filière canadienne : Barbade, Caïmans, Bahamas, Nouvelle-Écosse, Ontario.
Includes bibliographical references and index.
Issued in print and electronic formats.
ISBN 978-0-88922-836-8 (PBK.). – ISBN 978-0-88922-837-5 (EPUB)

     1. Tax havens – Canada. 2. Tax shelters – Canada. 3. Tax havens – West Indies.
4. Tax shelters – West Indies. I. Browne, Catherine, 1958–, translator II. Title.

HJ2337.C3D4613 2015   336.2'06   C2014-907421-2
                                                C2014-907422-0

Nobody knows what democracy really is,
but many know what it is not.

— FRANÇOIS-XAVIER VERSCHAVE

■ CONTENTS

◼ TABLES AND ILLUSTRATIONS

◼ ILLUSTRATIONS

◼ TABLES

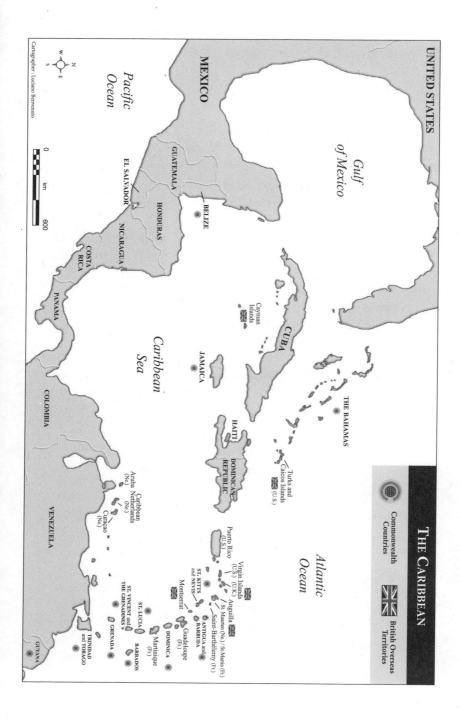

HEADLONG FLIGHT

In which investigative journalists release massive amounts
of data about owners of secret tax haven accounts, and
the Canadian finance minister hastens to Bermuda

On April 4, 2013, members of the International Consortium of
Investigative Journalists (ICIJ) in countries throughout the world
announced that they had gained access to the financial records of
over 100,000 investors with bank accounts in tax havens. Among the
ICIJ members were CBC and Radio-Canada journalists, who covered
the story at the national level.[1] This was by far the most spectacular
leak of offshore data the world had ever seen, but it was not the first.
In 2008, a systems engineer working for the HSBC Bank in Geneva,
Hervé Falciani, had given French authorities details of thousands of
accounts held by his bank,[2] and that same year, German tax authorities
had intercepted information about tax evaders in Liechtenstein.[3] In
short, although information on this topic is still relatively sparse, bank
secrecy is no longer as impenetrable as it once was.

By the time investigative journalists unleashed their thunderbolt,
the home states of major clients of offshore banks had already begun
to take action. After years of leniency, in March 2010 the United States
suddenly enacted the Foreign Account Tax Compliance Act, familiarly
known as FATCA. This law requires banks throughout the world "to
track down those who are evading American tax laws throughout all
of their subsidiaries and to take disciplinary action against them on
behalf of the United States tax authorities."[4] In 2013, the year FATCA
came into force, France was setting up a judicial body specializing in
international tax fraud[5] and tightening supervision of assets held by
elected politicians,[6] while the British government unexpectedly threatened to exceed its constitutional powers in order to challenge the bank
secrecy clauses defended by a number of highly permissive jurisdictions
under the direct authority of the British Crown.[7]

The Canadian government could not remain indifferent to this issue. By 2012, Canadians had "invested" more than $155 billion in seven offshore tax havens.[8] Under this practice of tax avoidance, citizens are deprived of money to fund public services, and the state as defender of the common good looks like a joke. Like its neighbours, Canada started by announcing a program to track those guilty of "fraud"[9] – or such at least was its ostensible purpose as it threatened to sue CBC journalists to make them disclose the information they had obtained.[10] The government also tabled a budget that closed a few peripheral loopholes,[11] then announced it would increase funding for the department in charge of detecting tax swindlers.[12] Having taken these measures, Ottawa felt entitled to include in its budget anticipated revenues from Canadians abroad amounting to $5.2 to $7 billion a year.[13]

The chief effect of all these decisions, however, was to transform a political debate into a legal issue. Focusing on tax cheats is a way of taking attention away from the fact that, for decades, Canada has been legalizing the use of tax havens under a wide range of circumstances and has also looked to them for inspiration in developing its own policies.

The federal government's real response to CBC and ICIJ revelations was expressed on April 12, 2013, when Finance Minister Jim Flaherty hastened to Bermuda to reassure the business community there. Flaherty was welcomed with open arms by Business Bermuda, an association dedicated to the promotion of investment in the archipelago. Bermuda, one of the most overtly criticized tax havens in the world, is also one of the states that has signed a Tax Information Exchange Agreement (TIEA) with Canada.[14] TIEAs may pierce the bank secrecy of permissive jurisdictions under some (rare) circumstances. Their chief purpose, however, is to enable Canadians to use these jurisdictions to register assets generated in Canada; the assets can then be transferred back to Canada as dividends, on which no tax is paid. The stratagem is made possible by Canadian tax regulations associated with TIEAs. As a consequence, by 2012, Canadians had moved close to $12 billion to Bermuda.[15] Flaherty's 2013 trip to Bermuda was intended to consolidate commercial relations between the financial establishments of the two countries.[16] During his visit, the finance minister acknowledged Bermuda as a "global leader" in the reinsurance field.[17] As we will see, hundreds of companies in the wider insurance field have incorporated in Bermuda in order to bypass the tax policies and regulations of countries such as Canada. The minister trivialized the relocation of a colossally profitable economic sector, which, at a moment when the world was becoming acutely conscious of the severity of the relocation problem, was nothing short of provocative.

What became clear in the spring of 2013 was that the Canadian federal government's policy is to *fight tax fraud by legalizing it*. The government simultaneously condemns the fraudulent use of tax havens and encourages their legal use by corporations and the very rich; in some cases, it even provides these users with benefits. As sociologist Pierre Bourdieu argues, the left hand of the state doesn't know what the right hand is doing. The principles that lead the government to fight tax fraud are obviously contradicted by measures that incite corporations and wealthy individuals legally to benefit from highly permissive legislative and jurisdictional regimes. And in order to satisfy the financial and industrial class whose interests are represented in Ottawa, Canada is now working unobtrusively to legalize what was formerly viewed as fraud.

TAX HAVENS AND HIGHLY PERMISSIVE JURISDICTIONS

A *tax haven* is commonly defined as a jurisdiction whose tax rate is or approaches zero and whose legal system (not that its unworthy rules really deserve to be known as "laws") creates a level of bank secrecy that conceals the identity of account holders as well as the nature of their transactions. No substantial activity takes place in a tax haven: its jurisdiction is used strictly for accounting and legal purposes to avoid laws and regulations in force elsewhere in the world. In this sense, it is a haven – a safe place – for corporations and "high-net-worth individuals" trying, by legal or illegal means, to avoid paying taxes.

But highly permissive jurisdictions include more than just tax havens. They also include other types of states: states that provide not only tax advantages, but also a wide range of privileges, and especially privileges of a regulatory and legal nature. Working to benefit banks, corporations, and wealthy individuals, these ultra-permissive states neutralize the laws, public policies, and regulations that hold sway in traditional states. We will refer to all these states as *accommodating jurisdictions*, a generic term we suggested in a previous work[18] to include not only tax havens but also legal and regulatory havens, free zones, and free ports. Each of these jurisdictions, of which there are dozens, in its own way enables privileged actors to bypass not only laws of taxation in their country of origin, but also laws applying to many other fields such as high finance, insurance, accounting, intellectual property rights, manufacturing, or maritime transportation.

Another type of activity merits consideration. Criminal trafficking is more likely to flourish in accommodating jurisdictions than in traditional states. The radical permissiveness of the former, established with the assistance of the latter, allows the gangrene of crime to spread. On the world market, political sovereignty is now a commodity. According to economist Raymond W. Baker, "The law in these places can be bought ... What is legal is commercialized by authorities and sold as a product. Many havens and enclaves are niche players in this business of legalizing subterfuge. Tax lawyers go 'treaty shopping' for the most favourable legislation protecting certain types of activities."[19] One such tax consultant, Alex Doulis, actually says that a tax haven is a "jurisdiction that is in the business of providing tax avoidance"[20] when it is designed, for example, to transform a process that should not be legal (*tax evasion*) into one that is (*tax avoidance*). Thus *global governance* pits states against each other as competitors, forcing them to satisfy international capital by every possible means, including extreme deregulation and legalization of acts that are viewed elsewhere as wrongful acts according to the spirit of the law.[21] Summing up the situation, Marie-Christine Dupuis-Danon, an expert long employed by the UN in the fight against money laundering, noted that the offshorization process in which we are now involved is inciting an increasing number of individuals and companies "no longer to ask if an act is wrong *in itself,* but to ask if it can be carried out in a completely legal manner somewhere in the world."[22]

What this means is that tax havens cannot be reduced to a cartoon representation of coconut trees and dazzling beaches on a distant island where anything goes. "Today, the traditional image is being replaced by an image of countries whose laws and tax administration are effective ... in that they have the power to attract. The idea of the tax haven, like any other concept, evolves over time,"[23] writes a group of accountants with a fondness for offshore activity. A less jovial definition that also recognizes the historical evolution of tax havens was provided by tax specialist Richard Gordon. In a report submitted to the White House in 1981, Gordon pointed out that a tax haven is simply any jurisdiction that is viewed as such by those who profit by it.[24] This definition tells us that tax havens aren't necessarily where we think they are. Today, unsuspected jurisdictions can sometimes be detected only by signs such as capital flows – especially when these flows bear no relation to the state of the real economy – or a high number of incorporations.

In the postwar years, many British dependencies and former colonies changed their laws to establish themselves as formal tax havens, but Canada did not do so. Rather, it chose to involve itself with a number of Commonwealth jurisdictions that were becoming tax havens, often instigated by Canadian emissaries and Canadian citizens present in the Caribbean. At home, however, Canada did not adopt comprehensive measures guaranteeing bank secrecy or providing tax-free status for foreign entities choosing to incorporate in Canada without carrying out any real economic activity there. This was to come sector by sector and in small touches, particularly in the extractive industry. During the crucial postwar years, Canada managed to maintain a credible facade, even urging corporate entities (corporations and their subsidiaries) and individuals active in Canada to report on their extraterritorial operations.[25]

In a thousand ways – progressive, subtle, and indirect – Canada has favoured, in recent years, the powerful and wealthy seeking to use tax havens to bypass public constraints. And yet these constraints are precisely what give substance to the principle of rights and freedoms that should apply fairly to all. Today, our country's laws and public policies apply only to citizens belonging to social classes unable to take advantage of the loopholes that our indulgent government has created for the benefit of the powerful.

CANADA, PIONEERING INSTIGATOR
OF CARIBBEAN TAX HAVENS

If we want to understand the relationship between Canada and today's tax havens, we need to understand Canada's direct contribution to the genesis of some of these jurisdictions. Because Canada had trade relations with British dependencies in the Caribbean long before they became tax havens, and because Canadian banks had played a key role in the Caribbean since the early twentieth century, Canada was a major player in their transformation.[26] As we will document in this book, beginning in the 1950s, at the instigation of Canadian financiers, lawyers, and policymakers, these jurisdictions changed to become some of the world's most frighteningly accommodating jurisdictions. In 1955, a former governor of the Bank of Canada most probably helped make Jamaica into a reduced-taxation country. In the 1960s, as the Bahamas was becoming a tax haven characterized by impenetrable bank secrecy, thanks to a former Canadian minister of finance the Bahamian finance minister was a member of the board of administrators of the Royal Bank of Canada (RBC). A Calgary lawyer and former Conservative Party honcho drew up the clauses that enabled the Cayman Islands to become an opaque offshore jurisdiction. Later, in the 1980s, the Canadian government itself made Barbados into the tax shelter of choice for Canadians. Our country has also asserted itself as an imperialist power in states that are notorious drug-trafficking hubs, such as Trinidad and Tobago.

Canada eventually began to experience the impact of creatures that it had helped beget. In the 2000s, the government of Nova Scotia encouraged subsidiaries of Bermudian companies responsible for routine accounting tasks to establish themselves in the province, while the Toronto Stock Exchange acquired a stake in the Bermuda Stock Exchange. Persistent rumours indicated that Canada was about to annex accommodating jurisdictions such as the Turks and Caicos Islands and make them into Canadian territory. Canada also signed a free-trade agreement with Panama, world centre for laundering the proceeds of drug trafficking, and today is attempting to sign similar agreements with all the countries included in the Caribbean political community (CARICOM). A number of Caribbean tax havens currently share Canada's seat at the World Bank and the International Monetary Fund.

Given its history of leniency, it's hardly surprising that Canada is now seen as a tax haven itself. This is a reality that is increasingly difficult to conceal. Not only is the corporate tax rate in Canada one of the lowest in the industrialized world, but some of the loopholes in its laws induce foreign companies to relocate their activities to Canada, just as if it were Luxembourg or Belize.

Early symptoms of Canada's seamless incorporation into the world network of tax havens were described in the early 1990s by investigative and forensic accountant Mario Possamai (who was close to an RCMP source) on the CBC's *Fifth Estate* television program and in his book *Money on the Run: Canada and How the World's Dirty Profits Are Laundered*.[27] Possamai's findings ought to have come as a bombshell; however, his work was quickly set aside. Reading his book even today is enough to send a chill down the spine. One story concerns Haitian kleptocrat Jean-Claude Duvalier and his wife, Michele. When they were forced by popular unrest to leave Haiti on February 7, 1986, their first move was to empty government bank accounts. The Duvaliers, whose colossal fortune is particularly shocking and scandalous in that it originates in a country of extreme poverty, helped themselves even to money owed by the state to foreign institutions. In the 1980s, while nine out of ten children in Haiti were malnourished,[28] two hundred local families had gradually acquired wealth that made them into millionaires.[29] The Duvaliers, as everyone knows, entrusted a significant part of their assets to Swiss banks. In April 1986, the Swiss authorities and courts – at a time when Switzerland was already under scrutiny for similar affairs – took the highly unusual step of freezing the Duvalier accounts.[30] The Duvaliers now "required a fail-safe system for replenishing their cash supply from their deeply buried fortune. And there was a complicating factor. Things were heating up on the legal front."[31] The couple turned to Canada. On September 23, 1986, Alain Le Fort, a lawyer from the Geneva law firm of Patry, Junet, Simon, and Le Fort, showed up at RBC headquarters in Toronto.[32] Le Fort was one of a handful of advisers who had successfully laundered some of the millions that the Duvaliers and their entourage required to enjoy a pleasant life in exile. The goal of these advisers was now to convert into cash a sum of $41.8 million held by their famous clients in Canadian treasury bills. Most importantly, they proposed to do so "without disclosing the funds' origins or owners."[33] The use of Canadian financial documents made the money more difficult to trace, and perhaps more importantly, Canadian treasury bills are the kind of security that doesn't attract the attention of international inspectors because they are seen as respectable. This is how the RCMP and the U.S. Drug Enforcement Agency, in a joint report, explained why the funds had been moved through Canada.[34] To put it in a nutshell, Canada's worthy reputation was for sale.

Once converted into Canadian treasury bills, the Duvaliers' assets could no longer be scrutinized. Internationally, these securities are acknowledged money-laundering tools. "Canadian treasury bills – popular internationally for, among other things, the ease with which they're bought and sold – are virtually anonymous. The Duvaliers' bonds could have been purchased anywhere."[35] Le Fort worked with a Swiss colleague, Jean Patry, and John Stephen Matlin from the British law firm of Turner and Company to take full advantage of the Canadian connection as part of an operation that would involve as many jurisdictions as possible. The dictator's money was moved from Canada to the tax haven of Jersey,[36] where it was received by the Royal Trust Bank, a subsidiary of Canada's Royal Trust Company. A deposit was then made to an account that was part of a larger account held by the Manufacturers Hanover Bank of Canada, a financial institution with its headquarters in Toronto a few steps away from the RBC where the whole operation had been set in motion.[37] The operation became more complex, with securities being split from their ownership records[38] and further movements between the HSBC Bank in Jersey, the RBC in London, the Banque Nationale de Paris, and sundry Swiss institutions.[39] Despite guidelines requiring banks to determine their customers' identity, the RBC admits that it simply relied on the impeccable credentials of the two lawyers, Le Fort and Matlin, who were conducting the operation. The bank later claimed that it would have refused the money had it known who the true beneficiaries were. According to Possamai, "That it did not highlights the limitations of a cornerstone of the strategy used by both the federal government and Canadian banks to combat money laundering." He also says that it is unlikely any other Canadian bank would have turned down the Duvaliers' money,[40] and that all this happened before the 1989 law "intended to crack down on the practice."[41]

An American investigator from the Stroock & Stroock & Lavan firm, sent to Port-au-Prince in 1986 to audit government accounts, remarked with bitter irony that "the exiled Duvaliers were probably better off than they had been in Port-au-Prince: they had all the benefits of the Haitian treasury with none of the headaches of governing."[42] While Haitian government representatives were trying to track down public funds wherever they might be, financial technicians in the Duvaliers' pay "had set up an intricately concealed flow of money through a bevy of banks and accounts, most of them Canadian."[43]

In 1992, then, we already had all the information we needed to understand that Canada – like many other former colonies – was completely incorporated into the network of tax havens that it had played a key role in developing. Today, we are finally tackling the job of studying this phenomenon. Each chapter of this book details the connections established by Canada with one of the tax havens in the British Caribbean, from the late nineteenth century to today. In each case, we identify the agents involved and analyze the offshore stratagems they developed with the help of local authorities, until the time when Canada began to model entire sections of its own laws on this offshore model.

WARNING

The chapters in this book can be read independently of each other; some repetition has been tolerated to make this possible. All the cases described as part of our analysis of the overall issue are based on highly serious investigations involving primary sources such as bank and corporation annual reports, court decisions, governmental department press releases, official publications of international organizations, MPs' circular letters, statements from police sources, journalists' reports on public bodies, government investigations, and Parliamentary reports. Few secondary sources originating in "critical" or "activist" organizations are available on this topic. Throughout we name the public personalities and well-known institutions and companies. We do not believe that a claim to being "scientific" can be based on censorship of the names of those responsible for a given model and those who benefit from it – agents and beneficiaries who would then only be known through portmanteau words approved by the organizations that give research grants. Nor have we found it necessary to summarize their views of the actions attributed to them by our sources, except in cases where, to our knowledge, they provided an official and public response. There are no grounds for viewing this book as defamatory, except possibly in the basic sense of the original word: *diffamare*, to say that something is inglorious. If actors from the legal field have any reason to be concerned with this book, it should be because their professional order is part of the structures of power that have made it possible, in recent years, to transform states into accommodating jurisdictions radically hostile to any democratic principle. May this book enlighten them, and their clients, on this topic.

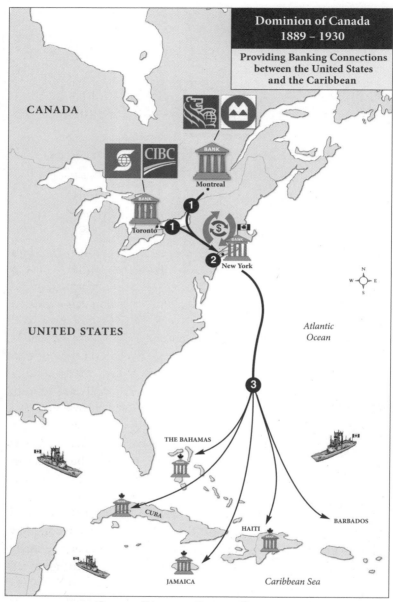

CAPITAL FLOWS TO BRITISH CARIBBEAN
1889 – 1930

THE DOMINION OF CANADA

WELL-OILED BANKING HINGE BETWEEN
THE UNITED STATES AND THE CARIBBEAN

*In which the Bank of Nova Scotia, the Royal Bank of Canada,
and the Canadian Bank of Commerce step in to answer the
needs of American companies in the Caribbean at a time
when American banks are prevented from acting abroad*

What if Canada itself were a regulatory haven before such things were established? What if the activity of Canadian banks in the Caribbean colonies were the prelude to their transformation into tax havens? What if Canadian banks had played an active role in this mutation?

Canadian laws governing private companies were extremely permissive in the early twentieth century, and in 1913 the Parisian daily *L'Humanité*, published by Jean Jaurès, published a series of articles in which Canadian permissiveness was vehemently denounced. On October 16, the paper's description of Canadian laws made the Dominion of Canada sound like one of today's tax havens: "Where corporations are concerned, Canadian law is particularly elastic: it authorizes the most random combinations, giving businessmen the freedom to channel French savings toward more or less fictitious businesses operating in foreign countries."[1]

A European financial scandal was the trigger for this unusual focus on Canadian corporate law. The Barcelona Traction company had been incorporated in Toronto in 1911 on the basis of essentially imaginary share capital. It then entered the Paris Stock Exchange to sell bonds. The company was described as having been "founded in Canada by cosmopolitan American, English, and Belgian parties, against and in opposition to French laws, in order to issue 75 million francs' worth of bonds." *L'Humanité* found the Canadian system astonishing:

"They had to go all the way to Canada to find a jurisdiction that would allow them to create a corporation with a capital of 125 million francs of which not a single share has been subscribed in cash, and whose founders and promoters have not scrupled to assign to themselves 125 million francs' worth of shares. Where do these 125 million francs go? To wheeler-dealers and con artists of international finance..."[2]

L'Humanité attacked again on October 21 and November 1, pointing out that Barcelona Traction's Canadian incorporation was an obstacle to a lawsuit brought against the company in France. The newspaper stood up for French bond holders "swindled out of 75 million francs thanks to methods used on the other side of the Atlantic":

> Twice already, *L'Humanité* has dealt with the Barcelona Traction affair involving a company whose activities are centred in Spain, but whose founders have located its head office in Canada to take advantage of "more convenient" Canadian laws...The affair will not be suppressed, since the complaint filed by bondholders remains. And if by chance this complaint too were smothered, there remains a question about the way in which Canadian laws are used in France by certain financiers – a question that was put several months ago and that the Chamber [of Deputies] will soon be required to discuss. Whatever happens, the Barcelona Traction affair will be brought before the public – this affair and other, similar Canadian affairs that truly deserve to be known.[3]

In other words, in the early twentieth century, Canada was known abroad as the equivalent of one of today's tax havens: an anonymous jurisdiction that attracted foreign head offices because it provided regulatory advantages unequalled by any other country.

▧ FLAGS OF CONVENIENCE

Around the same period, Canadian shipowners inaugurated a system that was to have a profound impact on the management of maritime transportation: the flag of convenience. Like the founders of Barcelona Traction, they took advantage of discrepancies between jurisdictions. In this case, Prohibition in the United States was the source of their profits: "When approaching American territorial waters with barrels of rum in the hold, it was better to fly a foreign flag. The Canadian flag often proved suitable, since America's northern neighbour had not found it necessary to ban alcohol."[4] In some cases, the ships anchored in international waters not far from the U.S. coast and provided gambling facilities and a place to drink. Canada developed a taste for legislative and regulatory attenuations – an intoxicating beverage for the financial class. This maritime practice gave rise to the word *offshore* as it is used today to qualify operations taking place in various accommodating jurisdictions.[5] During the same period a whisky producer, Samuel Bronfman, made a fortune in Canada by massively exporting his production to the United States with the help of smugglers associated with the mafia.[6]

A REGULATORY HAVEN LONG BEFORE THE TERM WAS COINED

In the nineteenth century, businessmen and bankers active in Canada were already operating in an undefined mental space at the junction of the British Empire and the United States. For them, the primary meaning of the word *Canadian* related to the place in which they were incorporated. The Bank of Montreal, for example, was originally a joint venture involving American merchants and the Montreal representatives of major British mercantile houses. Almost half the capital subscribed when the bank was established in 1817 came from the United States,[7] and throughout its early years it exported the colony's most valuable assets to the United States: gold, hard currency, and "the very best paper in the world," that is, pound sterling bills of exchange drawn by the colonial government.[8] Members of Canada's financial establishment presented their institutions abroad as British or American. Coming from nowhere, they could claim to be at home wherever they went.

Nineteenth-century Canada belonged to a coterie of hucksters and wheeler-dealers, and the laxity of Canadian laws is not surprising when you consider who wrote them. Canadian bankers themselves were the authors of the comprehensive act that defined their activities in 1871, and they formulated all its subsequent revisions,[9] just as they later developed, in the Caribbean, the clauses that made these territories into tax havens. The forty-odd men who governed Canada's financial system in the early twentieth century[10] were well aware of their disproportionate power over the country's political life. Because they were so few, they found it easy to co-operate to assure their ascendancy, as the president of the Canadian Bank of Commerce (today's CIBC) ingenuously explained in 1901; he went on to observe sagaciously that American bankers, unfortunately for them, were too numerous to enjoy this advantage.[11]

The prosperous financial oligarchy we are describing was oriented to international investment. In the early twentieth century, Canadian banks owned shares in foreign corporations, invested large amounts in call loans in New York, and opened branches abroad, while Canadian insurance companies invested in the United States and other countries, and Canadian railway companies purchased hundreds of kilometres of railway track in the United States.[12] While officially Canadian, these institutions did not view development in Canada as a priority of any kind: in 1911, Canadian banks owned more foreign (and especially American) securities than Canadian.[13] Despite their colonial moorings, from the start they acted like transnational corporations. The colony's stateless financial rulers assessed investment prospects strictly in terms of profits, following the logic already observed by Karl Marx: "If capital is sent abroad, this is not done because it absolutely could not be applied at home, but because it can be employed at a higher rate of profit in a foreign country."[14]

Shaping the laws that governed them, Canadian financial institutions made sure these laws were permissive. Canadian laws enabled them to act in other countries as "*de facto* American banks" without "the constraints of American banking," according to Duncan McDowall, the official historian of the Royal Bank of Canada (RBC).[15] American national banks were legally forbidden either to accept drafts arising from international transactions or, until 1913, to open branches abroad.[16] As a consequence, even in the United States, their involvement in the foreign exchange market and in financing foreign trade was small.[17] Meanwhile, Canadian banks had been dealing with pound sterling (the main currency of international trade in the nineteenth century) from the moment they were established; in New York, Canadian banks were accustomed to buying and selling bills of exchange in

THE DOMINION OF CANADA

foreign currencies; and under Canadian law, they were allowed to open branches abroad. The forte of Canadian banks was their ability to take advantage of discrepancies between Canadian and American banking laws. In 1874, well-informed observers believed that they might soon channel most of the funds required for the foreign trade of the United States.[18] In the last years of the nineteenth century, Canadian high finance had far more capital than it knew what to do with. Suddenly "awash with cash," chartered banks (whose assets increased fourfold between 1890 and 1910)[19] and Canadian insurance companies were "desperately searching for new vehicles for idle capital."[20] According to Mira Wilkins, in 1914 Canada was the third-greatest recipient of capital in the world after the United States and Russia,[21] but at the same time, Canada also exported large amounts of capital to the United States.[22] The Canadian Bank of Commerce probably financed between one-quarter and one-half of American cotton exports,[23] as well as a significant proportion of the country's exports of grain, lumber, steel, and farm machines.[24]

Canadian banks were in the habit of playing several games at once as they adroitly profited from legislative differences between countries. While acting as "American" banks in other countries, they were "foreign" banks in the United States, which entitled them, in some cases, to fiscal privileges. In the 1880s, for example, the Bank of Nova Scotia enjoyed an informal agreement with the State of Minnesota that reduced its tax payments. The fear of losing this advantage was a significant factor in the bank's decision to close its Minneapolis branch in 1892.[25] At the same time, Canadian banks played a part in the British financial system: they channelled British investments in North American capital assets.[26] In the late 1860s, the Bank of Montreal's London branch was "the coordinating centre for British investments in North America"[27] and was viewed as the bank "responsible for half of the portfolio investments from Great Britain from 1860 to 1914."[28]

The "Canadian" ruling class had always wanted to be part of a ruling class that included both Great Britain and the United States, and to play a pivotal role within this class. London, far more than Canada, was the horizon to which members of the Canadian propertied classes looked. Around 1900, the Bank of Montreal was obliged to adopt a collegial management style because its chief executives were in the habit of suddenly making off to London to become English lords.[29] Men born in Great Britain became millionaires in Canada, invested large amounts of money in the United States, and retired in Great Britain. It was impossible to say whether they were Canadian or British.[30]

The fact that the banks of British North America were part of an international system was not without consequences for people living in the Dominion of Canada.[31] Banks we now view as "Canadian" had no more concern for Canada's development than foreign banks with headquarters in the Bahamas have any concern today for the Bahamian economy and population.

NORTH AMERICA – GREAT BRITAIN – CARIBBEAN: THE TRIANGLE

The economic group ruling the colonies that would eventually become Canada had always had an eye on the Caribbean. This was especially true of Halifax merchants, who were interested in the West Indies trade. From the eighteenth century on, these merchants grew wealthy by exporting salt cod and lumber to the islands and importing coffee, sugar, molasses, and rum.[32] Halifax banks were also involved in the West Indies trade, and in 1837 the Halifax Banking Company became a partner of London's Colonial Bank, an institution that was at the heart of the Caribbean banking system throughout the nineteenth century. The British bank asked the Halifax bank to develop an interbank clearing system that would provide liquidity to Colonial Bank branches in the Caribbean. The Halifax Banking Company was also asked to become the Colonial Bank's source of financial knowledge in North America, providing Caribbean bank managers with analyses of the money market and its fluctuations and rates of exchange for the currencies of Europe, the United States, and the colonies of British North America.[33]

The Halifax Banking Company was well acquainted with the Caribbean. The stuff of Caribbean folklore, the bank was founded by a privateer who had sailed Caribbean waters. Around 1814, Nova Scotia privateers – violent seamen authorized by the British government to attack merchant ships designated as enemy vessels – deplored the lack of proper banking services in the port of Halifax.

The privateers complained that they had to rely on private money-changers to dispose of the foreign exchange accumulated as they went about their professional duties. One of these moneychangers, Enos Collins, himself an ex-privateer, had the idea of creating a real bank and was able to carry out this project in 1825. Such was the origin of the Halifax Banking Company.[34]

With the Halifax Banking Company–Colonial Bank deal as a forerunner in 1837, Canadian banks massively entered the Caribbean in the late nineteenth and early twentieth centuries. At the time, the major Canadian banks were seasoned international players with an acute sense of the advantages they might reap from their pliant identity. Their overabundant supply of capital was yet another reason to invest in the Caribbean.

The first Canadian banking branch in the Caribbean was opened by the Bank of Nova Scotia in Kingston, Jamaica, in 1889.[35] The Merchants' Bank of Halifax (soon to become the Royal Bank of Canada) opened in Havana in 1899;[36] the Union Bank of Halifax opened in Port of Spain, Trinidad, in 1903;[37] the Canadian Bank of Commerce opened in Havana, Kingston, and Bridgetown in 1920.[38] Each of these institutions found itself in a strong position in the Caribbean market.

Trade between Canada and the Caribbean was not sufficient, in itself, to justify the arrival of Canadian banks. True, Canada imported sugar, rum, and fruit and exported flour, lumber, and fish, but trade between Canada and the islands, even when it was increasing, remained modest in scope. The reality was that the banks came to the Caribbean to finance trade not with Canada, but with the United States. The geo-graphical location of the Canadian bank branches bears witness to this fact: Cuba, Puerto Rico, Haiti, and the Dominican Republic, where the largest number of branches were located, belonged to the American sphere of influence.[39]

In 1889, an American stockbroker told the chief accountant of the Bank of Nova Scotia that it would be a good idea to open a branch in Jamaica because an American consortium planned to build a railway on the island. The bank took his advice and opened in Kingston a few months later.[40] When the railway was not built, the bank dedicated itself to financing trade between Jamaica and the

United States. In 1899, it opened a branch in Boston to provide better service to a major client, the pugnacious United Fruit Company.[41] The RBC was similarly influenced by American advice: it began to think of opening in the Caribbean when encouraged to do so by New York's Chase Manhattan Bank,[42] and in 1902, it was able to buy a Cuban bank because it had received capital from New York and Chicago industrial investors.[43]

Canadian banks were also integrated into the British banking system in the Caribbean and had multiple ties with the Colonial Bank, the British bank that dominated the British West Indies. Having acquired the Halifax Banking Company in 1903, the Canadian Bank of Commerce took on the role of agent of the Colonial Bank that the Halifax institution had played since 1837. In 1911, the Royal Bank toyed with the idea of buying the Colonial Bank; when this fell through, British-Canadian financier Max Aitken became the Colonial Bank's majority shareholder, a position he retained until 1918. Throughout the 1920s, the Bank of Montreal was a major shareholder in the Colonial Bank.[44]

Thanks to their floating identity, Canadian banks in the Caribbean demonstrated an extraordinary plasticity. Duncan McDowall, RBC historian, openly acknowledges that in Cuba, "from the outset, the Canadians saw themselves as an 'American' bank."[45] The bank's American identity ensured peace of mind for Canadian bankers, since it was American military power that enabled them to carry out their work in Cuba, Puerto Rico, and the Dominican Republic; they were "snugly covered" by the Platt Amendment, protected by the recurring interventions of American battleships or Marine contingents, and appreciative of the pleasingly stable political climate provided by "ruthless" dictators such as Trujillo of the Dominican Republic.[46] At the same time, as McDowall explains, "in the British West Indies, it [the Royal Bank] was a 'British' bank," and in South America "the British ambassador was usually its best friend in town."[47] But the Royal Bank was not only American or British. In Guadeloupe, Martinique, and Haiti, it presented itself as a "French" bank. After all, did it not have a branch in Paris, and a number of French Canadian employees?[48] At work behind the scenes of multiple empires, Canadian bankers donned multiple personalities.[49]

The U.S. victory over Spanish forces in Cuba in 1898 favoured the expansion of *Canadian* banks in the region. The American military and political occupation of the island was associated with massive investments on the part of American corporations.[50] Given the legal obstacles preventing American banks from intervening in Cuba, what could be better than a Canadian bank to manage these investments? Edson Pease, managing director of the Merchants' Bank of Halifax office in Montreal, hurried to Havana as soon as the peace treaty was signed in order to take full advantage of Cuba's ruined economy. Touring the devastated city in a carriage, he chiefly noticed not the distress of the population but the opportunity to rebuild Havana's port facilities, buildings, bridges, and warehouses. "Among the wreckage, Pease could see opportunity," the bank's historian cheerfully reports in 1993.[51] Pease developed an instantaneous "friendship" with the American consul and carried out the "brilliant coup"[52] of appointing him co-director of the branch opened in Havana in 1899. In 1900, the bank adopted an impressively imperial new name: known henceforth as the "Royal Bank of Canada," it opened an agency in New York to support its Cuban projects and proceeded to open branches on the island "wherever it could facilitate the spread of foreign [that is, American] investment entering Cuba."[53] One of its clients was the United Fruit Company,[54] which as we know from previous discussion was already doing business with another Canadian bank, the Bank of Nova Scotia, in Jamaica.[55] The Royal was also the bank of major American corporations that now controlled sugar production in Cuba, and in 1902, it was contracted by the Cuban government to distribute the pay of soldiers in the Cuban army. From then on, the bank enjoyed "a favoured relationship" with Cuban governments "both democrat and dictator,"[56] as McDowall serenely remarks. This kind of favoured relationship contributed to the bank's prosperity throughout the twentieth century.

The RBC's single most important client in the Caribbean was Sir William Van Horne's Cuba Company.[57] A perfect representative of the Canadian-American-British business class, the wealthy Van Horne was an American citizen who had made his fortune in Canada as president of the Canadian Pacific Railway. His chief residence was in Montreal, and having become a Canadian citizen (and therefore a British subject), he was raised to the peerage in Great Britain. In 1900, he incorporated the Cuba Company in the United States,[58] with primarily American but also Canadian and later Scottish capital. The company's project was to build a railway to transport sugar produced and refined in eastern Cuba.[59] There was no local contribution to this development; the Cuba Company's projects were supported by a business network that included the United States, Canada, and Great Britain.[60] As a friend of the RBC, Van Horne designed the facade of its branch in Camagüey.[61] He also showed his affection for Cuba by drafting its railway law, which he based "largely on Canadian railway law." The law, which came into force in 1902, allowed his company to expropriate a number of "unreasonable" parties.[62]

From Cuba, the RBC extended its activities throughout the Caribbean and South America.[63] Among the bank's foreign branches, those of Rio de Janeiro, São Paulo, the Dominican Republic, Colombia, British Honduras (today Belize), and Jamaica generated the bank's highest profits throughout the 1920s.[64]

IMPERIAL BANKS

The 1920s marked the peak of the international networks of Canadian banks in the first part of the twentieth century: close to 20 percent of their assets were located abroad, and they had two hundred branches outside of Canada.[65]

During this period, Canadian banks had few competitors in the Caribbean,[66] and to the extent that they did face competition, they worked to neutralize it by forming cartels. In the British Caribbean, a cartel was formed no later than the 1920s between the Canadian banks and their only rival, the Colonial Bank. The banks colluded to fix interest rates offered to depositors and bank fees. Their collusion was even put into writing in the 1950s, and there is every reason to believe that the cartel still existed in the 1970s.[67]

Canadian banks were undeniably part of the colonial system in the British West Indies, where they literally played the role of central banks. This was the case of the Royal Bank in Cuba[68] and the Bank of Nova Scotia in Jamaica.[69] The Royal Bank, the Bank of Nova Scotia, and the Canadian Bank of Commerce produced the banknotes, in pound sterling or in dollars, that served as local currency in the Caribbean.[70] In Cuba and Jamaica, these banknotes circulated until the late 1930s.[71]

From the moment they entered the Caribbean, Canadian chartered banks were free from any kind of regulation. The United States, which imposed strict rules on their activities in its own territory,[72] was indifferent to their action anywhere else. British authorities saw no reason to regulate what they did in the Caribbean: they were viewed as innately virtuous, on a par with British banks. (In contrast, any Caribbean bank attempting to establish itself during this period was subject to strict supervision by British authorities.) As a result, Canadian banks were completely untrammelled in the Caribbean until Jamaica's central bank was established in 1961.[73] But even after the Jamaican banking law was enacted and other islands followed suit, British dependencies were unable to coordinate their efforts and adopt uniform banking laws at a regional or supra-regional level. As a consequence, it was easy for Canadian banks to threaten to leave any jurisdiction that showed a propensity to enact even minimal regulation of the banking sector.[74]

There was only one force that might have regulated the banks, and that was the Canadian government. Canada's financial institutions owed their existence to charters granted by Ottawa under the Bank Act. As a consequence, in Jamaica, Puerto Rico, the Bahamas, or elsewhere, Canada was in a better position than local authorities to regulate the banks. By default, it controlled the banking sector in the islands. As law professor Daniel Jay Baum was to point out, "The greater part of Canadian banking is conducted in Canada even though the banks are world enterprises. Thus, in a legal and a realistic sense, the federal government has the power to control banking behaviour in the Commonwealth Caribbean."[75] However, Canada remained faithful to its habits and continued to behave like a banking haven: choosing not to employ its jurisdictional power, it organized laissez-faire,[76] giving complete freedom to Canadian banks abroad. With the Canadian government as their sole regulatory power, vulnerable populations were left utterly without protection. Baum describes the Canadian government's position as "a total absence of any control, restriction, recommendation, or even comment on how they [Canadian banks] may or may not carry on their foreign operations."[77] The passivity of the Canadian state thus ensured anomie, an absence of all standards, for Canadian banks as they operated in other countries.

Free of all constraints, Canadian bankers showed no compunction in doing business with regimes practising torture and assassination. In 1920s Venezuela, the RBC was associated with dictator Juan Vicente Gómez, with whom it shared profits from Lake Maracaibo oil.[78] In 1933, the Cuban dictator, Machado, asked for political asylum in Canada; this request was twice granted on a temporary basis, enabling him, in 1935, "to straighten out his financial affairs with the Royal Bank" in Montreal.[79] Batista's reign of terror in 1950s Cuba did not prevent the RBC from opening new branches on the island.[80] In the Dominican Republic, Trujillo's dictatorship provided a "stable political climate" ensuring the profitability of Canadian banks,[81] which may explain the "tens of millions of dollars" loaned by the Bank of Nova Scotia to the regime in 1958–1959.[82] While the bank might claim ideological neutrality, we note that it made loans to Machado, Batista, Trujillo, and Somoza, but that it refused to lend to Jamaica's centre-left government under Michael Manley.[83]

Banks do not make available the content of their archives on issues of this kind; the history of their relations with dictators remains shrouded in silence. Nor do they tend to publish information about anticolonial protests directed against them. Peter James Hudson, a historian who has worked to document popular opposition to the Royal Bank in the Caribbean, notes that "the near-total restriction on public access to the Bank's archives in suburban Toronto ensures it is a history that cannot be told in its entirety."[84] Hudson is nonetheless able to show that throughout its history in the Caribbean, the bank faced "demonstrations and attacks, and on occasion robberies and heists," of which he presents the following examples:

1931:   Opponents of Cuban dictator Machado detonate a bomb inside an RBC branch in a Havana suburb.

1934:   Protesting the forcible eviction of 5,000 families to benefit a sugar company financed by the RBC, Cuban peasants from the district of Realengo 18 attack the Royal's Santiago de Cuba branch.

1948:   Opponents of Cuban dictator Batista stage an armed attack against RBC headquarters in Havana.

1967:   The PUCH (Unified Party of Haitian Communists) holds up an RBC branch in Port-au-Prince in order to fund urban insurgency against Duvalier.

1968:   In Kingston, unemployed Black youth attack an RBC branch and other foreign corporations and financial institutions, to protest the expulsion of left-wing intellectual Walter Rodney.

1970:   During the February revolution in Trinidad, student protesters storm RBC headquarters in Port of Spain.[85]

At the political level, Canada at the time remained unconcerned with its image as an exemplary democracy – an image that it finds valuable today. In contrast, throughout the twentieth century, Canada provided the United States with military support in the region, sending battleships on several occasions to support regimes threatened by invasion from the outside or by the anger of their own citizens. Thus, Canadian forces occupied Bermuda twice, in the mid-1910s and again in the early 1940s; St. Lucia from 1915 to 1919; the Bahamas and Jamaica in the 1940s; and Barbados in 1966. Canadians have also been involved since the 1970s in training soldiers in Jamaica and Trinidad and Tobago. "The sentiment that Canada has imperial tendencies in the Caribbean is widely held there," notes political analyst Yves Engler, quoting an External Affairs official of the 1970s saying that "'we're not colonialists by intent, but by circumstances. We've taken on a neo-colonial aura there'."[86]

Canada went even further when it actively claimed the right to annex various islands in the British West Indies. Should not we too have colonies? This project, fiercely debated in Canada at the end of the nineteenth century, showed a last flicker of life in 1917: Ottawa asked London to give it the Caribbean as a reward for its role in defending the Empire during the First World War. The request was refused, partly because Canada's political class did not unanimously support it. Prime Minister Robert Borden was worried that he might have to give Black citizens of the Caribbean the right to vote in Canada.[87]

Just as they did in Canada's Maritime provinces, "Canadian" banks siphoned the capital of Caribbean islands, blocking the development of the local economy.[88] The banks almost never made long-term investments in the region. The Bank of Nova Scotia had a few Havana municipal debentures, but the holdings that really mattered to it were United Fruit bonds.[89] In terms of loans, it favoured large exporting firms and worked to create the financial framework required, in the Caribbean, for direct American investment and trade. The RBC did the same. The banks did not like to lend to primary producers; they preferred to finance the storage, transportation, marketing, and processing of crops.[90] After the Second World War, they drew criticism for financing imports of luxury products and consumer goods for the middle class instead of supporting industry or housing construction.[91]

In fact, the Canadian banks that controlled capital flows in the Caribbean islands where they were active[92] were opposed to any kind of local project. They viewed loans to peasants or small cane producers as too risky, even when applications were presented through the intermediary of state-controlled agricultural co-operative banks.[93] Like any self-respecting bank, they had higher standards of solvency for the poor than for the rich.[94] Deposits made by Caribbean savers were systematically greater than loans made in the region.[95] In the case of the Bank of Nova Scotia, the excess of deposits over loans was a constant,[96] and when it did lend money locally, it was to large producers: in 1910, for example, lending activity in Jamaica "was mainly confined to the United Fruit Company."[97]

Profits realized by Canadian banks in the Caribbean were transferred to Canada, the United States, or Great Britain. Economist, historian, and criminologist R. T. Naylor has estimated that none of the surplus generated by the Royal Bank in the Caribbean ever reached Canada: "The Royal took its large, free surplus from the West Indies and loaned it on call in New York."[98] Bank surpluses not sent to New York were generally sent to London and became part of the institution's reserves. From there, they were redistributed to the most credible borrowers, wherever they might be. In competition with all possible borrowers throughout North America and the Caribbean, small Caribbean borrowers just weren't impressive enough.[99] As for the shareholders who received the banks' dividends, they were rarely citizens of the Caribbean.

The international expansion of Canadian chartered banks favoured banking concentration within Canada. The four banks most active abroad – the Bank of Montreal, RBC, CIBC, and the Bank of Nova Scotia – became dominant between 1900 and 1930, forming an oligopoly as they swallowed up almost every rival Canadian bank.[100] Their lucrative foreign operations provided the capital they needed to finance these acquisitions.[101] The exponential growth of RBC and the future Scotiabank between 1900 and 1914, and their emergence as major national and international banks, are directly related to their expansion in the Caribbean.[102]

While Canadian banks were increasing their power, the Canadian state continued to display its extreme passivity. As a state, Canada was a tool that powerful actors in the countries to which it was subservient – Great Britain and the United States – used to allow them to benefit from an alegal regime that they did not want to set up themselves. This explains Ottawa's indifference in the Caribbean despite the highly significant presence of Canadian financial actors. When, in 1931, Cuban rebels detonated their bomb in an RBC branch in Havana, the minister who protested to President Machado was British, not Canadian.[103] Generally speaking, Canada seemed to be the state least concerned by actions taken by its own banks in other countries; it offered them no protection.[104] Often it did not even have diplomatic representation in the countries where the banks were active.[105] When the banks needed support, they looked to the British and American governments.[106] According to historians Christopher Armstrong and H. V. Nelles, the British government was the most helpful: "Capital may have been stateless, but the government of Great Britain was its most consistent friend."[107]

CANADIAN ADVENTURERS

Chartered banks were not the only Canadian businesses turning up in the Caribbean in the early twentieth century. Beginning in 1897, the islands saw the arrival of Canadian promoters looking for concessions to operate streetcars, power plants, and telephone companies. The promoters created private companies misleadingly known as "public utilities." These companies benefited from monopolies ensuring that their early years were extraordinarily profitable.[108] Companies incorporated in Canada were responsible for streetcars, trolleys, electrical power stations, and street lighting in cities such as Kingston (Jamaica), Georgetown (Guyana), Port of Spain (Trinidad), Camagüey (Cuba), and San Juan (Puerto Rico).[109] Canadian promoters also set up public utilities in Brazil, Venezuela, El Salvador, Bolivia, Mexico, and Barcelona.[110] Initial profits were so high that between 1900 and 1910, Canadian shareholders continued to invest more money in utilities abroad than in Canada.[111]

The arrival of Canadian companies operating streetcars and other utilities in the South became possible when Canadian railway entrepreneurs who were looking for new worlds to conquer (they had already electrified Canadian streetcars)[112] encountered a new type of financier making its appearance at that moment in Canada.[113] Specializing in the search for financing packages that would ensure a quick profit at the very beginning of an enterprise, these financiers were often seen as foolhardy in comparison with Canadian chartered banks.[114] When they issued securities, the new financiers were paid not in money, but in ordinary shares: they were speculating on the rising value of shares for which they had not paid a cent.[115] While the financiers' potential profits were enormous, the shares did not represent any real investment in the company. This was the swindle denounced by *L'Humanité* when it pointed out the fictitious nature of Barcelona Traction's share capital. And as *L'Humanité* noted, the investment companies established by financiers under Canadian law were not subject to any genuine regulation.[116]

Canadian promoters had initially attempted to launch public utilities in American or English cities, but many of these efforts proved fruitless as they came up against a world of standards, regulations, and competition: "a maturing economy densely populated with expensive lawyers, feuding politicians, litigious property owners, and treacherous rivals."[117] When they turned their attention to the Caribbean, they were delighted with the freedom provided by a colonial system.

Promoters' profits derived essentially from the strength of the monopoly they were granted by a city or state to operate a streetcar system or produce electricity. Hence, a new kind of lawyer was needed to create these companies: it was the lawyer's job to negotiate the deals and draw up the contracts. The rise of corporate lawyers in North America was meteoric in the early twentieth century at a time when huge conglomerates were being established.[118] Corporate lawyers did not just practise law. They combined their technical knowledge and ability to draw up contracts with access to powerful networks that included businessmen, investors, and politicians.[119] Far more often than their European counterparts, North American lawyers became entrepreneurs and financiers themselves, launching their own investment companies and managing streetcar or electricity companies.[120] Charles Cahan, for example, the Halifax lawyer who provided support for financier Max Aitken's companies, set up the Demerara Electric Company in Georgetown, Guyana, then went to Port of Spain to establish the Trinidad Electric Company, and from there went to Mexico to become vice-president of Mexican Light and Power, a company of which he was also a major shareholder.[121] Another Canadian lawyer active in Toronto, Zebulon Lash, extolled as "the foremost Canadian corporation lawyer of his day," was the chief legal architect of a range of public utility companies created in Canada at the instigation of American engineer F. S. Pearson. Lash was also vice-president of Mexico Tramways, vice-president of the Brazilian Traction, Light, and Power, and vice-president of the Canadian Bank of Commerce.[122]

Over the years, Canadian public utility companies became known to populations in the South for their greed and their brutal view of labour relations. "In Barcelona, Mexico City, São Paulo, and especially Rio de Janeiro, the very word *Canadian* became an epithet for the exploitive, authoritarian, reactionary, dictatorial foreigner, especially during times of labour strife."[123] The most famous of these companies, the Brazilian Traction, Light, and Power, was known to Brazilians as "the Canadian octopus."[124]

To ensure their profits, the new financiers created a new kind of organization, the syndicate, that was also associated with new forms of financial crime.[125] A group of shareholders maintaining a "tight, secretive discipline" was able to affect a security's price.[126] The syndicate also gave its members free shares:[127] this practice, common in Canada, was illegal in other countries.[128] Equally frequent was overcapitalization (also known as stockwatering), the process by which promoters claim that a corporation's shares (that is, its capital) are worth a certain, fictitious amount, higher than is justified; this allows them to boost shareholders' entitlement to returns.[129] And finally, Canadian law did not promote disclosure when securities were issued, and insider trading was widely accepted. Historian Gregory Marchildon, who studied the Canadian career of the most famous of the new financiers, Max Aitken (a.k.a. Lord Beaverbrook), states that Aitken's methods would probably land him in jail today.[130]

Although their improbable financing packages were initiated in Canada, the new financiers quickly realized that the Dominion was not home to enough investors to support them in their rise to stratospheric levels of wealth. As a consequence, they moved to London where they had access to abundant capital. Max Aitken's company, established in London in 1910, was one of a dozen Canadian investment houses opened in the City between 1905 and 1912, and by 1915, close to sixty organizations offered Canadian securities in London.[131] While Canadian financiers were viewed as adventurers by staid British bankers, they nonetheless helped consolidate the power of British finance: they confirmed the importance of London as a place to finance public utility securities, strengthened the City's connections to Brazil and Mexico, and brought to London the techniques of North American finance.[132] As we will see, Canadian financiers and lawyers again played a supporting role when the time came to help the City of London set up tax havens in the Caribbean.

Fully a part of an international political and financial system, Canadian adventurers made fortunes in the London financial market. The "Canadian" identity of the public utility companies whose shares they sold became more and more tenuous. These companies hired American or British engineers to look after equipment built in the United States or Germany.[133] Shareholders were no longer Canadian, but British or European; a Belgian conglomerate owned companies whose head offices were located in Toronto.[134] Decisions at the highest level were made in London or Brussels, while everyday decisions were made on-site in Latin America or Barcelona.[135]

The companies' Canadian headquarters were addresses of convenience. In 1909, the head offices of Demerara Electric, Porto Rico Railways, and the Camaguey Company were located at 179 St. James Street in Montreal, in the offices of Max Aitken's Royal Securities Corporation.[136] In Toronto, the head offices of Brazilian Traction, Mexican Light and Power, Mexico Tramways, and Barcelona Traction were housed in the offices of the Blake, Lash, and Cassels law firm dominated by Zebulon Lash. Within the law firm, no more than two or three employees were needed to deal with the four companies' official correspondence.[137]

But in any case, the "Canadian" identity of these companies had always been unreal, even when their shareholders were Canadian. As Armstrong and Nelles point out, from the beginning their link to Canada was an arbitrary one: "The place of domicile of most of the founding entrepreneurs and the laxity of company law alone made them Canadian." For the promoters who created these companies, "Countries … were things to use – and they were interchangeable."[138]

THE CANADIAN MODEL

The 1920s marked a high point in the activities of the four great Canadian chartered banks in the Caribbean and Latin America. In the 1930s, they scaled down their operations.[139] Despite their relative sluggishness, however, they never left the Caribbean.[140] And during their first foray in the South, they acquired habits that they were never to lose. The first of these was the habit of instrumentalizing the Canadian jurisdiction. Canada for them was a tool, no more, no less. Canadian laws provided ways of creating structures that channelled foreign capital; presenting yourself as American or British was always an option.

Another habit was unconditional support for the hegemonic power governing the place in which they were operating. Sub-imperialists have the absolute requirement that a true imperialist protect them. In this respect, the Canadian state was completely passive: it acknowledged that Canadian banks were free to operate abroad, but did not provide them with any kind of protection. The banks were thus necessarily complicit with a greater power (United States or Great Britain) that ensured their safety and the stability of their profits. Relations with this greater power took precedence over any other consideration. Support for local dictatorships was part of the same logic based on the pre-eminence of profit.

Finally, the banks that were always faithfully devoted to the interests of the propertied classes were always indifferent to local populations. The well-being of shareholders took priority, and this was the case not only in the Caribbean, but also in Canada: Halifax bankers, for example, stopped lending money to Nova Scotia factories because they viewed Chicago and Jamaica as more profitable markets.[141] "Their primary loyalty was not to their region, but to their class."[142]

As for the paradox of a country dominated by foreign capital, but that nonetheless continued to export capital, it merely deepened in the twentieth century. In the late 1950s, at a time when some Canadian intellectuals were starting to worry about the hold of American foreign direct investment on the Canadian economy, Canada was a major source of direct investment abroad. By 1971, it had become the sixth capital exporter in the world, surpassed only by the United States, the three largest economies of Western Europe, and Switzerland.[143]

▉ RELAUNCHING THE BANKS OFFSHORE

In the late 1950s, Canadian banks showed signs that they were about to rise again in foreign parts. Something new was happening in the Caribbean as a consequence of a crucial event that had taken place in London in the late 1950s: the birth of the Eurodollar market,[144] a first step toward a world financial system based on "the circulation of capital offshore without public regulation."[145] Tax havens were called on to play a key role in the Eurodollar market, and this made them into the essential protagonists they are today. London bankers were the first to accumulate significant amounts of Eurodollars generated by the Marshall Plan as massive sums flowed from the United States to Europe to rebuild it after the Second World War. The Eurodollar market appeared in 1957 when the Bank of England agreed that it would not regulate transactions taking place in London in dollars if they were carried out by two non-residents.[146] For the first time in modern financial history, banks could deal with very large amounts of money in a currency not supervised by their government. However, the colossal sums flowing into the City under this regime became embarrassing. For this reason, financial institutions began to move very large sums to the British Caribbean, where they were received by Canadian bankers. By the late 1950s, Canadian financiers were becoming active again in the islands.

Meanwhile, the American mafia that had been expelled from Cuba was moving to the Bahamas. The flows of money variously associated with organized crime and Eurodollars arrived in the British Caribbean at the same time. The Bahamas and Cayman Islands were particularly well positioned to receive and combine, beyond the reach of the law, the two streams of financial and criminal capital.[147] Each in their own way, these jurisdictions represented a new junction between British and American financial systems. Canadian banks naturally found they had a role to play as a well-oiled hinge between the two systems. In the early 1960s, Canadian institutions worked with American and British banks to transform the Caribbean into a vector for Eurodollars and illicit transactions, thus launching the great project of moving the entire world offshore.

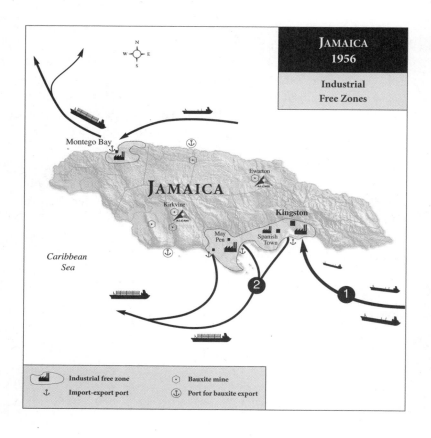

JAMAICA
1956

Industrial
Free Zones

N
W   E
S

Montego Bay

JAMAICA

Ewarton
ALCAN

Kirkvine
ALCAN

Kingston

May
Pen

Spanish
Town

Caribbean
Sea

2

1

Industrial free zone   Bauxite mine

Import-export port   Port for bauxite export

JAMAICA

INDUSTRIAL FREE ZONE

In which an ex-governor of the Bank of Canada mysteriously
intervenes in Jamaica as the colony reshapes its financial
institutions and tax laws, and multinationals such as
Alcan consign the country to economic oblivion – so that
becoming a free zone looks like the only way out

In 1956, the Canadian government did everything in its power to make sure Canadian financial institutions continued to dominate the Jamaican banking system. This is apparent when we consider the report published by the Canadian establishment's envoy to Jamaica, a former governor of the Bank of Canada, during this crucial year. Graham Towers's presence in Jamaica also coincided with significant changes to Jamaica's tax laws, prefiguring the development of a highly permissive free zone in 1977.

Jamaica had been a key territory for Canadian banks in the Caribbean since the late nineteenth century. The Bank of Nova Scotia opened a branch in Kingston as early as 1889; this was the first time a Canadian bank opened a branch other than in Canada, the United States, or Great Britain.[1] The Royal Bank of Canada (RBC) joined the Bank of Nova Scotia in 1911,[2] and the Canadian Bank of Commerce came to the island in 1920.[3] These three Canadian banks, and a British bank, Barclays (DCO), were the only commercial banks in Jamaica at the end of the Second World War, and no American banks operated on the island until First National City Bank of New York arrived in 1961.[4] In 1956, everything happened exactly as if the Canadian financial establishment were attempting to consolidate its supremacy by defining both the financial institutions and the tax laws of the emergent Jamaican state. During that same year a Canadian multinational, Alcan, was one of several that worked to shape the colony's mining code.

When Graham Towers was formally asked to advise the Jamaican government, he was already familiar with the region. He had lived in the Caribbean from 1922 to 1929 as a manager for RBC,[5] before becoming the first governor of the Bank of Canada (1934–1954) and sitting as alternate governor of the International Monetary Fund (1946–1954). In 1955, the Jamaican government asked him to "review the role of Jamaican financial institutions, to see if they could better mobilize the island's resources for development purposes, and to examine whether a central bank should be created."[6] Towers was officially appointed by the United Nations Technical Assistance Administration, but Ottawa was fully involved in his response: the Bank of Canada (which Tower had just left) and Canada's Ministry of Finance gave their opinion through "consultation" sessions on the reforms that the Jamaican colony ought to undertake.[7] Towers was also seconded by J. L. Fisher, adviser to the governors of the Bank of England.[8] The outcome of the process was Towers's 1956 report,[9] indicating how the colony's private and public credit system should be developed to foster investment in Jamaica's real economy.

The Towers Report was an attempt to restrict the range of action of political authorities while giving (foreign) bankers more freedom. Jamaican authorities were advised not to create a central bank that would allow them to influence economic decisions.[10] Towers asserted with paternal benevolence that Jamaica would probably be better off if it were unable to influence the money supply: "where monetary independence exists in so-called underdeveloped countries, the anxiety to move ahead rapidly often leads to inflation, instability, and retardation of the development that is so keenly desired." Fortunately, any kind of independent action on the part of Jamaica was unnecessary, since Towers "[could] not foresee any situation in Jamaica in which the Government of the day would lack the whole-hearted co-operation of existing banks."[11] Given that three of the colony's four "existing banks" happened to be Canadian,[12] this advice amounted to saying that everything should be left in wise Canadian hands. Towers's report stated that the Jamaican government should invest in certain businesses or industrial projects without, however, being involved in their management.[13] It also included a number of proposals that were less than impartial, such as the invitation to

Jamaica, a British colony, to borrow outside London in places like Canada, the United States, and Switzerland – a banking haven.

What is probably even more significant than Towers's recommendations with regard to banking, however, is the fact that Jamaica was radically reshaping its tax rules exactly at the time he was staying on the island. It is hard to believe that this is mere coincidence. In 1956, the colonial government adopted two laws that reduced the cost of labour and provided tax exemptions for foreign companies.[14] One of the laws was explicitly designed to support corporations creating manufacturing zones in Jamaica, strictly for export purposes. Already, the goal was to make Jamaica into an industrial free zone in which labour would cost almost nothing, taxes would be derisory, labour unions non-existent, and social and environmental legislation a joke.

Finally, 1956 was also the year in which the Jamaican legislative assembly enacted Law 36, creating a type of offshore corporation known as the International Business Company (IBC). Companies or shareholders registered in Jamaica under this status could receive funds from abroad without paying taxes. The 1956 law "is designed to encourage influential international and other organisations to set up their management offices in Jamaica," according to a government paper, issued six years later by the Jamaican minister of finance, that reiterated the principle of the law.[15] This was a first in the British Caribbean. IBCs opened the island to foreign investors who enjoyed legislative advantages without displaying any interest in Jamaica's real economic activity. And should there by chance be any significant economic activity, the tax rate established in the new provisions was not to exceed 2.5 percent of declared profits.[16] As critical historian Yves Engler writes in the *Black Book on Canadian Foreign Policy*: "These laws, which became a model for the rest of the newly independent English Caribbean, pleased Canadian banks."[17] While the nature of these laws may not have been immediately apparent, they were the first step in a process that was to lead to the transformation of almost every territory in the British Caribbean into an offshore jurisdiction.

It is also worth noting that the year 1956 was the moment when the Jamaican government began negotiating with aluminum producers, including a Canadian company (Alcan), to develop a mining code. The resulting law proved outrageously favourable to aluminum corporations. Companies were to pay the government only 2.10 percent of the value generated by their business between 1960 and 1973, according to an arrangement intended to remain unchanged for twenty-five years.[18]

His mission completed, in 1958 Graham Towers joined the board of directors of RBC, where he would presumably be in a position to ensure that the bank reaped the benefits of his knowledge of Jamaican banking structures.[19] In 1963, the institution discovered a new purpose in Jamaica: the Royal Bank of Canada International Limited, a corporation entirely controlled by the bank, provided Jamaica and Trinidad with "trust and fiduciary facilities" through its subsidiaries. In that year's annual report, the bank announced its intention to increase its operations in these areas as well as in other areas of international finance.[20] In 1964, the bank opened three new branches in Jamaica for a total of eleven.[21]

The Bank of Nova Scotia went through a similar process, with seventeen branches in the colony in 1953 and ten more in 1961.[22] In 1967, the Halifax institution created a limited liability company, the Bank of Nova Scotia Jamaica Limited, and brought the number of its Jamaican branches up to 35.[23] Relying on the usual banker's rhetoric to announce in veiled language that Jamaica had become a tax haven, the bank describes this as a "natural development in the light of the expanding Jamaican capital market and the growing national strength and maturity."[24] Since then, Canadian financial institutions have continued to play an important role in Jamaica.[25]

UNEXPECTEDLY INDEPENDENT

Meanwhile, however, the Towers plan to consolidate the pre-eminence of Canadian banks in Jamaica was running into a few problems. In 1959, the Jamaican people put an end to colonial rule and achieved self-government, three years before becoming completely independent. Two years later, the Jamaican government rejected Towers's advice and established a central bank that would enable it to support economic development and a full employment policy for Jamaica.[26] The principle of the central bank was adopted in 1960 as part of the Bank of Jamaica Law. For the first time, a Caribbean institution was subjecting Canadian banks to its authority.[27] Before the creation of the Jamaican central bank, the Bank of Nova Scotia, which was the colonial government's bank,[28] was also the colony's de facto central bank,[29] as it determined the size of Jamaica's money supply. The bank received as deposits the colony's balance of payments surplus and could choose either to increase the monetary mass by increasing the number of local loans, or, on the contrary, to reduce it by investing surplus funds in short-term assets in London or New York.[30] The Jamaican economy was subject to whatever jolts or upheavals might be caused by the business decisions of a Canadian bank that had no particular reason to care about their local impact.[31] But in 1961, the situation was reversed, with the Bank of Nova Scotia now answerable to the Jamaican minister of finance.

For the Canadian financial establishment, this was a slap in the face, and Towers's biographer Douglas Fullerton petulantly asserts that Jamaica's subsequent economic difficulties were caused by its failure to abide by Towers's precepts.[32] From this point on, Jamaica seems to have lost its status as the favoured Caribbean territory for Canadian banks. Hostile to its emancipatory politics, the banks expanded in other directions in the British Caribbean, giving priority to the Bahamas and Cayman Islands, then later to the Turks and Caicos, Barbados, Bermuda, and Trinidad and Tobago.

The Jamaican national emancipation movement was at its peak in the early 1960s, with Jamaica reaching full independence in 1962. Once equipped with a central bank, the Jamaican state no longer co-operated in the same way with Commonwealth lobbyists. While foreign bankers attempted to ensure that the British colony served the ambitions of international finance, the Jamaican population was heading in the opposite direction. In this context, the offshore financial culture failed to thrive: Jamaican authorities seemed to adopt the offshore model reluctantly and to apply it only half-heartedly. Even the clearly liberal industrial policies adopted by various governments from 1962 onward embodied the pursuit of autonomy. Their goal was to reduce imports by having consumer goods manufactured on the island.[33]

In 1972, the advent of Michael Manley's progressive government caused a severe chill in the banking sector. The Jamaican government was now attempting to follow the example of industrialized countries by managing economic activity. Manley's timid policies – he was described by American writer Russell Banks as a kind of "Christian Democrat" with an awareness of social justice issues[34] – were sufficient to make him known as a wild socialist. His showdown with international big business elicited the contempt of tax haven eulogists, including the authors of various tax haven guides.[35] In some cases this contempt was overtly racist: tax consultant Édouard Chambost, for example, described Jamaica as "a racial hell to be avoided at all cost,"[36] while his fellow analyst André Beauchamp appeared troubled by its "very great ethnic diversity."[37] According to Beauchamp, who published a guide to tax havens in 1981, "Jamaica's legislation is similar to that of Antigua, Barbados, and Granada with regard to International Business Companies, but the current [Manley] government does not provide them with a warm welcome and the law has never really been applied."[38] Attempting to steer a different course, the government had crossed an invisible line: it was clear that the newly independent state must be broken.

▓ POLITICS ACCORDING TO ALCAN

Although their actual outcome was negligible, the 1956–1957 negotiations between Jamaican officials and the mining industry were nonetheless a trial of strength between the two parties. At a time when Jamaica was still under colonial management, the island's political representatives wanted to take advantage of increased interest throughout the world in bauxite, a mineral used to produce aluminum and of which Jamaica had an abundant supply. In 1957, Alcan's Kirkvine factory produced more than 500,000 tons of alumina,[39] the product obtained at midpoint in the process of manufacturing aluminum. Jamaica decided to maintain a tax of 40 percent on assumed profits, but to increase the assumed profit from US$0.60 to US$2.30 per ton.[40] In the end, under this system, aluminum companies were still taxed at the laughably low rate of US$0.35 per ton,[41] and they still paid virtually no royalties.[42] This is to say that the authorities' show of force remained somewhat symbolic: "The revenues which accrued to the Government were relatively modest," according to Robert Conrad of Syracuse University, citing government sources.[43] However, thanks to these measures, the state's annual income derived from taxes did rise from US$6.9 million to over US$29 million between 1957 and 1973.[44]

But to this day, it remains difficult to say if the aluminum industry makes a genuine contribution to Jamaican development, given that the community has to provide much of the infrastructure required by private companies to operate and given that these companies siphon resources that might be used in other ways. As an example, alumina production requires 30 percent of the oil imported by Jamaica.[45]

In any case, Alcan (known today as RioTintoAlcan) was not pleased with the Jamaican people's political aspirations. Duncan Campbell, the company's official corporate historian – a former military officer who became the company's public relations officer in 1945 – remarks condescendingly that bauxite is found in "underdeveloped or developing countries" and notes that, unfortunately, Alcan had to face "the realities of life as a multinational corporation concerned with natural resources." In order to explore and operate in the postwar period, the company was forced "to deal often with governments just emerging from colonial status."[46] Does anyone believe this kind of language, redolent with colonialist superiority, would be used in speaking of Australia or the United States? Many sentences carry more than a whiff of racism. While the chaotic economic conditions and tragic battles of the Second World War are presented as ordeals belonging to history's highest reaches, events in Southern countries are viewed as forms of "upheaval,"[47] or described as "quasi-hysterical howling" in the case of citizens supporting the anticolonial speeches of Guinean political leader Sékou Touré.[48] History, for Alcan, is the connection between an inert raw material to be exploited and unfortunate phenomena such as "oil shocks, foreign debts and political change."[49] The company clearly preferred Jamaica when it was "a colonial, somewhat backward, agrarian isle of beauty";[50] but alas, Jamaica was driven to "bankruptcy and despair" by factors such as "ill-advised theorizing," and unfortunately tried to find solutions in "left wing and socialist policies."[51]

Manley's government represented a break with the past that certainly was startling. Previously, when it was time to draft a bill, Alcan executives had been used to sitting down with the minister. Alcan's cozy relationship with Jamaican government officials had been established as soon as it arrived in Jamaica. When Alcan first carried out exploratory work in the colony in 1943, in the middle of the Second World War, there was no need to be punctilious about forms. However, the company was already anticipating what "future mining laws in Jamaica" might look like, suspecting that they "will probably provide that only the owners of land will be permitted to apply for mining rights."[52] Alcan therefore decided to acquire massive options on properties in Jamaica. To make this decision, no great business acumen was required on the company's part: since it was involved in drafting Jamaican laws, it was also in a position to make sure that its rivals would bite the dust.[53] In 1946, Alcan's managing director in the colony, Bryn Davies, was already "engaged in prolonged discussion with the government authorities over the formulation of a mining law"[54] that was adopted the following year. In 1952, Alcan joined forces with an American company, Kaiser Aluminium, to make sure the minimum wage on the island rose no higher than twenty-six cents an hour; after tense negotiations between the companies and the National Workers' Union, a British arbitrator eventually settled the matter in the companies' favour.[55]

Alcan was also a major landowner in Jamaica, and because Jamaican law required the company to make sure that land was not exploited to the detriment of farming, the Canadian mining giant became a major player in Jamaican agriculture. Under a program established in 1953, the company's 28,900 acres were farmed by almost 5,000 tenant farmers.[56]

Taken by surprise by popular demands in the 1950s, Alcan did its best to embrace a new cause: *Jamaicanization*. A policy bearing this name was attempted by the company at the time it was building and enlarging the Kirkvine facility and inaugurating the Ewarton plant.[57] However, the company's use of the word was Orwellian: Alcan was not adapting to Jamaica but adapting Jamaica to serve its own purposes. According to Duncan Campbell, *Jamaicanization* actually meant "to train and develop local Jamaican nationals, with all possible but prudent speed"![58] Referring to a country's citizens as "local nationals" surely reflects a certain unease. And from a Jamaican perspective, the word *Jamaicanization* surely means something quite different: the possibility for Jamaicans to become *owners* of the bauxite sector's development infrastructure.[59] Alcan was actually carrying out the Alcanization of Jamaican political demands. The most the company would do was put a few local actors in positions of prestige.[60]

Behind its insidious rhetoric, Alcan spared no effort to fight the anticolonial movement. In 1961, as Jamaica achieved self-government and was about to declare independence, Bryn Davies, the Alcan executive who had helped the colonial government in Kingston draft its mining laws, was appointed to a director's position in London. His mission was to lobby the British government regarding the fate of the British territories forming the Federation of the West Indies, and to counteract "the moves of several former colonies towards independence from Britain."[61] In economic terms, Alcan sought to shape the conditions of the international bauxite market in order to dominate the states where the resource was found. At the time, in the expressive words of historian Vijay Prashad, "the Third World was not a place. It was a project."[62] As part of this project, in the 1970s, Third World bauxite-producing countries established the International Bauxite Association (IBA) to ensure just compensation for the resources extracted from their territory.[63] Like the oil-producing countries united under the banner of the Organization of the Petroleum Exporting Countries (OPEC), they intended to halt the competitive dynamic that was causing all of them to race to the bottom. This common front was one of the "unusual number of uncertainties" that Alcan claimed to have been facing in early 1974.[64] When the Manley government enacted new taxes on the mining industry in 1974, Alcan made every effort to break the unity established between nations that had been impoverished by colonial history. Time was running out: the company had already lost its footing in Guyana when the government nationalized bauxite production in 1971.

In 1974, in the middle of an oil, inflationary, and budget crisis, the Manley government voted to increase the taxes paid by aluminum companies.[65] "In addition to indexing the price of bauxite to the price of the finished product (aluminum), the Jamaican government adopted the Tax Levy Act, which introduced a significant increase in operating taxes and enabled Jamaica to multiply its revenues from this mineral by six – from $24 million in 1973 to $150 million the following year."[66] This tax was to increase slightly over the next few years.[67] The government also began negotiations that were to continue until 1978 to gain equity in the multinationals' Jamaican mining facilities,[68] eventually obtaining a 7 percent share in Alcan's subsidiaries. [69]

In the early 1970s, Alcan was one of the aluminum companies that held extensive mining reserves in Jamaica and that were contributing to the public treasury.[70] Under the new tax regime enacted in 1974, the company paid the government $30 million, five times the amount paid in 1973.[71] Rejecting the country's "socialist policies," "mismanagement," and "ill-advised theorizing,"[72] Alcan tried to create competition between Jamaica and Guinea-Conakry, where the company had recently, and with difficulty, been able to obtain a concession. Alcan's argument was twofold. First, it claimed that because of the new Jamaican taxes, its Jamaican operations were now running a deficit: the company's official historian refers to "severe financial reverses."[73] However, no figures are provided on this topic. The Alcan historian's argument is bolstered by a second consideration which is clearly paramount: "these new taxes ... would imply a present price for bauxite ... far in excess of any arm's-length price anywhere in the world known to the companies at that time," and "to attribute a tax of this magnitude to the intrinsic value of bauxite was wholly unrealistic."[74] The lack of realism attributed by Alcan to Jamaican officials relates to a reality that Alcan was in a position to shape. The market, the price of bauxite, competition between states, and the stock market's favourable or unfavourable reactions[75] were all factors strongly influenced by Alcan and its fellow multinationals Kaiser, Reynolds, and Alcoa. The "cartel" of states with bauxite deposits, which Alcan denounced,[76] was opposed by the cartel formed by Alcan itself with the other aluminum-producing multinationals. By ensuring that bauxite-producing countries continued to compete with each other, the aluminum oligopoly favoured the lowest possible prices for bauxite. To assert, as Alcan did, that in Jamaica, "unhappily, the outcome in the decade after 1974 was almost identical to that predicted by the industry executives"[77] is a rhetorical device. The outcome "predicted by the industry executives" was actually produced by their policy of obstruction, as companies reduced their production levels and relocated their operations. Alcan's historian seeks to hammer the point home: "Australia and Guinea, despite their IBA membership, were slower to raise their taxation levels on bauxite, which contributed to their ability to attract investment."[78] Thumbing his nose one last time at efforts by Jamaican people to establish their country's economic independence, Alcan's corporate historian Duncan Campbell remarks that forming the IBA and establishing levies did enable Jamaica and other countries "to force up the delivered price of bauxite by some 200 percent, but at the cost of a diminished position in the world market," and he claims that "the decline [of production] in Jamaica has been more severe than in others because of the higher taxation."[79] As noted by mathematician Damien Millet and artist François Mauger, "these people's grudges are long-lasting."[80]

According to political scientist Bonnie Campbell, the winner in the competition was Guinea. One reason for this was the quality and density of its deposits;[81] even more important, no doubt, was a highly advantageous tax system that included a maximum export tax of 0.75 percent.[82] Overall, the corporations' divisive strategy was hardly a secret. Historian Vijay Prashad notes that "Transnational corporations sucked the benefits from the extraction of mineral resources like bauxite. The combined power of the companies worked against the mutual competition between states. Guinea and Jamaica, for instance, competed against each other to the benefit of transnational firms."[83] Carlton E. Davis, Jamaican government adviser and negotiator in the matter of the bauxite levy, reached the same conclusion.[84] To this day, orthodox economists believe that Jamaica, unlike Guinea, is not reaching its full potential in terms of bauxite exports.[85]

Under pressure from Alcan and the other members of the aluminum cartel, the Jamaican government finally abandoned its mining resources tax program in 1988.[86]

▓ YOUR FRIENDLY INTERNATIONAL MONETARY FUND

The various forms of resistance displayed by the Jamaican population and Jamaican officials failed to please international oligarchs, multinationals, foreign diplomatic corps, and financial institutions. Jamaica no longer offered what investors and bankers expected from a tax haven and, for this, it was to pay a heavy price.

In the 1970s, the United States took steps to bring the young independent state into line. A voluminous literature describes the vast "destabilization" campaign orchestrated from Washington against the Manley government, a campaign that included weapons for gangs connected with Colombian cocaine traffickers. Geographer Romain Cruse is one of the people who have documented this uneasy, opaque, and crime-fostering period. The uncontrolled proliferation of gangs with easy access to weapons created a state of permanent tension in Jamaica. These armed groups made political dissent impossible in districts where violence ensured their rule: significantly, during this period, many poor neighbourhoods in Kingston delivered an absolutely homogeneous vote in Jamaican elections.[87] In a paper written with economist Fred Célimène, Cruse argues that bauxite multinationals actively participated in destabilizing the Manley regime in the late 1970s.[88]

As the state's accounts went into the red, the Manley government enacted taxes on the prosperous middle class, involving greater tax monitoring of small merchants. To escape this burden, retailers shifted increasing amounts of capital abroad with the help of Canadian banks, as described by Russell Banks in his novel *The Book of Jamaica*. A character in the novel hears "of this 'capitalist' or that leaving the country," noting that such people had "at last…deserted their real property and debts here and fled to join their money, Canadian and American currency, if they were lucky, or jewels, as the Jamaican dollar kept on being devalued to comply with the conditions set by the International Monetary Fund."[89]

Jamaica's economic collapse left its political class with few options, and Jamaican leaders eventually chose to establish the Kingston free zone in 1976. This first free zone, located close to a container port, gave companies producing for export a permanent tax holiday and waived all duties on their imported inputs.[90] The Jamaican government even undertook to provide some foreign companies with subsidized rental of factory space.[91] This scheme brought the state very little money, and as ministers were given wide discretionary powers, its modest financial benefits were diverted by corruption. According to Jamaican tax expert Wayne Thirsk, the investment incentive policy "was largely uncoordinated and inconsistent in its application and, above all else, highly discretionary. Each separate ministry had its own clientele of firms and determined eligibility for incentives and the *actual* length of the holiday period using criteria that were frequently at odds with those used by other ministries."[92] In other words, incentives were more likely to be used to corrupt ministers and upper civil servants than to attract new business investors.

In the aftermath of Jamaica's economic crisis and the "destabiliz-ation" campaign led by the henchmen of big business, Edward Seaga and his ultra-liberal party came to power in 1981. Seaga immediately called on the International Monetary Fund (IMF) to underwrite an export economy. The structural adjustment program imposed on the country by the IMF at Seaga's behest was devastating. Thirsk notes that "there was an abrupt shift in emphasis from import-competing to export-oriented firms."[93] The IMF transformed Jamaica into a land where resources were sold off at bargain rates and cheap consumer goods were produced for Northern markets. Under policies designed for export-oriented multinationals rather than companies supplying the domestic market, Jamaica became, in effect, one big free zone. All that remained to be done was to seduce foreign companies by grant-ing them further tax holidays and endorsing laissez-faire in terms of labour standards and ecosystems protection. Such were the humiliating measures adopted to attract companies and create jobs.

To pay off its debt to the IMF, in the 1980s Jamaica enacted aus-terity measures that triggered a deadly downward spiral.[94] Economic self-destruction was ensured by the following policies:

- Subsidies for basic necessities were abolished.
- Public expenditure was drastically reduced in sectors defined as *unproductive* such as culture, education, health, housing, and public infrastructure.
- The local currency was devalued.
- Interest rates were increased to benefit foreign capital, ensuring hardship for local merchants.
- Exports were given priority over answering the population's needs.
- The domestic market was completely opened up, placing small local businesses in competition with powerful multinationals.
- The taxation system targeted consumers and workers rather than the earnings of large companies.
- State-owned corporations were massively privatized.[95]

UNICEF, the United Nations Children's Fund, sounded the alarm: these measures spelled disaster for the population. Malnutrition made its appearance, while ordinary consumer goods took on the status of luxury items.[96] "West Kingston is now home to Garbage City: a place where hundreds of people come every day with a hook to rummage through an open-air dump, searching for a scrap of rotten meat, a not-quite-empty bottle, or a piece of refuse that can be reused."[97]

Jamaica could not easily defend itself politically within the apparatus of the IMF. Not only had the IMF adopted free-market rules that provided companies such as Alcan with outrageous advantages, but Jamaica was not directly represented within it. In fact, only eight countries – the United States, Japan, Germany, France, the United Kingdom, Saudi Arabia, China, and Russia – have their own delegation to the IMF.[98] Jamaica belongs to a group of states, most of which are Caribbean, that are represented by – a Canadian.[99] And the ultimate trickery involved in all these measures is to blame the victimized state when it fails. The country is then required to spend decades paying back a debt that brought citizens no benefit of any kind, while stakeholding banks simply let the money flow in.[100]

The push for ever more ultra-liberal measures is felt today. Jamaican society, and the Jamaican Parliament, continue to debate the need to extend the country's offshore provisions.[101] Desperate for capital, the country is contemplating a more radical free-zone policy. The goal is to attract corporations to free zones where injustice is already the law, in Kingston and Montego Bay, and to develop the Spanish Town free zone near Kingston. IMF funds are used to develop these zones where businesses pay virtually no taxes, workers are paid the local minimum wage, and a pernicious legal framework forbids labour unions. Repression is total: "Anyone who dares to demand better conditions is put on a blacklist and will never again work in a free zone."[102] These penal colonies are located next to harbours, facilitating the entry of raw materials that will be transformed in factories and immediately exported to foreign markets. "The presence of commodities on the island is so fleeting that they could hardly be expected to bring currency or contribute to Jamaica's development."[103] Throughout the world today, there are approximately 3,000 of these free zones where the wretched of the earth are concentrated.[104] The Jamaican free zones are so permissive that they have been the focus of two documentary films.[105]

JAMAICAN FREE ZONE: AN ESCAPE ROUTE FOR CANADIAN MONEY

On March 30, 1978, Canada signed a double taxation agreement with Jamaica, incorporating into its own tax regime the benefits granted by Jamaican law. Canada has undertaken not to tax the funds that Canadian companies transfer from Jamaica to Canada. This is justified by the claim that they have already been taxed in Jamaica – which is obviously untrue if the company has been operating in a free zone. A Canadian company can deduct, from its taxable income, any returns on direct investments in Jamaica.[106] According to tax expert James Wozny, "Since virtually all nonfinancial Canadian subsidiaries have earned only active business income, none of the dividends they have paid to Canadian direct investors have been subject to Canadian federal tax."[107] Wozny adds that profits from activities managed by holdings in Jamaica are also exempt from taxation in Canada.[108] These measures have made Canada into a tax haven for Jamaica: income generated in Jamaica by the activity of companies belonging to Canadians will not be taxed in Jamaica as long as the dividends are registered in Canada, nor will they be taxed in Canada as long as they are generated in Jamaica. Today, 16.5 percent of the Jamaican population lives in extreme poverty and is dependent on external support.[109]

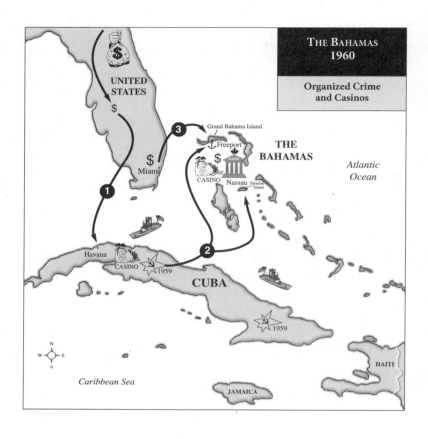

THE BAHAMAS
1960

Organized Crime
and Casinos

UNITED
STATES

$

Miami

THE
BAHAMAS

Grand Bahama Island

Freeport

CASINO

BANK

Nassau   Paradise
Island

Atlantic
Ocean

Havana

CASINO   1959

CUBA

1959

HAITI

N
W   E
S

Caribbean Sea

JAMAICA

THE BAHAMAS

DEN OF AMERICAN ORGANIZED CRIME

In which the Bank of Nova Scotia provides the Bahamas
with a trusted adviser, and the Royal Bank finds a
Bahamian finance minister to join its board

American tax authorities called it a "serious crime community"[1] –
a network embodying an unusual "illegal concentration of power,"
established in the Bahamas in the 1960s.[2] Lou Chesler, Wallace Groves,
and Meyer Lansky had arrived from Cuba, expelled by the 1959 Revolution.[3] The casinos they managed in Cuba had been used to launder
capital created through criminal operations in North America; now they
wanted to pursue their activities in the Bahamas. "Laundering capital"
means finding a way to bring illegally acquired money into the legal
economy, "justifying the money's origin by inserting a fictitious intermediary in the circuit."[4] Small-scale drug dealers hide their profits in
the cash registers of neighbourhood restaurants; above them, powerful
distributors conceal illicit earnings in the accounts of import-export
companies; and at the top of the chain, people move their dirty money
through casinos in the Bahamas. Much of the infrastructure required
to run these large-scale laundering operations in the islands was set
up in the 1960s with loans from two Canadian banks: the Royal Bank
of Canada and the Bank of Nova Scotia.

Our tale begins in the 1950s with the ambitious projects of a
well-connected Bahamian businessman, lawyer, and broker, Stafford
Sands. Sands was known in the Bahamas as one of the "Bay Street
Boys," a powerful group of wheeler-dealers who dominated the colony's
economic and political life in the mid-twentieth century.[5] Elected to
the House of Assembly of the Bahamas in 1937, he joined the Executive Council in 1945[6] and took charge of the Bahamas Development
Board, becoming the equivalent of a minister of tourism.[7] He was also

minister of finance. Still holding these two positions, after a few years he became involved in Canadian banking affairs. Among Sands's goals was to establish a casino and resort on the island of Grand Bahama, one of the few inhabited islands among the seven hundred that formed the colony. To carry out this project, he needed to convince the Executive Council of the Bahamas to liberalize gambling.[8]

Sands had a partner. Wallace Groves, a member of his intimate circle since the 1930s,[9] was an American lawyer who had gotten rich through repeated operations involving buying, merging, and selling (for a high price) companies that went through major transformations as soon as he acquired them.[10] In 1938, his illegal selling strategies caused him to be sued by the Securities and Exchange Commission, the U.S. stock market regulatory agency. At the time, he was selling General Investment Corporation shares at inflated prices and fraudulently pocketing large commissions.[11] Five of the companies he owned, of which two were located in the Bahamas, were convicted in this affair, and Groves himself spent two years in jail.

Groves was released from the federal penitentiary in 1943. Before going to jail in 1941 he had married a Quebecer named Georgette Cusson and made her his business partner.[12] After his release from prison, he left the United States and went off to conquer the Bahamas, where he met up again with his friend Stafford Sands.[13] One of Groves's enterprises involved Grand Bahama Island: launching himself in the logging business, he removed almost all the island's trees. That project complete, he decided to create a free port and an industrial complex on the island.[14]

The stars were aligned for the two hucksters. They had a project that suited them both, and Sands convinced the Executive Council to endorse the Hawksbill Creek Act, adopted by the Bahamian government in 1955. This act provided Groves with a 50,000-acre free port zone on Grand Bahama Island for the ludicrously low price of $2.80 an acre (the total price was $140,000 in 1955 dollars).[15] The free port zone covered approximately half the island. Journalist Bill Davidson described this act as "one of the most peculiar agreements ever concluded between a government and a private individual," adding that Groves was virtually "the Emperor" of Grand Bahama.[16] Groves had sole control over port facilities[17] designed to accommodate 77,000-tonne ships.[18] Under the

Hawksbill Creek Act, companies that settled in the port authority's free zone were "exempt until 2054 from export taxes and customs dues on imported products needed for their work."[19] Groves, however, had the right to impose a form of private taxation, and he also created an organization, the Grand Bahama Port Authority, through which he could grant any partner the right to take up residence in the port zone.[20] "This grant made the company a government," notes Alan Block, professor of criminology at Penn State University.[21] In addition, the tax exemptions increased the value of Groves's property. He eventually opened Port Authority capital to other investors in order to favour its growth and development, but he and his wife, Georgette, kept 50 percent of its assets.[22] The value per acre of the free port zone was now assessed at $2,800 – a 1,000 percent increase over the initial purchase price.

Groves was soon to return Sands's favour: he made no objection to Sands's promotion of a gambling house and resort on Grand Bahama.[23] In fact, Sands's project was so convincing that Groves set aside his own activities as a lumber producer to adopt his friend's business plan. Sands and Groves started looking for partners to make the island into a tourist destination.[24] As a British territory, the Bahamas already attracted British visitors, and the close proximity of Florida made it a promising location for tourist development.[25] However, the two schemers also had other, less honourable customers in mind.

■ A GALLERY OF SHADY CHARACTERS

This is where "Big Lou," Canadian citizen Louis Arthur Chesler, comes into the picture. Groves took him on as a partner in 1960 to open a luxury hotel on the Grand Bahama site,[26] and in 1961 the two created the Grand Bahama Development Company (Devco), of which Chesler was president.[27] Chesler soon took over all the company's shares through two Canadian corporations under his control.[28] A stockbroker at the Toronto Stock Exchange and owner of a mining development company in Canada, Chesler had been involved in providing capital to American investors who were close to power in Washington.[29] After becoming a millionaire, he pursued criminal activities in the financial world, handling stolen securities through offshore financial centres in Switzerland and the Bahamas.[30] According to French journalist Alain

Vernay, Chesler was "a 300-pound nabob whose friends included as many mafiosi as ministers and financiers."[31] CBC journalist Paul McGrath named Chesler as one of the "men initially responsible for corrupting the Bahamas with the introduction in the 1960s of mob-run casinos."[32] Mario Possamai, a forensic accounting investigator and CBC consultant with close ties to an RCMP informer,[33] corroborated this information in the 1990s, writing that Chesler had established "organized-crime-tainted gambling in the Bahamas."[34] The stated mission of Chesler's company was to attract retailers and residents to its part of the free zone.[35] But in fact, under cover of tourist operations, the goal was to attract illegal traffickers.

Groves and Chesler received from the Bahamas Executive Council a permit to build a luxury hotel in the zone,[36] as well as a Certificate of Exemption authorizing them to run a casino on Grand Bahama for ten years.[37] In 1963, they set up the Bahamas Amusements Limited.[38] The preferential treatment they were given was actually quite expensive, based as it was on the unrestrained bribery of politicians. Chesler's Devco and Groves's Port Authority provided the funds.[39] Stafford Sands, who worked tirelessly to get Executive Council approval for his friends' projects, received a huge sum.[40] "Sands was paid anywhere from $519,000 to $1,090,000 for legal services"[41] – fees that were also presented as "consultancy fees and political contributions."[42] In 1967, Sands told a Bahamian commission of inquiry that he had been paid $1 million for his "many services," but according to Vernay, he was alleged to have been given almost twice this amount.[43] Having paid for the goods, Groves and Chesler got what they wanted: their project was supported by five of the Executive Council's eight members.[44] There was some opposition because "everyone knew mobsters were running the casino,"[45] and one concession was made: casinos would have to pay taxes.[46] Hotels, however, would not have to pay taxes or even customs duties.[47] This arrangement led to many accounting scams ensuring that casinos officially ran deficits.

Chesler helped bring Meyer Lansky into the group.[48] During Prohibition, Lansky had made a fortune as a bootlegger selling Canadian hard liquor in New York.[49] In partnership with Cuban dictator Fulgencio Batista, he played a key role in ensuring that American organized crime dominated Havana until he and his associates were expelled by the Castro revolution in 1959.[50] A friend of Bugsy Siegel and Lucky Luciano, Lansky had studied the accounting errors that enabled an American federal court to convict Al Capone of tax fraud in 1931. He started by using Canada, then Cuba, to launder capital generated by his illegal activities in the 1930s.[51] Lansky eventually developed a range of techniques for transferring illegal funds to Switzerland and Liechtenstein: suitcases full of bills, travellers' cheques, bogus bank loans, direct investments by fictitious companies, and exploitation of Cuban casinos. He is viewed today as the father of the first great international money-laundering circuits.[52]

Thus, Sands brought in Groves, who brought in Chesler, who brought in Lansky – who brought in John Pullman, a racketeer who had become a Canadian citizen in the 1950s.[53] During Prohibition, Pullman had been part of some of the most sordid affairs in the New York crime world. As Chesler moved to the Bahamas to run casinos, Pullman was leaving for Switzerland to create a bank designed to handle Mob funds – the International Credit Bank (ICB).[54] When Chesler's Bahamian venture prospered, Pullman's bank opened a subsidiary in the Bahamas.[55] Pullman later participated in operations with South American smugglers so noxious that he attracted the attention of both American tax authorities (the IRS) and Canadian police officers.[56]

Lansky co-operated with Chesler in building the Grand Bahama casino.[57] He had been secretly discussing the project with his coterie for several years, and his confederates, previously active in the gambling and hotel business in Cuba,[58] helped shape the Bahama casino company's accounts in a way that would make it easier to launder criminal funds.[59] At the time, Interpol suspected the Lansky clan of managing the heroin trade in North America and Western Europe and was also trying to investigate its involvement in prostitution.[60]

Work was proceeding on the Grand Bahama luxury hotel. A Canadian corporation, Atlantic Acceptance, was in charge of financing the project in exchange for 850,000 shares in the company building the hotel. Within a few years, Atlantic had been fleeced by Groves and Chesler and was driven to bankruptcy.[61] The two swindlers caused construction costs to skyrocket. They were the owners of the Lucayan Beach Hotel and Development Company that was building the hotel,[62] and as Alan Block explains, "The inflation and corruption

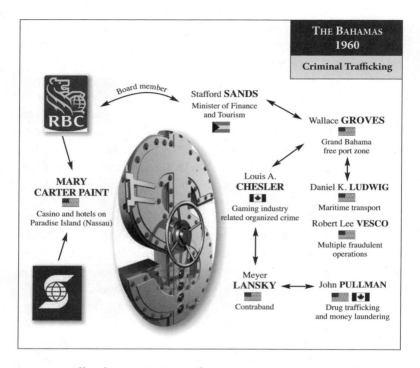

RBC

Board member

Stafford **SANDS**
Minister of Finance
and Tourism

Wallace **GROVES**

Grand Bahama
free port zone

**MARY
CARTER PAINT**

Casino and hotels on
Paradise Island (Nassau)

Louis A.
CHESLER

Gaming industry
related organized crime

Daniel K. **LUDWIG**

Maritime transport

Robert Lee **VESCO**

Multiple fraudulent
operations

Meyer
LANSKY

Contraband

John **PULLMAN**

Drug trafficking
and money laundering

were visually obvious in just a few years; construction quality was
quite shoddy and soon the hotel had the tinge of real squalor. Atlantic's stocks in the Lucayan development company weren't worth very
much after all."[63] Other Canadian companies such as the Montreal
Trust also held overvalued Lucayan stock, as did the American mafia
clan headed by Frank Nitti.[64] The not-quite-finished hotel, and the
casino, finally opened on January 11, 1964.[65]

In the spring of 1964, the plot twisted: Wallace Groves took control of Devco after a dispute with Chesler, who sold Groves his shares
and probably also sold his interest in the Lucayan Beach Hotel and
Development to Canadian financier Allen Manus.[66] More sharpsters
kept showing up. One of the "investors" attracted by the gambling
industry was Robert Lee Vesco.[67] His biographer locates him "at the
pinnacle of white-collar thieves,"[68] and he is said to have corrupted
Bahamians in every walk of life, transforming "as much of the population as he could into criminal accomplices."[69] A highly aggressive
investor, he prefigured the glory years of ruthless financier Michael

Milken. Vesco's initial technique had been to use borrowed money to enable one of his obscure corporations to acquire a prosperous firm, then to pay back the loans with which he had conquered the firm by looting its treasury and selling off its assets.[70] When in 1972, for example, the Investors Overseas Services (IOS) was experiencing this treatment, Vesco sent $392 million from his Luxembourg accounts to those of his own bank in the Bahamas.[71] His predatory operations were sheltered by the protective laws of offshore countries: Switzerland, Panama, Luxembourg, and, of course, the Bahamas.[72] Vesco's peace of mind was guaranteed by the hundreds of thousands of dollars he had contributed to Richard Nixon's election campaign.[73] Regulatory authorities were unable to determine how many hundreds of millions of dollars he had accumulated through his secret operations.[74] One reason was that he dabbled in everything: gun running, contraband high-tech equipment in Cuba, LSD trafficking, and so on. He was helped in his undertakings by two acolytes from Quebec, Norman LeBlanc (an experienced accountant trained at Montreal's McGill University) and Conrad Bouchard,[75] with whom he was connected to a major heroin-trafficking network in Canada,[76] and who was thought to be involved in drug purchases in Europe.[77] With the help of LeBlanc, not only did Vesco multiply fraudulent operations to plunder the assets of private firms, but in the Bahamas he also created a bank known as the Columbus Trust that received millions of dollars' worth of profits made by selling cocaine,[78] among other operations made possible by this structure.[79] American authorities put enormous pressure on the Bahamas to neutralize Vesco's dubious bank.[80] Another of Vesco's projects was a vain attempt to wrest control of Paradise Island from businessman Howard Hughes in order to make it into a gambling haven.[81]

Another key player was Daniel Keith Ludwig, owner of the world's second-largest private shipping fleet.[82] Already familiar with offshore management of maritime shipping, he was running ships under Liberian flags and managing his business through Liberia- and Panama-based holding companies. These companies controlled coal mines, oil wells, shipyards, and fishing concerns.[83] In the Bahamian free port, Ludwig established a fuel depot,[84] providing shippers with substantial savings over prices charged by suppliers located in the United States. At one point, Ludwig's oil bunkering company was moving over a million barrels a month through the island.[85] The free port also attracted other large companies such as Shell, which adopted a Bahamian flag of convenience for a number of its oil tankers.[86]

By the late 1960s, the colony's penchant for organized crime was well known. "Sir Stafford Sands as attorney for Bahamas Amusements Ltd. negotiated a licence fee for the casinos with Sir Stafford Sands, the minister of finance," the *Saturday Evening Post* mockingly reported in February 1967.[87] Other American publications such as *Time* magazine and the *Wall Street Journal*, as well as British newspapers, published devastating stories on the unhealthy developments to be observed in the Bahamas. But the IRS missed the opportunity to neutralize the network while there was still time.[88] In the early 1960s, the Bahamas started functioning as a base for establishing multiple connections between criminal channels and legal economic activity.[89] By the time the IRS acted, setting up Operation Tradewinds (1963–1965) to understand illicit financial activities in the colony, it was too late.[90] During the same period, British tax authorities were trying to put an end to bank secrecy as financial institutions active in Great Britain escaped government control. The British state itself was home to one of the world's most opaque offshore financial centres (the City of London), but as soon as banking institutions acted outside this specific framework, they could be sued. The Royal Bank of Canada (RBC) was to learn this lesson in 1972 when Great Britain's tax authority, the Inland Revenue Commissioners (IRC), took it to court over transactions generated in the Bahamas,[91] but the consequences for the bank were minimal.

As for Canada, its attitude to the Bahamas was one of indulgence. Ties between the two jurisdictions were so close that Bahamian premier Lynden Oscar Pindling, today described as the "Father of the Nation," started thinking in 1967 that maybe the Bahamas should forget about independence and become part of Canada. Canadian stewardship was viewed as "even more tolerant" than British rule,[92] and Canada had historic ties with the Bahamas. Since the arrival of Canadian institutions in the early twentieth century, the Bahamas had been functioning as a kind of tax haven for Canadians, even before the term was coined. Alain Vernay notes the advent of "subsidiaries, with wide-ranging powers, of Canada's best-known institutions,"[93] clearly referring to RBC, active in the Bahamas since the early twentieth century. This phenomenon was to become even more significant as time went by. By 1930, as the United States government enacted major tax increases to counter the Depression, massive numbers of investors discovered the appeal of the Bahamas as developed by Nassau's Canadian-run banks. In his book *Offshore*, William Brittain-Catlin, an investigator for London's Kroll Associates, a corporate investigations firm, notes that the trusts they established for their clients "ensured wealthy Americans maximum protection from onshore tax authorities."[94] Along with financial services, the colony offered a set of British-inspired laws which, since 1866, had enabled non-resident companies to avoid disclosing either their financial statements or their shareholders' names.

▇ "WE LIKE TO TAKE CARE OF YOU AT THE ROYAL BANK"

Taken over by outlaws in the 1960s, the Bahamian jurisdiction was now out of control. For Alan Block, facts spoke for themselves: "The Bahamas had been infiltrated by the most sophisticated band of professional criminals this century has produced."[95] The Grand Bahama casino project quickly found imitators: the culture of gambling and luxury hotels spread to other islands in the archipelago, including Paradise Island. Wallace Groves was involved in this project along with the Mary Carter Paint company.[96] Similar manoeuvres were taking place in Nassau, the capital, thanks to connections cynically developed by the Lansky clan with the Black emancipation movement that was soon to take power.[97] Meanwhile, Lou Chesler was quietly developing his own projects on Berry Island, hidden behind real estate and development companies.[98]

Criminal networks had made the Bahamas into a giant laundromat for dirty money. "Mingling with tourists, gangsters laden with banknotes flew in to Grand Bahama where they spent a few hours at the casino, then left the next day for New Providence island [that is, Nassau] to deposit their dollars in a private bank."[99] Often, these funds were immediately transferred to Switzerland in order to outwit "every American effort to detect criminal money."[100] Upscale villas and apartments proliferated, as did luxury shops and clinics[101] and hotels[102] (including those of Quebec investor Jean Doucet, later to be active in the Cayman Islands).[103] These were followed, of course, by banks, law firms, and accounting firms. "Still no courts of law, however,"[104] observes Alain Vernay. Every deal depended on influence peddling organized by Stafford Sands, Lou Chesler, Wallace Groves, and their associates: "The Bahamas must be run like a family concern by men who know how to run a business," intoned Sands, presumably with a straight face.[105]

As for the Lansky network in the Bahamas, its members were busy managing the Bank of World Commerce, entirely dedicated to the capitalization of its criminal activities.[106] One of their imitators, naturalized Canadian citizen John Pullman, established not only a branch of his Swiss bank in the Bahamas, but also company subsidiaries and trusts.[107] This was the moment when traditional financial capital – Canadian banks first and foremost – broke into what we might call "irregular affairs." A certain amount of surprise was caused when the instigator of the original venture, Stafford Sands (or *Sir* Stafford Sands as he was now known), was admitted to the RBC board. He was a director of the bank from January 13, 1966, to January 11, 1968,[108] while still a member of the Bahamas' Executive Council as minister of finance and tourism. Sands held these two positions while also acting as legal adviser to an American bank (Chase Manhattan) and a British bank (Barclays).[109] He also owned an insurance company[110] and was involved in the food, liquor, and gas and fuel retail trades.[111]

The Royal Bank of Canada would seem to have appointed Sands to its board in order to make him the bank's "representative in the Bahamas."[112] In other words, as an administrator, he was formally appointed to speak to his country's political institutions on behalf of the bank. As Alain Vernay remarks: "He acquired his knowledge of the world by acting on behalf of international corporations as they dealt with government and on behalf of government as it dealt with international corporations."[113] It is clear that the Canadian bank was in a position directly to influence Bahamian policy. To nobody's great surprise, the Bahamas was extremely indulgent to foreign financiers, providing a political space that was tailor-made to suit their exclusive interests. Vernay's comment in 1968 remains true to this day: "Nowhere in the New World can major investors find lawmakers more likely to regard them with favour and more eager to serve them."[114] Regulatory mechanisms in the Bahamas seemed to have been invented by Lewis Carroll. To create a private bank, for example, all you had to do was mail in an investment of a few hundred dollars; your initial capital might consist of five shares, each of which was worth five cents.[115]

RBC was perfectly at home in the Bahamas' arcane and permissive byways. It had been operating in the Bahamas since 1908 and remained the colony's only bank until 1947.[116] The bank's Bahamian activities took off in the late 1950s at a time when massive amounts of Eurodollars were appearing on the London market. In the early 1960s, the bank's annual reports discuss its presence in the Bahamas in the most conventional economic terms. The free movement of capital in offshore jurisdictions is first mentioned in 1963 under the "Widespread International Organization" heading: "During the past few years, with the increased convertibility of major world currencies, with the formation of new trading blocs and the general lowering of barriers to freer world trade, and with the movement of free funds becoming more sensitive to changing conditions in the principal money markets of the world, the international field has become more and more important in banking operations."[117]

This is how the bank explained why it had opened a new regional office for the Caribbean in Nassau while continuing its expansion in British Honduras (today Belize), Jamaica, St. Kitts and Nevis, and Trinidad and Tobago.[118] In 1964, RBC opened three more branches in the Bahamas for a total of eighteen.[119]

In 1968, the Royal Bank became involved in an undertaking related to the projected casino on Paradise Island, Nassau's neighbour. The undertaking was to build a bridge between the two islands, to be carried out by the Bridge Company. Along with Power Corporation, the Montreal Trust Company, and a few other international banking corporations such as the Westminster Bank, RBC was a shareholder in the RoyWest Bank consortium.[120] This entity, incorporated under Bahamian law, not only held a mortgage on the Bridge Company but also owned shares in the company.[121] Building the bridge was a condition imposed on the Mary Carter Paint company, "a chain of large hardware stores with a yen for diversification,"[122] when it obtained a licence to run a casino after a meeting with Stafford Sands.[123] To get the licence, the company also had to put Sands himself on the payroll[124] and provide the business coterie already present on Grand Bahama with a minority participation (four-ninths) in its Paradise Island operations.[125] In all, Mary Carter Paint amassed $33 million to fund the infrastructure supporting its casino in the Bahamas. Over half of this amount, to which the Canadian bank contributed, came from criminal assets.[126]

With what we can't help suspecting is black humour, in the RBC 1965 annual report, just before Stafford Sands's arrival as a member of the board, the bank's chief executive writes: "RoyWest was formed to undertake mortgage and development financing in the Bahamas and the British Caribbean territories and we expect that it will help to fill a long-felt need in these areas."[127] We may also note that on at least one occasion during this period, the RBC board met in Nassau,[128] and that this was a period when the RBC faced allegations of money laundering in the Bahamas.[129] However, as Inspector General of Banks William Kennett said in the 1980s of RBC chairman Rowland Frazee: "By the time you get to be CEO of the Royal, you're no longer running the bank on a day-to-day basis, you [are] a statesman."[130]

THE BANK OF NOVA SCOTIA: "WE'RE RICHER THAN YOU THINK"

As its network of partners grew, Mary Carter Paint became more ambitious. Having paid a speculator $12.5 million for 75 percent of the land on Paradise Island, the company invested $3.5 million of its own money and "picked up a $9 million mortgage held by the Bank of Nova Scotia" (today's Scotiabank).[131] This Canadian institution was now part of the Bahamian venture along with RBC. Taking up the euphemisms suited to high finance, in 1960 the Bank of Nova Scotia had explained its Caribbean activities by referring to its expertise and long experience,[132] rather than the sudden availability of capital in crime-producing tax havens where money can always be washed clean.

In the Bank of Nova Scotia's 1960 annual report, its general manager did acknowledge in somewhat ambiguous language that "it should be recognized that some of the deposits obtained are of a fluctuating character."[133] However, what the bank was chiefly called on to recognize in later years was the fact that U.S. tax authorities and Department of Justice were on its tail. In the late 1960s, the IRS suspected the International

Credit Bank (the institution managed by naturalized Canadian citizen John Pullman for the benefit of organized crime) of having deposited money with the Bank of Nova Scotia and another Canadian institution, the Canadian Imperial Bank of Commerce (CIBC).[134] The IRS was also interested in a $15-million loan made by the Bank of Nova Scotia to the Bahamian subsidiary of Resorts International Inc. in order to fund a casino project in Atlantic City.[135] The suspicions of American authorities continued to mount, reaching a peak in the 1980s. U.S. grand juries now thought that the Bank of Nova Scotia's Miami branch might be opening accounts for American clients in its Bahamian branches.[136] The Bahamas at this point were subject to close surveillance by the United States, since they were thought to channel 50 percent of the cocaine entering the country.[137] In addition, American federal authorities had been told by a 1983 Senate report that losses of $75 billion in U.S. balance-of--payments data were largely due to "errors and omissions" associated with money-laundering operations, and specifically operations in Caribbean tax havens.[138] The U.S. Senate report noted in passing: "In the Caribbean, one major Canadian international bank has a consistent reputation for encouraging dirty money."[139]

Of the five major Canadian banks, the Bank of Nova Scotia was by far the most active in the Bahamas and the one that had the most to lose from the U.S. government's unwanted attention. In 1982, its "international" activities accounted for over 50 percent of its profits.[140] The previous year, a grand jury in Fort Lauderdale had demanded to see the records of one of the bank's Bahamian branches to investigate an alleged connection with drug dealers.[141] At the time, the bank's name was associated with a variety of drug lords such as Salvatore Amendolito, Bruce Griffin, and Leigh Ritch,[142] as well as Carlos Lehder and his cartel.[143] In the late 1970s and early 1980s, Lehder deposited profits from massive heroin-trafficking activities in Bank of Nova Scotia accounts in the Bahamas, under cover of managing a marina in the archipelago.[144] "In the 1970s and 1980s, the Bahamas must have been a paradise for drug dealers: Carlos Lehder actually owned one of the archipelago's islands," according to criminologist Patrice Meyzonnier.[145] This island, Norman's Cay, was used for cocaine transshipments.[146] Lehder was both one of the period's major drug dealers and a manager of companies located in the Bahamas such as International Dutch Resources.[147] The Bank of

Nova Scotia did not bat an eyelid as US$11.4 million passed through Lehder's accounts in less than two years. In contrast, an American money-laundering expert concluded that these transactions were, at the very least, suspicious.[148] According to forensic accountant Mario Possamai, many of Lehder's financial outflows "took advantage of the Canadian bank's vast international network. Tens of thousands of dollars, for instance, were routinely wired between Scotiabank branches in Nassau, Miami, Panama [another tax haven] and New York."[149]

In short, the bank made it possible for the money to go from shadow to sunlight. In a final twist of the plot, Bahamian prime minister Lynden Oscar Pindling was also suspected of corruption in connection with the Lehder affair.[150] The Bank of Nova Scotia's actions did nothing to lay these suspicions to rest: the bank had loaned Pindling over $1 million and "seemed to do little to annoy [him] with interest payments."[151] None of this prevented Pindling from hosting a 1985 summit at which he welcomed Commonwealth prime ministers, including Margaret Thatcher from Great Britain and Brian Mulroney from Canada.

Subpoenaed in the United States in 1981 in connection with the affairs of drug dealer Robert Twist, the Bank of Nova Scotia was reluctant to provide American courts with relevant bank records, claiming that the Bahamian law on bank secrecy required it to withhold all information on its clients in the Bahamas. In 1982, the U.S. court responded by imposing a $500-a-day fine, which was increased to $25,000 a day in 1983. The bank finally gave in.[152] In all, the case cost the bank over $100,000 in fines,[153] but the symbolic price was even higher, as the bank's reputation was tarnished by charges of contempt of court arising from its stubborn refusal to co-operate.

In March 1983, American tax authorities began a second set of legal proceedings against the Bank of Nova Scotia, this time in a case involving an American marijuana trafficker, Frank Brady.[154] "In January 1984 twelve persons were indicted on charges of importing marijuana into Florida. The leader of the ring later claimed to have incorporated businesses in Florida and the Bahamas and washed the funds through several secret accounts in the Bahamas and Cayman Islands branches of the Bank of Nova Scotia."[155]

The bank argued that it was caught between a rock and a hard place: American injunctions violated Bahamian laws on bank secrecy.

The scenario of the Robert Twist drug-dealing case was enacted a second time. When the bank in 1984 grew tired of paying the $25,000-a-day fine, it finally agreed to co-operate. At that point, it had paid fines totalling US$1.825 million.[156]

The president of the Bank of Nova Scotia, Cedric Ritchie, explained in the 1980s that his institution was subject to the contradictions of international law and the historical moment. His defence was a touching statement of helplessness: "Because of both the nature of our business in the Caribbean and the unique vulnerability of that region to drug traffickers, it was inevitable that criminals would attempt to use our bank for their nefarious purposes."[157] This kind of premise could only lead to a plea of innocence: "In hindsight, there can be little doubt that some of our branches were used unwittingly to launder drug-related profits."[158]

GOODBYE, FROSTY CANADA

It was in fact true in the 1970s and 1980s that the Bank of Nova Scotia found itself caught between two legal systems: American law demanding that it produce its clients' records, and Bahamian law that forbade this in the name of "bank secrecy."[159] However, this situation was of the bank's own making. In the late 1970s, its representative in the Bahamas, Donald Fleming, worked to convince the Bahamian government to enact, in relation to banks, the most permissive and protective tax laws and regulations conceivable. These turned the Bahamas into a formidable offshore state competing with traditional politically sovereign countries. Fully conversant with constitutional law and the workings of Western states, Fleming knew exactly how a tax haven could develop a negative set of laws that would neutralize them. Serving as Canada's minister of finance in the Diefenbaker government from 1957 to 1962,[160] then as first Secretary-General of the Organisation for Economic Co-operation and Development (OECD) in 1961[161] and a governor of the World Bank and the International Monetary Fund in the 1960s, Fleming ended his public career as president of the International Bank for Reconstruction and Development (IBRD).[162] He also aspired to high political office: on three occasions, he vainly attempted to become the leader of the federal Progressive Conservative Party.[163] In

1968, as his political career was ending, the Bank of Nova Scotia offered him a position as managing director of the Bank of Nova Scotia Trust Company in the Bahamas.[164] From Nassau, this institution controlled a group of trusts, all of which were located in tax havens: the Bahamas, Jamaica, Trinidad, Barbados, and the Cayman Islands.[165] (The bank was later to open offices in the British Virgin Islands and Guyana.)[166] In 1977, Fleming wittily remarked to Prince Philip, who happened to be in the Bahamas: "I have found that being a banker in Nassau is more profitable than being Minister of Finance in frosty Ottawa."[167] The prince laughed heartily. Tax consultant Édouard Chambost, also a great wit, commented that Fleming "did not lose his presence of mind when he became director of the Bank of Nova Scotia Trust Company."[168]

Fleming's full title was comprehensive: "General Counsel to the Bank of Nova Scotia in executive, financial, public relations and other matters in the Bahamas and the Islands of the West Indies and the Caribbean."[169] In this location characterized by "freedom from income tax,"[170] his job was to advise not only the bank on practically every matter, but also the Bahamian government. "My duties under this title offered unlimited variety. I sometimes ... met ministers of governments, advised on legislation, consulted on tax matters," he says in his memoirs.[171] In fact, his role was more active than this would imply, encompassing far more than mere lobbying. Along with American lawyer Marshall Langer,[172] Fleming was one of the people who designed the Bahamas tax haven in its contemporary form. For anyone following current events in the offshore world, it would have been obvious that his 1977 public speech in Nassau on the importance of bank secrecy and a zero tax rate was made to support the Bahamas against any attempt on the part of American tax authorities or courts to intervene in whatever schemes were being hatched in the islands. According to the highly knowledgeable Édouard Chambost, the "state of mind" prevailing in the Bahamas, inasmuch as it was "opposed to that of the United States," was precisely what was "summarized in a speech by Mr. Donald M. Fleming."[173] Two years earlier, Fleming had published a panegyric on the Bahamas in *The Tax Executive*, subtly titled "The Bahamas (Tax) Paradise."[174]

Mario Possamai notes that "in the Bahamas, much credit is ... given to a former Canadian finance minister, Donald Fleming."[175]

Throughout his years in the Bahamas, Fleming helped make bank secrecy watertight.[176] In the early 1980s, when the Bahamas was under investigation by American drug enforcement agents,[177] and the Canadian government had timidly begun "probing in a tax case,"[178] Fleming was there to advise Bahamian policymakers. According to McGill University criminologist R. T. Naylor, "On the advice of a resident former Canadian finance minister, Donald Fleming, the Bahamas passed the Bank and Trust Regulation Act, which closed most of the loopholes through which confidential client information could be obtained."[179]

Fleming's intervention in the Bahamas shows the evolution of the Canadian establishment's projects for the Caribbean. Offshorization, a project blocked to some extent in Jamaica by the population's political will to achieve political emancipation and greater economic independence, was here carried out to a far greater extent. RBC and the Bank of Nova Scotia, fully at ease in their dealings with the Bahamas as the "serious crime community" was emerging in the 1960s, continued to flourish in the congenial atmosphere created by Fleming's watertight bank secrecy.

The strong pressure exerted by American tax authorities on the Bahamas since the 1960s put Bahamian officials on the defensive. Because of this pressure, Stafford Sands scrambled to protect appearances as scandals continued to rock the colony. "The only thing that concerns us," he said to Alain Vernay, "is to preserve our reputation for honesty and efficiency."[180] The sentence reads like a revealing slip of the pen: *only our reputation matters – regardless of what we may have done.* It is a sign of embarrassment arising from the debasement of Bahamian public institutions. Even when he wants to be reassuring, Sands's conclusion is autocratic in tone: "If someone threatens to damage the Bahamas' reputation and honour, I'll get rid of him. There's no need for explanations – it's enough."[181] This turned out to be his swan song: the business sharper-cum-politician left the colony for good in 1967, having been "charged with taking a $1.8-million payoff."[182] The United States forced archipelago authorities to undertake a modicum of efforts to ensure respectability,[183] including the gradual development of a program to fight the drug trade. In 2000, criminologist Patrice Meyzonnier noted that "the United States, which provide the archipelago with 150 DEA [Drug Enforcement Administration] agents and an equal number of U.S. Customs and U.S. Army personnel, have created throughout the territory a radar detection network using tethered balloons."[184]

The United States was also putting pressure on its northern neighbour, convincing Canada to provide a minimal degree of regulation for the offshore activities of its banks. By 1968, the two countries had already signed an agreement stating that "Canadian authorities agreed to co-operate with the United States in ensuring that Canada did not become a capital conduit whereby funds were passed through this country en route to third countries, in attempts to avoid the applications of the U.S. guidelines."[185] This agreement was sharply criticized by the Bank of Nova Scotia in its 1968 annual report.[186]

However, American pressure on Canadian banks was short-lived. Under the ultra-liberal presidency of Ronald Reagan, the U.S. financial lobby found it easy to convince Washington to give free rein to Canadian banking activity in the Caribbean. In 1981, Washington allowed American financial institutions to create their own Canadian-style institutions abroad, known as International Banking Facilities or IBFs.[187] Until then, anti-offshore sentiment in the United States had been "encouraged by the entrenched position of major Canadian and British banks in the Bahamas and Caymans."[188] From that point on, American bankers could benefit from tax havens through subsidiaries of corporations under their own control in the United States.

O BAHAMAS, OUR HOME AND NATIVE LAND

During the first half of the twentieth century, before any of these scams and swindles, two Canadian investors had created in the Bahamas the precursor of gated communities for millionaires. These lairs were surrounded by "the high walls of rising prices" that kept passing tourists at bay. They proved to be "pygmy havens for gigantic fortunes." Sir Harry Oakes, "the king of Canadian mining,"[189] über-rich discoverer in 1912 of Canada's largest gold mine in Kirkland Lake, Ontario, appreciated the fine points of the Bahamian island of New Providence: settling there in 1935 enabled him to avoid both death duties[190] and $3 million a year in Canadian taxes.[191] (In 2012, the Niagara Falls History Museum was still presenting him as a great philanthropist.)[192] After the Second World War another Canadian investor, Edward Plunket Taylor, also settled in New Providence. Taylor's investment company, Argus, controlled a number of the finest representatives of Canadian capitalism, including Massey Ferguson, Canadian Breweries, the St. Lawrence Corporation, and Dominion Stores.

"The fact that the two biggest landowners of New Providence are Canadian is not due to chance," noted Vernay.[193] At the time, the Canadian government itself had established advantageous rules for its "non-residents" as part of an "agreement on non-Canadian double taxation."[194] According to these rules, non-residents paid no tax on their Bahamian income and only 15 percent on their Canadian income.[195] Canadians could obtain these rights as long as they did not own a house in Canada or sit on the board of directors of any Canadian company. They could also take full advantage of Canada's public services during the 183 days per year they were entitled to spend in Canada.[196]

These advantages were enjoyed by many. In 1978, after selling Siebens Oil for $120 million, Albertan oil tycoon Harold Siebens hurried to the Bahamas to avoid Canadian taxes.[197] In the 1980s, David Gilmour, Peter Munk's former partner in the Barrick Gold mining company, also settled in the Bahamas,[198] while Antoine Turmel, founder of the Provigo supermarket chain, spent his golden retirement years in the archipelago after stepping down as company chairman in 1985.[199] James Smith, former governor of the Bahamas Central Bank from 1987 to 1997 and minister of finance from 2002 to 2007, explained in *The Bahamas Investor* that these wealthy Canadians played a key role in the islands' political evolution.[200] The tax rules designed for their benefit in the 1930s helped the Bahamas gradually develop as a tax haven for wealthy individuals,[201] and Canadian expertise is still serving them for tax purposes today. Farhad Vladi, for example, is a Canadian broker whose unusual calling is to sell dream islands in offshore archipelagos, especially the Bahamas. Throughout the world, he has negotiated the sale of over 2,000 islands to ultra-wealthy purchasers.[202]

The Canadian banks' massive presence came later. While the Royal Bank of Canada had opened in Nassau in 1908 in the aftermath of the American invasion of Cuba,[203] it was not until the 1950s that Canadian financial institutions in the Bahamas asserted themselves as international institutions handling significantly larger volumes of transactions. RBC was joined in Nassau by the Bank of Nova Scotia in 1956,[204] the Canadian Bank of Commerce in 1957, and the Bank of Montreal in 1958.[205] In partnership with British interests, the Bank of Nova Scotia created a new company dedicated to "carrying out ... certain offshore deals and trust operations which were not open to a Canadian bank."[206] The new institution, known as the Bank of Nova Scotia Trust Company (Bahamas), then opened offices in New York, Jamaica, and Trinidad and Tobago in order to serve its American customers in the Caribbean. The CIBC merged its Caribbean operations with Barclays' in 2001.[207] (Barclays sold its shares in this concern in 2006).[208] As for the Bank of Montreal, it first established the Bank of London and Montreal (BOLAM) in partnership with the Bank of London and South America (BOLSA) in Nassau in 1958,[209] then founded the Bank of Montreal (Bahamas & Caribbean) Limited when BOLAM was dissolved in 1970.[210] Until the 1980s, "the four biggest Canadian banks controlled more than 80% of increasingly lucrative Bahamian domestic business."[211] Canadian financial institutions moved into the Caribbean to handle "complex international transactions that cannot be repeated" (this description by Alain Vernay sounds like a line from some corrosive satirist such as Jon Stewart).[212] Today, Canadian banks are still described by the Bahamian financial press as "an integral part of the financial services industry, offering trust and private banking services" along with other big banks in Nassau.[213] Scotiabank has six corporate entities operating in the Bahamas,[214] RBC, four,[215] and CIBC, two.[216]

THE BAHAMAS TAX HAVEN: WHO PAYS THE PRICE?

For Canadians, the existence of a tax haven in the Bahamas comes with a high price tag. Under Ottawa's benevolent gaze, Donald Fleming, the former Canadian minister of finance who moved on to act for Scotiabank, helped convince the Bahamian government to adopt a development model that would provide banks, multinationals, and wealthy individuals – whether Canadian or not – with a series of tax and legal loopholes. Today, the Bahamas are one of the world's most controversial tax havens. This dot-sized country offers multiple ways of registering assets, including banks, trusts, and shell companies. No tax is paid by companies or fortune-holders from abroad. And the country has its own stock market, the Bahamas International Securities Exchange (BISX).[217]

The Bahamas have also continued to be a drug-trafficking hub for the region,[218] used as a key transit point for cocaine entering the United States.[219] Fifty percent of the cocaine intended for the North American market is thought to pass through the Bahamas' hidden runways or one of its 120 ports.[220]

"The Bahamas, along with the Cayman Islands and Panama, are still the triumvirate of tax havens."[221] It is true that unrelenting pressure from the United States since the 1980s has led the Bahamas to eliminate bank secrecy for transactions involving that country. Thus, any transfer to the United States involving more than $5,000 must be declared.[222] However, there are countless ways of getting around this regulation. Criminologist Patrice Meyzonnier observes that "Bahamian banks are still a major refuge for banks throughout the world,"[223] especially Swiss banks, which continue to open branches in the Bahamas to serve customers who want the respectability of the Swiss regime. To no one's surprise, the Bahamas was on the earliest versions of blacklists dealing with tax havens and tax evasion produced by the Financial Action Task Force (FATF) on drug trafficking, the OECD, and the Financial Stability Forum (FSF).[224]

Several recent financial scandals in Canada reveal close connections between swindlers and the Bahamas. The Cinar affair is one example. In 2000, unknown to its board of directors, this children's animation company transferred some US$120 million to Bahamian bank accounts controlled by Cinar senior executives.[225] (Cinar is also known for "falsifying identities of scriptwriters to obtain millions in Canadian content subsidies"[226] and for a plagiarism affair involving creator Claude Robinson.)[227] In 2003, another Canadian company, Norshield, used the Bahamas' watertight bank secrecy rules to manipulate the accounts of a subsidiary in order to overstate the value of its assets to the tune of $300 million.[228] In 2006, the Bahamian firm Dominion Investment, owned by Canadian businessman Martin Tremblay, was part of a money-laundering operation involving US$1 billion, and in 2007, the company was convicted of having channelled US$20,000 from Russian double agents through the Bahamas.[229] All these schemers were able to carry out their plans by opening bank accounts with RBC in the Bahamas. And according to Revenue Canada, Nick Rizzuto, associated with the Montreal mafia, was able to open accounts with the same institution.[230] How can this be? "We're not our customers' accountants." This was the RBC spokesman's answer to *La Presse* in 2007, at the same time as he was praising his institution's "very strict standards of control." While seeking to reassure, during the interview the spokesman nonetheless expressed surprise that a mafioso such as Rizzuto was able to open an account, thus contradicting the bank's claim of stringency: "I don't know why... There's a lack of congruence between these principles and your question."[231]

In 2009, it was Progressive Management's turn to be charged with fraud: this fictitious investment company was accused of orchestrating, from the Bahamas, a giant scam to remove millions of dollars from its clients' pockets.[232] In 2013, the owner of the Gildan garment manufacturing company, Glenn Chamandy, was in the hot seat as the Canada Revenue Agency launched a suit against the company for having transferred tens of millions of dollars to an obscure company in the Bahamas. Quebec's large civil service pension fund, the Caisse de dépôt et placement du Québec, held 11 percent of Gildan shares, and the company was also funded by the Fonds de solidarité (an investment fund sponsored by government and the Quebec Federation of Labour) until 2003. In other words, this company seems to have taken full advantage of financial globalization. With the help of public funds, its wealthy owner runs a company whose T-shirts are manufactured in sweatshops in free zones in the Dominican Republic or Bangladesh, while its profits are recorded in the Bahamas so that he can avoid paying taxes.[233]

Almost every country in the world could provide us with similar tales of criminality made possible by the Bahamas' highly permissive laws. The Bahamian system, in existence throughout the twentieth century but whose development took off in the 1960s (largely through the agency of Canadians), wrongs the Canadian population. When Canadians today are called on to compensate, through tax increases, the loss of government revenue caused by tax flight; when they accept the fact that institutions designed for the common good are weakened and public services are deteriorating; or when they endure the presence of criminal dealers who have become obscene investors after having laundered their ill-gotten gains offshore, they are experiencing the harmful consequences of the Bahamian regime.

The people of the Bahamas also pay a price. One aspect of the system's financial colonialism is that they pay astronomical customs duties to make up for the lack of a corporate tax.[234] Agriculture in the Bahamas is marginal, industry is concentrated in the Freeport free zone, and major economic sectors have generally been abandoned in favour of tourism. Canada's colonial power has established, as a horizon that can never be transcended, the idea that people living in the Bahamas must be the willing servants of the great. Politically, Bahamians have been left high and dry. Even Prime Minister Pindling, "Father of the Nation," who in the 1960s paved the way for Bahamian independence in 1973, never opposed his country's metamorphosis into a tax haven. The furthest he went was to suggest, when in opposition, that banks might provide islanders with better credit services![235] The group of foreign bankers that controlled the Bahamas was never seriously bothered by the Bahamian independence movement supported by the Black community. According to Alain Vernay, the "president of a great Canadian financial institution" that had been "the chief employer of the Bay Street Boys" found it very easy to come to terms with the defeat of the Bahamas' White financial establishment: he said it was probably better, in the long run, that "White casuists of taxation and law" be replaced by "equally qualified Black casuists."[236] Pindling himself was involved in shady deals, one of which involved fraudulent bookkeeping entries arising from the affairs of a corporation whose "real owner, a Canadian financier," remains unknown.[237] The Bahamian prime minister also enjoyed the favours of corrupt businessman Robert Vesco,[238] who at various times was funding him to the tune of $100,000 per month.[239] *Time* magazine asserted in 1964 that a member of the Bahamian opposition party claimed a close relation with a Canadian institution: "Nine out of 33 seats in the island assembly are held by the all-Negro Progressive Liberal Party, whose membership includes one man who campaigned in last year's general election on a promise to distribute the Royal Bank of Canada's money among his supporters."[240]

The truth about this affair, like so many others taking place in the Bahamas, will remain unspoken – because that's the way it's supposed to be.

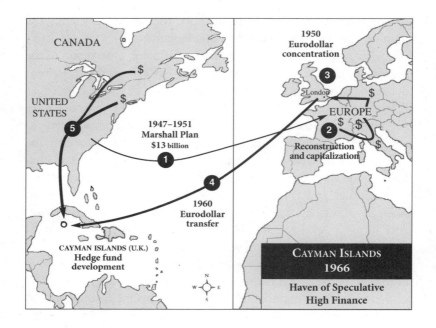

CANADA

UNITED STATES

1950
Eurodollar
concentration

3

London

EUROPE

$

5

1947–1951
Marshall Plan
$13 billion

1

$ $
2
$
Reconstruction
and capitalization

4

1960
Eurodollar
transfer

CAYMAN ISLANDS (U.K.)
Hedge fund
development

N
W ⬥ E
S

CAYMAN ISLANDS
1966

Haven of Speculative
High Finance

CAYMAN ISLANDS

HIDEOUT FOR SPECULATIVE HIGH FINANCE

In which a lawyer from Calgary lays the
foundations of hedge-fund law

Europe was awash in credit during reconstruction after the Second World War. Washington alone poured $13 billion into the Old World between 1947 and 1951 in an effort to relaunch the European economy. Out of the European Recovery Plan, also known as the Marshall Plan, was born a strange new currency: the Eurodollar. This new currency appeared when the United States, fearing inflation, chose not to bring its money back home once this money had activated exchanges in Europe. Dollars circulated freely in Europe, unregulated by any state.[1] For the first time, bankers handled massive amounts of money in a currency that did not belong to their home country. The financial world – that considerable share of the planet's assets that are managed by financial institutions without governmental supervision – began to flourish.

Thanks to the Marshall Plan and the United States' carefree approach to creating money abroad, the American dollar proved a highly volatile world currency. This volatility was confirmed when President Nixon ended the dollar's gold convertibility in 1971. "National states no longer had the means to fight financial markets, which had been freed from all constraint with the creation of Euromarkets," writes Jean de Maillard in a book published by a group of European judges under the grim title *Un monde sans loi* ("a world without law").[2] Economic journalist Nicholas Shaxson makes a similar point. Before this metamorphosis, he writes, "exchange rates were mostly fixed, banks were not supposed to trade in foreign currencies unless it was for the purpose of financing specific trades for their clients and not allowed to take deposits in foreign currencies, and governments were tightly controlling how fast financial capital could flow in and out of their economies."[3]

The market itself then produced, in rapid-fire succession, a series of complex mechanisms designed to neutralize the risks associated with deregulation. For example, you could now acquire options to buy securities or currencies at predetermined rates, independent of market fluctuations. These contracts themselves became the object of further transactions based on highly complex calculations. The massive development of this new currency, without any basis in reality, gave tax havens a new impetus. According to Jean de Maillard, "Tax and banking havens, in the afterwar years, were control valves for politics, the economy and finance. In fact, they were slush funds. But computers, satellites, and emerging financial markets gave these banking places an unprecedented scale."[4] Speculators claiming to improve on the workings of the international financial system now put the savings of entire populations beyond the reach of traditional states. Decisions to buy or sell massive amounts of a currency or stock – either to turn a quick profit from high-speed movement of large amounts of capital, or to avoid the impact of a feared price collapse – were now allowed to escape any form of control, no matter how destabilizing this might prove to the world order.

According to McGill University criminologist R. T. Naylor, Eurodollars and deregulated markets led companies to pay more attention to how they were viewed by speculators, who buy and sell at unimaginable speed, than to actually extracting profit from industrial or tangible production. Even worse, companies were able to use financial products based on the Eurodollars concentrated in tax havens to avoid the basic rules prevailing in their jurisdiction: they no longer needed to ensure minimum shareholder equity. For banks, meanwhile, Eurodollars were a favourite financial tool, providing abundant reserves of cash in the form of dollars as long as they were channelled to tax havens – that is, as long as they were sheltered from traditional monetary requirements and taxes. Naylor's chapter on this topic is titled "Eurodollars and Nonsense."[5]

For financiers, this was a hot, libidinous time. Traders were as frenzied as the casino crowds described by Dostoevsky in his novel *The Gambler.* The game was all about pride and distinction: not so much about gaining wealth as about taking pleasure in beating the system by profiting from its flaws. The speculators had their own story. Unlike the surrounding mafia, who were involved in so many sordid affairs, specu-lators, on the contrary, developed what they saw as pure, abstract ways of getting rich and, like George Soros, they posed as "philosophers."[6]

The place where Eurodollars first converged was London or, more specifically, its business district, the City, literally a state within a state. The City was in fact a tax haven that had been controlled for almost a thousand years by merchants, and later banks, that settled there independently of the British government. The corporation man-aging the financial district provided banks with many legislative and regulatory advantages.[7] The Bank of England acted as a pressure group or, in the words of journalist Nicholas Shaxson, "a sort of praetorian guard protecting the City of London and its libertarian world view."[8] The Eurodollar market exploded in 1957 when the Bank of England agreed not to regulate transactions carried out in London in U.S. dollars, as long as they took place between two non-residents.[9] From the City, it then became possible to manage currencies other than the British pound sterling. While this had previously been done on a small scale,[10] the volumes now generated began to flood the market. City banks recorded $1 billion in deposits in 1960, compared to $200 million the previous year. The total rose to $3 billion in 1961, $46 billion in 1970, and $500 billion in 1980; today, nobody even tries to measure it.[11] By 1997, close to 90 percent of the world's international loans were made through this market that had no standards.[12] Eastern bloc countries would rather invest their U.S. dollars in Europe than in the United States, and American companies preferred London's higher interest rates, avoiding the legal maximum to which they were subject at home.[13]

Of particular importance was the fact that City bankers had direct connections with British territories and colonies overseas that were subcontracted to carry out embarrassing operations such as money laundering and fiscal avoidance. In these territories, the banks also developed fantastic financial products such as Eurobonds, used by European states to borrow money.[14] Entirely unregulated and strictly speculative in nature, these offshore bearer bonds were worth whatever price the market was willing to pay. With no record as to who owned them, they were an ideal vehicle for anyone practising tax evasion.[15]

One of the major architects of the Eurodollar markets, George Bolton,[16] a former executive director of the Bank of England who became the chairman of the Bank of London and South America (BOLSA) in 1957,[17] established a partnership with the Bank of Montreal to free his activities from the pound. In 1958, he organized a joint venture between BOLSA and the Bank of Montreal, creating the Bank of London and Montreal (BOLAM). BOLAM spread throughout the Caribbean, opening branches in Nassau, then Jamaica and Trinidad and Tobago.[18] This partnership afforded Bolton, an investor with close ties to the Canadian financial establishment,[19] a certain level of protection as he launched his institution into the volatile Eurodollar market. The Montreal bank provided him with access to Canadian currency[20] and enabled BOLSA managers "to tighten their connection with the U.S. and the dollar."[21]

Among Canadians, however, bankers were not the ones chiefly involved in developing the highly speculative sector that was eventually to have such a devastating impact on economies affected by Eurodollars.[22] A key role was played by a Canadian lawyer who was determined to make the Cayman Islands into one of the riskiest financial investment centres in the world.

 ## "A FEW PHILOSOPHICAL IDEAS ON HOW YOU MAKE A TAX HAVEN WORK"

London bankers used tax havens governed by the British Crown to coordinate operations that the City itself did not allow. From within the City's perimeter, affairs that needed to remain in the shadows were managed offshore with the lightest of touches. Shaxson offers the following summary:

> The formal empire did not quite disappear; fourteen small island states decided not to seek independence, becoming British overseas territories with the Queen as their head of state. Exactly half of them – Anguilla, Bermuda, the British Virgin Islands, the Cayman Islands, Gibraltar, Montserrat, and the Turk and Caicos Islands – are secrecy jurisdictions, actively supported and managed from Britain and intimately linked with the City of London.[23]

The Euromarket and speculative finance were eventually to be dominated by the Cayman Islands. This colony was directly attached to the

Crown in 1962 after Jamaica, of which it had previously been a part, achieved independence. The Caymans provided ways of incorporating deregulated finance into major economic circuits, avoiding taxes, and laundering criminal funds that people did not want to handle in London.[24]

There is nothing fortuitous about the rush of Canadian banks to the Caymans during this period.[25] In 1964, only two banks served the population of 8,612 people scattered over three islands.[26] When the Royal Bank of Canada opened a branch in the Cayman Islands in 1965, it took deposits from seamen and small local businesses.[27] By 1976, there were 126 banks,[28] and by the early 1980s, 450.[29] Some 250 of these were subsidiaries of large international institutions. Insurance companies were established in the islands – there were 270 of them in 1983 – and companies appeared by the thousands, juggling dozens of billions of dollars. The Eurobond and Eurodollar sectors developed by leaps and bounds, and money laundering became routine.[30]

The transformation of the Cayman Islands into a formidable tax haven was the work of Calgary lawyer and Conservative politician Jim Macdonald. In a 1979 interview with Macdonald entitled "The Haven That Jim Macdonald Built," *Canadian Business* magazine notes that, though there were no banks on the Cayman Islands when Macdonald first visited in 1959, eventually he "wrote the Companies Tax Law that is the source of the islands' current prosperity," attracting "250 offshore banks...and about 9,000 offshore companies."[31] The City of Calgary, where Macdonald was alderman from 1955 to 1959, describes him as the first qualified lawyer to settle in the Caymans and the author of the law "which established the Island as a tax haven."[32] This claim is corroborated by forensic accountant Mario Possamai, who states that Macdonald wrote the Cayman Islands legislation on bank secrecy: he "deftly turned the Caymans into the region's preeminent tax haven," drawing on "the best features of more established rivals."[33] Inspired by laws from the neighbouring Bahamas and Bermuda, as well as the very permissive State of Delaware (a tax haven within the United States),[34] or perhaps even Ontario, Macdonald quickly reached his goal. "I had a few philosophical ideas on how you make a tax haven work. There was nothing particularly magical about it,"[35] as he told *Canadian Business*. This is certainly true: there is nothing overly complex about the

Caymans' business "philosophy." According to Monte Smith, who was in charge of the Bank of Nova Scotia in the Caymans in the 1970s, "There is no law in the Caymans that has any reference to tax, because there *are* no taxes."[36] The bank under Smith's management provided clients with a guarantee of complete secrecy in a legal void. When all forms of control, taxation, and regulation based on ideas of fairness disappear, the system is childishly easy to understand.

Macdonald moved to the Caymans in 1960. Without electricity, telephone service, or running water, life in the islands was lacking in amenities; only one street was paved, and swarms of mosquitoes were so dense they were said to suffocate the cows.[37] "The colonial government was disposed to go along with Macdonald's plans to turn the place into an international tax haven. Better still, there were no lawyers on the islands," relates the *Canadian Business* article.[38] William Brittain-Catlin, investigator for a corporate investigation firm, confirms the Canadian's role: "Macdonald took the Bahamas as his tax haven model, and the authorities in Cayman, looking to their future, embraced his ideas with open arms."[39]

Macdonald did not act alone: "He has been assisted, over the last two decades, by a variety of very talented Canadian lawyers."[40] *Canadian Business* names Bill Walker[41] (a "financial services industry pioneer" and founder of the Caledonian financial services firm),[42] Roy Dunlop, and brothers Don and Brian Butler, active in real estate.[43] Canadian banking institutions also followed in Macdonald's footsteps, opening offices in the islands. Three of the four major banks arriving in 1965 were Canadian: as usual, they were the Bank of Nova Scotia, the Canadian Imperial Bank of Commerce (CIBC), and the Royal Bank of Canada (RBC).[44] These Canadian individuals and institutions formed "a genuine Canadian Club which has transformed and now manages the Cayman economy."[45] According to tax specialist André Beauchamp, "The Cayman Islands tax regime would appear to be one of the most favourable in the world. There is no tax whatsoever on income or profits, capital or wealth, surplus value, property, sales, or inheritance."[46]

In its 1968 annual report, the Bank of Nova Scotia noted a growth in international activity.[47] The bank stated that "growth in our foreign currency operations has occurred largely in the off-shore Euro-dollar markets."[48] The current situation enabled the bank to provide loans and function successfully on the basis of Eurodollar availability at exceptional rates.[49]

The Cayman Islands are the perfect example of a tax haven tailor-made for capital. Tax fraud is child's play there. As a banker told *Canadian Business*: "It's really not my business to enquire whether you're going to report that income to the Canadian tax authorities. We don't bother to ask, and the Canadian tax authorities can't find out."[50] In the Caymans, Macdonald went into partnership with British national John Maples[51] – later a Conservative MP in the United Kingdom – to establish the Macdonald and Maples law firm, specializing not only in offshore financial services but in the actual configuration of highly permissive jurisdictions. Informally, the law firm was able to establish its hegemony on the Caymans. Cayman authorities did not enact laws that the law firm then observed; the law firm designed its own laws that Cayman authorities then endorsed. Changes to Cayman laws were drastic: "In 1966 and early 1967, the government passed several key pieces of legislation, including the *Banks and Trust Companies Regulations Law*, important revisions to the *Companies Law* – first passed in 1960 – the *Trusts Law* and the *Exchange Control Regulations Law*."[52] According to Cayman journalist Alan Markoff, Macdonald worked with Paul Harris (founder of the first accounting firm in the Caymans, a subsidiary of British firm Pannell Fitzpatrick & Co.) to develop "important legislation that allowed for offshore banking and exempt offshore companies."[53] This dream legislation enabled corporate executives to circumvent their country's laws, and Macdonald and Maples lawyers were there to develop the exclusive financial products most suited to such clients.

PURE CONSERVATISM

According to economist Thierry Godefroy and law expert Pierre Lascoumes, Macdonald's construct is the ultimate tax haven. "It includes all of the classic ingredients of commercial offshore companies: minimum formalities (shell companies incorporated within twenty-four hours), management from abroad, no taxes, no restriction on capital movements (no currency control), minimal accounting constraints, etc. This regime is described by local law firms as a 'modern and comprehensive' system."[54]

Under Cayman law, ordinary resident companies are not required to publish accounts or keep a shareholders' ledger. They are also free of any limitation regarding the composition and distribution of funds.[55] "Since trusts have no moral personality, they cannot be sued, no matter what act is committed in their name."[56] The islands also welcome non-resident companies that may be incorporated without anyone knowing who owns them; the name of a company lawyer is sufficient. The category of the "exempt company" is even more popular: these are entities that can obtain a tax-exemption certificate that is legally binding, no matter how Cayman tax law might evolve.[57]

One original characteristic of the Caymans has been to enable capitalism to benefit from an archaic legal system. In offshore trusts, to quote William Brittain-Catlin, "the link between premodern forms of ownership and control and their modern equivalent is preserved."[58] Some forms of incorporation are unambiguously archaic and are intended to remain so. In the Caymans, residents and merchants have been tax exempt for a long time. Legend has it that in 1794, island dwellers rescued a shipwrecked crew that included a cousin of George III; to thank them, the king allegedly granted them the freedom from taxation from which they still benefit today.[59] On the basis of this tradition, in the 1960s the Caymans made the old British law of trusts available to wealthy owners looking for ways to conceal their assets abroad. The Caymans' bogus legality, "stuck in a kind of time warp," protects finance from time itself. As was pointed out to William Brittain-Catlin with great satisfaction by a lawyer from the law firm founded by Macdonald and Maples, "It's as if the clock was stopped on English law some time in the nineteenth century – certainly before the dawn of the welfare state."[60] British common law had developed the structure of the trust to enable asset-holders to transfer their assets to a management corporation for the benefit of a third party. For example, landowners gave land to a trust so that the Church might benefit, because the Church itself was not entitled to hold property. This structure was still present in the Caymans in the 1960s, but its purpose was completely transformed: it now enabled asset-holders to conceal their assets to avoid not only taxation, but also any kind of regulation, control, or even investigation in their country of origin.[61] Trusts were the entity that attracted tax cheaters in the 1960s by offering them absolution.[62] The attraction was heightened by the fact that, in the Cayman Islands, trustors transferring assets to a trust are allowed to be named its beneficiaries. In this secretive and incestuous system, the three parties involved in a normal trust – trustor, trustee, and beneficiary – are merged into one.[63]

Exempt companies established under Cayman law have invented new ways of doing things. These companies create a financial vacuum enabling people involved in manipulating money and securities to escape from the political sphere. The companies, set up as discrete entities separate from their founders and owners, are beyond the reach of tax authorities. According to Godefroy and Lascoumes, Cayman law "ensures opacity by separating three elements: the legal entity, its legal representatives, and its economic beneficiaries."[64] Exempt companies do not carry out any substantial activity in the islands; their purpose is simply to neutralize the power of the state in which their owners are found.[65] In this legal no man's land on "the island that time forgot,"[66] a corporation escapes its responsibilities in its own community entirely without belonging to any other community. Finance here has reached the fantasy stage. Withdrawal from the world is viewed in the Caymans as the pre-eminent financial form. It embodies what was once unforgettably described as the "truly neutral ground" of capitalism by the head of Dow Chemical – an American corporation that hastened to the Caymans to create its own *captive bank*.[67]

The obsolete quality of Cayman law makes it appear authentic. "What we have in Cayman is a purer, more essential form of capitalism, where business isn't distorted by tax, and the conditions for doing a deal are perfect," muses Henry Harford, member of the law firm cofounded by Macdonald in the Caymans.[68] Having reached this ideal stage characterized by liberal legality and in which law has been successfully reduced to contract relations, finance can merrily flout the collective, cultural, and political requirements that it could never ignore as part of a traditional socially defined state.

The fantasy of purity has another advantage: it helps conceal the stain of criminal activity. Macdonald's legal provisions included not only the creation of structures that made it easier to dodge taxes and laws, but also a highly resistant bank secrecy.[69] For many years it was impossible for tax and regulatory agencies of other countries to gain access to the data of clients of Cayman institutions, and even today a breach in this secrecy has barely been opened. A former anti-money-laundering adviser for the United Nations Office on Drugs and Crime, Marie-Christine Dupuis-Danon, sees the Cayman Islands as a jurisdiction that embodies all the "excesses of offshore finance."[70] The number of financial institutions in the islands has been seen as disproportionate since the 1990s. This was the place where everything seemed possible, where the Bank of Credit and Commerce International (BCCI), for example, was left undisturbed to handle the drug-trafficking funds of Panamanian general Manuel Noriega. As a consequence, the Caymans were the first tax haven inspected in the 1990s by the Financial Action Task Force (FATF), an intergovernmental group established in 1989 to fight money laundering.[71]

SMALL ISLANDS AND HUGE FINANCIAL INTERESTS

The Bank of England actively promoted the conversion of British dependencies into tax havens, tacitly supporting initiatives such as Macdonald's. As for the British government, it behaved as if it were under an obligation to remain silent, which was strange since the issue was the transformation of a territory under the Crown's direct authority.[72] As Shaxson observes, "Just as the Bank of England had officially tolerated but quietly encouraged the growth of the offshore Eurodollar market from 1955, so Britain adopted a policy of official tolerance and quiet encouragement toward its new secret empire."[73] Both financial and political London worked to protect the idea that everything that was happening was simply part of the evolution of capitalism.[74] But in fact, at the same time, there were high-ranking members of the British civil service who thought that the laws bearing Macdonald's imprint went too far. "A confidential Foreign Office memorandum from 1973 expressed the concern. 'The Cayman Islands set up as tax haven in 1967 and passed appropriate legislation which went considerably beyond what the U.K. Treasury was prepared to wear', it said. The bill quietly passed after an unnamed desk officer failed to submit the legislation to London for consent."[75] London came to dread the creature created by its own political regime, fearing that the regulatory, fiscal, and legislative liberalities granted the Caymans would lead to loss of revenue in amounts sufficient to affect even the British Treasury. "Britain later patched the holes in its own tax code as best as it could … leaving the elites of Latin America, the United States and the rest of the world free to use the Caymans' offshore facilities."[76] The tax havens of the British Caribbean had become a weapon turned against all economies not using the pound sterling.

The Caymans' legislative measures also came to antagonize U.S. authorities. A 1970 report from the House of Representatives is crystal clear:

> Secret foreign bank accounts and secret foreign financial institutions have permitted proliferation of "white collar" crime; have served as the financial underpinning of organized criminal operations in the United States; have been utilized by Americans to evade income taxes, conceal assets illegally and purchase gold; have allowed Americans and others to avoid the law and regulations governing securities and exchanges; have served as essential ingredients in frauds including schemes to defraud the United States; have served as the ultimate depository of black market proceeds from Vietnam; have served as a source of questionable financing for conglomerate and other corporate stock acquisitions, mergers and takeovers; have covered conspiracies to steal from the U.S. defense and foreign aid funds; and have served as the cleansing agent for "hot" or illegally acquired monies.[77]

Some Canadian and American bankers had ways of throwing tax investigators off the scent: "American bankers were referring U.S. customers to their Canadian colleagues, and the Canadians were returning the favour."[78] However, the U.S. justice system eventually broke through the bank discretion erected in the Caymans by the laws of 1966 and 1967,[79] as it had done in the Bahamas.[80] As part of legal proceedings against the Caymans' Castle Bank, in 1976 a U.S. grand jury subpoenaed the bank's managing director, Canadian citizen Anthony Field, to force him to disclose information.[81] The American investigation showed that the Castle Bank was notorious for its links with organized crime[82] and that it was widely involved in tax evasion and avoidance operations in the United States.[83] The bank helped launder money derived from shady operations in the real economy.[84] Originally established in the Bahamas, the Castle Bank created a duplicate structure for itself in the Cayman Islands when it became clear that the United States was taking aim at it. The CIBC was said to have helped the Castle Bank move from the Bahamas to the Caymans by preserving copies of Castle Bank archives in its vault.[85] Field argued that he had to remain silent because if he were to disclose information about bank clients in the Caymans, he would then be subject to judicial punishment in a territory that defined breaches of bank secrecy as criminal offences.[86] Pro-offshore tax expert Édouard Chambost described the American grand jury as "relentless" in its efforts to compel Field to give evidence "despite the fact that his testimony in the United States was a criminal offence in the Cayman Islands where he worked and lived."[87] Chambost also insisted on the fact that Field "was a Canadian citizen."[88] Field was eventually successful in withholding information and withdrew to a reclusive life in the Caymans as soon as he was able to leave the United States. He had nonetheless been the main character in a key episode redefining the balance of power between the two jurisdictions.

Macdonald designed new measures in the 1970s to consolidate the set of laws developed in 1966 and 1967: the Cayman Islands must not in any way "bow down"[89] before the United States. Macdonald was acting in support of Godfrey Johnson, chairman of the Cayman Islands Monetary Authority (CIMA), the official regulatory agency of the archipelago's financial markets.[90] On September 13, 1976, the Cayman Islands adopted a law extending bank secrecy to "all confidential business or professional information" produced in or brought to the islands, and to any person staying in the islands or leaving them with such information in his or her possession.[91] The Confidential Relationships (Preservations) Law reaches heights of absurdity as it attempts to define every imaginable circumstance in which Cayman Island laws can forbid bankers to disclose information about their clients.[92] It is now illegal not only to disclose bank information, but even to request its disclosure![93] Paranoia was the name of the game and still is today, as revealed by this quote from 2014:

The Confidential Relationships (Preservations) Law 1976 makes it a criminal offence to divulge confidential information or to willfully obtain or attempt to obtain confidential information relating to a Cayman Island company. The law imposes a maximum penalty of a fine of CI$5,000 and/or a term of imprisonment of up to 2 years.[94]

This law was aptly described by William Brittain-Catlin as a "money launderers' charter."[95] The law stated explicitly that no bank information could be disclosed as part of investigations carried out in other jurisdictions. The goal was to provide the law with an extraterritorial reach that would neutralize the laws of traditional states – even in relation to events taking place on their own territory. The only concession in the Cayman law was to say that when foreign governments were investigating crimes other than tax offences, they might solicit the assistance of Cayman authorities.[96] In the best case scenario, this would allow criminal investigation of money laundering, but Cayman would nonetheless keep operations and account-holders secret. A citizen who goes to the Cayman Islands General Registry to try and understand what a company does will learn only the company's name, registration state, file number, agent, and type and status of company. "This is the only information we provide," as the Registry explains.[97] Brittain-Catlin's conclusion is that "with this new law, Cayman codified its secret realm and told the outside world to leave it alone and mind its own business."[98]

The severe penalties set out in Cayman criminal law concern a literally infinite category of agents. Any resident or transient person who betrays bank secrecy, for example, may face criminal charges and risk up to four years in jail.[99] Even pro-offshore Édouard Chambost describes as "absurd"[100] the occupational categories covered by the bank secrecy law, which mentions not only professionals in the area of trade or finance but also all professionals "belonging or not to the previous categories, licensed or not, habilitated or not to act in such capacity."[101]

Cayman financial authorities acknowledged that these legal measures were an attempt to make bank secrecy impervious to American political power. Commenting after the fact in 2007, the chairman of the Cayman Islands Monetary Authority (CIMA) asserted that "in 1976, the *Confidential Relationships (Preservations) Law* ... was a response to aggressive action by the U.S. authorities at the time to obtain information from offshore banks."[102] In 1980, Chambost added the following highly accurate comment: "Bank secrecy is a basic principle in the Cayman Islands and there is every reason to believe that in order to keep on attracting banks and their clients, it will continue to be energetically defended."[103] Under Macdonald's direction, the Caymans attempted to take over from other experienced offshore financial centres, in particular the Bahamas. "The Caymans were latecomers to the offshore banking game, springing into action when the Bahamas seemed to be getting into financial and political difficulties, and accepting business that the more 'respectable' offshore centres would not touch."[104] Against all likelihood, the Caymans' legislative arm-wrestling match with the American giant ended favourably for the islands. In another legal joust in 1982, the British bank, Barclays, successfully blocked American judicial authorities by invoking the Caymans' right to bank secrecy.[105] That same year an American holding company, Citicorp, asserted that Bahamian laws on bank secrecy took precedence over laws enacted in Washington.[106]

The legal action taken by American tax authorities in 1982 against the Bank of Nova Scotia, this time for operations carried out in the Cayman Islands, also came to nothing. The bank was accused of "participating in a scheme to defraud the U.S. government through $122 million in phony tax-shelter claims" in the Caymans,[107] a case the U.S. government lost on appeal two years later.[108] This kind of judicial decision makes it seem that little has changed since the era when U.S. courts favoured the rise of the powerful and unscrupulous businessmen known as the robber barons.[109]

Washington was politically weak. Procedures against the Castle Bank showed that American secret services, and many politicians and multinationals, were swimming in the same waters as the mafia that was so well served by Canadian banks. "The IRS investigation that had led to grand juries and subpoenas for tax evasion and money laundering was soon closed down, prompting allegations that Castle Bank was a front for the CIA and that many of the offshore tax evaders were in fact Republican fat cats and Nixon cronies."[110]

Meanwhile, the Caymans were still "innovating." Exchange-control restrictions were abolished in the late 1970s,[111] so that by 1980 the Caymans and the Bahamas provided fierce competition for London as a financial centre.[112] Hundreds of companies were attracted by 1979 insurance law[113] that allowed insurance company founders to insure – themselves. Today, 760 insurance companies are based in the Caymans.[114] The Harvard Medical Group, for example, established an insurance company that protects it from the legal consequences of medical errors.[115] "Today, about half of the captive insurers in Cayman are U.S. health-care companies."[116]

During this period, the International Monetary Fund was providing Cayman authorities with assistance in organizing the islands' banking sector along tax haven lines,[117] at the same time as it was forcing countries in the South to carry out deep cuts to their already meagre public services.[118]

In 1985, these fronts were stabilized. Courts adopted new strategies, targeting individuals suspected of tax evasion and requiring them to eliminate the confidentiality clause protecting some of their accounts. In one particular case, this approach "quickly resulted in the surrender of documents to a Florida court by the Bank of Nova Scotia."[119] The increased pressure led to a compromise: the Caymans would provide access to bank accounts on questions related to drug trafficking, but would not co-operate in any way with regard to tax evasion.[120] It sounded as if the Caymans' financial secretary could direct the American empire as he pleased.[121] "Inhabitants of the tax-free islands regard taxation as 'repugnant' in principle"[122] – a view shared by the American financial barons who dictate Washington's political line.[123] The Bahamas also resisted[124] and also established their status as a first-rate tax haven.

THE RESISTIBLE RISE OF JEAN DOUCET

Throughout the years when American institutions were trying to limit, however minimally, the perverse effects of Cayman Island laws, Montreal banker Jean Doucet was promoting their benefits.[125] In 1968, he founded the International Corporation of the Cayman Islands, subsequently to be modestly renamed the International Bank, also known as the InterBank.[126] Later, in the early 1970s, he also created the Sterling Bank and Trust,[127] just in time to catch the Eurodollars pouring into the Caymans.[128] These were the first financial institutions in the Caymans to computerize bank data,[129] a cutting-edge initiative for a tax haven at the time.[130] Doucet, the colony's second-largest employer after the government,[131] had a flair for marketing. Starting with nothing, he printed 20,000 copies of an information booklet praising Cayman tax laws, and distributed them to the investors that were the object of his lust. As part of his charm offensive, he staffed his establishment with lovely young women and made sure it was decorated to suit the macho taste he might imagine to prevail among investors. He also produced a documentary film extolling the colony's merits.[132] This postmodern banker supplied the gaudy aesthetic often associated with the image of tax havens: palm trees, flowers, gold ingots, and ostentatious kitsch.[133] Some felt that Doucet was the one who raised Cayman's profile:[134] "Doucet, with his own distinctive style and ambition, was going to be the man who put Cayman on the map of international capital, who would break the mold of the old staid world of finance and banking and give it a bit of tax haven panache, flair, and cosmopolitan glamour … He made the world of offshore capital look sexy."[135]

Doucet's fall was as spectacular as his rise had been meteoric. In 1974, he invited a thousand businessmen to a Grand Cayman hotel to celebrate the opening of a bank dedicated to mortgage loans. Just two months later, his Sterling Bank collapsed and Doucet made off to Monaco. The problem was that his clients were making short-term deposits that Doucet was using for long-term investments. Such hedge fund methods were still in their infancy at the time. The Sterling Bank collapse had the merit of providing an accurate picture of the kind of operations taking place in the Caymans. No procedures were in place for winding up the bank, which was unfortunate in a context where, as certified accountant Michael Austin explains, "Sterling was not just a local bank; it had subsidiaries and all sorts of investments. It was a very complicated structure with companies all over the world."[136] Doucet was finally extradited to the Cayman Islands, where he was convicted of fraud and sentenced to nine months in jail. While serving his time, he was often visited by government representatives. When his time was done, he went back home to Quebec.[137]

Such accidents were unfortunate but mattered little: the groove was established. By the time Macdonald left his law firm in the early 1970s, his pet project was alive and kicking. The firm became known as Maples and Calder with the arrival of another partner, Douglas Calder, in 1969.[138] The law firm, eventually to be known simply as Maples, almost single-handedly developed the industry of speculative funds. The *Hedgefund Journal* rightly describes it as one of the pioneers of the Cayman offshore colony.[139]

Maples has a high profile in a jurisdiction that it knows inside out. Providing "Cayman Islands expertise,"[140] it presents itself not as a rival of other firms but as the one and only indispensable partner for offshore ventures.[141] The firm's growth reflects the growth of the financial industry that it generated in the Caymans. "It is obvious that Maples has been around for a long time, [and that the firm] has helped to design the offshore hedge fund blueprint."[142] In fact, the Cayman Islands are run by the law firm. Jim Macdonald told *Canadian Business* in 1979 how he personally had settled a money-laundering affair involving $1 million; it was obvious that he had full discretionary powers.[143] Exactly as if they were heads of state, Maples executives today do not beat around the bush when asked for their opinion in public about the political affairs of the Cayman Islands, including their controversial reputation or any steps taken to regulate and legalize their financial system. "[The firm's] success is in no small part due to the efforts of those law firms and other service providers that have worked with the Cayman Islands government to ensure that its legal regime meets the standards required, as well as those government officials and regulators who started out working in Cayman law firms, amongst them some former Maples lawyers."[144]

This is how the Cayman Islands became the jurisdiction with the largest number of hedge funds in the world – 775 of them in 2012.[145] According to the *New York Times,* the Caymans actually harbour more capital than all New York banks combined.[146] Maples deserves full credit for this. A survey of hedge fund professionals working in traditional states identified it as "the number-one law firm" working offshore.[147] The firm is an active member of the Offshore Magic Circle, a select club of law firms without whom tax havens would never be able to work as they do today.[148]

Entirely corrupt, hedge funds have made a significant contribution to the disruption of the economy as experienced by ordinary people. Managers of these unconventional funds multiply often risky strategies to earn higher yields than can be reached in traditional markets, and to earn them faster. The word *hedge* embodies their claim to provide cover – that is, security: they may, for example, establish in advance the price of certain financial securities or goods. But in a deregulated system, they have generated a market based on insecurity. The framework of commercial exchanges, established in the past by public authorities so that the community might handle economic relations, is now replaced by financial products guaranteed by private actors. A contract, for example, states that a certain quantity of oil – or wheat, or government bonds – will be available at a fixed price until a certain date. This document is exchanged on the market on the basis of hopes, calculations, and gambles, with hedge-fund managers providing a mathematically optimized way of constantly tempting fate.

Havens, Cayman first and foremost, give maximum leeway to financiers' fantastical imagination. "Hedge funds try to limit regulatory constraints as much as possible so that they can have great freedom in terms of management. The will to minimize the effect of taxes is another motivating factor. This explains why a high proportion of the funds are legally located offshore, often in a tax haven," to quote the proliferating euphemisms of two researchers active in investment firms.[149] Those who designed hedge funds did not always measure the impact of the methods they were developing to produce yields in the very short term, and brokers themselves did not understand the algorithms that over time would manage the market's subjectivity.[150] The perverse effects of these methods have been spectacular. For hedge funds, the real assets and real credit of our tangible economies are the stakes of their stock-market speculation. Improbable debts become commodities and are *securitized*, to use the accepted terminology, as *derivatives*. Thousands of heterogeneous elements are combined and sold as packages: bundles of mortgage debts, including those of impoverished households; options to buy oil (which the seller does not yet own) at a fixed price; transactions intended to reap marginal benefits on foodstuffs, as if food were no more than a chip in a poker game; and government bonds. Capitalization strategies are equally bold: in the process known as selling short, you sell securities that you don't own. Tax havens enable this unfettered explosion of speculation, since no state can set any limits on it by restricting the quality or quantity of wealth at stake, the record speed at which these transactions take place, or the terms of the exchanges that are negotiated.

Families buying rice in the actual marketplace, as well as the Western middle class aspiring to real estate ownership, see hedge funds putting the elements of their survival and their personal debts on the market, more or less in the spirit of a gambling casino. "What is true of oil is true of all other raw materials, agricultural products, rare or precious metals. If a product is sought out on the world market, then around it is created a whole financial market made up of complex, exotic, and esoteric instruments," writes French judge Jean de Maillard.[151] Worse yet, what is at stake is not even a traditional trading relationship in which a seller owns products and transfers them to buyers for profit, but a speculative gamble on the expected evolution of prices – an evolution that is, in fact, affected by speculation. Arbitrage strategies play on the difference between the real price of a resource (rice, oil, cotton) and an option to buy at some other (for example, lower) price. Speculation on the future price of raw materials can make prices rise. On September 22, 2008, for example, the price of a barrel of oil rose implausibly from $108 to $130.[152] In the same way, a powerful commodity trading firm, Glencore, played a key role in causing the price of wheat to rise by 15 percent over two days during the summer of 2010.[153]

Tax haven hedge funds allow bankers to bypass U.S. regulations forbidding speculation on the basis of their own assets. In tax havens, banks are free to create hedge funds of which they are the fundamental creditors, the "prime brokers." Marc Roche notes that "before the crisis, hedge funds were relatively unregulated actors on which national supervisory authorities had no information, in particular concerning risks and the leverage effect."[154] These funds have become so large that they sometimes earn more revenue than the banks that created them, as was the case in the second half of 2010.[155]

The key move is to use cunning to artificially free an ever greater amount of capital in order to increase the volume of activity in the markets. Offshore, hedge funds have discovered that they can create an extraordinary leverage effect thanks to "the possibility, provided by certain financial products or techniques, of multiplying the gains or losses associated with an initial investment. For example, you can buy a security when you only have part of the money, then sell it for a higher price. The leverage effect is the relation between the surplus thus realized and the initial amount."[156] Thus, a leverage effect of a hundred means that someone who invests $1,000 can benefit from the same return as if he or she had put in $100,000. In the Caymans, the exponential increase of this factor verges on sheer insanity: "In this market, proposed leverage effects generally vary between 100 and 500."[157] According to financial authorities, leverage effects stabilized around 135 percent in 2011.[158]

A financial subsidiary of Maples, MaplesFS, provides its clients in Grand Cayman with the services of independent investment fund managers capable of generating leverage effects.[159] Thanks to the Cayman Islands' exceptional regime in which "the moving parts...make the sum greater than its parts,"[160] and through a form of financial alchemy based on complex combinations of accounting entries, corporations access capital flows that allow them to cover extended territories of ownership. All this is described by admirers in a pontificating tone, with grave allusions to English common law as the basis for Cayman companies law and securities law.[161]

The Caymans also favour the development of financial products providing some with the pleasure of watching others break their necks. These sorcerer's apprentice products were a significant factor in triggering the financial crisis that began in 2008. Basically, they are products that help you to get rich by speculating *against* a security. *Selling short*, for example, is what occurs when a hedge fund sells a security at market value but does not actually own the security; it borrows it from a third party to whom it will be restored at a later date. To restore it, the fund will buy it on the market; it hopes that, in the meantime, the price will have gone down. A juggling act of this kind was performed in the 2000s with the development of the Abacus CDO. A CDO, or Collateralized Debt Obligation, can be a set of debts that have been fragmented and transferred as securities to an ad hoc structure whose shares are then sold on the stock market. When this kind of asset package is created by unscrupulous parties in jurisdictions where they are entirely unregulated, anything can be put in the package, whose fancy wrapping promises high returns. Abacus, a CDO set up in the Cayman Islands, perfectly embodies the insanity that seized financial markets in the 2000s. Goldman Sachs sold its clients Abacus shares through the intermediary of the Paulson and Co. hedge fund, at the same time as it was buying insurance for itself in case the value of these shares crashed on the stock market. (You can acquire this kind of insurance, known as a CDS or Credit Default Swap, even for securities that you don't own. This is akin to insuring your neighbour's house, hoping it will eventually burn down, and possibly giving things a nudge to make this happen.)

In 2007–2008, when the value of the Abacus CDO did collapse as expected, leaving thousands of investors who had lost their savings high and dry, Paulson and Co. made a profit of $3.7 billion at the same time as they bankrupted an insurance company. This episode has been well described as "a record – perhaps of all time – for financially profiting from the misery of others."[162] The Cayman Islands are the largest protectors of these funds, skilled in channelling the savings of the middle classes of traditional states into hazardous projects. In 2011, there was more hedge fund activity in the Caymans than in the territory's two main rivals, Luxembourg and Dublin, combined.[163]

ANYTHING AND EVERYTHING CAN BE DEPOSITED

Maples emerges as the de facto government of this permissive jurisdiction. Ugland House, the colonial-style building where Maple has its offices, is the official address of close to 19,000 companies.[164] During the 2008 election campaign, presidential candidate Obama made this building the symbol of tax fraud, arguing that it was "either the biggest building…or the biggest tax scam in the world."[165] Journalist Mélanie Delattre of the French weekly *Le Point* was equally scathing: "The law firm's chief activity, as I'm sure you realize, is to set up legal shells based on local law in which absolutely anything and everything can be deposited."[166] Everything, indeed, is on offer or can be designed in the Caymans: banks able to operate everywhere in the world,[167] insurance companies insuring their own founders, dummy corporations concealing anonymous agents in another country, English-style trusts benefiting their founders, flags of convenience for ships that will never come close to Cayman shores, limited partnerships on the U.S. model – and so on. All these structures are characterized, to various degrees, by tax rates approaching zero, ironclad discretion, an almost complete absence of regulation, and the support of indulgent supervising "authorities." The Caymans' goal today is to serve as a supermarket of unsupervised financial products – the ideal type, or as close to it as possible, of an offshore jurisdiction.

In 2011, Maples described itself as "proud of the offshore fund structures it has helped to formulate for hedge funds in the Cayman Islands, in close consultation with the Cayman Islands regulatory authorities."[168] Who are these authorities? The Cayman Islands Monetary Authority (CIMA), created in 1996,[169] was designed by none other than – Maples and Calder! Maples "recognises that its close co-operation with government and regulators in Cayman have helped it to succeed, and for Cayman itself to remain the jurisdiction of choice for hedge-fund managers."[170] In the aftermath of the 2008 financial crisis, the firm congratulated itself on the "relatively little litigation in the Cayman Islands" under laws it had designed.[171] Regulation of hedge funds was deemed sufficient, and Maples asserted that local "regulatory authorities" had the "ability" to co-operate with regulators from other countries[172] (if they wanted to). The government itself promotes the tax advantages conferred by its bank secrecy laws.[173] Since everything is upside down in the Caymans, offshore operators direct regulatory operations with the support of financial regulators such as CIMA,[174] whose chairman gives speeches under the recurring title "What Makes the Cayman Islands a Successful International Financial Services Centre?"[175] This is the organization that is supposed to enforce the law's new criminal penalties! "Under the Monetary Authority Law, CIMA has operational independence with rights of access to relevant client information held by financial institutions. If requests are not complied with within three days, the regulator can obtain a court order for disclosure."[176] We can easily imagine the passionate, blazing conviction with which these financial "regulators" will damage their offshore image by pestering their high-class clientele.

Since the beginning of the twenty-first century, the Organisation for Economic Co-operation and Development (OECD) has claimed to exercise a form of control over tax havens. First in 2000 and again in 2007, it drew up "black" and "grey" lists, categorizing offshore financial centres according to whether or not they were "co-operative."[177] Retired Swiss judge Bernard Bertossa has strongly criticized these international lists, arguing they are far more likely to whitewash tax havens than to weaken them. "Targeted states have reviewed or extended their laws to comply with international standards as required. But in many cases, everyone knows that the main objective is to put up a good show before supranational bodies. Nobody has ever really looked at how these laws are actually put into practice ... Removal from 'black lists' has generally been based on purely formal, or rather purely political, criteria."[178] In claiming to regulate tax havens, the OECD is actually answering for them within the world economic order. Tax evasion, tax avoidance, and abusive tax planning are no longer seen as controversial *opportunities* to accumulate wealth: they are now structural *necessities* related to the practices developed by businesses and fortune holders. The OECD claims the authority to distinguish, on arbitrary grounds, between *legitimate* and *illegitimate* tax havens. Legitimate, in this context, means that a tax haven has signed a dozen Tax Information Exchange Agreements with OECD members: these are supposed to do away with bank secrecy when highly detailed requests are presented from the outside world. Thus, by 2010, the initial blacklist consisting of thirty-five tax havens now included only three, the others having apparently repented.[179] To these agreements have been added a series of rules vainly enjoining banks themselves to run checks with regard to money laundering.[180] So far, nothing has changed, except that managers in the world of offshore secrecy have been made slightly uneasy by this unusual amount of attention.[181]

While CIMA may adopt operational rules that are formally compliant with international requirements, nothing is done to enforce them. According to *Le Monde*'s correspondent in London, Marc Roche, the Cayman Islands regulator is simply "unable to understand the sophisticated financial packages" designed by the engineers of finance.[182] Hallowed traditions are respected: "Bank secrecy and banks are supervised by the Inspector of Bank and Trust Companies, himself subject to bank secrecy," as Édouard Chambost noted approvingly in the 1980s.[183] In the Caymans, directors of hedge funds cannot be sued for any reason.[184] The slight legislative changes made in the 2000s to fight financial crime leave criminologist Marie-Christine Dupuis-Danon skeptical. In her view, it is doubtful whether anyone will actually call on the "very considerable human and financial resources" that would be needed to ensure "effective supervision of these financial institutions."[185]

So what, if anything, is actually forbidden? In the Caymans, a company's losses can be recorded off-balance sheet,[186] enabling it to embellish the financial results presented to shareholders. "It was not so much the Caymans' opacity that attracted the large players – though that helped – as its 'flexibility'. When tax haven supporters say they promote 'efficiency' in global markets, this is the kind of thing they are talking about. At the heart of this efficiency is these jurisdictions' flexibility – which, as we have seen, is really about their political capture by financial capital."[187] By suppressing bad news, the managers of large corporations are constantly manufacturing time bombs,[188] as was apparent in the case of Enron and Parmalat – two companies whose sensational collapse in the 2000s followed on their use of risky methods designed by Maples lawyers.[189]

Above all, given the massive semantic distortions we now are witnessing, it is pointless to rely on a company's status to understand its vocation. It is not unusual, for example, for a foreign bank to create a Cayman Islands trust in order to use it as a mutual investment fund (which is tax exempt like everything else).[190] Some of the unlikeliest asset transfers involve charitable organizations. Consider this example: "Airbus does not sell its planes to Air France or Qantas, but to a charitable organization on the island which then rents them to the airline."[191] The French journalist following the story quotes an expert from Maples, who explains that this bizarre operation, based on the idea that an air transportation broker is a charitable concern, allows the company to rent planes to itself. The company can then post a loss to its domestic accounts, leading to further tax deductions.[192] Manoeuvres of this kind are so common that the BNP Paribas bank is still present in the Caymans despite having boasted that it no longer has any branches in tax havens. According to BNP Paribas chairman Baudouin Prot, "If you're financing airlines, you have to be there."[193]

For economist Christian Chavagneux, one fact summarizes the Caymans' dubious activities: "While the City of London generates only three times as much capital (5,670 billion in assets versus $1,400 billion [US$]), its financial sector employs a hundred times as many people: 360,000 people versus 3,650! Either Cayman employees are exceptionally productive, or the islands' 'financial sector' has little real activity and is used to record fictitious transactions designed to avoid taxes or handle dubious risks."[194]

Toronto brokers have a particular gift for dubious activities in the Caymans and neighbouring tax havens. Even Édouard Chambost, the Swiss tax consultant capable of outrageous cynicism, finds them sleazy, referring to "the Toronto School" to describe the disgraceful operations of con artists. Chambost cites the example of three Toronto brokers who, in 1993, used their Grand Cayman address to sell Canadians indium, a rare mineral. "Indium... sells for about US$5 an ounce. They sold it to Canadian marks for $40, then used another dummy corporation to charge them $90, getting credulous customers to write them two or even three cheques." He adds: "In most North American and Caribbean con jobs involving shares, securities, or futures markets, you'll find characters from Toronto."[195] Another of Chambost's examples is the Investors Overseas Services (IOS) mutual fund scam directed by Bernie Cornfeld, whose best sales people – most of whom were to end up in court – convened in Toronto.[196] The tradition continues to this day: the Ontario Securities Commission's Annual Summary Report is a sorry compendium of shady practices by financial dealers, advisers, and investment fund managers.[197] The Caymans were also the location from which Toronto hedge-fund manager Paul Eustace engineered a fraud that bilked investors of $200 million until the U.S. Commodity Futures Trading Commission filed an injunctive action against him in June 2005 and shut down his funds immediately afterwards.[198]

In 2013, the IRS followed a time-honoured tradition by taking legal action in the United States against the FirstCaribbean International Bank in the Caymans. (The bank, owned today by the CIBC, was jointly controlled at the time by Barclays and CIBC.) The IRS suspected that the institution's accounts "may have been used by tax evaders."[199]

The Cayman Islands are criticized today as one of the most permissive tax havens in the world, and their ultra-liberalism is at the very least tolerated, if not knowingly supported, by politicians in the North. A New York prosecutor recently expressed surprise that states based on the rule of law allow the existence of jurisdictions that are dedicated to making their rules irrelevant: "After all, the Cayman Islands belong to the British Crown. London appoints their Governor and their Attorney General. The United Kingdom therefore has the power to put an end to the laissez-faire in its colony, but it doesn't." [200]

The quaint and folksy period in the last thirty years of the twentieth century, when criminals arrived in the Caymans with boxes of money of illicit origin stacked on wooden pallets, is now over. Today, many of the suspect or criminal actions allowed by the Caymans take the form of high finance and insurance management. In March 2001, a Cayman banker told a subcommittee of the U.S. Senate that 100 percent of his clients were engaged in tax evasion. [201] Tax authorities have no way of flushing out tax dodgers since the names of company directors do not appear in any registry. Some people belong, anonymously, to over a hundred boards of directors! Agents cannot be identified, and suspicion of fraud is itself illegal in the Caymans. [202]

Appearances, however, have been preserved. In 1986, the Caymans buried the hatchet with the United States by signing a treaty of mutual assistance against drug trafficking. [203] Ten years later, the territory added anti-money-laundering measures to its Criminal Code. [204] Under international pressure as a country on "blacklists" issued in 2000 by the FATF, the OECD, and the FSF, [205] and cited again on the OECD's 2009 "grey list," in the last decade the Caymans have signed Tax Information Exchange Agreements with twenty countries, including Canada and the United States. [206] This has enabled them to vanish from OECD lists [207] and obtain the FATF's blessing. [208] But these are purely formal measures. Laundering of money from drug trafficking was so significant in the late 1990s that the United States put the Cayman Islands on its list of high priority countries. [209] The Caymans' two international airports are described as "sieves," and their bank secrecy regime is highly suited to laundering drug traffickers' profits. [210] "The Cayman Islands are by far the wealthiest territory in all Central America and the Caribbean."[211] While both the Bahamas and Caymans have signed bilateral agreements (the Bahamas has one with Canada) to fight the transfer of criminal funds to the islands,[212] these measures do not seem to lead to concrete results. In late 2008, former Swiss judge Bernard Bertossa was still including the Bahamas and Caymans among the handful of offshore states that appeared most problematic.[213]

The creation in 1997 of a Cayman Islands Stock Exchange, CSX,[214] affiliated with the London Stock Exchange International Equity Market, gave reason to fear the worst as to what companies the exchange might list. Ten years later, "the number of active registered companies had grown to 84,500. The CSX has 1,760 listings with total market capitalisation of US$169 billion."[215] In 2009, the Caymans were the fifth-largest financial centre in the world, immediately after London, New York, Tokyo, and Hong Kong.[216] Today, Jim Macdonald's legacy is impressive: over 93,000 companies are registered in the Cayman Islands.[217]

While Canada is no longer as present in the Caymans as it once was, it still keeps close ties with this offshore territory. Worse yet, Stephen Harper's government actively recognizes the Caymans' virtues as an accommodating jurisdiction. A Tax Information Exchange Agreement (TIEA) between the two jurisdictions came into force on June 1, 2011.[218] In theory, these agreements instigated by the OECD are intended to make an offshore territory's information available when a highly specific request is presented. In true Canadian fashion, however, TIEAs signed by Canada lead to very different consequences: they allow Canadian corporations to benefit from the permissive laws and regulations of tax havens. Maples, of course, is there to help its clients enjoy the tax haven's advantages. Since the Caymans have earned the status of "designated treaty country" by signing the agreement, subsidiaries of Canadian companies that record their profits in the Caymans can now transfer them to Canada without paying any taxes – a clear incentive to practise transfer pricing. Dividends paid to a Canadian corporation by an entity registered in the Caymans are automatically tax exempt. "With no income, corporate or capital gains tax, no estate duty, inheritance tax or gift tax and no withholding tax, the Cayman Islands is well situated to be used in structuring investments for Canadian corporations," as Maples tells its clients.[219] The firm emphasizes that "Maples has many years' knowledge and experience of the business environment in the U.S. and Canada, and provides legal advice on the laws of the Cayman Islands, Ireland and the British Virgin Islands to North American based clients with global international focused businesses."[220] John Dykstra, who studied business and law in Kingston and Toronto,[221] works with the firm to help Canadians benefit from the Caymans' legislative munificence.[222] He is one of many Canadian brokers or employees of Canadian corporations[223] who work in the hidden byways of outlaw power, subjecting the world's populations to the upheavals resulting from their decisions.

Thanks to the Canadian government, financial exchanges between Canada and the Cayman Islands are now so well lubricated that Canadian citizens "invested" $25.8 billion there in 2011. These cash flows, hugely disproportionate to the size of the Cayman economy, make it the fourth-largest destination for Canadian capital abroad. In the Caymans in 2013, the Royal Bank controls three entities,[224] Scotiabank one,[225] and CIBC four.[226] In addition, Canadian businessman Michael Lee-Chin acquired 75 percent of a less well-known banking institution, NCB Jamaica, in 2002, and sold it in 2009 to a Canadian-based financial services group, Manulife.[227] The National Commercial Bank (NCB), whose main shareholder is AIC Financial Ltd., is also there.[228] Maples has opened an office in Montreal with the support of the Quebec Ministry of Finance. The firm specializing in the creation of offshore entities will pay only 22 percent tax on its income to provide advice to Quebec businesses. "Maples has been recognized as an International Financial Centre (IFC), which gives it the right not to pay taxes on certain earnings and to a 75% reduction in its contribution to the Quebec Health Services Fund."[229] Faced with criticism of Maples, the chairman of the Montreal International Financial Centre, Jacques Girard, who oversaw the arrangements for the firm's arrival, showed a disconcerting naïveté: "I don't want to make a judgment. We're making judgments on firms here and I think that's a little awkward."[230] The Quebec minister of revenue, Robert Dutil, preferred to take cover behind a pretence of legality: "In our society, you have to give people a chance and allow those who behave legally to establish themselves."[231] As for Maples itself, it appeared to be practising black humour in its statement to Radio-Canada: "Maples and Calder made it clear that the 18,000 client corporations registered at their address in the Cayman Islands were not registered for the purpose of avoiding taxes in their country of origin."[232] Meanwhile, MaplesFS, the entity heading the Montreal office, describes itself in two paragraphs, of which one focuses on its offshore skills: "Operating from key onshore and offshore jurisdictions, we provide professional and timely advice that draws upon the jurisdictional knowledge and experience of our professional staff."[233] In celebrating its ability to create various structures, including trusts, the firm implicitly recalls those designed by Canadians in the Cayman Islands a few decades earlier.

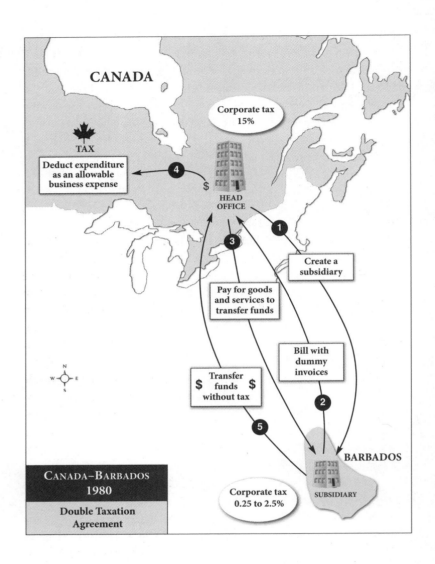

CANADA

Corporate tax
15%

TAX

Deduct expenditure
as an allowable
business expense

4

$

HEAD
OFFICE

1

Create a
subsidiary

3

Pay for goods
and services to
transfer funds

Bill with
dummy
invoices

2

$ Transfer
funds $
without tax

5

BARBADOS

SUBSIDIARY

CANADA–BARBADOS
1980

Double Taxation
Agreement

Corporate tax
0.25 to 2.5%

BARBADOS

HOME GROUND FOR CANADIAN OFFSHORE FIRMS

In which the Canadian government creates a tax-amnesty corridor leading straight from Barbados to Canada

Just as Switzerland is the tax haven for France and Liechtenstein has adapted its laws to become Germany's negative mirror image, Barbados in the 1980s became the tax haven whose job is to neutralize Canadian tax laws. This small island with a population of fewer than 300,000 people is the third-largest destination of Canadian capital in the world, after the United States and the United Kingdom. By 2012, Canadian business people had invested close to $60 billion in Barbados, an increase of almost 80 percent compared to 2007.[1]

Needless to say, there is no emerging market or large-scale undertaking in Barbados that would justify the convergence of billions of dollars on the island. Barbados tax rules, and the benefits they provide for Canadians, are the one and only reason for this phenomenon. There is no need to dissect the arcane reports of the Organisation for Economic Co-operation and Development (OECD) or check its "black" or "grey" list[2] to understand that Barbados is a tax haven. The facts speak for themselves.

A genuine domino effect was visible in the Caribbean in the 1960s as jurisdictions, one after another, morphed into tax havens. The Barbados banking law, enacted in 1963, reproduced many passages of the Jamaican law.[3] In 1987, the Barbados minister of finance said that his country had looked to Canada when independence was proclaimed in 1966 in order to pursue Barbados's interests in terms of exports." Economic policies established at the time included "attraction of investment capital for industrial development" and "promotion of the Barbados as an offshore financial centre."[4] The Bank of Nova

Scotia was among the first to understand this new thrust, locating trust services on the island in 1967.[5] It also opened a new branch in Barbados the following year.[6]

During this period, Barbados started to look like a free zone. Beginning in 1974, it reduced corporate income tax in order to attract export-oriented companies.[7] Food processing, paint, metallurgy, oil refining, furniture, and electronics plants opened in Barbados.[8] The island's free-zone status was confirmed in 1980 with the creation of the Barbados Industrial Development Corporation (BIDC). This agency established three industrial zones covering several hectares near international transportation points: one in Grazettes, north of Bridgetown (the capital), five kilometres (three miles) from a deepwater harbour; another in Bridgetown itself; and a third at Pelican near an airport built by the BIDC.[9] In all, ten industrial parks were to open on the island,[10] at Newton, Wildey, Pine, Six Roads, St. Lucy, and again in suburban Bridgetown, never too far from international transportation points. Today, the BIDC owns twelve industrial estates.[11] Since 2001, businesses relocating to these sites have been given tax holidays for periods of eleven to fifteen years,[12] and for nine years following the end of the tax holiday, they will be entitled to deduct from their profits the net losses of previous years.[13] These companies pay ludicrously low wages to Barbados workers, with an hourly rate that does not even reach US$4.[14] As is clearly stated in a guide to employee rights, "Barbados does not have legislated minimum wages."[15]

Given fierce competition in the job market and the context of a worldwide race to the bottom in terms of social standards, these free zones are harmful to workers everywhere[16] – which makes them highly beneficial for companies. Even in Canada, in any case, people from Barbados are often confined to the category of cheap labour. According to a Canadian government source, "Barbados participates in the Canadian Seasonal Agricultural Workers Program (SAWP), an organized labour mobility program, which allows for the entry of foreign workers to meet the temporary seasonal needs of Canadian agricultural producers. Barbados has participated in the SAWP since 1967."[17] In January 2012, the Canadian government website also indicated that Canada's Temporary Foreign Worker Program had led to agreements between Barbados and several prestige hotels in Ontario as well as the Staples

Business Depot chain store, and that the Barbados government wanted to extend these partnerships.[18] The free-zone pattern reproduces itself beyond the island, to the benefit of business, wherever it may be located.

Once the free zones were established, Barbados set to work to attract capital. In 1977, a year after taking power, Tom Adams's Labour government set up the International Business Companies system, essentially designed to help companies avoid the demands of Canadian tax authorities. As long as an International Business Company is not involved in selling or buying securities, it is not taxed at all, and when it handles investments, it is subject to a meagre tax rate equal to or less than 2.5 percent.[19] In 1979, Adams enacted the Offshore Banking Act and the International Business Companies Amendment Act, confirming Barbados's status as a tax haven. There is good reason to believe that these laws were influenced by advice from abroad.[20] The laws enabled "international business groups not controlled by Barbadian residents, but having established their head office in the island – banking institutions, foreign holding companies, international corporations – to benefit from tax insolvency."[21] Here is the offshore principle in its purest form: as long as you don't plunder us directly, we'll allow you to deposit with us the booty you acquired through plundering or embezzlement somewhere else.

A CANADIAN ESCAPE ROUTE TO BARBADOS

The following year, in 1980, Canada's short-lived Conservative government under Joe Clark signed a controversial treaty on avoidance of double taxation that allowed Canadians to register their assets in Barbados, where they paid virtually no tax, and then transfer them to Canada without paying tax in Canada either.[22] Depending on the type of activity and the rate of profit declared, taxes in Barbados range from 0.25 to 2.5 percent.[23] This agreement allows any Canadian company active in Barbados to pay taxes only in Barbados – which is a tax haven. Thus, when a Canadian corporation creates a subsidiary in Barbados, "there shall be attributed to that permanent establishment the profits which it might be expected to make if it were a distinct and separate enterprise engaged in the same or similar activities" (Article VII.2 of the treaty). In consistency with the agreement, tax regulations allow the business group to act as if the entities that it controls in the two jurisdictions are separate – even though the group's annual reports present in a consolidated, that is, cumulative, form the earnings derived from all its subsidiaries and the tax advantages it enjoys.

To some, the Canada-Barbados agreement may initially have seemed justified: Canada should be prevented from taxing capital returning from a country where it has already been taxed. Justified, especially, because Barbados gave the impression, after 1979, of applying responsible tax laws (even though this was not in fact the case).[24] But not many people were duped. Geographer Maurice Burac, for one, notes that these agreements against so-called double taxation, signed between Barbados and Canada and later between Barbados and thirty other countries,[25] are actually designed to "encourage tax reductions for corporations owned by nationals of the countries that invest in the island and would like to bring their profits back home."[26]

In 1994, less than a year after he was appointed Canada's minister of finance, Paul Martin strengthened the role of Barbados as tax haven of choice for Canadian companies. As sole shareholder of a maritime transport company (Canada Steamship Lines [CSL], registered at the time in the tax haven of Liberia, in Africa), he was particularly sensitive to asset holders' interest in registering their assets at a distance from states operating under the rule of law, including the state for which he was responsible. He introduced more specific rules in his 1994 budget, stipulating that Canadian companies could not bring back to Canada income generated in a foreign country unless that country had signed with Canada a tax agreement based on the 1980 Canada-Barbados agreement. By 1995, CSL's international fleet had been moved to Barbados by the trust responsible for managing Martin's affairs while he was in power.[27] On a more general level, Statistics Canada indicates that Canadian direct investment in Barbados increased by more than 3,600 percent over a dozen-odd years, from $628 million in 1988 to $23.3 billion in 2001.[28] In the late 1990s, Canada reinforced the tax agreement by signing a Foreign Investment Protection Agreement (FIPA) with Barbados. The FIPA enshrined the "freedom of transfer of investment returns" and included a mechanism for settling disputes similar to the one in the North American Free Trade Agreement (NAFTA).[29]

One sure sign of the nature of the Canada-Barbados agreement is the approval it has received from Swiss tax lawyer and tax haven enthusiast Édouard Chambost. Chambost notes that it is "unusual" for a state to flout its own anti-tax–haven measures in this way.[30] He rejoices in the fact that "with this country [Canada], an International Business Company under Canadian control sees its profits treated in Canada as exempted surplus, which can be distributed as such in Canada without being subject to Canadian income tax."[31]

Barbados clearly has a vocation to attract "free loaders." This is the expression used by Jean-Pierre Vidal, professor in the department of accounting studies at Hautes études commerciales (HEC) Montréal, the Université de Montréal business school.[32] Vidal notes that, unsurprisingly, since the 1980s, tax havens that have signed tax agreements with Canada have received a constantly rising share of Canadian "investments": between 1987 and 2006, this share has gone from 6.8 percent of Canadian investments abroad to 16.5 percent. "This growth is for a very large part explained by an increase in the proportion of Canadian investments in Barbados, which has risen from 0.7 percent in 1987 to 7.7 percent in 2006."[33] Today, of the $603.2 billion invested by Canadians in the fourteen top countries in which they are present, $155.5 billion – that is, over 25 percent – goes to highly accommodating jurisdictions.[34] Faced with this kind of data, Vidal works tirelessly to demonstrate the obvious: all these investment flows cannot be explained by investment in tangible industrial concerns or social projects such as buildings, roads, or other forms of infrastructure. And even when investments are channelled to real projects, these projects may have been designed to favour tax flight. One thing is blindingly clear: Canadian investments in Barbados are completely disproportionate to the Barbados economy. "In 2006, Barbados received Canadian direct investment totalling $89 million per square kilometre, or $136,653 per capita."[35] This is insane. In conclusion, Vidal once again states what is perfectly evident: "Clearly, some investments are not used to buy factories."[36]

While the 1980 Canada-Barbados agreement took Canadian non-interference one step further in the area of international tax rules, Ottawa's policies have always been anemic in this area. In 1972, the Canadian government had enacted a set of provisions on "foreign accrual property income" (FAPI), which were "intended to prevent Canadian residents from diverting certain income from Canada to controlled foreign corporations, especially those established in tax havens."[37] A Canadian resident who owned at least 10 percent of a foreign entity could be required to pay tax on this income in Canada. To this law was added another set of regulations on foreign investment and trusts, also intended to extend tax principles to passive entities abroad.[38] This last set of regulations, however, was defective in that the status of foreign affiliate already made tax avoidance possible.[39] Despite all this, since 1972, the Canadian government has not produced any serious study of international taxation issues,[40] confining itself to enacting minor changes to the law through its budgets. At most, the government's Technical Committee on Business Taxation, or the Advisory Panel on Canada's System of International Taxation, sometimes ask independent groups to carry out studies,[41] but this amounts to no more than "tinkering," in the words of tax expert Brian Arnold.[42]

Formally, the escape routes created by the federal government are open only to business: similar manoeuvres by individuals would be punishable by law:

> For individual Canadian citizens ... there is really no way to permanently (and legally) shelter foreign investment and business income from Canadian income tax. International Business Companies (IBCs) seem to offer a viable alternative, and may even prove effective in sheltering assets from Canadian tax. However, the CCRA [Canada Revenue Agency] requires that there must be some "bona fide purpose" other than merely tax avoidance for the establishment of an IBC, so their legality for individuals in a Canadian context is usually questionable, and you are sure to reap the whirlwind if caught out by the CCRA. Immigrant and emigrant trusts, where properly structured, provide partial and temporary protection for foreign assets, and becoming non-resident in Canada is always an option, but other than that, there are no real solutions for individuals.[43]

Meanwhile, Canadian companies benefit from an agreement against double taxation which limits their tax rate in Barbados to 2.5 percent of their income and ensures they do not have to pay tax when they bring the money back to Canada. This makes Barbados the ultimate tax haven for Canadian firms,[44] while individual citizens must make up for the loss to the public purse by paying higher taxes, experiencing a loss of public services, or both.

Canada's Auditor General, Sheila Fraser, noted in her 2002 report that Barbados had constantly adapted its laws in order to attract ever larger amounts of Canadian funds: "Barbados and Malta changed their tax rules to bypass our law – to accommodate foreign affiliate investments. Tax arrangements for foreign affiliates continue to erode Canadian tax revenues."[45] Playing Barbados's game, in 2010 Canada even extended to the entire insurance sector the right to send funds through Barbados in order to avoid taxes.[46]

As in Bahamas and Cayman Islands, tax flight jointly authorized by Canada and Barbados has now created a market for banking services. The ink had hardly dried on the measures enacted by Barbados in 1979 when the Royal Bank of Canada (RBC) hurried to the scene, establishing the Royal Bank of Canada (Barbados) Ltd. Within five years this institution, along with a British bank, Barclays, had assets of $1.5 billion.[47] Less than ten years after the measures had been enacted, the island was home to five great banking corporations specializing in offshore transactions, and 260 IBCs.[48] The RBC today manages six entities in Barbados.[49] Other Canadian financial institutions in Barbados include the Canadian Imperial Bank of Commerce with six entities,[50] Scotiabank with two,[51] the Toronto Dominion Bank with three,[52] and the Bank of Montreal[53] and the National Bank[54] with one each. Barrick Gold, the gold mining company, also has a financial institution in Barbados.[55]

TRANSFER PRICING AND DOUBLE-DIPPING

The Canada-Barbados agreement facilitates a favourite corporate tax-avoidance technique known as transfer pricing. First, the corporation creates one or more subsidiaries in a tax haven. Then it maintains business relations with the subsidiary as if it were an independent party. Transactions are always designed to benefit the subsidiary, because money earned by the offshore entity will not be taxed. In other words, the goal is to establish bogus operations with the subsidiary in order to record a large proportion of the corporation's earnings in offshore accounts, removing them from taxation in countries where the corporation has real and substantial activities. Or, to quote the summary provided by French senator Éric Bocquet, commenting as president of the 2012 French Senate inquiry on tax evasion, "simply put, for businesses, tax evasion means locating losses in countries with high taxation, where losses are tax-deductible, and locating profits in tax havens, where taxes are low or non-existent."[56]

Barbados is a choice destination for this type of operation because of its agreement with Canada on avoiding double taxation. As astute observers explain, while in 1980 there were no international regulations on transfer pricing:

> The global enterprise could simply inflate or deflate the value of any transaction passing between its Barbados corporation and the related Canadian corporation, so as to transfer the profits from Canada into the lower tax jurisdiction. Imagine the Barbadian subsidiary selling [supplies such as] a light bulb to the Canadian subsidiary for $102 rather than at its $2 cost price. This would result in the entire $100 profit being transferred to the Barbadian company. The same result could be achieved by inflating or deflating the value of services or intangibles passing between these related parties.[57]

Occurrences of what is known as *mispricing* can easily be as crude as that in the example given. There are no logistical problems involved, since the commodities are exchanged only in a virtual sense: the light bulbs artificially sold to the subsidiary never actually left the company warehouse. The ploy occasionally becomes visible when it backfires, as in the case of Tregaskiss, a Canadian company that created a Barbados subsidiary, Tregaskiss International Corporation, in 1995. Canadian tax authorities charged the company with transferring over $14 million to its Barbados subsidiary between 1995 and 2000; the Barbados entity had four employees. The company argued in court that it was transferring its activities to Barbados in order to benefit from the enlightened leadership of a senior executive who happened to live there.[58]

As early as the 1980s, scrupulous accountants were expressing concern about the ease with which corporations were carrying out transfer pricing. An arsenal of Canadian laws (Income Tax Act, Customs Act, Anti-Dumping Act) could not prevent the use (or misuse) of this technique: "Despite the aggressive tone of such rules, the large number of options for structuring multinational corporate finance invariably gives the edge to the corporations," wrote tax expert Donald J. S. Brean in 1984 in an issue of *Canadian Tax Paper* dedicated to international tax issues.[59] The truth is that the Canada-Barbados agreement negates the basic principles of taxation. Historically, "neutrality" was the prevailing principle in international taxation theory. In optimal terms, this meant that money moving from one place to another should be subject to the same tax treatment in each jurisdiction.[60] With the 1980 agreement, this idea of equilibrium was abandoned. Treaties to counteract alleged double taxation provide states with an opportunity to ensure that their own legal system is completely distorted and debased.[61] Brian Arnold describes how the treaties have made it possible to bypass Canadian laws: "Canadian multinationals have used international business corporations in Barbados as international holding companies or international finance companies. The corporation can be used to earn intragroup income, which is not subject to the FAPI [foreign accrual property income] rules because of paragraph 95 (2) (a) [of the Income Tax Act] and which can be repatriated in Canada tax-free despite the fact that the rate of tax in Barbados is very low."[62] In ensuring that its own system would be unable to counteract tax havens, Canada was championing private corporations against citizens, and especially ordinary citizens in need of a state that would make sure it had the revenue to fulfill its social responsibility. Providing companies with easy access to accommodating jurisdictions such as Barbados may make these companies more competitive,[63] but who are their competitors today now that states throughout the world, caught in a downward spiral, have become reluctant to tax anyone but wage earners? In Canada, corporations contributed only 13.4 percent to the national budget in 2014 (that is, $37 billion out of a budget of $276 billion), while income tax paid by individuals accounted for half of government income ($137 billion or 49.9 percent). The GST paid by these individuals accounted for 11.3 percent of the whole ($31.3 billion).[64] The Canadian tax system has long offered business some of the lowest tax rates prevailing in countries defined as industrialized.[65]

The conclusions reached by Arnold in 2009 were also those of Sheila Fraser, the Auditor General of Canada, in the two decades following the 1980 Canada-Barbados agreement. In 2002, she sharply criticized the complacent relationship between Canada and Barbados, quoting the following example: "We also observed a transaction, for example, where a foreign affiliate of a foreign-owned Canadian corporation was used to move $500 million in capital gains from Canada to Barbados tax-free. In 2000, Canadian corporations received $1.5 billion of virtually tax-free dividend income from their affiliates in Barbados (compared with $400 million in 1990)."[66] She identified the cause as follows: "Two special rules were also introduced in 1995 that provide exceptions to the general rule. One allows dividends from Barbados international business corporations and other similar corporations to qualify for tax-free treatment."[67] Fraser found that the government had managed in this way to legalize misdeeds noted in her 1992 report.

Canada's openness to Barbados also enables Canadian companies with sister companies abroad to deduct from their taxes the loans they make to each other. This system, denounced by Sheila Fraser in 2002, is still in operation today. Company A borrows money in Canada and invests it in company B, its Barbados subsidiary. Company B then lends the money to company C, another subsidiary of the same company, this time located in the United States. Company C invests the money and deducts from its taxable income, in the United States, the interest paid on the loan. "For a single investment, company A gets two tax deductions on the interest and Canada will not have been able to charge any tax on the income produced by the investment in the United States."[68] Thanks to this method known as "double-dipping," interest on a single loan is deducted *twice* from taxable income. This single flaw in our tax laws cost the public purse $3.5 billion in 1994 alone, and a number of foreign corporations have registered in Canada simply to benefit from this sleight of hand. The conclusion is unavoidable: through its relations with Barbados, Canada itself is part of the offshore network and is used by foreign corporations as a tax haven.

The federal government has always ignored such considerations, and this tax loophole went unchecked for a considerable length of time, until 2007. While article 18.2 of the 2007 budget was designed to make double-dipping impossible beginning in 2012,[69] business, brought together by the government itself in a lobby group known as the Advisory Panel on Canada's International Taxation System, loudly protested, claiming that this loss would seriously damage its "competitiveness" at the global level.[70] *Competitiveness,* as we know, is a word that will justify anything. Ottawa abolished the measure two years later, agreeing to let companies continue to abuse their prerogatives.[71] On January 1, 2010, the United States and Canada brought into force a Fifth Protocol to the Canada-U.S. tax treaty that was supposed to end the practice, but according to tax lawyer Lyne Gaulin, "the tax implications [of the new rules] should not be material."[72]

PERMISSIVE LAWS ... AND A CONCILIATORY SUPREME COURT

The scheming around transfer pricing was so crude that states eventually felt the need for some kind of intervention, however minimal. Beginning in the 1990s, a company seeking to reduce its tax bill was no longer allowed to sell supplies to itself (in one case, a company sold plastic buckets to itself at $1,000 per unit; rolls of toilet paper were sold at $4,121 for a package of four).[73] To provide rich countries with guidelines, the OECD decided to update deficient international tax provisions that it had not reviewed since 1984[74] or, before that, since 1979.[75] In 1995, it approved OECD Transfer Pricing Guidelines for Multinational Enterprises and Tax Administrations.[76] Using these as inspiration, Canada in 1998 enacted a requirement that entities of a group must invoice each other on the same basis as entities dealing at arm's length; transactions that could "reasonably be considered" to be intended primarily to gain a tax benefit were forbidden.[77]

However, corporations continued to refine their tactics to keep on practising transfer pricing and mispricing. Only a little scheming is required for a corporation to move its funds to jurisdictions where tax institutions are a joke. For example, the offshore subsidiary of a Canadian corporation may be assigned exclusive rights to a trademark used by the group to which it belongs. It may then charge the parent company millions of dollars every year for the right to use the trademark, with the purpose of removing these sums from the parent company's declared income. At this point, laws no longer have any bite, or, if they have any, Canadian courts will make sure they are neutralized. The courts are required to distinguish between legal and illegal practices with regard to undeclared transfers by Canadian companies to tax havens, at a time when these transactions are increasingly impenetrable. As usual, however, what is "reasonable" in law is not what would seem reasonable to a critical mind or even to a person endowed with ordinary common sense. From 1990 to 1993, for example, Glaxo, a Canadian subsidiary of the British firm with the same name, sold an antihistamine to its Swiss subsidiary at a price varying between $1,512 and $1,651 per kilo, that is, five times the price of the generic product. The Canada Revenue Agency estimated that losses to the public purse totalled $51 million.[78] But in the end, the Supreme Court of Canada rejected the tax authorities' claim and ruled in the company's favour.[79] Glaxo argued that the high price paid by its Swiss subsidiary was justified because the transaction gave the Swiss entity the right to use the Zantac trademark. The Supreme Court accepted the merits of an intragroup transaction on intellectual property rights even though the transaction was, in fact, a stratagem to bypass Canadian tax laws.[80]

The justification based on intellectual property rights obviously does not solve the problem – in fact, it *is* the problem. In the United States, Glaxo's disputed transfer-pricing practices between 1989 and 2000 led to an out-of-court settlement in which it paid American tax authorities $3.4 million.[81] In France, the Senate studied transfer pricing as part of a fact-finding commission on tax evasion. The commission's report[82] quotes economist Christian Chavagneux describing the discretionary power of multinationals to bill themselves for services whose price is not clearly defined by the market. What is the value of the right to use a famous trademark? What is the value, for example, of the right to use the "Google" trademark, which Google appears to have transferred to its Bermuda subsidiary? "Since this right, which is extremely expensive, must be purchased by all Google subsidiaries, all profits can be channelled to Bermuda where, of course, there is almost no tax. But what is the international price for using the Google trademark? This is not easy to define. What standards can tax authorities use to say that a price is too high when there is no world market for the

Google trademark?"[83] The profits recorded by Google in the Bermuda tax haven, after they have passed through Ireland and the Netherlands, are colossal – close to $10 billion, in fact.[84] In 2013, the public was surprised to learn that another information technology giant, Apple, had used similar ploys. "Instead of bringing the money back to the United States, the company preferred to borrow the record amount of $17 billion to pay for dividends and stock buybacks that shareholders had been promised."[85] In his book *La Grande Évasion*, journalist Xavier Harel showed that transfer pricing was used by an impressive list of companies, including large agrifood corporations (Chiquita, Fresh Del Monte, Dole), mining companies (BHP Billiton), and oil and forestry companies (ExxonMobil and Danzer).[86] In Washington, Citizens for Tax Justice also cited Nike and Microsoft,[87] and Ikea was later named.[88] In Montreal's *Le Devoir*, Éric Desrosiers added IBM, Facebook, Pfizer, Johnson & Johnson, and Citigroup to the list. For Desrosiers, the most important question was: "Will popular pressure be sufficient to force governments to find a solution?"[89] The problem of transfer pricing has become so blatant that, in July 2013, the OECD published a white paper suggesting ways for its member states to counteract it and create the basis for a simplified international taxation system.[90]

On the related issue of *treaty shopping* – the process by which a company knowingly registers its operations in the tax haven most adapted to its needs, in order to bypass Canadian taxes – the courts have been so favourable to major taxpayers sued by the CRA that even the federal Department of Finance appears discouraged. Since 2006, Canadian judges have ruled three times that the general anti-avoidance rule, which is supposed to penalize abusive strategies involving transfer of funds to tax havens, should not prevent corporations from registering their assets in tax havens such as the Cayman Islands, Luxembourg, or the Netherlands. The science of law merely says that "there is nothing inherently proper or improper with selecting one foreign regime over another."[91] These three cases (MIL [Investments] S.A., Prévost Car Inc., and Velcro Canada) are now highly significant elements of case law.[92] According to a Department of Finance document, "Collectively, these three cases indicate in relatively strong terms that the courts in Canada are not currently inclined to find against taxpayers in treaty shopping cases."[93] As a consequence, the department has undertaken a vast project to make the law more specific, without any assurance that Canadian judges will understand the impact of their decisions when it comes to penalizing the wealthy, whose use of tax havens is depriving Canadian society of resources.

These legal decisions also indicate the courts' confusion, which lawmakers have done nothing to dispel. The confusion stems from the fact that, in the mind of those who exercise public power of various kinds, the issue of tax havens is not related to any particular ethical system. Today, we decide to neutralize tax benefits associated with trusts; tomorrow, we authorize an outrageous technique such as transfer pricing. As a consequence, a court may sometimes do something unexpected – as did Justice Judith Woods in a decision given for the Tax Court of Canada in 2010. Woods refused to view trusts registered by Canadians in Barbados as foreign corporations,[94] and her ruling was endorsed by the Supreme Court of Canada in 2012.[95] Despite such encouraging decisions, it is still easy to bypass Canadian law through sophisticated operations combining several jurisdictions to create trusts or other structures.[96] Thus, the money in a trust will be taxed in a tax haven if the trustee and the beneficiary demonstrate that they are not in any way involved in its management; this is what the interested parties failed to do in the case Justice Woods decided. In other words, the legal situation remains highly uncertain. Diane Francis argues that "Revenue Canada regards any cash distributions from such offshore trusts as non-taxable even when sent back to Canadian tax residents, as long as those individuals have nothing to do with the trusts or how they are run. Canadian courts have ruled that these are distributions of capital, not of income, a technicality that has never been corrected by Canadian lawmakers."[97] However that may be, not even lawmakers know, or seem to know, how to frame laws in a way that will make it clear from the start how they will be enforced.

In the Glaxo case, nobody knows how much Canadian tax authorities vainly spent on lawyers' fees to try and recover the amounts involved. Nor does anyone know if the costs of these judicial sagas are not potentially larger than the sums the CRA hopes to collect. Like Parliamentary Library researcher Sylvain Fleury, we may say that "the delicate task" that is "left to the courts" is caused by "the lack of clarity in legislative provisions."[98] We may also think that the profoundly corrupting influence of money on the judicial system, given its central role in organizing evidence, is not experienced as an ethical problem by either lawmakers or corporate lawyers.

TRANSFER PRICING: WORLDWIDE PROBLEM, CANADIAN ZEAL

Thanks to the common practice of transfer pricing, 40 percent of international transactions today take place among entities belonging to the same economic group. Hundreds of billions of dollars thus bypass the tax system of states based on the rule of law.[99] The worldwide ramifications of finance directly affect national tax structures and are far ahead of theoretical and legislative responses. At this point, a strictly national attempt to counter tax revenue shortfalls affecting the public purse is no longer relevant.[100] Real investments in economic undertakings abroad, which create revenue within a national territory, are combined with offshore investments that are intended to bypass taxation – and to benefit from the legal impenetrability of these legislative zones.

Multinationals benefit when legal frameworks view their subsidiaries and components in dozens of jurisdictions as independent units, despite the fact that they are seamlessly integrated into the main unit. In fact, as Australian lawyer Kerrie Sadiq points out, "the multinational entity is an indivisible whole rather than a mere sum of its separate parts."[101] We would be well advised to view it as such in legal terms. Taxes would then be levied on the consolidated earnings of a corporation and not on the earnings of each of its structures, viewed separately. Today, governments are simply patching up an inadequate legal system that provides multinationals with all the leeway they could possibly need. Both Jomo Kwame Sundaram, author of a report published by the German Friedrich-Ebert Stiftung foundation,[102] and the international research and advocacy group Tax Justice Network believe that the transfer-pricing issue should be brought directly to the United Nations, with a guarantee of independence.[103] All this is to say that the tax agreement between Canada and Barbados is designed to reinforce a structural error.

There is a market in Canada for pedagogical explanation of the transfer-pricing technique. Tax lawyer Jonathan Garbutt, for example, gives lectures with unambiguous titles such as "Transfer Pricing and Tax Planning for Barbados Subsidiaries of Canadian Parent Companies" (a 2011 seminar presented by the Royal Bank of Canada).[104] The proliferation of a certain kind of job offer also provides food for thought. In 2011, for example, accounting firm Deloitte posted a job offer for a transfer-pricing analyst: "Deloitte's transfer pricing practice is one of our fastest growing service areas worldwide," explains the advertisement, adding that the jobholder "must manage all of the intricate details in local jurisdictions, while strategically planning the global flow of transactions."[105]

This phenomenon will probably be exacerbated now that Barbados has decided, in its 2012 budget, to reduce virtually to nothing the taxes paid by international financial corporations registered in its territory. "The budget proposes to reduce the corporate tax rate for International Business Companies (IBCs), Societies with Restricted Liability (SRLs) and International Banks. The rate will drop to 0.50% (from 1.00%) in 2012 and to 0.25% in 2013."[106] In its inimitable style, the KPMG accounting corporation states that "The budget proposes special entry permits to assist high net worth individuals and other property owners who wish to invest in Barbados."[107] In Barbados, these are people who enjoy complete freedom from taxes on dividends, capital gains, wealth, and inheritance.[108]

Canadian financial institutions are the lynchpin of the whole system. In 2012, the Canadian government boasted that Canadians represented 75 percent of the international financial community in Barbados.[109] In the same breath, it underlined the congruence between Canadian and Barbadian financial rules, without bothering to discuss tax issues as such.

 DOING IT DIFFERENTLY IN FRANCE
AND IN THE EUROPEAN UNION

In its 2012 report on tax exile, the French Senate makes sure that the question is framed in political terms, viewing tax evasion in a "non-technical sense."[110] This puts an end to the distinction between tax "flight" toward tax havens, viewed as legal, and tax "evasion," which is against the law.[111] "There are obviously practical connections between these two processes."[112] The distinction between what is legal and what is illegal is not necessarily relevant and may in fact be harmful – especially since it favours a mindset that limits itself to the legal issues surrounding "fraud."

The French Senate frames the issue according to the spirit, and not the letter, of the law. The objects of its investigation – fiscal optimization (tax planning) and revenue transfers (income shifting) – become a problem "if the profits earned abroad include a profit that should have been associated with France."[113] Transfer pricing may lead to a loss of national sovereignty if a country can no longer accurately define its own earnings. The senators revert to the basic principles of political thought: corporations are supposed to pay taxes according to the location in which they are registered because as they carry out financial, industrial, or commercial operations, they are indebted to the instituted public framework for ensuring the possibility of their private enrichment. "Values exist in a space of sovereignty that helps them take form."[114] When states begin to compete with each other to attract corporations, whether or not these corporations carry out real activities, the traditionally instituted political structure is damaged. The offshorization of states makes regulation impossible. "Tax laws must be viable, and this viability does not depend only on the state's sovereignty, since the fiscal competition of other states limits its power."[115] A state damaged by such operations must create new legal mechanisms to prevent them. These are the terms in which the French Senate formulates the problem after having consulted the French population.

The French Senate asserts that the issue of fiscal competition between sovereign states is an area of concern in and of itself, and that "international fiscal competition, and analysis of it, are of genuine interest to help us consider the forms of action to be taken against international tax evasion."[116] Lawmakers and agents of the state should focus, for example, on businesses posting phenomenal profits in tax haven subsidiaries where they do not have a single employee, and should treat them as cases of tax evasion. In these cases, the relocation of activities is not related to "the transnational conditions of the group's activity"[117] or "the new international division of labour,"[118] but to "an effect of pure optimization."[119]

From this perspective, the problem of tax evasion caused by opportunistic planning is seen to be considerable. In the French government's

2007 budget, the largest companies – those with 2,000 employees or more – were paradoxically those that contributed least to the public purse. They provided only 4.1 percent of total taxes, while companies hiring fewer than 250 people contributed 47.4 percent.[120] Less than 50 percent of France's 1,132,500 companies actually paid taxes that year, and only 500 of its 12,100 largest corporations paid corporate income tax.[121] Tax fraud deprives the French government of 60 to 80 billion euros a year, while European countries as a whole are thought to lose up to 2,000 billion euros annually.[122] These data produced by the French Senate's commission have no equivalent in Canada. Although grassroots organizations have requested them,[123] our country refuses to provide such estimates.

Who is responsible? Certainly those who give advice to corporations, "selling plans for tax optimization, at best, or tax evasion, at worst."[124] These firms play on the advantages offered by various sovereign jurisdictions that compete with each other, in the context of a "total fiscal heterogeneity,"[125] enabling corporations to "construct" their own tax rate,[126] providing them with absolute sovereignty in the current framework of economic and financial globalization. The French Senate could have cited France Offshore, a firm specializing in relocating businesses, which in 2012 presented its clients with a range of jurisdictions providing offshore-type tax shelters; Canada was one of these jurisdictions.[127] The work carried out in France led to important legislative measures such as the adoption by the French National Assembly, in 2013, of a law forcing French banks to disclose the value of their foreign assets, country by country.[128]

A similar approach is apparent at the Parliament of the European Union in Strasbourg. In 2013, for instance, the Committee on Economic and Monetary Affairs published its *Report on Fight against Tax Fraud, Tax Evasion, and Tax Havens*,[129] which gives priority to the fight against transfer pricing and its reliance on tax havens.

In Europe, the commission has undertaken to hear evidence about firms that break a basic civic rule: paying taxes. Work has also been done on a law on the erosion of corporate taxation that would establish a minimum tax level for resident corporations. This approach, which is the opposite of that taken in Canada, shows that our country's actions are dictated not by some inexorable fate, but by choice.

The 1980 Canada-Barbados agreement also had repercussions in the maritime sector. Like the Bahamas, Barbados in the late 1970s developed a flag of convenience[130] that made it a formidable free port, to be feared by traditional states. Since shipowners must, in international waters, obey the laws of the jurisdiction where the ship is registered, the fact of registering a ship in a "free port," which is to maritime transportation what a tax haven is to taxes, is a way of guaranteeing the ship's impunity. Flying the flag of Liberia, the Republic of Malta, or Barbados guarantees release from any kind of meaningful state regulation. There is no need, of course, to declare earnings or pay taxes on the operation of these ships. Health and safety at work, and sailors' working conditions in general, are barely regulated, and laws on making ships safe for ecosystems are virtually non-existent. Choice of flag is dictated solely by bookkeeping considerations: few ships registered in Barbados are likely to be seen in Bridgetown harbour. And unlike earlier jurisdictions providing flags of convenience (such as Liberia), Barbados and other Caribbean territories provide a full range of offshore accounting services.[131] These territories allow registration of entire maritime fleets active anywhere but in their own waters, with shipowners benefiting from the territories' legal and regulatory void.

The 1980 Canada-Barbados agreement includes a section dealing with maritime transportation, ensuring that Canadian shipowners will enjoy the island's legislative generosity. Article VIII, paragraph 1, states that "Profits derived by an enterprise of a Contracting State from the operation of ships or aircraft in international traffic shall be taxable only in that State."[132] These are terms that enable a state to create a free port in its territory. In other words, Canada has legalized and even encouraged the registration of industrial transportation vessels far from its own jurisdiction – an initiative that benefits shipowners, but has no relevance to the common good of which the government is officially the steward.

The Canadian minister of finance Paul Martin later personally profited from this section of the treaty. While he was a member of the federal government from 1993 to 2002, and in fact responsible for the budget in the government of Jean Chrétien, he was also the sole shareholder of a maritime transportation company, Canada Steamship Lines (CSL). For shipowners such as CSL, the chief attraction of off-shore jurisdictions lies in the regulatory advantages they offer in terms of labour: "In countries providing flags of convenience, the absence of any kind of social regulation brings the cost of labour down even more – especially since these countries also avoid imposing the rule of crews' nationality, to which Western seamen's unions long clung with the energy of despair."[133] The minister's company justified the relocation of its fleet on the basis of international competition,[134] as if this were a situation that could not be countered by any policy, and especially as if it were a worldwide condition that political institutions had done nothing to create. By managing its fleet, officially, from tax havens, CSL was able to disregard Canadian standards for toxic waste disposal, Canadian regulations on ship maintenance, and Canadian laws on safety at work and minimum wages, in addition to avoiding the tax obligations that Paul Martin, as minister of finance, was actually responsible for enforcing over a period of ten years.[135]

Martin's actions are part of the offshore realities that create a race to the bottom among Northern jurisdictions. The International Transport Workers' Federation (ITF) estimates that over 51 percent of the world's tonnage is registered under a flag of convenience.[136] To avoid losing their fleets, states based on the rule of law, such as France, the United Kingdom (through the Isle of Man), Norway, and Japan, have now developed flags that imply almost no regulation.[137] The race is on.

The *Amoco Cadiz*, a Liberian vessel responsible for an oil spill on the coast of Brittany in 1978 – the logical outcome of great negligence – prefigured the dark future of maritime transportation in terms of environmental protection. Citizens' worst fears were confirmed by environmental disasters on the coast of Brittany (*Erika*, 1999), in Abidjan, Côte d'Ivoire (*Probo Koala*, 2006), and in the Gulf of Mexico (BP oil-drilling platform, 2011). Each of these catastrophes was brought about by a chain of entities registered in free ports and tax havens.

"The sea covers two-thirds of the planet, and this 'no man's land' is the merchant marine's business asset."[138] Low-cost maritime shipping also favours relocation of businesses. Because the labour of maritime crews costs almost nothing, and because ship maintenance is neglected, it still makes sense for Western corporations to manufacture low-end products of first necessity in the free zones of China, Indonesia, or Jamaica, rather than in North America or Europe.

CONNECTING WITH THE OFFSHORE NETWORK

For the Canadian establishment and Canadian small business, the Barbados-Canada corridor was for many years the gateway to offshore regimes. Not only do our capital-holders legally and merrily benefit from the advantages granted by Barbados, but through Barbados they are connected to the worldwide network of tax havens. This is made explicit by financial adviser Alex Doulis: "My Barbados company can set up a trust in the Turks and Caicos Islands for us and it will be tax free." [139] Once funds have been located in Barbados, they can move on to a trust in the Turks and Caicos and then to a broker in the Channel Islands, pass through the Caymans, and then return to Barbados to re-enter Canada legally. For Canadians, Barbados is a bridgehead for illicit operations, favouring the movement of Canadian capital in and out of the offshore financial system in a completely legal way. According to Doulis: "As it is, I pay 2.5 percent to the Barbadian government and nothing to Canada, but I have the use of the money here. I could get myself in a real tax mess with a non-treaty country when I tried to get hold of the money. It would probably be taxed at full rates." [140]

Jean-Pierre Vidal, economics professor at Hautes études commerciales (HEC) Montréal, makes a similar point. Money placed by Canadians in Barbados, in order to remove it from the reach of tax authorities, is "redirected elsewhere, where substantial activities are then actually deployed." [141] The funds may be mobilized for risky stock market operations managed by Cayman Island hedge funds or for Panamanian drug trafficking, then return to Canada through the Barbados corridor. Bank secrecy is not as well protected in Barbados as in some other places, because dubious manoeuvres are more likely to be entrusted to companies and banks in other parts of the Caribbean. Barbados, however, has been home to several import-export firms suspected of irregularity by the European Union. Another interesting story about Barbados involves Norshield, a Canadian company that carried out a gigantic fraud in the early 2000s. As part of this fraud, Norshield sent $60 million to third parties, for unknown reasons, from a Barbados bank; investigations associated with investor lawsuits indicated the presence of the Royal Bank of Canada in the background.[142]

▮ KEEPING UP WITH THE JONESES

Many of these problems could be eliminated simply by repealing the Canada-Barbados agreement. But this agreement today is seen as a model to be imitated. The Conservatives in power in Canada have been working in the most insidious way possible to develop multiple corridors of this kind between Canada and other tax havens. Under pressure from the Organisation for Economic Co-operation and Development to sign Tax Information Exchange Agreements (TIEAs) with offshore states, with the explicit intention of breaching the bank secrecy prevailing in these jurisdictions, the Canadian government resorted to duplicity. The principle behind TIEAs is to allow the tax agents of one country, under certain conditions, to investigate parties potentially guilty of fraud in another jurisdiction. However, compared to other agreements throughout the world, Canadian-style TIEAs have one distinctive feature. The Canadian government's 2007 budget made explicit the fact that under section 5907(11) of Canada's Income Tax Regulations, Canadian investors who put their assets in a tax haven that had signed a TIEA with Canada could then bring their money back to Canada in the form of dividends without having to pay taxes on it. This astonishing measure is intended "to increase the incentive for countries to enter into TIEAs with Canada,"[143] according to the Ministry of Finance. In other words, while these tax measures remain in effect, the government is stimulating offshore activity while pretending to fight tax havens. The federal directive is perfectly clear, as explained in 2009: "dividends paid by foreign affiliates operating in a jurisdiction with which Canada has a tax treaty in force are generally exempted from tax in Canada. Canada's policy in respect of TIEAs is to extend the same exemption in respect of dividends paid by foreign affiliates that operate in jurisdictions with which Canada has a TIEA in force." And this reference document adds: "The availability of such benefits could make these jurisdictions more attractive for Canadian investment."[144] In other words, the Barbados model is spreading.

Meanwhile, the provisions that are supposed to provide access to information protected by bank secrecy have no real impact. A former Manhattan district attorney now active in the Caymans comments: "Even when they cooperate to eliminate the fraud … it takes so long that when the door is finally closed, the horse has been stolen and the barn has burned down."[145] A member of the French Parliament, Vincent Peillon, who chaired a 2000 Parliamentary commission on tax havens, comes to a similar conclusion: "How many judges, in affairs relating not to benign and banal tax evasion, but well and truly to transnational criminality, have found themselves faced with situations in which, because they didn't know the exact account number, their investigation was brought to a halt by the rigidity of bankers and national judicial authorities? Taken to the extreme, refusal to authorize this kind of investigation means that assistance is provided only when investigators already have the evidence in their possession!"[146]

If Canada were to ask Switzerland, with which it has signed a TIEA, for access to bank information on a presumed Canadian tax evader, it would first have to provide detailed information on the subject's banking operations. This information is almost impossible to obtain since the TIEA does not allow the exchange of information when it involves "any trade, business, industrial, commercial or professional secret or trade process, or information, the disclosure of which would be contrary to public policy."[147] Gilles Larin, holder of the Research Chair on Tax Issues and Public Finances at the Université de Sherbrooke, notes that "Canadian tax authorities, despite their official line, may not get what they want from the process of information exchange established with the Swiss Federal Council."[148] The Royal Bank of Canada agrees in a reassuringly upbeat circular produced by one of its tax experts in the tax haven of Guernsey: "TIEAs should have no effect on compliant confidentiality." After all, the only information that a TIEA might lead the bank to disclose to "appropriate authorities" would be information about "the income earned by a trust" or the moment "when a distribution is made to a beneficiary in a particular jurisdiction."[149] (A trust, as we know, is a structure whose beneficiaries in tax havens are generally unknown.)

Tax havens couldn't line up fast enough to enjoy the benefits of a Canadian-style agreement, including the certainty of attracting money seeking to escape the taxman. Anguilla, the Bahamas, Bermuda, the Cayman Islands, Dominica, St. Lucia, the Netherlands Antilles, St. Vincent and the Grenadines, San Marino, St. Kitts and Nevis, and the Turks and Caicos Islands have all signed an agreement. These agreements wipe out any steps the government may take to fight tax havens[150] and confirm Canada's official role as a tax sieve.

Instead of closing the permanent tax-amnesty corridor between Barbados and Canada, the Conservative government chose to appease competing jurisdictions by reproducing it. Barbados representatives deplored the loss of their monopoly, and Barbados then decided to reduce its minimum tax rate for international corporations. The president of the Barbados International Business Association (BIBA), Melanie Jones, applauded this decision, which constitutes "a meaningful response to Barbados' recent loss of its competitive advantage in the Canadian market, due to the extension of the exempt surplus treatment to subsidiaries established in TIEA jurisdictions."[151] The logic of racing to the bottom now applies, relentlessly, everywhere.

TURKS AND CAICOS ISLANDS

TRUE SOUTH STRONG AND FREE

*In which Liberals and Conservatives try to create an
eleventh province offering sun, sand, and bank accounts*

The political class of the Turks and Caicos Islands might look a little
dubious in some lights. In 1985, the islands' chief minister, Norman
Saunders, was arrested in Miami and sentenced to eight years in jail
for conspiring to bring cocaine into the United States.[1] The minister of
commerce and development, Stafford Missick, was arrested along with
him.[2] This unsavoury episode had no effect on Canadian Conservatives and Liberals eager to make the archipelago – currently a British
overseas territory with a population of fewer than 50,000 full-time
residents[3] – into the eleventh Canadian province, the fourth Canadian
territory, or perhaps, simply, a Canadian dependency. Beginning in the
mid-1980s, this initiative was repeatedly brought to the forefront by
its Canadian advocates.

Although the flirtation between Canada and the islands began in
1917,[4] it was in 1974 that the Turks and Caicos officially expressed their
willingness to become part of the Canadian confederation. At the time,
even the New Democratic Party joined in the game. A bill to annex the
islands, tabled by New Democrat MP Max Saltsman, was eventually
rejected by the House of Commons[5] amid whispers that an agreement
of this kind would lead to massive immigration from the islands to
Canada.[6] In his 1980 *Guide des secrets bancaires*, however, pro-offshore
tax consultant Édouard Chambost still presented the Turks and Caicos
as pretenders to the title of "future Canada in the Caribbean."[7] Pierre
Elliott Trudeau's second Liberal government finally turned down the
offer, but had taken it seriously enough to consider it for six years.[8]

Business circles tried again in 1986 with intensive lobbying.[9]
Dan McKenzie, Conservative MP from Winnipeg, joined forces with

Ralph Higgs of the Turks and Caicos Islands Tourist Board and Delton Jones, an economist who was to become the islands' minister of finance in the 2000s, to address the Progressive Conservative Caucus Subcommittee on External Affairs in April of that year. They had little impact, however,[10] as the subcommittee chair, David Daubney,[11] merely recommended that Canada create closer ties with the Turks and Caicos by increasing foreign aid and encouraging private sector investment.[12]

Higgs and Jones were back in 1987. This time, they worked with the Turks and Caicos Development Organization to try and stir up enthusiasm for the project in the Canadian population. At the end of his career as an MP in 1989, McKenzie went on a mission to the Turks and Caicos and produced a document entitled *Report on Practical Measures Which Might Be Taken to Increase Trade, Investment, and Economic Cooperation Between Canada and the Turks.*[13] His work was left unfinished when he died suddenly of a heart attack in 1989.[14]

Over a decade later, the cause was taken up by Peter Goldring, Conservative MP for Edmonton East.[15] The birth of two civil associations – A Place in the Sun, founded by businessmen Brad Sigouin and Richard Pearson and of which Goldring became a member, and Canadians for a Tropical Province – was carefully staged.[16] Speaking in perfect synchronicity, these worthy analysts asked the government to create the "eleventh province" in order to provide Canadians with something truly important: a recreational bathing spot. Goldring, a former vice-president of the Canada-Caribbean Parliamentary Committee[17] who travelled regularly to the Caribbean (he has specified that he does so on a private basis and "using [his] own funds),"[18] advocated annexing the islands in a Parliamentary circular called "Turks and Caicos Update." In November 2003, he tabled a motion in the House of Commons stipulating that "the government should commence exploratory discussions to determine whether there is a social and economic will for a union of the country of the Turks and Caicos Islands with Canada as Canada's eleventh province."[19] The following year, he led a fact-finding mission to the archipelago,[20] and in the fall of 2004, he became the Conservative opposition's foreign affairs critic for the Caribbean. The same year, the three parties represented in Nova Scotia's legislature, still enamoured with offshore relations, unanimously voted to make the Turks and Caicos Islands part of their province.[21] A Conservative member of the provincial legislature, Bill Langille, talked of a "natural union" between the province and the archipelago and lauded their "historic trade connections" while ignoring the many controversies that were the cause of the Turks and Caicos's distasteful reputation. Goldring received reinforcements in 2005 from young federal Liberals who were in favour of making the archipelago part of Canada.[22]

It is asserted that this activism, purely intended to support tourism, has absolutely nothing to do with capital transfers to islands characterized by reduced taxation. Who are the activists? Brad Sigouin has worked in the financial sector since 1996 and acts today as wealth manager for the Royal Bank of Canada, or, to be more specific, for a branch of RBC Dominion Securities Ottawa.[23] In 2004, the Royal Bank presented him to clients as "well versed in market and economic trends, and working closely with RBC Equity Analysts, Fixed Income Specialists and Tax Professionals."[24] As for Richard Pearson, although he was interviewed by *Tax-News.com*, a British website dealing with tax havens, he claimed to view the Turks and Caicos integration project strictly in terms of benefits to the real economy: "The Turks and Caicos would become not only a sales centre for Canadian business people supplying products to the Caribbean, but an excellent trans-shipment point for Canadian goods sent into the area."[25] In an equally revealing moment of humour, Goldring stated in 2004 that Prime Minister Paul Martin, who was also the sole shareholder in Canada Steamship Lines – a maritime transportation company whose international fleet was registered in Barbados – would find it advantageous to support the project: "It would give Canada Steamship Lines the opportunity to register its fleet in a part of Canada."[26]

Prime Minister Martin and Stephen Harper, the opposition leader who was to succeed him less than two years later, declared themselves willing to meet the chief minister of the Turks and Caicos, Michael Misick, to discuss the project.[27] Stephen Harper had told French weekly *L'Express international* the previous year that "discussions" between the Turks and Caicos government and the Canadian government, in view of "negotiations," had already taken place.[28]

Meanwhile, the greatest scandal in the history of the Turks and Caicos was brewing. In March 2009, Chief Minister Misick fled to Brazil, accused of having gained undue profit from the sale of public property. The London *Telegraph* commented in 2013: "The corruption scandal – the biggest in Turks and Caicos history – is believed to have left the islands, which have a population of just 31,000, on the verge of bankruptcy, with the British government forced to provide $260 million in loan guarantees."[29] At the time, however, instead of causing concern among Canadian politicians and business circles, the revelation of a state of chronic corruption in the islands appears, on the contrary, to have revitalized the charm offensive. In June 2009, Liberal MP Massimo Pacetti tabled a new bill in the House, seconded by the Conservative Goldring, stating that "the government should immediately mandate two Members of Parliament, one from the governing party and one from the official opposition party, to begin discussions with representatives of the Turks and Caicos Islands in establishing a framework in order to determine areas of enhanced partnership in trade, social and economic development."[30] The following month, Stephen Harper, by this time elected as prime minister of Canada, asked Goldring to organize a meeting between him and the islands' new premier, Galmo Williams.[31] The archipelago's entire political class was so obviously corrupt, however, that four months later, in August 2009, the British government suspended self-government and imposed direct rule, making the governor responsible for managing the territory for the next two years[32] – just like in colonial times – and putting an end to vague Canadian desires. There were to be no further elections in the Turks and Caicos until November 2012.

Meanwhile, Brant Hasanen of the Kamloops Chamber of Commerce in British Columbia estimated that Canada's annexation of the Turks and Caicos would automatically provide Canada with benefits amounting to $9 billion. What methods were employed in producing this estimate? Nobody knows. According to Goldring, ever fascinated with what he believes to be the march of history, "this encouraging conclusion is certainly worthy of follow-up."[33]

Although the annexation project may have been indefinitely postponed, Canada nonetheless came to colonize the islands economically. Canadian firm FortisTCI is the electricity provider,[34] while InterHealth Canada, a private health care firm, manages the hospital.[35] The RCMP seconded two high-ranking officers to the jurisdiction's affairs.[36] Canadian business people own many hotels, restaurants, and recreational venues in the islands and play a key role in the real estate sector.[37] In addition, many Canadians settle in the islands not only to escape their own tax obligations in Canada, but also to establish law firms or accounting offices that enable others to do the same.[38]

ULTERIOR MOTIVES

The tourist project is perhaps more than just an alibi. Turks and Caicos casinos are thought to profit from the massive Canadian presence, and accountants, who are often required to make the round trip, benefit from cheaper flights thanks to tourist demand. And, certainly, large numbers of travellers would help break the monotony. Nonetheless, Canadians need to know that the Turks and Caicos are not just a sun and sand destination for the middle class. A March 1989 edition of the magazine for Paris newspaper *Le Figaro* presented the archipelago as a group of "desert islands for billionaires" where companies also carry out criminal activities. This is where, between 2003 and 2005, Canadian hedge fund Portus Alternative Asset Management diverted some $35 million of the $800 million it had received from 26,000 investors in Canada.[39] It was later understood that the company had created a gigantic pyramid fraud scheme. This hedge fund appeared to offer "the fastest growth in Canada" until the Ontario Securities Commission began to look into its capital transfers, amounting to millions of dollars, abroad.[40]

It is also possible, in the Turks and Caicos, to create "exempted companies" with "minimal" restrictions and administrative requirements,[41] and there are over 10,000 companies of this kind in the archipelago.[42] Asset holders do not have to reveal their identity. Hybrid combinations of criminal funds and corporate assets are set up without scruple. As tax expert Grégoire Duhamel notes, "North American and Canadian tax lawyers provide visitors with a warm welcome. The question of the origin of the funds would generally appear to be ignored."[43] In addition, Édouard Chambost observes that there has been no attempt to supervise corporations since 1994. "It is no longer necessary to draft a document indicating a social purpose: companies can do anything!"[44] The Turks and Caicos are also a haven for life insurance investors, with between 1,000 and 2,000 companies registered in this sector.[45] These companies carry out their business through subsidiaries in the Turks and Caicos, ignoring the constraints operating in a sane economy: they have no hesitation in reducing "the provisions (reserves) and capitalization rates that are required in regulated countries."[46]

Thus, the Turks and Caicos attract highly suspicious assets, operations, and transactions. Even Grégoire Duhamel, author of a guide to tax havens, warns his readers against the "dubious money" transiting through the Turks and Caicos and gives the islands a low rating of twelve out of twenty, because the jurisdiction is an important relay point for smuggling drugs from Colombia. Patrice Meyzonnier, member of the French judicial police force, gives the following example: "On February 24, 1999, a three-party United States-Great-Britain-Bahamas operation led to the inspection of *Nicole,* a freighter registered in Honduras, that was supposed to deliver cement loaded in the port of Barranquilla, Colombia, to the United States. Two tonnes of cocaine, worth between $200 and $300 million, were discovered. In the Turks and Caicos, 1,500 companies benefited from offshore status at French Cay, Grand Turk, and Providenciales."[47] The jurisdiction provides owners of ships of 150 tons or less with a flag of convenience that makes it easier to incorporate drug trafficking into maritime transportation.

The Turks and Caicos have naturally made bank secrecy impenetrable. This secrecy "is jealously protected by a law intended to compete with the Cayman Islands in terms of penalties. The law of 1979, known as the 'Confidential Relations Ordinance', establishes, for violations of bank secrecy committed by individuals, a fine of up to US$10,000 and a jail term of up to three years (this is unusual for criminal offences under banking laws), and a fine of up to US$50,000 for corporate bodies."[48]

And this is not even the worst. The Turks and Caicos have a vocation: they specialize in reinsurance, rivalling Bermuda for pre-eminence in this sector. "The Turks and Caicos Islands has more than 70 percent of the world's reinsurance companies in the country's financial services industry, which is second in investment only to the tourism industry."[49] Reinsurance companies do not converge by the hundreds on the Turks and Caicos in order to insure the islanders' fishing boats. They come to carry out large-scale operations that may not be authorized elsewhere – for regulation is minimal in the Turks and Caicos. A company will create a *captive* corporation whose purpose is to "create customized insurance policies," "cover risks that are difficult or impossible to insure in the market," and "reduce the overhead associated with contracts," as French firm Aon, specializing in this business sector, explains.[50] In plain words, a *captive insurance company* is one that is managed directly by the company that it insures. By insuring itself, this company is infringing the spirit of the law in its own country. Captive companies "cover the risks of the group to which they belong and that this group cannot or will not have covered by a traditional insurer. The constitution of a captive company makes it possible to reduce the corporation's overall insurance costs and to benefit from the tax and regulatory flexibility of the country in which the captive is established. If no loss occurs, the company can recoup its investment."[51] Under this system, the insured party is able, of course, to charge itself highly advantageous premiums. And in the Turks and Caicos, the law allows an offshore insurer to cover an insuree in sectors not included, or actually prohibited, by the laws of the state in which the insuree operates.

A company may also go into the reinsurance business in order to cover other insurance companies registered in conventional jurisdictions.[52] Reinsurance enables insurance companies to shift part of their responsibilities to the reinsurer; this gives them the leeway to sign more contracts than their capital would in fact authorize. In other words, reinsurance companies are to insurance companies as hedge funds are to banks: they provide a leverage effect, enabling the insurance companies to act on ever larger and riskier scales. Establishing this practice in tax havens makes it easy to bypass regulations established in conventional states. And in tax havens, accounting methods make it easy to launder money. The Financial Stability Forum (FSF) and the European Central Bank (ECB) have formally stated their concern with the resulting financial instability.[53] Fortunately, this need not concern us, given that the Turks and Caicos Islands claim to rigorously supervise these controversial practices.[54]

▨ MILITARY BASE AND FREE ZONE?

Why on earth have Canadians gotten involved in the annexation project? As Goldring sets out his arguments, it becomes obvious that he has many unspoken thoughts. For example, he notes with approval that "the Turks and Caicos Islands currently have one of the most successful economies in the entire Caribbean region."[55] To quote Grégoire Duhamel, however, "sole responsibility for this rests with offshore investment activity,"[56] and this in fact is what Goldring is praising. Goldring also sees the Turks and Caicos as potential sites for military bases that would facilitate Canadian military interventions in countries such as Cuba or Haiti.[57] The past augurs well for the future as, according to him: "In March 2004, the Turks and Caicos Islands gave permission to Canada to stage its troops before landing in Haiti,"[58] just like in the good old days when Canada invaded British dependencies to protect its commercial and industrial monopolies. Goldring also extols the islands' potential in terms of port facilities: he notes that their deep waters could harbour maritime container transportation[59] – by which he means, implicitly, that the islands could become a free zone. And finally, he insists that the Turks and Caicos, in this projected union, must become a province and not only a territory.[60] This would give them maximum legislative leverage and enable them to wield power as a tax haven within Canada itself, just as Delaware does within the United States.[61] It is also apparent that Goldring, who is absolutely determined to bring the two jurisdictions together, would be willing to carry out his project in a roundabout way – through a free-trade agreement, for example.[62]

Canadians are still behaving like monarchs in these islands. In a money-laundering affair related to narcotics smuggling in Canada, RCMP officers carried out a raid on Grand Turk in 1999 against Ontario businessman Richard Hape, presumed to be a guilty party. The affair was greeted with outrage in the local business community.[63] That day, Canadians showed that they could interfere as much as they wanted in the internal affairs of the Turks and Caicos Islands, and they also demonstrated that only under exceptional circumstances would they take action against potential criminals, whether tax swindlers or others.

ALBERTA

PETRO-STATE POLITICS

In which the government of Alberta embraces the oil and gas
industry, leaving citizens and the environment to fend for themselves

O ver the past twenty-five to thirty years, the general trend in Alberta
has been to deregulate the oil and gas sector, loosen environmental
regulations, and reduce the so-called "fair-share" return to the electorate
established in 1976 by Premier Peter Lougheed, leader of the Alberta
Progressive Conservatives, through the Alberta Heritage Savings Fund.
Since Lougheed's retirement in 1985, deregulation has ensured an ever
more permissive environment as subsequent governments have bowed
to the interests of international oil. The North American Free Trade
Agreement (NAFTA), in effect January 1, 1994, further liberalized
the oil and gas sector through expanded trade and enhanced opportunities for investment by large multinational corporations despite
minimal benefit for Alberta citizens and increased health risks through
environmental damage. Reducing taxes on natural resources has made
it impossible to reinvest in public infrastructure and education. But the
consequences of Alberta's development as a petro-state are even more
profound than this. As the provincial government frames its laws to
suit the interests and desires of the great petroleum- and gas-producing
corporations, Albertans find themselves without an institution that
would represent them in dealing with political, fiscal, economic, and
environmental issues.

Like all Canadian provinces, Alberta has full jurisdiction over
the exploration, development, and management of natural resources.[1]
Royalties and taxes are payable to the Alberta government in exchange
for use of these resources,[2] mainly because they exist on government-
-owned land.[3] However, instead of benefiting from the resulting
resource revenue as have other jurisdictions such as Norway with its

Petroleum Fund, Alberta has developed as a *petro-state*, where "institutions are weak and wealth and power are concentrated in the hands of a few", as the dictionary says.[4] Petro-state nations are recognized as countries where:

1. Oil exploitation generates considerable revenue that automatically flows into the pockets of government, thus reducing the need for direct taxation of the population. This leads to democratic fracture. To reverse the famous principle that inspired American revolutionaries in the years leading up to 1776, there is "no representation without taxation": any government that is funded by oil revenues can safely ignore its citizens.

2. Because exploration and exploitation in the oil and gas sector call for massive investment and technological advances, the corporations involved are extremely powerful. With enormous resources at their disposal, the pressure they exert on states to ensure their expectations are met – through processes that may often include corruption – is consequently very strong. In a petro-state, the outcome of this pressure is the virtually complete deregulation of the energy sector.

3. Exploration and exploitation companies want to have their say in the day-to-day administration of the government's energy policies. The state's petro-revenue-dependent status blurs the lines between public and private, allowing the private sector to shape decision-making and legislative processes. This in turn leads to a vicious cycle of "oilification" that reinforces the two previous trends.[5]

A petro-state is a state for corporations: for the population, it tends to disappear. The low level at which it taxes the population helps make it non-existent and unaccountable. In many cases, the facilities used by citizens and the services they receive – such as sports facilities or cultural events – are directly funded or massively sponsored by oil companies. Surrounded by corporate sponsors, the state seems to dissolve and vanish.[6]

Bruce Campbell of the Canadian Centre for Policy Alternatives notes that petro-states "are highly dependent on petroleum for 50% or more of export revenues, 25% or more of GDP, and 25% or more of government revenues."[7] Alberta revenue easily matches these figures. Energy accounted for roughly 72 percent of its total exports in in 2011,[8] 28 percent of its GDP[9] for that same year, and 26 percent of its government revenues in 2012.[10] It is also worth noting that Alberta boasts of having the lowest rate of income tax in Canada, and that the province still does not have a sales tax.[11] All of this helps dissolve the government's connection with its citizens.

Meanwhile, the industry's power over public authorities and public opinion in Alberta has never been greater. Public policy in Alberta is entirely dedicated to serving international capital, independently of any local consideration. Like the states that were created specifically to provide a framework for the oil industry in the former Ottoman Empire after the First World War, Alberta no longer represents anyone except petroleum corporations looking for the right regulatory context. Even the province's minimalist environmental regulations, developed under international pressure, are the product of discussions with industry. Citizens become aware of this minimalism when they are exposed to environmental hazards.

Demand for oil remains high throughout the world, and according to an Alberta government source – Alberta Energy – the tar sands contain the equivalent of 168 billion barrels.[12] Instead of practising greater regulation of the industry, and especially its environmental consequences, the Alberta government has become "oilified," reducing taxation of the oil and gas sector and turning a blind eye to its environmental damage. Journalist Andrew Nikiforuk has clearly demonstrated how opaque the regime is when it comes to information about gas and petroleum production.[13] Thus, as a province, Alberta has turned into a deregulated zone for the energy sector, in the manner of offshore jurisdictions where everything is permitted.

AN AD HOC ROYALTY SYSTEM

During the 1960s and 1970s, oil was abundant, pipeline management was a sensitive issue, and federal policies were designed to exercise control over oil exploitation projects. As the price of oil rose between 1971 and 1985, Alberta oil began to be exploited by a mixed private and public enterprise (through the 50-percent publicly owned Alberta Energy Company). At the time, the Alberta government had control over upstream and downstream petrochemical industry sectors (including transformation and refining of bitumen), and was in a position to develop them.[14] When Peter Lougheed took office in 1971, the price of oil was $3 a barrel; it tripled to $9 with the first oil shock in 1973 and again to $27 in the second oil shock in 1979.[15] Taxation revenues multiplied as royalties poured into government coffers for use of the resource – with individual Crown Agreements royalties running at 40 percent of revenue from oil production. Consequently, in 1976, the Alberta government created the Heritage Fund, a sovereign trust fund based on royalties, to save a share of the state's oil money (30 percent of all its annual oil revenues) for following generations.

By 1992, however, under new Progressive Conservative leader Ralph Klein and within the federal framework of the Mulroney administration,[16] pro-petroleum officials occupied key positions in the Alberta government and the Alberta legal system was used to prevent and discourage dissent, reduce taxation and royalty regimes, and weaken the environmental regulation process.[17] When the Klein administration took over the mandate to lead the province in 1992,[18] the oil sands royalties system was based on multiple ad hoc royalty agreements with each individual oil sands project.[19] According to the government of Alberta, this led to substantial discrepancies and a lack of transparency.[20] The system set up a decade earlier may have had other flaws: according to Bruce Campbell, the Lougheed government failed to achieve most of its goals in terms of royalties collection, and while the goal of 35 percent of revenues from energy extraction was reached in the late 1970s, it soon fell back to roughly 20 percent around the mid-1980s.[21] These were not the deficiencies that the Klein administration set out to correct. In 1993, the Alberta Chamber of Resources formed the steering committee for the National Task Force on Oil Sands Strategies, a select group composed mainly of the oil sands and supporting industries' finest representatives.[22] The group's mission was to "be a catalyst for the further development of Canada's oil sands resources through identification of a clear vision for growth and preparation of a plan of action."[23]

The practical implications of the new royalty regime were clearly stated ten years later by former Klein administration energy minister Murray Smith, who told a Texas audience it was a "give-it-away formula."[24]

The basic elements of Klein's new royalty regime included a minimum 1 percent fixed royalty payable on all production; a royalty on production equivalent to 25 percent of net project revenues after the developer had recovered all project costs, including research and development costs; and a return allowance (after "payout") set at the Government of Canada long-term bond rate. All project cash costs, including capital, operating, and research and development, were 100 percent deductible in the year incurred.

The royalty rate increased depending on the price of oil, and projects were subject to a lower royalty rate, calculated on *gross revenues*, until the project had reached *payout*, or recovered its capital costs. Once *payout* was reached, the project was subject to a higher royalty rate, calculated on *net revenues*, where the amount owed to the government was determined by oil revenue after operating and sustaining capital costs were deducted.[25]

When the new Oil Sands Royalty Regulation came into effect on July 1, 1997, it established royalty terms for all new oil sands projects at 25 percent (considerably reduced from the 40 percent of oil-production revenue required under Lougheed in the 1970s). Through the end of the 1990s and into the 2000s, royalty rates continued to be reduced in the province by government after government. By the time Ed Stelmach was elected premier in 2006, rents and royalties were at an all-time low of 9 percent[26] – with considerably reduced revenues to support important public investments needed in Alberta's infrastructure, educational system, and other areas of public concern.

Another interesting fact is that Alberta has failed to collect even the very modest royalties to which it claims to be entitled. As the provincial auditor general pointed out in 2007, the province's inadequate accounting methods have been associated over the years with losses in the billions of dollars. Civil servants had pointed out the problem to various ministers, but in vain.[27]

Alberta tax law also provides corporations with generous deductions, even though corporate income is taxed at the low rate of 10 percent. As PricewaterhouseCoopers explained in 2012, "For years before 2007, a royalty tax deduction could be claimed, equivalent to the excess Crown royalties disallowed for federal income tax purposes over the 25 federal resource allowance. This deduction cannot reduce Alberta income tax below zero. Unused deductions from years before 2007 can be carried forward to the subsequent seven taxation years, but expire on December 31, 2013. For eligible expenditures incurred by qualifying corporations after December 31, 2008, Alberta allows a SR&ED tax credit of 10% on up to $4 million of eligible expenditures incurred, for a maximum annual credit of $400,000."[28]

It is worth mentioning that Alberta is not the only Canadian province to show profound subservience to giant corporations in the extractive sector. While Ontario and Quebec do not have oil, they do have mineral resources, and they are extraordinarily generous to mining companies: the royalties they require are ludicrously small, they provide multiple ways of reducing these royalties to even lower rates, and they sometimes fail to collect even the amounts due.[29] As we have argued elsewhere, this systemic bias in favour of resource extraction multinationals is rooted in Canada's past as a colony created to provide such resources to its metropolitan masters.[30]

▮ THE NORWAY ALTERNATIVE

Things could have developed differently in Alberta. Ironically, Alberta's Heritage Savings Fund was the model used by the Norwegian administration early on in its petro-boom to establish a sovereign wealth fund based on 94 percent of all resource-based revenues.[31] Established in 2001, Norway's oil fund exceeded $905 billion in 2014. The Alberta fund by that time had reached only $16.7 billion, a tiny fraction of what Norway had accumulated in a shorter period of time, mainly because the Alberta government had stopped paying into its oil fund by 1986.[32]

Under the Norwegian policy based on its "Ten Oil Commandments," oil exploitation is nationalized up to 78 percent, with the Norwegian government taking control of both regulation and exploitation of oil under the government-owned Statoil company. Public authorities regulate and control upstream and downstream sectors related to petroleum.[33] Norway does not have a royalty system, but captures petroleum rent through taxes and direct ownership. Companies are subjected to an ordinary tax of 28 percent plus a special tax of 50 percent. Deductions are allowed for costs associated with exploration research and development operations, and there is a six-year depreciation allowance. A carbon tax was introduced in 1991.[34]

As an oil producer and exporter, Norway is a major contributor to the world's greenhouse gas emissions. However, one of its Ten Oil Commandments requires that petroleum development must take environmental protection into consideration. To resolve this contradiction, Norway has taken many steps to attenuate the harm caused by its oil production. "Under the Copenhagen Accord, Norway's carbon reduction targets are the most ambitious in the industrial world. It has plans to become carbon neutral by 2050, possibly earlier, and is contributing to international efforts to encourage the transition to a low carbon world." While environmentalists may legitimately argue that these efforts are insufficient and that Norway should in fact reduce its oil production, in Alberta there is nothing to argue about in the government's record.[35] Alberta, and Canada generally, has a deplorable environmental record when it comes to regulation of the oil and gas sector, particularly as it impacts First Nations and their territorial land.[36] Environmental deregulation puts at risk the health of those living in rural areas, including territories of First Nations, who are most affected.[37] A study on water pollution in the Athabasca River, reported in *Proceedings of the National Academy of Sciences*, found air pollution from the tar sands industry to be five times greater than reported, with bitumen particles and toxins from smoke stacks coating snow in a thirty-kilometre radius of the project, sufficient to create water contamination at carcinogenic levels.[38]

The bitumen from Albertan deposits is made up of 15 to 25 percent of petcoke, a much higher proportion than conventional oil deposits. From an environmental perspective, petcoke is even more of a problem than coal. According to a 2013 study, "Petcoke is like coal, but dirtier. Petcoke looks and acts like coal, but it has even higher carbon emissions than already carbon-intensive coal."[39] The authors add: "Because it is considered a refinery byproduct, petcoke emissions are not included in most assessments of the climate impact of tar sands or conventional oil production and consumption. Thus the climate impact of oil production is being consistently undercounted."[40]

The consequences of tar sand exploitation can devastate people's lives. A peer-reviewed report published in 2009 found that people in the northern community of Fort Chipewyan had higher than expected incidences of rare cancers. Many of the study participants worked in the tar sands.[41] In 2006, and again in 2011, the Plains Midstream company's pipeline, insidiously known as the Rainbow, ruptured in Cree Lubicon territory, spilling 1 million litres (the first time) and 4.5 million litres (the second time) of petroleum products under the highly polluting form of "dilbit" (diluted bitumen): "The soluble fraction consists of highly toxic light aromatic composites."[42] Because of the toxic effects of evaporation, spreading, dispersal, dissolution, sedimentation, and bio-degradation, the Cree are also afraid that these spills will lead to massive forest fires.[43] The Lower Athabasca region – covering 90,000 square kilometres in northeastern Alberta – is no longer home to the healthy ecosystems that once surrounded First Nations communities, but a territory profoundly contaminated by the oil industry.

Thus, in environmental terms, Alberta has become a counter-model to Norway, its standards the complete opposite of Norwegian standards – and even Norway is not able to neutralize the noxious effects of the oil industry, which include both the toxic pollution it inexorably generates and the intellectual inertia it encourages. This inertia is what prevents us from developing the imaginative means we will eventually be forced to adopt in order to emancipate ourselves from petro-dependency. "Hydrocarbons block the development of renewable energies, and not vice versa," notes Kim Cornelissen, a regional development consultant in Northern countries.[44]

■ ENVIRONMENTAL LAWS AND THEIR (NON) ENFORCEMENT

A law and its enforcement may be two very different things. The Canadian Environmental Protection Act (CEPA) is a matter of criminal law. Its most recent version, enacted in 1999, asserts that is intended to prevent acts of pollution, in particular through "processes to assess the risks to the environment and human health posed by substances in commerce."[45] The act "provides a wide range of tools to manage toxic substances, other pollution and wastes" and "ensures the most harmful substances are phased out or not released into the environment in any measurable quantity."[46] All these excellent intentions and considerations, written into the law, are not followed by any particular effects, however.[47] True, Canadian law criminalizes forbidden acts that lead to pollution of ecosystems, but in the judicial process, the onus is on the party plaintiff. Because of the *mens rea,* or culpable intent, level of requirement, any claimant (which usually means the government in cases of this kind) must be able to prove that the party defendant actually wanted to do harm – that there was an intentional act to damage the environment.[48] Canadian law does include penalties for parties guilty of negligence, but only in extreme cases. Thus, an agent who shows "wanton or reckless disregard for the lives or safety of other persons," thereby causing "death or bodily harm to another person," is subject "to prosecution and punishment," with all the legal requirements this entails. Offenders may be sentenced to five years in jail.[49] The law focuses on spectacular acts, completely ignoring cases where pollution is slow but steady. And it is very easy for corporations who have ranks of lawyers working for them to hold forth endlessly on the true meaning of terms such as "intention" or "reckless disregard." In 2011, the Auditor General of Canada was less than impressed by the way in which CEPA was applied throughout Canada. The following "significant shortcomings" were identified in their report: "regulations that are difficult to enforce, inadequate intelligence information to inform enforcement planning and targeting, and inadequate training to support enforcement officers."[50]

The situation is worse in Alberta. The Environmental Protection and Enhancement Act (EPEA) appears to have no more weight than a rumour. According to section 228(1), the court cannot sentence a person responsible for an offence to two years' imprisonment unless proof of *mens rea* has been established.[51] And, just like the "regulatory" public bodies in tax havens, the Alberta Energy Regulator (AER), which is supposed to enforce Albertan environmental laws, is in fact inclined to flout these laws itself. When Brion Energy – a joint venture between PetroChina and Athabasca Oil Corporation – wanted to exploit a deposit in northern Alberta and treat the bitumen on site, it anticipated a production of some 250,000 barrels a day for 65 years. The Cree, who were directly exposed to the project, presented a very moderate requirement for a 20-kilometre buffer zone around their reservations to protect biodiversity and prevent pollutants from coming too close to where they lived. Brion Energy, showing its sense of priorities, refused this demand: the buffer zone would entail the loss of 1.4 billion barrels.[52] The AER found in favour of the oil company, declaring that the natural boundary was not required. Showing an equally strong sense of priorities, the AER asserted that it would be contrary to public interest to fail to exploit the petroleum deposits found in the proposed buffer zone.[53] The Cree communities, astonished and angered by this outcome, have taken the AER to court and the case is now pending before the Alberta Court of Appeal.[54]

PEDDLING ENVIRONMENTAL INFLUENCE

Since the early 1990s, Alberta's regulatory body, the Energy Resources Conservation Board (ERCB), has approved nearly a hundred projects, worth tens of billions of dollars in investment, and has done so without a general and cumulative risk assessment for either environmental or social impacts.[55] This approach fully complies with legal standards. Thus, the ERCB has helped certify over the years that major oil projects, which have not been carefully assessed, are perfectly legal.

It is increasingly difficult to believe in the independence of Alberta's political class: signs of its complicity with industry continue to multiply. The documentary film *Fort McMoney* shows former Albertan environment minister Diana McQueen saying the province "controls" oil companies with respect to environment issues; this "control" is chiefly based on data provided by the companies themselves.[56] Andrew Nikiforuk relates that less than six months after leaving office as premier, Ralph Klein became a petro-consultant for Borden Ladner Gervais LLP (BLG), a Canada-wide law firm representing several corporations involved in the energy business in Alberta.[57] As Nikiforuk points out, Klein does nonetheless have principles: as he explained in 2008, he was willing to represent business, but only when they pay him.[58] Also notable is the ambiguous role played by Peter Elzinga, who moved from Premier Klein's entourage in 2004 to the private sector, working as a lobbyist for Suncor Energy, and then grotesquely came back to public service nine months later as general director of the Progressive Conservatives.[59] The pro-oil cast of the Klein government is also apparent in the case of Greg

Melchin, Klein's energy minister (2004–2007), who later joined the board of EnMax, an energy corporation, and former Economic Development Minister Mark Norris, who after leaving office became president of Westcrop Energy Inc.[60]

There are other indications that the marriage between the government of Alberta and the oil industry has now been fully consummated. In July 2012, after three major oil spills in Alberta in May and June,[61] Energy Minister Hughes announced that it was time to act in order to prevent subsequent spills.[62] A review of the province's pipeline infrastructure by a third party, under ERCB supervision, was set in motion. Communications acquired by Greenpeace under the Freedom of Information Act showed that Minister Hughes had convened various stakeholders to a meeting to discuss the situation, including CEOs of fourteen pipeline companies as well as the Canadian Association of Petroleum Producers and the Small Producers and Explorers Association of Canada.[63] However, not a single landowner or environmental organization was invited to the meeting, although they were the ones who had called for the review in the first place.[64] It appeared that they were not deemed "interested" enough, even if a spill might entail complete loss of their land and its value as well as severe damage to the environment. As noted by Greenpeace campaigner Keith Stewart, "it looks like industry got to write the terms for [the] review."[65] The government's partiality toward the industry and its alignment on the industry's "best practices" were apparent – despite the fact that the job of an environmental regulatory body is to inquire into violations of the laws and regulations under its responsibility. In the Albertan petro-state, there is nothing illegal about calling a completely one-sided meeting to discuss a review of pipeline operations, since environmental assessments on such issues are not compulsory.[66]

Political parties have received a substantial amount of money from the oil patch. According to documents available through the Chief Electoral Office of Alberta, the Progressive Conservative Party received almost $600,000 in donations from the oil industry for the years 2011–2012. This does not include private donations from individuals who might be aligned with the industry.[67] Oil companies in 2012 contributed roughly 10 percent of the party's $2 million budget, with Suncor Energy at the top of the list with donations of nearly $15,000.[68] According to the Polaris

Institute, Mark Rudolph, a long-time lobbyist representing Suncor Energy and Shell Canada, said that "lobbying the province of Alberta is virtually unnecessary since…the government is entirely on the industry's side."[69] Ian Urquhart, a University of Alberta professor specialized on petroleum politics, notes that the party-financing regime in Alberta is marked by leniency, setting almost no spending limits in provincial elections, and allowing corporate and personal donations up to $15,000, or $30,000 during a campaign.[70] According to numbers compiled over six years (2004–2009) by Stewart and Sayers, two University of Calgary professors, this lax system has consistently given a constant significant edge to the Progressive Conservatives, who had roughly three to four times more funding than other parties.[71] Perhaps spurred on by the popularity of an even more conservative party, the Wildrose Alliance, in 2007–2008, the Progressive Conservatives intensified their efforts to attract the favours of the industry: they enacted a set of policies to please major extracting corporations, reducing royalties for high-cost drilling enterprises and conventional exploitation.[72] In short, it is obvious that Alberta's elected officials and political parties are highly likely to be influenced by oil companies, which are in a position to support them financially thanks to the Albertan petro-state's lax political party financing law.

Alberta's politics are intrinsically oil-based. In *Fort McMoney*, filmmaker David Dufresne quotes a lobbyist who establishes complete identity between politics and his industry, arguing that the Western economy is based on oil in countless ways. The filmmaker, attempting to express this idea, comments, "Oil companies are democracy, and democracy is oil. It's as if one flows into the other, and in this game, the companies lead the world and the dance."[73] Alberta's development as a petro-state has gone so far that there is little reason to expect that the NDP government elected in May 2015 will be able to reverse it, even if the election results show a healthy desire on the part of citizens to end their government's dependence on oil and its unstable economy.[74]

CALGARY: MULTINATIONAL CORPORATIONS UNDER FEDERAL OVERSIGHT

Sections 91(2) and (12) of the Constitution Act (1867) establish that the federal government has jurisdiction over inter-provincial and international trade and the management of natural resources on federal lands and the ocean floor. The federal government also holds lands in trust for the First Nations, whose approval is required for resource exploration and exploitation projects on their lands, as recognized under section 35 of the Constitution Act of 1982 and by jurisprudence. This means that Ottawa is a key player. It is therefore significant that the federal government is slowly but surely moving toward the formalization of pro-oil politics nationwide, in a process of "Albertanization," while also contributing to the current offshorization of Alberta's legal system.

During the first decade of the Lougheed administration, in the 1970s, the federal government established Petro-Canada and the National Energy Program, proposing policies similar to that of Norway's Ten Oil Commandments in order to maintain Canadian ownership over oil resources and appropriate a greater share of oil wealth.[75] Through its publicly owned oil company and policies giving it a degree of control over the oil industry, the state was in a position to make political decisions, and potentially to reduce or halt production for environmental reasons, instead of being entirely ruled by multinationals' search for profits.

By 1985, the Mulroney Conservatives had eliminated most measures previously adopted to keep control of energy extraction in the government's hands. However, the key elements in the scuttling of previous federal regulatory activity in the oil sector were the 1989 U.S.-Canada Free Trade Agreement and Chapter 6 of the subsequent 1994 North American Free Trade Agreement (NAFTA). The provisions of Chapter 6 explicitly eliminate any possibility for governments to establish any kind of export tax, price controls, or quota on the export of oil. The agreement includes a principle of proportional sharing that forces Canada forever to maintain the same ratio of oil exports to production, whatever the real volume of production may be; this means, for example, that oil exports cannot be reduced in order to favour domestic consumption. In recent years, the Harper government has further extended free trade by signing new agreements including Foreign Investment Promotion and Protection agreements, the Trans-Pacific Partnership, the Trade and Investment Partnership, and the Comprehensive Economic and Trade Agreement, among others.

NAFTA and other free-trade agreements include investment protection chapters that can prevent takeover of private interests by the state. Seventy percent of the world's known oil reserves are controlled by state-owned companies; well over half of the remaining 30 percent, which are privately owned, are in Canada, which means that Canada's oil "is uniquely accessible to private capital." As a result, the companies that own Canadian oil are based in countries all over the world, from the United States to Malaysia and China, and include most major European state-owned oil companies. The Mulroney administration's policies are now in full flower.[76]

The Albertan petro-state has fully embraced its corporate masters, to whom it is more accountable than it is to its own citizens. If new laws are not enacted, and if nothing is done on a political level, Alberta and Canada will suffer, rather than organize, the energy transition that is inevitable throughout the world. The wealthy classes are well aware of the fact that this transition must occur, given the ongoing destruction unleashed on ecosystems. New measures of this kind would also be a way for Canada to break with its colonial past and for its citizens, at last, to begin to establish a genuinely independent political community.

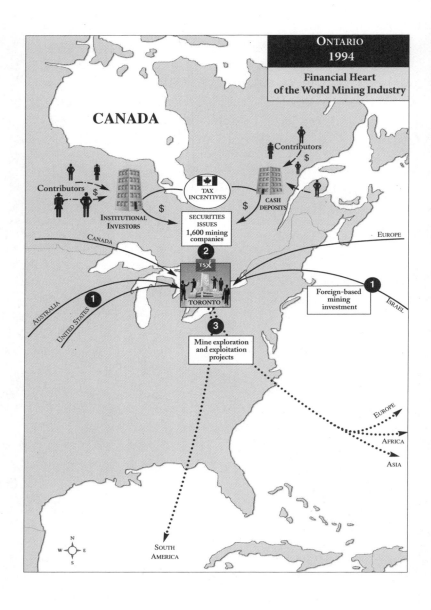

ONTARIO
1994

Financial Heart
of the World Mining Industry

CANADA

Contributors $

INSTITUTIONAL
INVESTORS

TAX
INCENTIVES

Contributors $

CASH
DEPOSITS

$ $

SECURITIES
ISSUES
1,600 mining
companies

EUROPE

CANADA

2

TSX

TORONTO

AUSTRALIA

1

UNITED STATES

Foreign-based
mining
investment

1

ISRAEL

3

Mine exploration
and exploitation
projects

EUROPE

AFRICA

ASIA

N
W   E
S

SOUTH
AMERICA

ONTARIO

FINANCIAL HEART OF THE
WORLD MINING INDUSTRY

*In which the majority of the world's extractive corporations
flock to Toronto to enjoy investment tax incentives*

René Nollevaux, Belgian manager of a copper mine in the Democratic Republic of the Congo, clearly believed he was stating the obvious when he remarked that "in the mining industry, venture capital usually comes from Canada." The comment was made to filmmaker Thierry Michel, who was shooting a documentary about Belgian neo-colonial relations in the African Great Lakes area.[1] Canada (begging the question) is the favourite jurisdiction of mining companies.[2] According to a 2012 publication of the Toronto Stock Exchange (TSX), 75 percent of the world's mining companies choose to register their activities in Canada, and 60 percent of those who issue stock market shares register in Toronto, which is far ahead of its direct rival, the London Stock Exchange. In 2011, 90 percent of the shares issued in the mining sector throughout the world were administered by the TSX, and through shares, Toronto financed the mining sector to the tune of $220 billion between 2007 and 2011.[3]

The romance of Canada's universal goodness, partly arising from Canadian peacekeeping operations, begins to unravel as soon as we are confronted with the sorry environmental, social, political, safety, and tax record of the extractive industry hosted by Canada. Throughout the world, Parliamentary commissions, courts, UN experts, independent observers, specialists in the economy of the South, and experienced journalists have testified to the injustices – and sometimes the crimes – committed or massively supported by Canadian mining companies active in countries in the South. When we say "crimes," we are not using anthropological nuance; we mean that people are reporting cases of corruption, tax fraud, institutionalized plundering, massive pollution, injury to public health, violent expropriation, murdered demonstrators, complicity in the assassination of people opposed to mining projects, strategic lawsuits against public participation (SLAPPs), criminalization of political opposition, arms trafficking, and collusion with warlords and other belligerents involved in conflicts centred on control of mining deposits. If you take a look at the abundant literature supporting allegations against the mining industry, you will have enough information to grasp this reality.[4]

With the claim that extractive industries "make a major contribution to Canadian prosperity,"[5] the federal government bends, twists, or stretches every one of the principles that it promotes in international forums. Ably assisted by the Ontario government, it has made Toronto into the nerve centre of the mining haven that Canada represents at the global level. Mining corporations defined as "Canadian" often do not have any substantial activity in Canada: many of them originate in other countries and operate mines in countries other than Canada. They are incorporated in Canada in order to benefit from the regulatory, legal, and tax advantages provided here. Hence, an abnormally high number of mining managers from Australia, Israel, Sweden, Belgium, and the United States, among others, converge on Ontario to create prospecting or mining companies. These companies work mining claims obtained in Ecuador, Chile, Zambia, Haiti, Burkina Faso, Indonesia, Romania, or elsewhere. Close to half the mining projects registered on the TSX are located outside of Canada, and many companies registered in Canada do not have a single claim on Canadian soil.

The TSX is first and foremost an institution fostering the frenzied speculation that the industry loves. On this exchange it is notoriously easy for a company to list presumed deposits and magnify their value. The great majority of the 1,600 mining companies registered in Toronto are "juniors," which means that they are exclusively involved in finding new deposits. Lacking the financial, technical, human, and political resources to run mines themselves, these small companies make their profits from stock market speculation. Their goal is to discover deposits and sell them to the majors who alone are in a position to operate mining facilities; a sale will cause a junior's share price to go up. The juniors sometimes invest more in marketing campaigns aimed at potential investors than in the actual search for mineral deposits, because in this field, speculation is more important than development.[6]

In giving juniors more leeway than they have anywhere else to cultivate ambiguity around the true potential of their mining deposits, the TSX favours the interests of mining companies. The TSX advocates disclosure of both a mine's *reserves* and its *resources*. *Reserves* are supposed to be a detailed and precise estimate of a deposit's exploitable potential, while *resources* – this is the thorny concept – are a crude estimate of everything the deposit may contain. The information on *resources,* essentially based on possibly altered excerpts from geological studies, provides investors with a glowing picture of a potential for exploitation that is higher than the real potential, based on the idea that a mineral's price may rise or extraction techniques may become more sophisticated. Disclosure of *resources* encourages stock market speculation and makes the price of mining stocks go up.

In this context, there is nothing surprising about the many frauds and scandals that have characterized the TSX throughout its history.[7] Now-forgotten stories include the 1960s Windfall affair,[8] in which the "discovery" of copper, silver, and zinc caused an uproar at the TSX but turned out to be nothing but unfounded rumour. The Bre-X swindle in the 1990s is another example. The company had sprinkled gold over its rock samples to give the impression it had acquired a high-quality deposit.[9] Toronto stood revealed as a temple of the casino economy, this according to the statements of financial advisers themselves. The reality is that no one can say what is in the ground until a mine is actually dug, and outcomes depend on such a wide range of factors that buying shares in a junior is like gambling at the casino. The actual geology of the claim, how easy it is to access, variations in world prices, technological advances, and the local political climate may all have an impact. Mining experts estimate that the odds of success are somewhere between 1 in 500 and 1 in 1,000. Mining exploration is a risky business, by essence speculative, as French taxpayers learned to their cost in 2007 when a publicly owned company, Areva, bought a Toronto-based junior, UraMin, only to find that the company's reserves were far more difficult to exploit than had been foreseen. Areva also discovered that UraMin's key deposit had been overestimated by 42 percent, and all this was taking place at a time when the price of uranium was dropping.

How much did this affair cost French taxpayers? All we can say is that having acquired UraMin for 1.8 billion euros, Areva in 2011 announced a 1.46-billion-euro writedown on the UraMin assets.[10]

According to Wilfrid Laurier University economists William J. McNally and Brian F. Smith, both the Toronto Stock Exchange and the Ontario Securities Commission (OSC) that is supposed to regulate it are negligent when it comes to illegal insider trading. Unlike practice in the United States, such trading is rarely investigated. As a matter of fact, investors themselves worry about Toronto's weak enforcement of regulations. In 2004, the governor of the Bank of Canada, David Dodge, said that his colleagues in New York, Boston, and London spoke of Toronto as a financial Wild West because of its lax regulatory framework. In 2006, a Harvard law professor, Howell Jackson, observed that in terms of effectiveness, Canadian measures did not bear comparison with the United States. The following year, even Finance Minister Jim Flaherty expressed similar reservations about the powerlessness of Canadian regulatory agencies.[11] Also in 2007, the president of the Ontario Teachers' Pension Plan, Claude Lamoureux, and Barbara Stymiest, former head of the Toronto Stock Exchange and chief operating officer of the Royal Bank of Canada, deplored the fact that securities laws are simply not enforced in Canada.[12] According to McNally and Smith, on the rare occasions when guilty parties are arrested, penalties are sometimes less than the proceeds of the crime, and "almost half of the repurchasing firms fail to report their trades to the OSC."[13] The Ontario regulator is certainly not trying to frighten anyone: it recently established a new way of punishing wrongdoers – while making sure that cases remain confidential.[14] The OSC's particular brand of compassion may derive from the fact that it has been headed by people who are particularly indulgent to the financial sector, including (from 2005 to 2010) David Wilson, an investor who was previously vice-president of Scotiabank.[15]

▣ CONNECTING TO CARIBBEAN TAX HAVENS

The shares of a company registered on the TSX may be bought and sold in Ontario while being held by people with accounts in the Bahamas, the Cayman Islands, Barbados, or the Turks and Caicos Islands. The TSX and the Ontario and Canadian governments work to convince companies in the extractive sector to incorporate or establish subsidiaries in Canada or register in Canadian stock exchanges, but they do nothing to induce these companies to accumulate their profits either in the country where they sell their shares or in the countries where they carry out their prospecting or run their mines. Companies in the extractive sector appreciate Ontario laws because they allow them to easily raise capital through stock market speculation; this way of raising money has nothing to do with the actual profits they record. As a consequence, they may pay almost no taxes in Canada.[16]

Canadian mining companies often use subsidiaries in Caribbean tax havens to negotiate the acquisition of mining claims. The tax havens' secrecy laws make it impossible to find out how widespread this practice is, but a few documents provide a kind of sampling. When the terrible war in the African Great Lakes region officially came to an end in 2003, Democratic Republic of Congo MP Christophe Lutundula was appointed by the Congolese Parliament to investigate the value of the mining contracts signed during the conflict. Lutundula found that many contracts involving mining deposits, which had been the basis for a war that killed millions of people, had been signed by belligerent parties with mining company subsidiaries incorporated in tax havens. According to the commission chaired by Lutundula and several independent organizations, Kinross registered its business partnership in the British Virgin Islands,[17] the Lundin Group's subsidiaries were located in Bermuda,[18] and Emaxon, a Montreal company belonging to Israeli diamond magnate Dan Gertler, was run from Panama.[19] Agreements between the Congolese state and Canadian mining companies such as Anvil Mining (whose tax rate was 0 percent) were so advantageous to the mining company in terms of taxes that DR Congo itself was now, in fact, a tax haven. The term *contrat léonin* was used to describe these agreements: one-sided contracts in which the most powerful party took the lion's share. Resources were sold to offshore entities during a war in which the fighters were trying to get money and arms. Other examples of mining contracts with offshore companies occasionally come to light, such as the first industrial contract negotiated by the president of Mali, Moussa Traoré: the agreement was signed with a Canadian exploration company, AGEM, whose Barbados subsidiary was officially responsible for closing the deal.[20]

This phenomenon sometimes leads to obscene situations. Congo-lese decision makers, for example, signed an agreement with a company called Vin Mart Canada: nobody knows to whom this company belongs nor even where, finally, it is incorporated.[21]

Under this system, it is very easy for companies to corrupt their partners in the South. Raymond W. Baker, a Harvard-trained consultant and businessman active in Africa, estimated at the time of the conflict in the Great Lakes area that spending related to political corruption deprived poor countries of $500 billion a year.[22] Baker also found that the World Bank and the International Monetary Fund (IMF) were doing nothing to block corruption or money laundering, even though it was obviously the money they were providing to Southern countries that was being diverted to tax havens. When corruption is associated with the corrupted party, the corrupter is easily forgotten. So far, noth-ing has been done to punish the Western actors with whom the bribes originate. "For the World Bank and also the IMF, discussion of illicit cross-border transfers is addressed almost exclusively to developing and transitional countries and occasionally offshore financial centers but virtually never to Western banks and corporations."[23] James Henry of the Tax Justice Network also notes the flow of money from poor countries to tax havens:

> We estimate that the amount of funds held offshore by individ-uals is about $11.5 trillion – with a resulting annual loss of tax revenue on the income from these assets of about $250 billion. This is five times what the World Bank estimated in 2002 was needed to address the UN Millennium Development Goal of halving world poverty by 2015. This much money could also pay to transform the world's energy infrastructure to tackle climate change. The World Bank has reported the cross-border flow of the global proceeds from criminal activities, corruption, and tax evasion at $1–$1.6 trillion per year, half from developing and transitional economies.[24]

Over the past ten years, a very large number of serious documents have been published deploring the harm caused by tax havens in the South. In 2009, Oxfam International estimated that developing countries faced a shortfall of $124 billion because of offshore activities. "This money could pay for health and education services, for protection against the deepening impact of the economic crisis such as safety nets to help those who have lost jobs and for projects to protect poor people already affected by climate change. $16bn a year would be sufficient to give every child a school place and $50bn a year is needed to help poor countries protect their people from climate change."[25]

CANADIAN LAXISM

In 2011, the OECD blamed Canada for reneging on its commitment to fight corruption. Canada has done nothing within its own territory to punish any company for political corruption in other countries, even though it attracts the majority of the world's mining companies, which, as the OECD points out, are notorious for participating in influence peddling abroad.[26] An anonymous representative from "one of Canada's most well-known and respected companies globally" told the OECD that Canadian companies abroad face "pressures ... to engage in corrupt practices."[27] As a true legal and regulatory haven, Canada protects mining companies incorporated under its laws from the consequences of their wrongdoing abroad.

UN experts have asked Canadian political authorities to investigate the role of Canadian companies in DR Congo, after having duly cited these companies on a list of businesses considered to be in violation of OECD's "Guidelines for Multinational Enterprises."[28] As the UN observers state without any equivocation, "The OECD Guidelines offer a mechanism for bringing violations of them by business enterprises to the attention of home Governments, that is, Governments of the countries where the enterprises are registered. Governments with jurisdiction over these enterprises are complicit themselves when they do not take remedial measures."[29] The only response by Stephen Harper's Conservative government has been to issue a directive in 2009 entitled *Building the Canadian Advantage,* providing the mining industry with a Corporate Social Responsibility counsellor who is explicitly deprived of any real power: "The Counsellor will not review the activities of a Canadian company on his or her own initiative, make binding recommendations or policy or legislative recommendations, create new performance standards, or formally mediate between parties."[30]

Rules on financial disclosure in Canada explicitly force companies to make public any information about ethical crises, political instability, and environmental risks that they provoke in the South – but only if these phenomena might have an effect on the price of their shares on the stock market.[31]

Oxford Pro Bono Publico is surprised at how difficult it is for citizens to launch civil lawsuits against Canadian corporations in cases of alleged abuse occurring outside Canadian borders.[32] Claims are often rejected because of the *forum non conveniens* rule. The situation is different in the United States, where the Alien Tort Claims Act authorizes lawsuits for serious cases. We hope that the rules of the game may be changed by a precedent set in 2013, when an Ontario Superior Court judge ruled that Hudbay, a Canadian company, could be sued in Canada for crimes allegedly committed in Guatemala. Since then, Guatemalans have filed three related lawsuits against the company in Ontario, and lawsuits have also been filed in Vancouver against two other Canadian mining companies, Nevsun Resources and Tahoe Resources, over events in Eritrea and Guatemala, respectively.[33]

◼ COLONIZING THE SOUTH THROUGH MINING POLICIES

Over the past twenty or thirty years, the great ore-consuming areas of the world – China, Europe, and North America – have joined in a race to control metals, including base metals such as aluminum, copper, zinc, and iron; rarer metals such as lithium, tantalum, and molybdenum; and precious metals such as gold, silver, and platinum. While OECD countries' high consumption patterns were stable, China's consumption of refined metals increased seventeen-fold between 1990 and 2011.[34] In other words, the current mining boom is driven by Chinese growth. These metals are used in products we use every day, from electronic gadgets to cars, and to produce energy (such as nuclear energy) and weapons.

Southern states are subjected by the World Bank, the IMF, and the World Trade Organization (WTO) to a competitive logic that forces them to open their borders. The juniors have taken advantage of these open-border policies to establish the "free mining" system, which provides them with guaranteed unlimited access to underground resources. The free mining principle is largely based on a colonial model rooted in Canadian history. Once a profitable deposit has been discovered by a junior and ceded, for a high price, to a major, the major generally sets a large-scale mining project in motion.

An exponentially growing demand combined with the deteriorating quality of deposits leads to a system that produces hundreds of millions of tonnes of waste every year and uses massive quantities of toxic processing agents (such as the cyanide used to extract gold). The use of open-pit mining techniques, involving craters several kilometres in diameter and hundreds of metres deep, is one of the stigmata most representative of the system's predilection for intervention on a gigantic scale. In terms of the environment and public health, devastated lunar landscapes and accumulated waste have consequences that will be felt for dozens or, more likely, hundreds of years to come. The damage we can anticipate, and the accounts we receive from areas close to the mining sites, are alarming: ecosystems destroyed; species eliminated; soil, air, and water massively polluted; as well as increased incidence of cancers, respiratory ailments, and spontaneous miscarriages.

In relation to this long list of serious issues, Canada presents itself to the international mining sector as a regulatory haven enabling multinationals to act with impunity in Southern countries. Canada's diplomats and co-operation agencies spare no effort in pressuring these countries' governments to carry out the acts of dispossession required by industrial mining activity: expropriating, violently if need be, people living on mining claims often acquired by corporations through dubious means; developing tailor-made mining codes; and providing corporations with facilities and infrastructure such as access to energy, water, and transportation networks.

The Canadian International Development Agency (CIDA), today merged with the Department of Foreign Affairs, Trade, and Development, funded the reform of Peru and Colombia's mining codes, as well as a major dam in Mali that provides energy for mines in the western part of the country. Between 2011 and 2013, CIDA also undertook to fund projects identified as "development" that went no further than providing compensation for communities abused by large-scale mining projects. As an example of such abuse, in the 1990s, Canada's High Commissioner in Tanzania pressed Tanzanian officials to expropriate people living on land that had been ceded to the Sutton corporation. The result was the massive eviction of the population of Bulyanhulu, a process during which dozens of artisanal miners are alleged to have been buried alive.[35] Documents disclosed in 2013 by American whistleblower Edward Snowden also indicate that Canada has spied on the Brazilian Ministry of Mines and Energy,[36] confirming once again the tight connections between the Canadian government and the mining industry.

CASHING IN ON THE STOCK MARKET

In 1994, the mining lobby and the Canadian government undertook to attract even more capital to the Toronto Stock Exchange, sending every possible signal to seduce investors. The stock market is "an important source of capital for the mineral industry in general, but is the *only* source of capital for the 'junior' sector."[37] Pension funds, insurance companies, and banks to which Canadians entrust their assets, as well as Canadian individuals (wealthy and less wealthy), were encouraged to invest massively in shares issued by mining companies in Toronto. Investors of all kinds were drawn into creating the mining industry's nest egg in Toronto, regardless of where this industry was acting in the world. The industry learned that it was easy to get venture capital in Toronto. In 2011, some 185 corporations active in Africa, 286 in Latin America, 315 in Europe, and 1,275 in the United States went through Toronto specifically to raise money for their often controversial projects.[38] The Canadian government actively supports investments in the mining sector, particularly by drawing on its employees' pension funds or the budgets of its public development agencies.

The mining lobby is clearly the driving force in the game. In 1994, the Canadian government was so profoundly subjugated that it allowed the industry to speak on its behalf in its own communications. This was the year the mining industry redefined the concept of government regulation in terms that were endorsed by political authorities. In a spirit of "good governance," the mining lobby's leading voices in Canada, the Mining Association of Canada, and the Prospectors and Developers Association of Canada, organized a series of discussions with various social partners as part of what they called the White-horse Initiative. This kind of "discussion," legitimized by government participation, is a specious form of political deliberation, providing a basis for political decisions that are supposed to reflect a so-called partnership between highly unequal partners.[39] In this context, the state is seen as just one partner among many. The mining industry's goal was an obligatory "consensus": it wanted the principles, measures, and guidelines it was promoting to be endorsed by everyone in sight, including representatives of "federal, provincial and territorial governments; business, including the banking community; Aboriginal groups; environmentalists; and labour."[40]

The Canadian government made itself one with the process, adopting the mining companies' rhetoric to the point where it completely lost any semblance of autonomy. The industry became the speaker making statements on the government's behalf, with the federal Department of Natural Resources explaining that "the mining industry concluded that it needed support, assistance and advice within a non-adversarial framework to help it develop a new strategic vision and to create solutions for the 21st century."[41] Industry, in other words, is the source of all action and decisions, as is explicitly stated by political authorities themselves. Political discourse bows down before the unrelenting logic of the globalized market: the "challenges" faced by industry are "outside Canada's control." The department also states, "We cannot escape the reality of the nature of global competition" – leaving it unclear to whom "we" might refer. "Numerous mineral-rich countries have liberalized their economic and political systems to attract investment,"[42] adds the department (or the mining lobby that causes it to speak). Domestically, these exchanges led to an agreement between the Canadian government and Aboriginal peoples on mining issues. Overall, as a British and Uruguayan research group observed, "these deliberations seem to have moved little beyond the industry's opening gambit,"[43] which was to "see its opportunities expanded, instead of reduced," in Canadian territory (as John Carrington, vice-president of Noranda Minerals, candidly observed).[44]

A year later, in 1995, a representative of Natural Resources Canada, speaking to a House of Commons Standing Committee, went one better by expressing himself exactly as if he were a mining industry lobbyist. Keith Brewer placidly remarked: "Canada has lost some ground in attracting mining investment as a result of an increasing burden of mining taxation."[45] And yet, government had fully adopted industry demands, "improving the investment climate for investors" and "streamlining and harmonizing regulatory and tax regimes."[46] During the same Standing Committee session, a participant had drawn attention to two exorbitant tax deduction programs, the "Canadian exploration expense" (CEE), in which mine exploration and some development costs may be written off at 100 percent, and the "Canadian development expense" (CDE), in which mine development and some operating costs are deducted at 30 percent.[47] But the government was not going to listen to anyone but the mining industry.

Another federal government program involves what are known as *flow-through shares*. This is a tax program specifically encouraging investors to put money in mining shares or, to put it another way, a program that indirectly subsidizes stock market speculation on the securities of junior companies. Flow-through shares are a way for mining companies to provide shareholders with tax deductions for expenses that the companies themselves cannot claim because they have already deducted over 100 percent of their income[48] (this testifies, of course, to the incredible generosity of Canadian tax laws for mining companies). The goal is to induce investors both big and small to support mining securities. There is no way this program can be justified according to the arguments used when it was introduced in 1954 as a way of stimulating investment in mining. Today, the program allows mining, gas, and oil companies to issue shares that are entirely tax-deductible in Canada. In our country, investing in a mining company is tax-free, just as a charity donation is tax-free.

In 2000, the federal government, judging that investment in the mining sector was slowing down, increased the rewards provided by the program through what are now known as *super-flow-through shares*. This involved an additional tax deduction of 15 percent for investors holding shares in a mining exploration company incorporated in Canada. Most Canadian provinces then also gave investors an additional tax credit.[49] This improved Canadian program did not even require that the exploration and mining projects be carried out in Canada. For those investors who earn a living by playing the market, this is a rare and beautiful opportunity for tax avoidance. Thanks to double flow-through share programs, spending on mining exploration went from $300 million in the late 1990s to $1.72 billion in 2006, and the discovery of new deposits rose from 15 in 1999 to 268 in 2005.[50] While these tax incentives may not always lead to actual mining projects, there is absolutely no doubt that they are keenly enjoyed by speculators. This way of organizing capital leads to severe social and environmental damage of the kind inflicted by Barrick Gold in Papua New Guinea – damage that led both the government of Norway and Quebec's credit union federation, the Mouvement Desjardins, to withdraw their investments from this company.[51]

In any case, Canadian companies dedicated to exploiting mining wealth outside the country are fiscal shape-shifters. All they have to do to avoid taxes in Canada is to incorporate themselves as income trusts. Theoretically, beneficiaries of the trust will be landed with the tax bill – but as long as these beneficiaries open accounts and incorporate entities in tax havens, no tax is paid by anyone. This is a quirk of the Canadian model adopted in 2011: income trusts are taxed like any other entity, except when they do not have any assets in Canada.[52]

The rhetoric of the Canadian government can no longer be distinguished from that of the Caribbean tax havens Canadians did so much to develop. The closeness between the two makes perfect sense: Canada, as a jurisdiction providing mining companies with legal protection and open financial channels to the tax havens of the Caribbean and elsewhere, has more similarities than dissimilarities today with offshore states. The international offshore order makes it possible, for example, for national or foreign arms merchants to establish a mining corporation in Canada. Through a subsidiary in a tax haven, this corporation will then be able to sign a "lion's share" contract with a Southern state, manage its tax evasion strategies, and handle the cost of political corruption and arms deals. It can transport commodities or minerals on ships using flags of convenience, and eventually process raw materials in free zones. It will also be in a position, using offshore accounting practices beyond the reach of any law, to trade in dangerous or strategic materials such as uranium.[53] Populations injured or wronged in other countries will find very few channels open to them in Canada to oppose what the corporation is doing in their country. In Toronto, the corporation's stock may well be rising throughout this process.

CANADA

TAX HAVEN

In which the federal government decides to imitate
tax havens by reducing corporate taxes

Sylvain Fleury, Parliamentary researcher for the International Affairs, Trade, and Finance Division, points out the contradictions of Canadian politicians in their so-called fight against "abusive tax avoidance." In 2010, he wrote: "The Canadian federal government intends to take part in international efforts to combat tax havens, but it is not planning to amend its statutory tools to combat abusive tax avoidance. Some experts think, however, that the government could be better equipped in this regard."[1] Ottawa views corporate tax avoidance as a problem, but it also defends corporations' tactics as a way of ensuring their "competitiveness."[2] In some federal government documents, Canada itself is presented as if it were a free zone, and Ottawa has even modified its law on trusts in a servile imitation of tax-haven statutes.

On the issue of competitiveness, Fleury finds himself obliged to reverse the proposition, reminding the government that it is precisely an effective tax regime that enables a country to finance its political authorities and public services and "remain economically competitive on the international scene."[3] This is not exactly what Ottawa has in mind: the government is committed to "shutting down...tax avoidance structures" only when they are "inappropriate."[4] In other words, the government believes that some types of tax avoidance are "appropriate" – those being the ones it helps make possible because it wants companies to remain competitive! The minister of finance asserts that "the modern economy does require that Canadian businesses be internationally competitive. To sustain competitiveness, Canada must have a tax system that, in its overall impact, is generally in step with the systems of major competing jurisdictions."[5] We are reminded of the tale of Frankenstein, the eccentric scientist. This is no longer Canada making British territories in the Caribbean into tax havens; now Canada's creatures are forcing it to weaken its own jurisdiction. Instead of fighting tax havens, Canada is bringing its own regime into compliance with the pattern established by its formidable rivals. Canada's own revenue agency declared in 2008 that aggressive tax planning is one of five "key priority risk areas" threatening "to erode Canada's revenue base,"[6] but does this matter?

Canada chooses powerlessness every time it has to take a position on the issue of tax havens. The government's rhetoric, fatally, consists of setting in opposition the principle of fighting tax avoidance and the principle of helping Canadian enterprises "compete" – and the government makes sure, in the end, that the second principle wins. Even when all the G20 countries together decided "to reduce their tax losses, in particular by more vigorously discouraging the use of tax havens, or by tightening their legislation so they can better fight abusive tax avoidance at home, or both,"[7] Canada remained on the sidelines. The most Parliament was able to do was to give the Standing Committee on Finance a mandate to study tax fraud and the use made of tax havens. At the committee's hearings, the erosion of Canada's tax base through offshore transfers was documented by many participants. The outcome of the sessions, however, was an insignificant report,[8] with which opposition MPs refused to be associated.[9] The committee did not recommend any steps to assess the revenue shortfall caused by tax evasion. The Parliamentary budget officer himself admits that "Canada is an international outlier on this matter: fourteen OECD countries, including the United States and the United Kingdom, estimate their tax gaps."[10] But the only data we have indicate that the assets of Canadians registered in tax havens amount to something like $170 billion, according to Statistics Canada figures published in 2013.[11]

The committee also remained silent on the necessity of establishing, at the international level, a mechanism for the automatic transfer of information between countries to replace ineffective Tax Information Exchange Agreements.[12] Nor was there any recommendation to fight transfer pricing, despite the considerable body of evidence now available at the international level about this widespread practice,[13] that the United States, the United Kingdom, Europe, and China have all made a commitment to oppose. The committee did recommend that the government launch a propaganda initiative to conceal its inaction: "That the federal government continue to maintain taxpayer morale by ensuring clear messaging of ongoing efforts directed to ensuring fairness and transparency in Canada's tax system."[14]

On the subject of fighting tax evasion, the Canadian government continues to manifest its contradictions. In its 2013 budget, it announced with great fanfare that it would provide the Canada Revenue Agency (CRA) with resources to tackle tax fraud;[15] at the same time, it cut 3,000 jobs within the CRA and closed its voluntary disclosure centre in Montreal, which was supposed to receive the confessions of repentant tax cheats![16] On the other hand, Canada is full of zeal when the time comes to ensure that Canadian businesses are "competitive" in terms of taxes. A 2014 report from the KPMG auditing firm states that among the ten jurisdictions studied, our country has the lowest corporate tax rate;[17] with a Total Tax Index[18] of 53.6 percent, Canada is ahead of the United Kingdom, Mexico, and the United States. In addition, the study establishes that among fifty-one major cities with more than two million inhabitants, the top three in terms of tax leniency are Toronto, Vancouver, and Montreal. Another study published in 2014, this one by PricewaterhouseCoopers, provides similar findings: among 189 economies, Canada is ninth in the world for "ease of paying taxes"[19] for medium-size businesses (see Table 1).

In 2013, conditions were felt to be so advantageous in Canada that Chinese investors planned to open a world trade centre in Laval, Quebec, so that something like a thousand Chinese companies could sell their products as retailers in North America without having to go through local intermediaries. Roger Pomerleau and Martin Cauchon, former federal MPs from, respectively, the Bloc Québécois and the Liberal Party, and former Canadian prime minister Jean Chrétien on behalf of the Heenan Blaikie law firm, were said to be actively involved in the project.[20]

The corporate tax rate is in fact so low in Canada that when fast-food giant Burger King entered into a friendly takeover agreement with major Canadian fast-food company Tim Hortons on August 25, 2014, the American corporation chose to merge with Tim Hortons in order to relocate its head office north of the 49th parallel. This operation was designed for no other purpose than to reduce the corporation's tax bill. The corporate tax rate in Canada is around 25 percent: this includes a 15 percent federal tax, to which is added a provincial tax that is usually around 10 percent. If Burger King had left more than an empty shell in Miami, it and its main investor, 3G Capital of Brazil, would have faced an American corporate tax rate closer to 40 percent.[21] Then in November, Quebecers learned that Valeant, a pharmaceutical company that had been American before it acquired Bausch & Lomb in 2012, was subject to a real tax rate of 3 percent in Canada while it would theoretically have paid 36 percent in the United States.[22] Valeant first relocated to Ontario, then moved to Quebec, where the Quebec government welcomed it with an $8-million subsidy.[23] The corporation, whose total profits in 2013 were expected to be nearly $3.4 billion,[24] obviously knows exactly what to do to reduce almost to zero its debt to the society that welcomed it. "Valeant's strategy involves the use of offshore subsidiaries in places

TABLE 1.

Ease of paying taxes in the G7 countries (2015)

Country	Overall ranking	Total tax payments	Time to comply (number of hours)	Total tax rate (%)
Canada	9	8	131	21
France	95	8	137	66.6
Germany	68	9	218	48.8
Italy	141	15	269	65.4
Japan	122	14	330	51.3
United Kingdom	16	8	110	33.7
United States	47	11	175	43.8

SOURCE: PricewaterhouseCoopers with the World Bank, "Canada Tops All G7 Nations in Ease of Paying Corporate Taxes," press release, March 11, 2015.

such as Barbados, Bermuda and Ireland."[25] Canada is becoming a tax haven because its economy is integrated with jurisdictions in this category. In an unusual connecting moment, Canada's two solitudes spoke with one voice, each discussing its own corporate tax boondoggle. Thus the *Toronto Star* headline of August 26, referring to Burger King's administrative arrival in Canada, proclaimed that "Merger Talks Show Canada Turning into a 'Tax Haven,'" while in Quebec the *Journal de Montréal* headline, referring to Valeant, was "Le Québec: Paradis fiscal."

As a matter of fact, Canada is competing directly with the most well-known tax havens. In PricewaterhouseCoopers's overall ranking, Canada occupies ninth place globally (see Table 2) and finds itself ahead of notorious tax havens such as Switzerland (eighteenth), Luxembourg

TABLE 2.

Overall tax ranking: The first eight countries according to PricewaterhouseCoopers (2014)

Country	Overall ranking	Total tax payments	Time to comply (number of hours)	Total tax rate (%)
United Arab Emirates	1	4	12	14.8
Qatar	2	4	41	11.3
Saudi Arabia	3	3	64	14.5
Hong Kong	4	3	78	22.8
Singapore	5	5	82	18.4
Ireland	6	9	80	25.9
Macedonia	7	7	119	7.4
Bahrain	8	13	60	13.5

SOURCE: PricewaterhouseCoopers with the World Bank, 2014. Extract from *Paying Taxes 2015*. Available on <http://www.pwc.com/payingtaxes>. © 2014 PwC. All rights reserved.

(twentieth), the Republic of Malta (twenty-sixth), Malaysia (thirty-second), or the Seychelles (forty-third). As for the United States, the same study locates them in forty-seventh place.[26] And in terms of taxing profits, Canada's total tax rate is 3.9 percent compared to a world average of 16.3 percent.[27]

In short, there is absolutely no need to try and make the Canadian jurisdiction competitive: it already is. Canada's liberalities to business are noteworthy, to the point where some foreign planners view our country as a full-fledged member of the network of tax havens. Specialized websites name Canada as an offshore jurisdiction. In France, for example, we find surprising statements such as this: "Canada may be viewed as a new offshore jurisdiction, with some Canadian provinces offering a status resembling offshore status through an almost null tax rate (only 5%) for activities carried on outside Canada."[28] Nor should we forget this charming comment: "Canada is not an offshore country, but we know how to make a company created in Canada into an offshore company."[29]

▪ CANADA: JUST AS DELIGHTFUL AS A TAX HAVEN

To attract investors, the Canadian strategy is to provide enticing descriptions of tax benefits equivalent to those on offer in tax havens, while boasting of Canada's unrivalled access to all offshore jurisdictions.

Overall, Canadian tax measures favour the fluidity of capital flows and the accumulation of capital by wealthy individuals and large corporations,[30] whose real tax rate is particularly low in Canada. This point is confirmed by a study of ninety-nine of the largest Canadian companies that posted profits from 2009 to 2011, carried out by a research group at a Montreal university. On average, these corporations' real tax rate is 19.5 percent.[31] Canadian tax policies enable them to minimize this rate (see Table 3); in some cases, they can bring it down to zero or even get money back from the government. Despite all these incentives, government officials continue to warn us that companies may leave Canada and that it is impossible to tax big business at a higher rate.

Let's not be misled: of all the G8 countries, Canada is the one with the lowest corporate tax rate. At the federal level, this rate dropped from 37.8 percent in 1981 to 16.5 percent in 2011. Tax expert Brigitte Alepin notes that from 1961 to 2009, "the tax burden on individuals (that is, the share they contribute to the government's total revenue) went from 33% to 42%," while the tax burden on corporations dropped from 14 percent to 11 percent over the past few years.[32] In addition, in 2006, the federal government eliminated the tax on capital that business hated so much. This tax was set at approximately

TABLE 3.

Partial list of the largest profitable Canadian corporations, ranked by effective tax rate for fiscal years 2009 to 2011

Company	Before-tax profit (in millions of dollars)	Effective tax rate (%)
Cott Corporation	$193.20	-14.5
Emera Inc.	$639.20	-7.0
Canadian Pacific Railway	$2,199.00	-4.7
Molson Coors Brewing Company	$2,420.70	-1.9
Canadian Oil Sands Limited	$2,762.00	0.0
TransCanada Corporation	$5,914.00	1.7
Québecor Inc.	$1,822.20	3.8
Rogers Communications Inc.	$6,192.00	5.1
Enbridge Inc.	$4,764.00	5.3
SNC-Lavalin Inc.	$1,567.70	6.2

SOURCE: Adapted from a table in Frédéric Rogenmoser, Martine Lauzon, and Léo-Paul Lauzon, *Le réel taux d'imposition de grandes entreprises canadiennes : du mythe à la réalité. Analyse socio-économique de 2009 à 2011 des plus grandes entreprises* (report for the Laboratoire d'études socio-économiques, Université du Québec à Montréal, October 2012), 8–10 [our translation].

0.125 percent for capital in excess of $50 million, whether it belonged to an individual or a corporation.[33] Banks actively campaigned against this tax, which prevented them from fragmenting debts they had taken on for a plethora of financial products and hazardous stock market securities[34] – that is, derivatives. Abolishing the tax allowed Canadian banks to be active on the international markets for these products,[35] which made a very significant contribution to the 2008 financial crisis.

To justify the reduced taxation of corporations, it is claimed that eliminating corporate tax will enable corporations to reinject capital into the economy, thus creating jobs. This theory, however, remains highly debatable. According to Statistics Canada, corporations' cash reserves reached $630 billion in 2014.[36] Sociologist and economist Éric Pineault notes that in 2009, one-third of corporations' bank deposits were held as foreign exchange: "There is no longer any significant relation between the cash assets at the disposal of Canadian companies and their investments in the real economy of goods and services."[37] Economist Jim Stanford comes to the same conclusion: federal corporate income tax was reduced from 22.1 percent in 2007 to 15 percent in 2012, supposedly to lighten the burdens of capital, and yet the investments made by those benefiting from these tax reductions also declined.[38] A double standard is at work: the government never thinks of associating its tax reductions with any kind of obligation to invest, unlike its treatment of unemployed people, for example, whose benefits are always associated with an obligation to look for work.

A REDUCED CAPITAL GAINS TAX

Since 1998, the taxable portion of capital gains – gains including all profits made on investments (in the stock market, in real estate rentals, and so on) – has dropped twice: from 75 percent to 66 percent in 1998, then from 66 percent to 50 percent in 2000. While this may seem like an appropriate way of handling investments that will eventually support a retired person, Léo-Paul Lauzon, director of the Université du Québec à Montréal (UQAM)'s Laboratory of Socio-Economic Studies, emphasizes that the chief beneficiaries are a small group of very wealthy individuals.[39] Only those who derive their income from investments rather than a salary actually benefit from capital gains. "In 2007, those who declared taxable income greater than $250,000 and who also declared taxable capital gains accounted for only four-tenths of 1 percent (109,040) of Canada's 24,600,590 taxpayers, but they also accounted for 50 percent ($12.3 billion) of all declared taxable capital gains."[40] When wealthy individuals have this kind of income, their tax bill is reduced by half: for those in the highest federal tax bracket at 29 percent for income from wages, tax on their investment income will be 14.5 percent – which is less than the lowest federal tax bracket for wage earners!

Investors in the mining sector also have the privilege of tax-deductible status for a number of their stock exchange investments thanks to the flow-through shares program. This program, combined with other measures, explains why so many international mining companies are registered in Canada. By providing a tax shelter for mining companies from all over the world, and allowing them to benefit from it even if they have absolutely no activity in Canada, our governments have made the country into the world's most attractive tax and regulatory haven for the world extractive industry.

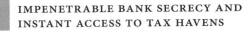

IMPENETRABLE BANK SECRECY AND INSTANT ACCESS TO TAX HAVENS

Surprising as it may seem, Canada allows financial institutions to conceal the identity of the owners of private corporations. In other words, we too have bank secrecy. Canadian tax lawyers, along with their American counterparts, are the ones that inquire the least about the identity of clients establishing companies on their home turf. This makes it very easy to create shell companies that can play a part in corruption or money laundering. Lawyer Marc-André Séguin goes straight to the point – forget about tax havens: "Canada and the U.S. are the two most lax jurisdictions in the world when it comes to the rules for preventing the incorporation of anonymous shell companies. What's more, corporate service providers operating in those two countries are less compliant than those operating in Ghana, Lithuania, or Barbados, and follow laxer rules than those in Malaysia or the Cayman Islands."[41] This conclusion is based on a study by Jason Sharman, professor of political science at Griffith University in Australia, whose team, impersonating consultants, approached 3,700 corporate service providers operating in 182 countries.[42] The service providers did not seem exactly terrified at the idea of penalties; they did not even comply with the standards of the Financial Action Task Force, of which Canada is a member.

In a similar vein, a 2013 investigation conducted by the CBC and Radio-Canada focused on the lack of ethics displayed by Canadian lawyers and financial advisers where tax evasion is concerned. When an investigator pretended that he wanted to carry out an illegal million-dollar transfer to Barbados and approached fifteen Canadian financial professionals for help with this plan, only four refused to give him advice. The news story shows lawyer Gilles Gosselin, a former employee of the CRA and now a financial adviser, urging the investigator to open an account in Barbados without informing Canadian tax authorities. Others advised him to use frontmen or told him that Barbados could be a launching pad toward other tax havens.[43]

Unsurprisingly in this context, Canadian lawyers recently joined forces against the government in a lawsuit before the Supreme Court designed to ensure that professional secrecy – needed for them to conduct their little affairs – remains intact. The federal government, as part of its Proceeds of Crime (Money Laundering) and Terrorist Financing Act, intends to force lawyers and notaries to identify and monitor their clients' financial operations. The professionals involved are against this,[44] whereas in countries like France, measures of this kind have been in effect for years.[45]

CUSTOMS DUTIES WORTHY OF A FREE ZONE

Canada's Department of Transport produced a document in 2009 with an eloquent title: *Canada's Tax and Duty Advantages: Enjoy the Benefits of Foreign Trade Zones ... Anywhere in Canada!*[46] Fearlessly adopting the offshore vocabulary, the government's program, known as Canada's Gateways, was designed to attract export companies to Canada by eliminating GST and customs duties. As the brochure says:

> Canada also offers three of the most export-friendly programs in the world. They are:

- the Duty Deferral Program;
- the Export Distribution Centre Program; and
- the Exporters of Processing Services Program. In combination
  with provincial and municipal incentives, Canada can offer the
  benefits found in foreign trade zones around the world – but
  with a key difference … Canada's duty and tax relief can be
  used anywhere in Canada.[47]

For example, a food-processing company, as long as it produces strictly for export, can get a refund for the customs duties it pays to import raw materials such as sugar and cocoa, and for the GST it pays on other raw materials purchased in Canada. The clauses that must be respected to ensure eligibility are custom-made for multinational corporations, especially those whose market is the United States. These tax advantages, similar to those provided by the most permissive free zones, are setting new standards for the Canadian economy. And yet, there are costs involved in having a company operate in Canada, and corporations benefit both from Canada's public infrastructure and its social programs. We have yet to see the figures demonstrating that it is advantageous to have foreign companies come to Canada in exchange for this level of generosity.

Canadian free zones win high praise abroad: "This destination is highly attractive in cases of trade with the United States and in the areas of processing, life sciences, advanced technology, the agri-food industry, plastics, hydro-electricity, mines, agriculture, or aerospace," according to a firm specializing in relocation of assets.[48]

In the same spirit, Montreal has positioned itself in recent years as a tax haven for the video game industry. American and other foreign companies whose assets are worth billions are given significant real estate advantages and tax benefits in Quebec's metropolis.[49]

TAX DEFERRALS FOR CORPORATIONS

In Canada, companies can also postpone tax payments. Given the astronomical sums involved every year, it is clear that government losses from these tax deferrals are considerable. According to Brigitte Alepin, corporations in Canada are allowed to defer tax payments for so long that payment becomes unimaginable. She carried out a quick survey revealing that in 2002, sixteen Canadian companies owed a total of $18 billion in deferred taxes.[50] Another study published by Léo-Paul Lauzon in 2008 estimated that between 1992 and 2005, "Canada's twenty largest tax deferrals increased by $29.4 billion, or 199%, going from $14.8 billion in 1992 to $44.2 billion in 2005."[51] The study noted that "these deferred taxes do not bear interest, do not represent a legal debt and have no fixed due date."[52] Given an interest rate of 8 percent in 1995, one tax dollar received ten years later, in 1995, was worth only forty-six cents.[53]

▨ INCOME TRUSTS MODELLED ON THOSE IN TAX HAVENS

In theory, a trust is used to protect a family's estate from being taxed until an heir takes possession of it. Trusts as such cannot be taxed; normally, only their beneficiaries are to be taxed when they receive payments from the trust. The problem today is that beneficiaries can open accounts in tax havens. And over time, companies have been given the right to establish trusts, like individuals, in order to reduce their tax rate to zero. When the dot-com investment bubble burst in the early 2000s,[54] a staggering number of corporations morphed into income trusts in Canada. In 2004, there were over 150 such trusts listed on the Toronto Stock Exchange for a total value of $91 billion. That same year, of a total of $4.6 billion raised by initial public offerings (IPOs) of newly registered shares, $3.8 billion was invested in trusts.[55] This change in legal form had little effect on companies' daily operations, but allowed a uniquely profitable level of tax avoidance.

Canada's minister of finance, Jim Flaherty, caused no little surprise in 2006 when he changed the rules for taxing income trusts. According to the new rules, from 2011, income trusts were to be taxed at the same rate as corporations – a rate which Flaherty reduced at the same time.[56] Today, the federal tax rate for corporations varies between 11 percent and 15 percent.[57] However, Flaherty made sure that a certain category of investor would still benefit from the tax advantages previously conferred by income trusts. You can still avoid taxes by creating an income trust as long as the trust does not own any assets in Canada. (This is the kind of loophole that gives Canada the reputation of a true tax haven.) The editor of the *Oil and Gas Investment Bulletin*,

Keith Schaefer, writes with cheerful confidence that despite the law enacted in 2006, "the market has found a loophole that may allow for many new trusts – especially in the energy sector: don't use Canadian assets … Last year, Eagle Energy Trust (EGL.UN) went public on the TSX, which was the first Canadian-listed oil and gas trust to launch since Flaherty's Halloween surprise in 2006. The company holds only foreign oil-producing assets … a loophole that excludes it from the new Canadian tax regime."[58] To no one's surprise, the areas where Canada continues to distinguish itself are energy and mining. An extractive company with no extraction projects in Canada (this is quite common), but that establishes its head office in Canada in the form of an income trust, will escape the corporate tax rate; only payments to shareholders will be taxed. According to Schaefer, "One other difference between the old and new trusts is that the previous had to limit the amount of non-Canadian shareholders to 50%. But this new class of trusts has no such restrictions."[59]

As the tax haven of choice for the extractive sector, Canada welcomes any corporation that wants to establish a trust from which it will manage its operations throughout the world. As long as it has no substantive activity in Canada, this corporation will be able to reduce its tax rate to zero and distribute, in the form of payments abroad – through conventional tax havens, for example – profits whose origin no one is in a position to trace. In addition, if a tax agreement exists between Canada and the territory to which these payments migrate, they will not be taxed when they eventually come back to Canada.

 LOWER TAX RATES FOR TAXABLE PROPERTIES OWNED BY NON-RESIDENTS

Until 2010–2011, a non-resident who proceeded, for example, to sell shares vested in a Canadian company (that is, *taxable Canadian properties*, or TCPS) was required to pay taxes amounting to 25 percent of the sale price. In his 2010 budget, Finance Minister Flaherty changed section 116 of Canada's Income Tax Act. As a result of this change, if an investor officially resides in a territory that has signed a tax agreement with Canada (this category includes tax havens), then all sums resulting from the sale of TCPS may legally escape taxation in Canada or at least be minimally taxed, within the limits established in tax agreements.[60] According to Brigitte Alepin, "The federal 2010–2011 budget…makes it easy for Canadian taxpayers to legally avoid Canadian income tax on the sale of Canadian shares by having them held by an intermediary residing in a tax haven."[61] The offshore detour thus enables Canadians to act as foreigners in their own country, benefiting from Canadian offshore-type liberalities normally reserved for non-residents! A Canadian resident, whether setting up a Swiss company operating with bearer shares[62] or simply opening an individual numbered account, may now buy TCPs anonymously from abroad and avoid all taxes when he or she sells them. This system also provides investors with the assurance that they will enjoy the guaranteed bank secrecy to be found in the usual tax havens.

■ ABILITY TO ACT FROM THE USUAL TAX HAVENS

We know that Canadian investors who register profits in an offshore account or corporation located in a country that has signed a Tax Information Exchange Agreement can move their assets to Canada without paying taxes. The financial channels between Canada and offshore centres are well lubricated, especially those used for foreign direct investment.

The share of Canadian direct investments[63] in tax havens and offshore centres (OFCs) has constantly increased over the past decades. "Between 1990 and 2003, Canadian assets in OFCs increased eight-fold … [accounting] for more than one-fifth of all Canadian direct investment abroad in 2003, double the proportion 13 years earlier… Among OFCs, the largest growth in Canadian direct investment during this time occurred in Barbados, Ireland, Bermuda, the Cayman Islands and the Bahamas,"[64] according to François Lavoie of Statistics Canada. Lavoie's study shows that during this period, Canadian assets in these countries increased from $11 to $88 billion;[65] other sources say they rose to $146 billion by 2008.[66] In 2003, the International Monetary Fund noted that "Canadian businesses held assets in 25 of these [offshore] jurisdictions."[67] Ten years later, Statistics Canada estimated these assets at $170 billion.[68]

In a 2010 study on harmful tax competition and abusive tax planning, Jean-Pierre Vidal, a tax expert from Hautes études commerciales

(HEC) Montréal, the Université de Montréal business school, classified jurisdictions in four groups: (A) relatively prosperous jurisdictions without significant tax incentives, (B) jurisdictions with significant tax incentives and an extended network of tax treaties, (C) jurisdictions with a generally low tax burden, and (D) jurisdictions with significant tax incentives and a limited network of tax treaties. Using Statistics Canada figures, Vidal estimated the proportion of Canadian direct investment going to each of the four groups (see Table 4).

This table shows that between 1987 and 2006, the share of Canadian direct investments going to Group A countries fell, while the share going to Groups B, C, and D increased. Countries and territories that we know are tax havens – Barbados, the Cayman Islands, Bermuda, the Bahamas, Vanuatu, Guernsey, Bahrain, Luxembourg, Switzerland, Andorra, Monaco, the Isle of Man, and so on – all belong to Groups B, C, or D. We may deduce that the Canadian position over the past decades has been favourable to direct investments in tax havens. To illustrate the scale of the amounts involved, Vidal notes that "each percentage point ... was the equivalent, in 2006,

TABLE 4.

Proportion of Canadian direct investment abroad in four markets

Year	Group A (jurisdictions that are relatively prosperous and do not have very significant tax incentives)	Group B (jurisdictions with significant tax incentives and an extended network of tax treaties)	Group C (jurisdictions with a generally low tax burden)	Group D (jurisdictions with significant tax incentives and a limited network of tax treaties)
1987	83.4%	6.8%	5.1%	0.0%
2000	70.0%	14.1%	8.4%	0.0%
2006	70.9%	16.5%	not available	0.1%

SOURCE: Jean-Pierre Vidal, "La concurrence fiscale favorise-t-elle les planifications fiscales internationales agressives?," in Jean-Luc Rossignol (ed.), *La gouvernance juridique et fiscale des organisations* (Paris: Éditions Tec et Doc – Lavoisier, 2010), 190 [our translation].

of some CAD$5 billion (or about 0.35 of a percentage point of the Canadian GDP). In 2006, Bermuda's share in Canadian direct investments abroad (3.1 percentage points) was thus the equivalent of about CAD$15.5 billion (over 1% of the GDP). In addition, the growth in this 1.0 percentage point share from 1987 to 2006 was even less negligible because Canadian direct investments abroad, during this period, generally increased sevenfold."[69]

A 2010 article by Walid Hejazi, associate professor of business economics at the Rotman School of Management, confirms that Canadian investment moving to offshore centres has continued to increase in the years from 2000 to 2008: "Three out of the top 10 destinations for Canadian FDI [foreign direct investment] abroad are OFCs (Barbados, Bermuda and the Cayman Islands). Together they received $86 billion in Canadian FDI in 2008, which constitutes 14 percent of total Canadian FDI abroad. This amount was up sharply from the 2000 total of $33 billion, which at the time constituted only 9 percent of total Canadian FDI abroad."[70]

THE CANADIAN FINANCIAL SECTOR IN TAX HAVENS

The share of Canadian assets abroad held in the strictly financial sector has increased significantly between 1990 and 2003, rising from 29 percent to 42 percent. In the financial services category, which includes insurance and investment services, the banking sector is the one that monopolizes the most capital. We also know that "two-thirds of bank direct investment assets" are held in offshore financial centres.[71] It is hardly surprising, then, that banks are enthusiastic about the possibility of opening subsidiaries and firms in tax havens. This fact was confirmed by a 2008 study by Léo-Paul Lauzon and Marc Hasbani, showing that the five largest Canadian banks with subsidiaries in tax havens were able to avoid $16 billion in taxes between 1993 and 2007.[72] This figure is based on the banks' audited financial statements, which include, among other things, a list of their offshore subsidiaries. "The five largest banks have at least 89 official subsidiaries in tax havens…and this is not to mention their associated companies, satellites, trusts, limited and general partnerships, etc."[73] From 2004 to 2007, these offshore subsidiaries enabled the five largest Canadian banks to triple the tax-exempt portion of their income, which rose from \$926 to \$2,432 million – that is, from 20 percent to 61 percent.[74] The authors do not hesitate to describe this way of getting around tax laws as fraud, even if "some will argue that this is not tax fraud from a strictly legal point of view."[75]

The Washington-based International Consortium of Investigative Journalists, which includes Radio-Canada and CBC journalists, discovered that Canadian banks were regularly named in the 2.5 million secret tax-haven files it acquired in 2013. The usual players – the Royal Bank, Scotiabank, and Canadian Imperial Bank of Commerce – are cited respectively 2,000, 1,839, and 1,347 times, and the CBC, using a cautious approach, came up with a count of 75 offshore subsidiaries for big Canadian banks. "Offshore havens rely for their existence on the financial infrastructure of the big wealthy countries," concludes the CBC, and "in Canada, our banks play a role." Along with other Western banks, they participate by "setting up accounts for offshore companies, or providing essential assistance to do so."[76]

TAX TREATIES AND TAX INFORMATION EXCHANGE AGREEMENTS

Tax treaties and Tax Information Exchange Agreements (TIEAs) are designed to standardize tax regimes for companies active both in Canada and in the signatory country. But when Canada signs such an agreement with a tax haven, its effect is to favour offshore transactions.[77]

We saw how Barbados made a travesty of the role of tax treaties intended to prevent money from being taxed twice as soon as it was transferred from one jurisdiction to another. Originally, in 1980, the United Nations promoted these tax treaties on double taxation to make sure that revenue earned in Southern countries was taxed in those countries rather than elsewhere. The treaties were supposed to act as incentives, allowing companies to pay taxes in the country where the activity took place without preventing them from bringing the money back to their head office. This seemed like a perfectly reasonable approach, but it backfired. Many companies relocated their operations – to Barbados, for example – to benefit from a zero or close to zero tax rate; they could then bring the money back to their country of origin without paying taxes there.

As for TIEAs, they are the product of an OECD initiative designed to counteract the bank secrecy prevailing in tax havens. Canada has also made a travesty of these agreements. Once the OECD had developed a model for them in 2002 to breach the legal secrecy surrounding tax haven bank records in specific cases,[78] Canada added a provision of its own. According to section 5907(11) of Canada's Income Tax Regulations, Canadian corporations that register their activities in tax havens that have signed a TIEA with Canada may bring money back to Canada tax-free in the form of dividends.[79] An advisory panel set up by the federal government emphasized the importance of this new loophole, even recommending that the clause exempting business income from taxes be applied to all countries, with or without a TIEA. These measures tend, of course, to reward foreign direct investment: "For the past 20 years, the portion of stock of Canada's direct investment abroad in treaty countries has ranged between 87 percent and 94 percent... Of the total amount of exempt and taxable surplus dividends paid by foreign affiliates of Canadian companies between 2000 and 2005, about 92 percent were exempt."[80] While the advisory panel shows perfunctory concern for the problem of unfair tax rates, it predicts that Canada will continue to sign tax treaties and TIEAs of this kind.[81] It is perhaps relevant that in 2008, the advisory panel included an ex-chairman of the board of the Royal Bank of Canada and ex-CEO of the SNC-Lavalin Group, a retired Scotiabank executive who was a director of Barrick Gold and Rogers, an international tax expert from PricewaterhouseCoopers, and a retired Shell Canada executive.[82] The panel produced a report whose title, *Enhancing Canada's International Tax Advantage*, would be perfectly appropriate for a tax haven.

Through these treaties and agreements, Canada is part of the same political space as tax havens. Tax havens, actively encouraged by the government, are fully a part of the Canadian economy. While claiming to fight tax fraud, Ottawa legalizes its every aspect. At the same time, its honour is untarnished in that it actively looks for TIEAs to sign and can therefore boast of being part of the international initiative instigated by the OECD. Fighting tax fraud by making it legal: this is truly Orwellian.

So far, ninety tax treaties signed by Canada with foreign countries have taken effect,[83] and since 2008, thirty TIEAs have been signed with tax havens.[84]

In a perfectly self-contradictory move, the minister of finance in 2013 launched a campaign to fight tax offences. While keeping a full range of bolt holes available (such as Barbados and TIEA signatories), he has made marginal gestures such as making it illegal for a company to reduce its tax bill by setting the accumulated losses of a company it has acquired against its own profits.[85] This kind of measure provides the government with a mask to hide its true political intention, which is to support corporations rather than taxpayers.

Tax expert Brian Arnold is categorical: TIEAs are of no benefit to Canada; they favour tax avoidance. "It is naive to think that tax havens that enter into TIEAs with Canada have any interest in providing information to the Canada Revenue Agency in any meaningful way. In fact, many of the countries with which Canada might enter into a TIEA probably do not have the resources to exchange information effectively."[86]

A TOOTHLESS POLICY: THE GENERAL ANTI-AVOIDANCE RULE AND VOLUNTARY DECLARATIONS

The General Anti-Avoidance Rule (GAAR) of the Income Tax Act is seen as the cornerstone of Canada's legislative efforts against tax avoidance. This rule is supposed to limit abusive tax avoidance on Canadian soil. However, as Sylvain Fleury points out, the GAAR has a number of flaws. According to him, it is difficult for tax authorities to enforce the rule because they are not allowed to use it until they have first proved that: "(1) the avoidance transaction under investigation gives rise to a tax benefit; (2) the avoidance transaction really is an avoidance transaction, that is, it is not undertaken for a bona fide purpose; and (3) the avoidance transaction is abusive."[87]

In other words, tax authorities must be able to prove the intention to commit fraud before a court instead of simply penalizing those whose manoeuvres lead to a certain effect, such as an unjustified tax benefit. This standard is even harder to meet in that "[the GAAR] does not give a specific definition of abuse."[88] In addition, even if the court rules that there is, in fact, "abusive" tax avoidance under the GAAR, those responsible for the fraud are not liable to a penalty: "the only amount claimed is the difference between the tax payable according to the self-assessment and the revised assessment and interest."[89] It is also worth mentioning that in Canada, taxpayers' tax returns are audited on a random basis. The likelihood of being investigated is therefore quite small. All in all, this means that a tax evader carrying out abusive tax avoidance is running very little risk.[90]

The government of Canada also allows authors of tax fraud who are seized with remorse, or perhaps unable to launder in Canada the money they have amassed in tax havens, to produce *voluntary declarations*. Tax expert André Lareau views this program as "a permanent amnesty mechanism established by tax authorities over forty years ago."[91] It enables parties to negotiate the conditions of their acquittal and makes sure nobody will be laying criminal charges – a clear indication that there are two legal cultures in our country, one for the rich, one for the poor.

In 2013, the federal Department of Finance acknowledged the pointlessness of its legal provisions against tax avoidance.[92]

THE FIGHT AGAINST TAX HAVENS: SMOKE AND MIRRORS

In the aftermath of the 2008 financial crisis, the issue of countries' taxation policies returned to the forefront of political discussion. In Toronto, the G20 countries signed a declaration in June 2010 in which they gave themselves until 2013 to reduce their deficit by half. To avoid being restricted to cutting public spending, they asserted their intention of forming a common front with the alleged goal of fighting tax havens. Canada joined in with extreme reluctance, a response that it also displayed at the 2013 G8 summit in Great Britain. According to information obtained by Dennis Howlett of Canadians for Tax Fairness,[93] Prime Minister Stephen Harper resisted for a long time before signing the final declaration of the Lough Erne summit. This declaration was supposed to tackle "the scourge of tax evasion," stating that "tax authorities across the world should automatically share information."[94] Well-placed sources also tell us that Canada is blamed by the French Ministry of Finance for hindering any kind of co-operation between states to deal with the problem.

Thus, Canada solemnly proclaims its principled opposition to tax havens while fostering their growth, and while deploring the fact that it no longer has enough money to fund the institutions of our common good as it once did. User fees for services and taxes levied on the middle classes continue to go up, while foreign investors are given advantages worthy of tax havens, and Canadian companies are given ever more loopholes enabling them to register their assets in highly accommodating jurisdictions with the full support of the Canadian government. It is hardly surprising, then, that private corporations continue to post record profits for every quarter. As for citizens, who understand perfectly well that governments are facilitating tax flight and who see potential government revenues vanishing in the name of an obscure ability to "compete," they are legitimately demoralized.

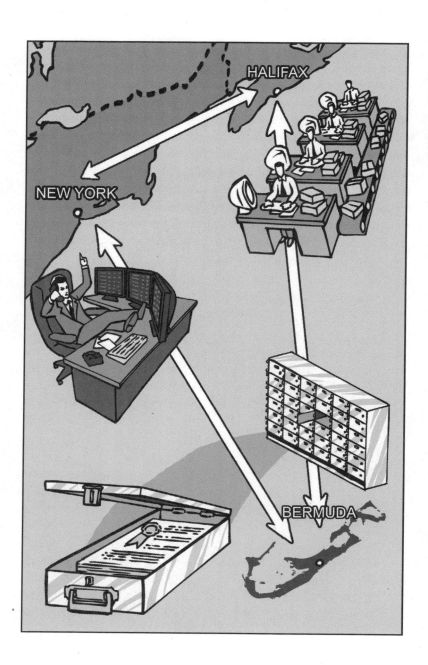

HALIFAX

BERMUDA'S BACK OFFICE

In which the Nova Scotia government helps
offshore firms hire professional accountants

In 2006, the winds began to change. No longer was it simply a matter of Canadian corporations opening offices in Bermuda to carry out their operations in utter freedom. Now, companies from Bermuda were opening offices in Canada to manage their murky operations – also in freedom. In November of this pivotal year, Nova Scotia's business development agency, Nova Scotia Business Inc., created a "financial services and insurance sector" in order to attract Bermudian companies' accounting jobs to Halifax. The reason given for this move was that real estate is expensive in Bermuda,[1] and that the provincial government was going to provide tax incentives to hire professional accountants. A company opening in Halifax could now count on bargain-rate, qualified middle-class employees who would carry out operations according to Bermudian law without having to be housed in Bermuda.

Nova Scotia Business Inc. (NSBI) is a public organization of a very particular kind. It is described as "private-sector led,"[2] and the government of Nova Scotia has always asked corporate executives to head it. After Douglas G. Hall[3] (who had previously been managing director of RBC Dominion Securities from 2003 to 2010) and Jim Eisenhauer (who chaired the NSBI board from 2010 to 2012), Janice Stairs,[4] legal counsel to the information technology and mineral resources sectors, took charge of the organization in the fall of 2012.[5]

Established in 2001, NSBI works to attract to Nova Scotia companies active in the finance, technology, aerospace, and weapons sectors (the latter is discreetly identified as the "defence, security, and aerospace" sector).[6] To carry out this mission, the organization provides candidates with specific advantages and sometimes puts its own money into projects through NSBI Venture Capital.[7]

Nova Scotia offers corporations "payroll rebates" amounting to 5 percent to 10 percent of "eligible gross payroll."[8] "This means that for every dollar a company spends in salaries and benefits, NSBI rebates back between five and ten cents."[9] Nova Scotia also gives tax credits for research and development equivalent to 15 percent of expenditures, to which are added deductions of a similar nature from the federal government for 20 percent to 35 percent of expenditures; these subsidies add up to "one of the most rewarding R&D tax credit programs in the world."[10] Deductions, which may reach 50 percent of expenditures, cover many types of expenses incurred in Canada and abroad, such as salaries.[11] Rebates are paid by the Nova Scotia government in cold, hard cash.[12]

Providing icing on the cake, the government boasts of providing businesses with qualified accounting experts and fostering synergy between the private sector and universities.[13] The Castle Hall Alternatives hedge fund is a perfect illustration: in 2010, the company chose to incorporate in Nova Scotia to benefit from tax holidays worth approximately $1.5 million in exchange for a commitment to hire fifty employees for six years. The company's owner, Chris Addy, congratulated himself on having gained access to "an experienced and stable pool of accounting and investment talent to support our ongoing growth."[14] But however much companies may benefit from Nova Scotia public spending, they are released from any obligation to contribute to it.

▮ HALIFAX: BACK OFFICE TO OFFSHORE HEDGE FUNDS

There were premonitory signs in December 2005 when a Bermuda firm, West End Capital Management, expanded the Halifax operations it had established in 1998.[15] Among the specialties of this financial management firm are derivatives,[16] the ultra-speculative products sold to investors gambling on changes in the value of shares or resources over time. The company's chief financial officer was Quebecer Patrick Boisvert, an accountant trained in Trois-Rivières with many years' experience in Luxembourg and Switzerland.[17] West End is chiefly known for the fact that one of its investors is Warren Buffett,[18] the billionaire who noted with surprise a few years ago that he was paying less tax than his secretary.[19] Nova Scotia's economic development minister, Ernest Fage, assured West End that it would find Halifax just as cozy as offshore. "By strategically locating its growth in nearby Nova Scotia and taking advantage of the highly educated provincial workforce, West End Capital will be able to increase its overall operations,"[20] declared Fage after congratulating himself on the expansion of centuries-old ties between the Maritimes and the Caribbean. NSBI promised more than $583,000 over three years through "payroll rebates" to support the creation of fifty jobs within the company.[21] In other words, West End was to get Halifax employees to manage $1 billion while still enjoying the full benefits of Bermuda's lack of regulation.[22] "Job creation," as we know, will justify anything.

In November 2006, three other hedge funds with headquarters in Bermuda – Citco Group, Butterfield Fund Services, and Olympia Capital – also opened offices in Halifax.[23] The global director of Citco Group made no bones about the fact that he was in charge of the process that led him to Halifax: "In the competitive world of site selection, we were looking for a location that would enable us to continue to expand our business meaningfully."[24] Citco, in a position to hire qualified staff at little expense – that is, at the expense of Nova Scotia taxpayers – was soon back for more, opening a Halifax office and training centre in 2007. In September 2009, it established a corporate residency MBA at Dalhousie University: the university, funded by citizens' money, was now at Citco's disposal to train future employees. The company opened its first North American real estate investment funds practice in January 2011 and increased its staff again in April 2011.

Butterfield Fund Services has a similar story. The company is happy to have access to "the many universities and colleges in the [Halifax] area" that "provide a large pool of qualified young candidates from which we can recruit."[25] Specializing in cross-management of offshore funds in a variety of tax havens, "Butterfield Fund Services (Bermuda) Ltd. provides a range of accounting, corporate, trustee, and shareholder services to offshore hedge funds, mutual funds, and pension funds. The company provides third party fund administration services in Bermuda, the Cayman Islands, and Guernsey, as well as in Hong Kong; and registrar and transfer agency services, as well as multi-currency net asset valuation and production of fund accounts services."[26] Nobody in Halifax inquired about the fact that these forms of management provide large-scale swindlers with a guarantee of impunity, with Butterfield's offshore services available to keep investigators, prosecutors, and other agents of the rule of law at a convenient distance. Nor did anyone seem troubled by memories of the murky schemes set up by Canadian investment funds such as Norshield or Portus Alternative, both accused of fraud in the mid-2000s.[27] On the contrary, the government of Nova Scotia congratulated itself on the arrival of the Fund Services Division of the mysterious Bank of N.T. Butterfield & Son Limited of Bermuda, which claims to administer assets "of over $65 billion serviced out of offices in Bermuda, the Cayman Islands, Guernsey and The Bahamas."[28] Halifax, the financial centre of eastern Canada, has light-heartedly chosen to become part of this shadowy business network. The managing director of Butterfield Fund Services in the Cayman Islands, John Lewis, confirmed that he "would be happy to hear from accountants in Cayman, Bermuda or elsewhere in Canada looking to move to the Maritimes,"[29] which would seem to indicate that the famous job creation that the province is subsidizing within this industry actually consists, at least in part, of bringing in employees from outside the province.

The third Bermuda hedge fund that came to Halifax in the fall of 2006, Olympia Capital, was founded by Oskar Lewnowski. Lewnowski was honorary consul of Austria in Bermuda, but he had no hesitation in stepping beyond his diplomatic functions.[30] His company was set to collect $1.5 million from the Nova Scotia government in "payroll rebates," as well as $300,000 offered by the province's Office of Economic Development as a "recruitment and training incentive package."[31] Olympia Capital is a controversial firm: in 2011, an investment banker accused it of having acted in the 1990s to help a Japanese camera manufacturer, Olympus Group, conceal losses in the area of $1 billion.[32] "Olympus invested hundreds of millions of dollars with Olympia. Generally investments were made in the closing days of Olympus' fiscal year, and usually earned Olympus a 33% dividend. But rather than reporting that return, Olympus would book its investment at cost and use the profit to offset older investment losses."[33] While the responsibility of Olympia Capital was not established in this affair, the evidence indicates the kind of operation that hedge funds are in a position to carry out in tax and legal havens. None of this prevented Nova Scotia's economic development minister, Richard Hurlburt, from implying that support for financial misappropriation is a price that must be paid to provide job opportunities for accounting students in eastern Canada.[34]

Another Bermuda hedge fund, Meridian Fund Services, arrived in Halifax two months later, in January 2007, to open an "operational support office."[35] The firm, which describes itself as a provider of strategic financial services, offers "a full range of services to hedge funds established in offshore jurisdictions."[36] It has offices in New York, where a significant proportion of its customers are to be found, and in the Cayman Islands,[37] a jurisdiction that attracts over 80 percent of the world's offshore funds. "In addition to supporting the valuation, accounting and investor relations needs of our other offices, our Halifax office is our major data processing centre."[38]

As it develops into a hedge-fund service location, Halifax is becoming a suburb of world finance where companies can use public money to bring low-level employees together in one location. According to the *Financial Post*, "a source working in the investment-management business in Halifax said not everyone is happy with the government subsidizing competition in the backyard. He added that tax dollars are being used to lure 'accounting labour rather than any real intellectual brain power'."[39] However, NSBI was still using the same rhetoric in January 2009 when it announced the arrival of another company from Bermuda, BF&M Insurance Limited. This firm, unhampered by restrictive laws as it manages a wide range of contracts from life insurance to risk management and property insurance, established "a strategic nearshore back office operation in Nova Scotia."[40] Another hedge fund from the Cayman Islands, Admiral Administration, made a similar move: as explained on its website in 2013, the company handles American business from Virginia and European affairs from Dublin, while its Halifax subsidiary is responsible for "back office administration services for the Cayman and U.S. offices."[41]

The instability of the tax haven economies makes these jobs particularly fragile, however. The ninety-odd employees of Flagstone Management Services, a Bermudian company established in Halifax in 2005 that had taken $1.68 million in "payroll rebates and recruitment incentives" from the Nova Scotia government, learned in November 2013 that their jobs would be abolished by Christmas, as soon as the ink was dry on the deed selling the company to Validus Holdings.[42] Some NSBI moves have also caused skepticism among Nova Scotians, such as a $2.8-million investment in a company selling Internet voting software; job creation considerations were obviously minimal in this case, since the company had only eight employees.[43]

NEARSHORING: TAKE TO THE WAVES, BUT DON'T GO TOO FAR

Taking up the rhetoric of his new guests, in 2006 the chief executive of Nova Scotia Business Inc., Stephen Lund, happily presented Halifax as "the next Dublin" – Dublin, of course, being a notorious tax haven.[44] Representatives of Nova Scotia's private sector show a recurring fondness for the tax haven vocabulary. In 2012, they openly congratulated themselves when a hedge fund analyst, eVestment (HFN), described Nova Scotia as "a new haven for fund administrators."[45] There was similar rejoicing when hedge-fund news service *Opalesque* described Halifax as "the next world financial centre"[46] and KPMG said that Nova Scotia was "the fastest-growing hedge fund administration centre in Canada."[47] The *Globe and Mail*'s Peter Moreira joined in the chorus: "Halifax is quietly establishing itself as a financial centre, capitalizing on the tight and expensive labour market in Bermuda to attract administrative operations from the tax haven's financial institutions."[48] Employment agency Hamilton Recruitment, which calls itself "the first choice for offshore professionals," is equally enthusiastic: "In recent years, a number of hedge funds and insurance companies have sought to move to Nova Scotia to take advantage of the high calibre of employees available, the excellent infrastructure and lower costs than in many other jurisdictions."[49]

Nearshore is the word that has gradually entered the vocabulary used in these circles as a rival to the word *offshore*. *Nearshore* suggests that, thanks to Canada, you can now find within close range a number of accounting services that were formerly available only in distant tax havens. *Close range* means *close to home* from the point of view of American firms. In communicating with this American target group, Nova Scotia authorities do not hesitate to present their jurisdiction as an outright tax haven.[50] They state, for example, in the case of a Nova Scotia unlimited liability company (NSULC), that "a U.S. taxpayer may be able to use losses from its Canadian business as a deduction against its income for U.S. income tax purposes."[51] There is no attempt to deny that advantages are associated with controversial transfer-pricing techniques: "A U.S. taxpayer could use the NSULC to limit transfer-pricing issues to Canada."[52] The province boasts of its ultra-permissive laws: "NSULCs do not have residency requirements for directors of Nova Scotia companies."[53] Raj Kothari, a PricewaterhouseCoopers senior executive in Toronto, says that Nova Scotia representatives "are trumpeting the concept of nearshoring." The Nova Scotia government hopes that American companies seeking to evade the restrictions imposed by the rule of law will choose Halifax over Third World countries because of cultural affinity. According to Kothari, among back-office havens, "Halifax is being boosted by two factors, a common language in English and understanding of the business model, which makes it more accessible to the U.S. marketplace than, for instance, operations in India."[54]

This pathetic descent into the logic of the lowest bidder is a sign that Caribbean tax havens, with their complete indifference to the common good and shared obeisance to financial power, are now colonizing eastern Canada. Evidence is provided by the Nova Scotia chapter of the Certified Management Accountants of Canada (CMA Canada), which now explicitly includes the Caribbean,[55] as if the two jurisdictions were one. The two CMA associations, with a membership of 50,000 accountants, have the same slogan: "Certified Management Accountants do more than just measure value – they create it." In the Caribbean, the CMA has joined forces with the University of the West Indies to train students in offshore accounting;[56] once trained, they can go into exile in Halifax to work on the accounts of firms enjoying the solicitude of tax havens. In the spring of 2013, for example, the CMA Caribbean website announced that an energy brokerage firm, Emera, was looking for a "Senior Manager, International Tax," to work in its Halifax office to "manage a challenging tax structure unparalleled in the Atlantic Provinces" and to "share acquisitions and a multitude of cross border and multi-jurisdictional issues." If not hired in Halifax, the newly trained professionals work in Caribbean tax havens that provide benefits for Canadian citizens and register their assets there in order to hide them from Canadian tax authorities, as is suggestively indicated in a CMA Caribbean brochure for 2012: "We See Opportunities at Every Stage of Your Career."[57]

■ BERMUDA: WHO BENEFITS? WHO PAYS THE PRICE?

Bermuda has long been a familiar feature of everyday life in the Maritimes. A dominant family in New Brunswick, the Irvings, has been making extensive use of Bermudian resources for many decades. Companies controlled by the Irvings were among the first in Canada to be overtly managed from a tax haven, and journalist Diane Francis presents the Irving family patriarch, Kenneth Colin Irving, as a "tax dodge pioneer." She observes that in 1972, he "moved to tax-free Bermuda and placed ownership of his empire into a series of Bermudian trusts that have never paid taxes to Canada."[58] Irving family interests include oil, shipbuilding, forest products, and media enterprises.

In Bermuda, the local establishment is grateful. According to the *Bermuda-online* website, "The famous Canadian dynasty, the Irving family, has a major offshore corporate base here in Bermuda. A $6 billion empire, it controls huge business concerns in New Brunswick. The 125-year-old dynasty has a number of J. D. Irving Limited Bermuda-registered entities, and the Island became the final home for company patriarch Kenneth Colin Irving before he passed away in 1992." The website gleefully notes in passing that Bermuda is a "main country of choice" among "tax haven countries for Canadians."[59]

Bermuda is in no sense a democratic country, and neither are the countries doing business with it. We may therefore legitimately ask whom the Halifax accountants are being asked to serve.

In 2006, the year in which Halifax and Canada became infatuated with Bermuda, Brigitte Unger of the Utrecht School of Economics, Greg Rawlings of the Centre for Tax System Integrity, and five other authors submitted to the Netherlands' Ministry of Finance a report describing Bermuda as the second-most-important jurisdiction in the world for laundering the proceeds of illicit or criminal activities.[60] Two years later, as enthusiasm in Halifax for Bermudian investors reached a peak, Unger and Rawlings published an article, "Competing for Criminal Money," in which they explained that tax havens such as Bermuda provide criminals with premium services. "Countries which were some of the first to compete for capital regardless of its origins had efficiency gains and are now some of the world's richest: Cayman Islands, Switzerland, Bermuda, Liechtenstein and Luxembourg."[61] Other sources indicate that the only thing forbidden in this jurisdiction may be riding a bicycle.[62]

Bermuda's well-established reputation for financial fraud was powerfully confirmed by the catastrophic failure of Enron, the giant energy brokerage firm whose collapse was largely caused by manipulations that accountant-cum-contortionist Andrew Fastow carried out first in the Cayman Islands, then in Bermuda and the Bahamas as discussed in earlier chapters. Bermuda's opaque regime supports a variety of tactics known as "off-balance sheet" that involve isolating, within a financial year, operations entailing a certain degree of latent risk and that may turn out to be hazardous.[63]

Bermuda also extends its hospitality to insurance companies, which may easily be created in Switzerland using a firm with ties to Bermuda in order to "maintain the anonymity and confidentiality of the insurance company's owner."[64] Offshore companies operating in this area also provide reinsurance: this means that insurance companies recognized in conventional states are insured in tax havens (Bermuda and the Turks and Caicos Islands are two prime locations). This system allows insurance companies to ignore the rules of conventional states regarding the cash reserves they must hold in order to be allowed to sell insurance.[65]

Financial crime seems to be a legitimate form of management in Bermuda, just as stupidity may be recast as wisdom. Scotiabank CEO Cedric Ritchie was strongly criticized in 1982 for joining the board of Mineral and Resources Corporation (Minorco), a Bermuda-based company with assets of $2 billion, not only because Minorco was in a position to avoid taxes in Bermuda, but also because the company's wealth was derived from apartheid in South Africa.[66] The solution for this kind of ethical problem is to make sure you don't think about it. "Ritchie may not be a brilliant man, but perhaps a banker does not need to be. As [his colleague] Harrison McCain puts it, 'Clever guys aren't running banks, they teach at university. They've got high IQs and read the classics. The guys who run banks have energy and can motivate people."[67] The source is obviously well informed.

The accounting manipulations that Bermuda allows multinationals to carry out are seen today as shocking. In 2011, Google moved $9.8 billion – over one-quarter of its annual revenue – to Bermuda even though the company has no substantial activity in this jurisdiction. This amount was twice what it had been in 2008.[68] By shifting its money to Bermuda, Google was able to avoid $2 billion in taxes that it would have paid if it had recorded profits in the countries where its operations actually took place.[69] Like many other multinationals, Google uses the techniques known as the *Double Irish* and the *Dutch Sandwich* to get its money to Bermuda. First, the right to use the Google trademark is sold to a Dublin subsidiary of a Bermuda holding "because Irish tax law exempts certain royalties to companies in other EU-member nations."[70] Then the Dublin firm sends the funds to a Dutch subsidiary in Amsterdam (which has no employees), and from there the funds are transferred to Bermuda. Bloomberg, the financial agency that first reported on the system, noted in October 2010 that Google was able, using this method, to keep its tax rate throughout the world at 2.4 percent.[71]

In another article focusing on pharmaceutical giant Forest Laboratories, Bloomberg investigated the financial circuit used in 2009 for profits from an antidepressant called Lexapro. The agency concluded that the manufacturer had been able to save $183 million in taxes – that is, about one-third of its U.S. tax bill – through transfer pricing. The money took the usual path from the United States to Dublin, where a company received the profits made from sales in the United States, then to Amsterdam to avoid taxes in Ireland thanks to a treaty between the two countries, and then to Bermuda, where it escaped taxation of any kind.[72] The case is interesting because it reflects a generalized drain: based on filings by only 175 companies, Bloomberg calculated that U.S. companies in 2009 had "amassed at least $1 trillion in foreign profits not taxed in the U.S."[73]

Tax evasion of this kind by multinationals has been documented over the past few years by Parliamentary investigations in several countries. In 2011, a British Parliamentary committee established to study tax evasion plied representatives of Google, Starbucks, and Amazon with detailed questions about the consequences of their administrative relocation outside the countries where the greatest part of their income is generated.[74] In 2012, the French Senate published two weighty tomes on tax evasion after hearing representations from corporations such as Paribas and Citigroup,[75] and in 2013, a U.S. Senate subcommittee required Apple's CEO to explain the company's controversial tax strategies.[76]

The Canadian approach is completely different. As scandal raged during the media coverage of ICIJ's "Offshore Leaks" in April 2013, Finance Minister Jim Flaherty flew to Bermuda to emphasize his friendship with the Bermuda business class and "promote deeper trade and investment ties between both economies."[77]

The Canadian government, in other words, is deliberately ignoring substantial political issues in this area. Canadians had "invested" over $13 billion in Bermuda by 2013,[78] essentially for the purpose of avoiding taxes. Where do the fortunes converging on tax havens come from? Who pays a price for this convergence? And why does the population of eastern Canada have to stoop to subsidizing this kind of activity? Some of these questions can be answered in the Maritimes. Kenneth Colin Irving, the local tycoon to whom the region was subject for decades, first made his mark as an oil importer, and his family's corporation mobilized the transfer-pricing techniques described earlier. From Bermuda, the Irvings signed trade agreements, recorded the revenues from their activities in their offshore corporations, and then sold to themselves the deliveries they were making to the Maritimes companies they controlled. Canadian tax authorities eventually tried to oppose the tactic, but in 1991 the Federal Court of Appeal ruled in the company's favour.[79] Once again, a Canadian court contradicted Canadian regulations by legitimizing the use of tax havens for tax avoidance. This kind of outcome has enabled the Irvings to rule their province as their private kingdom. Ultra-liberal financial journalist Diane Francis presents this as an obvious fact: "New Brunswick is a company town owned by the Irving family ... But technically, ownership is held in a series of trusts in Bermuda."[80] Before this elite, currently subsidized by Halifax to "create jobs," we are expected to bow down.

While Canadians continue to forge ever closer ties with Bermuda, the Bermudian government is more and more openly resistant to any international political negotiation focusing on the colony's policies. Bermuda publicly expressed its "reservations"[81] – this is surely an understatement – when British prime minister David Cameron proposed, at the time of the 2013 G8 Summit, to review the status of tax havens under the authority of the British Crown.

THE TORONTO STOCK EXCHANGE, PART OWNER OF THE BERMUDA STOCK EXCHANGE

The unexpected development of the Maritimes' chief city was noticed in Toronto, especially since Canada's Queen City was now forced to view Halifax as a significant rival. "The stars have never seemed so perfectly aligned" to make Toronto into "a new banking paradise," as business columnist Sophie Cousineau gushed in Montreal daily *La Presse* in 2010.[82] European governments that had mobilized massive amounts of public funds in the aftermath of the 2008 crash were now thinking of increasing taxes on banks, which might give Canadian institutions an advantage. Cousineau's blog post continues: "Will this make Bay Street into a more attractive financial centre, minus the snowy peaks of Switzerland?" Her witty comment indicates that she is several decades late in her grasp of the situation. She should know that the Toronto financial world is already seamlessly incorporated into the tax haven system. Canada's financial establishment recently displayed its ambitions in this area when the Toronto Stock Exchange became one of the largest shareholders in the Bermuda Stock Exchange (BSX), having acquired 16 percent of its shares on December 21, 2011; the CEO of the Toronto corporation, Tom Kloet, is now a member of the BSX board of directors.[83] The Toronto Stock Exchange press release announcing the decision notes that it is part of a political strategy developed by the Canadian government: "The announcement comes at a time of increased business activity between Bermuda and Canada. Most notably, a Tax Information Exchange Agreement was signed between the two countries earlier this year, effective July 1, 2011. In addition, the BSX gained recognition as a Designated Stock Exchange under Canada's Income Tax Act, effective October 31, 2011."[84]

Both of the advantages cited are tax benefits. As discussed earlier, the TIEAs that Canada has signed with tax havens as part of the international co-operative processes supported by the Organisation for Economic Co-operation and Development (OECD) are not mainly intended to breach bank secrecy in tax havens. Under paragraph 5907 (11) of Canada's Income Tax Regulations, Canadian corporations holding assets in an offshore country that has signed a TIEA can bring them back to Canada in the form of dividends without paying taxes. In other words, Canada is encouraging its wealthy citizens to transfer funds to accommodating states where, free of tax, the funds may be reinvested without being subject to any kind of regulation. The documents associated with these operations may even be processed by people working in Halifax, whose salaries are paid, in part, by Nova Scotia taxpayers, and who are satellites of Bermuda financial corporations that enjoy all the legal prerogatives of the indulgent Bermudian system. More easily and "legally" than ever, billions of dollars generated by the Canadian economy are recorded in jurisdictions with a zero or close to zero tax rate.

The TSX press release goes on to note that Canada's Income Tax Act recognizes the Bermuda Stock Exchange. As tax expert Grégoire Duhamel observes, "Bermuda's very advantageous tax regime allows non-resident investors to exchange shares and create investment funds without being subject to any kind of tax."[85] In addition, the Bermuda Stock Exchange is not subject to scrutiny by any public institution except the fantastical Bermuda Monetary Authority, which, on its website, is more interested in singing the praises of the various kinds of offshore entity you can create in Bermuda than in explaining how it might ever control these entities if they get out of hand.

CANADA, THE BAHAMAS, BARBADOS, BELIZE, ST. KITTS AND NEVIS, ETC.

OFFSHORE LOBBY AT THE WORLD BANK AND THE INTERNATIONAL MONETARY FUND

In which the Canadian government forms an alliance with a group of Caribbean offshore territories

The year 2000 was a turning point in the relations between conventional states and tax havens. Around this time, independent associations[1] and a number of intellectuals began to articulate a focused critique of the offshore phenomenon.[2] In addition, the Organisation for Economic Co-operation and Development (OECD), the Financial Stability Forum (FSF), and the Financial Action Task Force (FATF) each published a "blacklist"[3] intended to stigmatize tax havens (see Table 5). Tax havens were accused by these international institutions of obstructing investigations carried out by foreign tax authorities in cases of alleged fraud,[4] of abusively encouraging stock market speculation at the risk of destabilizing the world economy,[5] and of providing a way to launder the proceeds of drug-trafficking and "terrorist" activities.[6]

The OECD, however, transformed these blacklists into virtually blank sheets of paper by withdrawing one jurisdiction after another, using as a pretext the voluntary commitment of these micro-states to disclose certain kinds of information relevant to international investigations in cases of alleged fraud or crime. The FATF also reduced its blacklist, promising to analyze on a regular basis – discreetly – the provisions enacted by states against money laundering and "terrorism."[7] As for the FSF, it identified "good practice principles" that offshore jurisdictions were invited to adopt voluntarily as a matter of good faith.[8]

TABLE 5.

Countries on the blacklists of the Organisation for Economic Co-operation and Development (OECD), the Financial Stability Forum (FSF), and the Financial Action Task Force (FATF)

OECD	FSF	FATF
Countries and territories with harmful tax practices	Non-co-operative jurisdictions	Non-co-operative countries and territories
Andorra	Anguilla	The Bahamas
Anguilla	Antigua and Barbuda	Cayman Islands
Antigua and Barbuda	Aruba	Cook Islands
Aruba	The Bahamas	Dominican Republic
The Bahamas	Belize	Israel
Bahrain	British Virgin Islands	Lebanon
Barbados	Cayman Islands	Liechtenstein
Belize	Cook Islands	Marshall Islands
British Virgin Islands	Costa Rica	Nauru
Cook Islands	Cyprus	Niue
Dominica	Lebanon	Panama
Gibraltar	Liechtenstein	Philippines
Grenada	Marshall Islands	Russia
Guernsey	Mauritius	St. Kitts and Nevis
Isle of Man	Nauru	St. Vincent and the Grenadines
Jersey	Netherlands Antilles	
Liberia	Niue	**Jurisdictions placed under high surveillance**
Liechtenstein	Panama	
Maldives	St. Kitts and Nevis	Antigua and Barbuda
Marshall Islands	St. Lucia	Belize
Monaco	St. Vincent and the Grenadines	Bermuda
Montserrat	Samoa	British Virgin Islands
Nauru	Seychelles	Cyprus
Netherlands Antilles	Turks and Caicos	Gibraltar
Niue	Vanuatu	Guernsey
Panama		Isle of Man
St. Kitts and Nevis	**Moderately co-operative jurisdictions**	Jersey
St. Lucia		Malta
St. Vincent and the Grenadines	Andorra	Mauritius
Samoa	Bahrain	Monaco
Seychelles	Barbados	St. Lucia
Tonga	Bermuda	Samoa
Turks and Caicos	Gibraltar	
United States Virgin Islands	Lubuan	
Vanuatu	Macau	
	Malta	
	Monaco	

SOURCE: Compiled from OECD-CFA, *Towards Global Tax Co-operation* (Paris: OECD, 2000); FATF, *Report on Non-Co-operative Countries and Territories* (Paris: FATF, 2000); FATF, *Review to Identify Non-Co-operative Countries and Territories: Increasing the Worldwide Effectiveness of Money-Laundering Efforts* (Paris: FATF, 2000); FSF, *Financial Stability Forum Releases Grouping of Offshore Financial Centres (OFCs) to Assist in Setting Priorities for Assessment* (Basel: FSF, 2000).

Today, it is obvious that these statements of principle have had no effect. Tax expert Grégoire Duhamel overtly mocked them in 2006: "Although laws have recently been enacted saying that information must be provided on international criminal affairs, authorities generally do not answer requests for information related to tax issues or tax dodging."[9] Tax expert Warren de Rajewicz describes processes enabling jurisdictions to make sure that they don't even have the information that these new provisions might force them to disclose.[10] Political scientist Gilles Favarel-Garrigues, economist Thierry Godefroy, and legal expert Pierre Lascoumes have analyzed the many limitations of these guidelines that put the world's bankers in charge of monitoring money laundering.[11]

Restrictive measures whose ineffectiveness is obvious even to judges and MPs are aimed only at overtly criminal transactions such as money laundering, illicit trafficking, or funding terrorism. Often, investigators must already have the information they are looking for before they can pierce the bank secrecy of tax havens. Money-laundering techniques have become so sophisticated that it is usually impossible to detect fraud anywhere except in the offshore jurisdiction where it is recorded.

As for tax evasion, these measures leave it on the sidelines, enabling an exemplary tax haven such as Panama to boast: "In Panama, it is a criminal offense for any bank employee to divulge any information about a client without a court order, and those court orders are only written up if the person is suspected of financing terrorism, drug trafficking, money laundering or other serious crimes. *Panamanian judges will not issue court orders for tax issues.*"[12]

As it turned out, the movement to quell tax havens in the early years of the new millennium quickly got bogged down. Only when faced with the financial crisis of 2008 did states and international institutions again show concern. They started by publishing a set of laughable denunciations (with the OECD producing another set of black, dark grey, and grey lists).[13] The possibility of forcing businesses to declare their income and their subsidiaries' income for each country was also discussed; this would have more serious consequences for some parties. This method would make it possible to determine in which tax havens the holders of large amounts of capital have registered their assets.

But why did the fight against tax havens get stuck as early as 2000? This was the moment when George W. Bush and his friends moved into the White House; supported by the power of American capital, they were opposed, of course, to the use of blacklists.[14] The United States quickly put an end to OECD initiatives, and the offshore states themselves successfully made the OECD feel their power. Switzerland and Luxembourg were able to use their standing as OECD members to impose their authority for a time.[15] Tax havens that were not OECD members joined forces under the banner of the International Tax and Investment Organisation (ITIO). Canada stood by on the sidelines as one of its creatures, Barbados, took the leadership of the ITIO.[16] The ITIO, with undeniable legitimacy, turned the strategy of conventional states against them, telling them to preach by example with regard to Delaware, which is the exact equivalent of an offshore centre, or the City of London, in the heart of Britain, which gives the financial world complete regulatory freedom.[17] This form of blackmail allowed the tax havens to gain time: they continued to give birth to legally hazardous entities, including trusts, exempted companies, and the Special Purpose Vehicles[18] that serve to enrich multinationals, banks, and tax exiles. Godefroy and Lascoumes note that "Caribbean tax havens attempted to move discussions out of the OECD framework where they were not present."[19] Barbados protested as soon as it was mentioned in a critical way at the international level, challenging French president Nicolas Sarkozy's prediction when he announced the end of its offshore status in 2011.[20]

At the World Bank and the International Monetary Fund (IMF), the two institutions created at Bretton Woods in 1944 to redesign the world's economic framework, Canada shares its seat on decision-making councils today with Ireland and eleven Caribbean territories, each of which has become a tax haven. Thus, when Canada takes a position within these bodies through the voice of the Canadian minister of finance (who is a governor of the two institutions), it is also taking a position on behalf of the following states:

Antigua and Barbuda
The Bahamas
Barbados
Belize
Dominica
Grenada
Guyana
Ireland
Jamaica
St. Kitts and Nevis
St. Lucia
St. Vincent and the Grenadines[21]

These jurisdictions – and this is not a trivial matter – are dedicated to providing citizens of states based on the rule of law, such as Canada, with the entry points they need to bypass the constraints of social life in their own country. Tax havens prevent traditional states from enforcing both rights and duties in a spirit of fairness. A series of states whose format has been determined by bankers and corporate lawyers are special legislative zones for privileged people. In becoming their ally and de facto partner, Canada has developed within its own jurisdiction the escape clauses that enable its financial establishment to flout rules that members of other social categories are forced to obey.

From a strictly formal point of view, a number of these controversial micro-states – Antigua and Barbuda, the Bahamas, Belize, St. Kitts and Nevis, and St. Vincent and the Grenadines – are named on all the lists drawn up in 2000 by the OECD, the FSF, and the FATF, while Barbados, Dominica, and St. Lucia are each named on at least one list. At the World Bank that year, the joint representative of Canada and the tax haven coalition was Samy Watson, a man with a Ph.D. in "leadership studies" from Andrews University in Berrien Springs, Michigan, who was in charge of tax policy for the federal Department of Finance between 1990 and 1996.[22] Watson was supported in his functions, as is normally the case, by an alternate executive director from a Caribbean country;[23] at this time, it was Ishmael Lightbourne from the Bahamas, a character known for his involvement in a number of legal and financial intrigues.[24] In the meantime, at the IMF, the same position was filled by Canadian Jonathan T. Fried, former Canadian delegate on financial issues at international summits.[25]

In 2007, during the period leading up to the financial crisis, tax havens were in a vulnerable position. We are gradually coming to understand the active part they play in disturbing the workings of the global financial system. "These tax havens did not 'cause' the crisis, but they contributed powerfully to it," says the Tax Justice Network, a network of researchers and associations seeking to understand the effects of the offshore phenomenon on public life.[26] Tax havens in the British Caribbean are clearly part of the problem, especially those that released financial corporations from any form of scrutiny as they gambolled in the Euromarkets of the 1960s or gorged themselves on the risky subprime mortgage loans of the 2000s. The laissez-faire policies adopted by the City of London and the Cayman Islands, in particular, are a form of unfair competition leading conventional states to carry out ever greater deregulation of the financial sector. Among the obscure practices shaping the economy, we may include "leverage effects" that can artificially cause a firm's financial potential to swell, or, conversely, "off-balance sheet" items that allow them to remove some of their liabilities from their official financial accounts. "'Satellite' tax havens like some Caribbean islands or Britain's Crown Dependencies are conduits for illicit and other financial flows, often from developing countries into financial centres like London, New York, and these contributed to large macroeconomic imbalances. The mainstream economics profession has not measured these vast flows, many of which (such as transfer mispricing) simply do not show up'" in national statistics."[27]

In 2007, at a time when the world's major banks were carried away by their self-created frenzy, and financial products devised by sorcerer's apprentices were making it impossible to evaluate their assets, the Tax Justice Network published a detailed and rigorous list of countries that, in its eyes, were playing the role of tax havens.[28] Except Guyana and Jamaica, all Canada's allies in international financial institutions were on the list.

Officially, Canada did not take part in the debate. Not until 2009 did it formally commit itself to supporting the tax havens whose seat it shared at the World Bank and the IMF. But its intervention, though discreet, was absolutely unequivocal. In his 2009 annual report, Canada's minister of finance summarized Canada's official position with regard to representations he had made to the World Bank and the IMF:

> Some of our Caribbean countries have significant financial sector activities. There is a risk that changes to financial sector regulation in advanced countries could have negative unintended consequences on these activities. In particular, there is a risk that measures taken against non-co-operative jurisdictions, including tax havens, could have unintended negative impacts on well-regulated, transparent, financial centres. I believe that this should be avoided. Countries that comply with international standards should be protected from such measures.[29]

Meanwhile, in relation to these jurisdictions, the United States has taken the opposite direction. In March 2009, President Obama submitted to the U.S. Congress a bill explicitly aimed at inducing jurisdictions close to Canada to abolish their offshore legal system. Targets included Antigua and Barbuda, the Bahamas, Barbados, Belize, St. Kitts and Nevis, St. Lucia, and St. Vincent and the Grenadines – all states sharing Canada's seat at the World Bank and the IMF – as well as other tax havens with historic ties to Canada: Bermuda, the British Virgin Islands, Cayman Islands, Dominica, Grenada, and the Turks and Caicos Islands. It was understood that Jamaica, Trinidad and Tobago, and Guyana would also be added to the list.[30]

However, the U.S. attack on tax havens was only partial: the tax havens within, such as Delaware or the Marshall Islands,[31] were not greatly inconvenienced. Meanwhile, Canada put its weight in the balance to establish the legitimacy of the territories it is in the habit of befriending in international institutions, presenting them as "well-regulated, transparent, financial centres."

In 2010, Toronto hosted the summit of the world's twenty most powerful countries. The previous year had set the tone: the G20 countries had committed themselves, at least rhetorically, "to maintain the momentum in dealing with tax havens, money laundering, proceeds of corruption, terrorist financing, and prudential standards."[32] Nicolas Sarkozy, president of the French Republic, had even declared before the summit: "Tax havens, banking secrecy, that's all finished."[33] The following year in Canada, though, the G20 barely mentioned the subject, and its tone was noticeably softer: "We are addressing non-co-operative jurisdictions based on comprehensive, consistent, and transparent assessment with respect to tax havens, the fight against money laundering and terrorist financing and the adherence to prudential standards."[34] Only in 2012, at Cannes, did the G20 become somewhat caustic again,[35] and the G8 also showed more spirit at Lough Erne in 2013,[36] despite the extreme reluctance displayed by the Canadian prime minister.[37]

Current international plans to oppose tax havens include an automatic multilateral mechanism by which governments would exchange tax information, as well as new rules of accountability that would oblige financial institutions in tax havens to maintain a public registry. The registry would make it possible to identify the true beneficiaries of bank accounts, trusts, and companies – beneficiaries who are currently difficult to track down under the tax laws in force in highly permissive jurisdictions. These two measures would be a step in the right direction in terms of fighting tax avoidance through tax havens. And yet, Canadian prime minister Stephen Harper has been half-hearted in his support of these measures.

TURNING THE LEGAL SYSTEM INSIDE OUT

What are the *well-regulated, transparent, financial centres* to which Canada refers? Canadians have every reason to be concerned about the jurisdictions with which Canada shares its seat at the World Bank and the IMF, and in which Canadian banks are active. Accommodating jurisdictions are harmful to traditional states, and cases of fraud and other dubious operations have taken place in these territories in the past to Canadians' detriment. The evidence in support is clear.

- As discussed earlier, Barbados and the Bahamas are notorious offshore jurisdictions, while Jamaica has been forced to develop as a free zone. As for the jurisdiction of Antigua and Barbuda, it is a tax haven for wealthy individuals. "Income tax or taxes on the wealth of private individuals do not exist as such in Antigua."[38] It is also home to seventeen offshore banks, a handful of trusts and insurance companies, and, perhaps most importantly, twenty-three Internet gaming companies.[39] From this jurisdiction, American financier Allen Stanford coordinated a giant pyramid scheme,[40] estimated at $7 billion, whose harmful effects were felt by Canadian investors, among others.[41] The Canadian Imperial Bank of Commerce (CIBC), the Royal Bank of Canada (RBC), and Scotiabank are among the major international banks with branches in Antigua and Barbuda.[42]

- Belize has been a haven for people like Jean Lafleur, an advertising executive condemned by a Canadian court in 2007 to a $1.6-million fine and forty-two months in jail. Lafleur had embezzled public funds as a participant in what was known in Canada as the "sponsorship scandal," and Belize was the place where he stashed his ill-gotten loot.[43] Only his lawyers know how much money he has there, since Lafleur claims that Belize bank secrecy won't let him reveal the amount. "His lawyer, Jean-Claude Hébert, vigorously objected to the Crown's bringing into evidence his foreign assets. This information is confidential, according to Hébert, and disclosure could cause Mr. Lafleur 'irreparable' harm."[44] Here the tricks of the law verge on the obscene. Belize is also a free zone where tax exemptions and the lack of an exchange rate[45] provide for lucrative commercial activity. Companies created in Belize are entitled to a full array of measures providing for tax exemption, anonymity, bank secrecy, and freedom from any obligation regarding public disclosure or nomination.[46] Scotiabank is in Belize, as is the CIBC under the name CIBC FirstCaribbean International Bank.[47]

- Dominica was described by Édouard Chambost a decade ago as "the last-born of the major tax havens…able immediately to join the category of the 'other major havens'."[48] A tax haven for wealthy individuals, the island – according to Marie-Christine Dupuis-Danon, former anti-money-laundering adviser with the United Nations Office on Drugs and Crime – has also seen several of its bankers go over to the criminal side. A British offshore services firm, the MCE Group, is equally explicit in describing the advantages of Dominica for investors: "Establishing an offshore bank in Dominica will enable you to carry out legal banking transactions for companies based abroad or foreign nationals, and even for offshore companies such as IBCs (International Business Companies) that are registered in Dominica"[49] – all this without paying taxes on any kind of income. Another source indicates that RBC and Scotiabank are two of the region's four major banking institutions.[50]

- Grenada, a tax haven comparable to Antigua and Barbuda, prides itself "on being little known."[51] However, connoisseurs and firms specializing in relocating corporations are well aware that this island just off South America is "one of the most corrupt international financial centres in the history of offshore."[52] While Scotiabank and the CIBC are conspicuously present in Grenada,[53] the First International Bank of Grenada is perhaps better known: it was at the heart of a Ponzi scheme leading to losses of $170 million for Canadian and U.S. investors. Among the handful of rogues at the heart of the Ponzi scheme was Canadian Larry Barnabe, a marketing expert who was sentenced to six years in jail by an American federal court.[54] The regulator of Grenada's offshore industry at the time of the scheme was Michael Creft, an economist trained at the University of Manitoba who had previously spent over twenty years working as an analyst for the Canadian government. Creft admitted to the court that he himself had collected money from the First International Bank and personally delivered it in cash to a local political party.[55]

- Guyana was threatened in 2013 with remaining on the FATF dark grey list of countries that fail to adopt minimum anti-money-laundering measures.[56] Canada's main thrust in Guyana over the past few years, however, has not been to advocate stricter rules against money laundering, but to defend the interests of Canadian oil companies such as Calgary's Groundstar Resources, which in 2012 was about to begin drilling in

Guyana,[57] and Toronto firm CGX Energy, specializing in the operation of offshore oil wells.[58] In this context, it is hard to tell the difference between Canada's High Commissioner in Guyana, David Devine, and a mining industry lobbyist. Devine seems fully occupied in hawking Canadian companies' technology, claiming that it meets the high standards that Guyana ought to adopt.[59] Scotiabank is active in Guyana.[60]

- St. Kitts and Nevis, another free zone, offers corporations "complete freedom from taxes for fifteen years."[61] This jurisdiction also plays a key role in the economics of spam: it is home to one of three banks in the world that fund 75 percent of the world's transactions for spam-advertised goods.[62] Captive insurance companies are present in St. Kitts along with the usual branches of Scotiabank and RBC.[63]

- St. Lucia developed its financial and monetary sector in the 1990s.[64] It was estimated in the 1990s that over 40 percent of the industrial labour force in this former British colony worked in the two Vieux Fort free zones near the international airport,[65] which are still thriving today. The government has also made possible an offshore form of medical research. The Spartan Health Sciences University is a medical school whose high tuition fees ensure the de facto exclusion of almost anyone from St. Lucia. About 90 percent of the school's students come from the United States and Canada, while only 10 percent come from Africa and the Caribbean.[66] The CIBC,[67] RBC,[68] and Scotiabank[69] operate in St. Lucia.[70]

- St. Vincent and the Grenadines is known to Canadians as the home of PDP International Bank, to which hedge fund operator Portus Alternative Asset Management Inc. entrusted over $700 million worth of securities belonging to 26,000 Canadian investors, in an operation that gave rise to an investigation by the Ontario Securities Commission (OSC) in 2005. The OSC's efforts to obtain information on the possibly fraudulent activities of the hedge fund were fruitless under the islands' opaque bank secrecy rules.[71] Wealthy rock stars such as Mick Jagger and David Bowie find it advantageous to reside in St. Vincent and the Grenadines, and it is also possible to use this jurisdiction to create insurance companies or shell societies known as international business corporations. Corporate law governing these entities is utterly permissive.[72] Flags of convenience are also provided.

- Ireland, the only non-Caribbean country represented by Canada at the Bretton Woods institutions, is a tax haven specializing, among other things, in intellectual property rights. Its Shannon free zone provides tax exemptions for a wide range of activities.[73]

As is often the case in Canada, the left hand of the state does not know what the right hand is doing. While on the one hand Ottawa supports tax havens at the World Bank and the IMF, on the other it claims to help Southern countries deal with the direct consequences of these countries' lax fiscal policies. Thus in 2007, Canada became the promoter of the STAR (Stolen Asset Recovery) program designed to help developing countries recover funds embezzled by swindlers. The Canadian government indicated that "stolen assets are often hidden in the financial centres of developed countries," an implicit reference to the role of tax havens. The government even added that "bribes to developing country officials often originate from firms operating in both developing and developed countries."[74]

DRUG-TRAFFICKING HUBS

It is a notable fact that almost all these tax havens are used for drug trafficking. From Colombia, drugs are distributed through the many hubs provided by Caribbean islands or countries around the Caribbean. As a consequence, the drug economy and the islands' economies are inextricably involved. According to estimates carried out at the end of the twentieth century, the gross criminal product generated in the marijuana sector alone has reached $3 billion over a decade. These are funds that are subsequently laundered in part through real estate or transportation infrastructure.[75] While also asserting itself in the heroin trade, Colombia provides 80 percent of the cocaine consumed in the world. The cartels of Medellín and Cari, dismantled in the 1980s, re-established themselves as several small cartels, practising narco-terrorism or completely dominating the structures of the Colombian state, and it has become impossible to decapitate a movement that now takes the form of a tentacular network.[76]

Other sectors develop unrestrainedly in the Caribbean: "Kidnappings; racketeering (either purely criminal or wearing the colours of a revolutionary ideology that is now often nothing but a pretext); trafficking in arms, emeralds, protected species, gold or foreign exchange; manufacturing counterfeit products... these represent more billions. Tax evasion? At least 30 percent of what ought to be collected. Embezzlement of public funds, including funds intended for social purposes? Incalculable! ... [Offshore] criminal funds amount to a total of at least $300 billion."[77]

These states are undoubtedly negligent in fighting the drug trafficking that goes on in their territory, and in some cases their own institutions are active participants in the trade. According to criminologist Patrice Meyzonnier, chief commissioner at the central directorate of the French investigative police, ships registered in Belize carry heroin and cocaine, and Jamaica is a gigantic regional sorting centre for narcotics, with an ideal location close to the Bahamas, Haiti, and the Dominican Republic from which drugs are sent to the East Coast market in the United States and Canada. "Since 1998, it seems that shipments of cocaine and heroin [from Jamaica] to Canada surpass those to the United States."[78] The Bahamas are "the oldest and most direct route" for moving drugs to markets in the North.[79] Criminologists working to dissect the far-flung network connecting the countries involved in this traffic sometimes find themselves naming, in one sentence, almost every country with which Canada forms a coalition at the World Bank and the IMF. "This same cocaine also passes through Barbados, coming from Guyana, before moving on toward the United States and Europe on trawlers from Trinidad and Tobago and Grenada or yachts from private marinas in St. Lucia or the Grenadines... A highly structured network of complicity in the ports of Barbados facilitates the unloading and reloading of cannabis."[80] High-level complicity also explains the weak control exercised on this traffic by countries such as Barbados, or St. Kitts and Nevis, where "corruption is institutionalized,"[81] or St. Lucia, where everything "is paid in cash, including very large invoices,"[82] or St. Vincent and the Grenadines, where "the state is either non-existent, or corrupt."[83]

Criminologist Marie-Christine Dupuis-Danon observes that in Antigua, banks have no difficulty in laundering narcotrafficking money. "The island's bank secrecy has an unsavoury reputation, and there have been rumours of collusion with Latin American cartels, the Russian mafia, and other criminal organizations."[84] According to Dupuis-Danon, most of the tax havens allied with Canada are home to online casinos managed by various mafias, with connections sometimes reaching to Canada.[85] Where drug trafficking is concerned, it almost seems as if the legislative framework developed by states governed by the rule of law, such as Canada, is destined, paradoxically, to protect this highly lucrative trade.[86] In terms of the "war on drugs," Canada behaves exactly like the United States, making war on enemy states (such as Afghanistan) involved in drug production and trafficking while protecting "friendly" regimes that carry out similar activities.

A FREE-TRADE AGREEMENT WITH ALL CARIBBEAN COUNTRIES

Although the G20 countries themselves describe Caribbean states as a threat to the world economic order, and although many highly respected judges see them as threats to democracy, Canada shows no signs of turning back. Today, it is negotiating with the Caribbean Community (CARICOM) to sign a free-trade agreement that will connect it with some of the states with which it is associated in international institutions – Antigua and Barbuda, the Bahamas, Barbados, Belize, Dominica, Grenada, Guyana, Jamaica, St. Kitts and Nevis, St. Lucia, and St. Vincent and the Grenadines – as well as other CARICOM members such as Haiti, Montserrat, Suriname, and Trinidad and Tobago.[87]

Officially, discussions focus on trade in goods and services. However, the volume of this trade between the two zones is small, and tariffs are not really an issue.[88] In addition, it is clear that some part of the trade in services has little to do with the real economy: "Commercial services dominate the picture, particularly with Barbados. These are associated with the movement of capital to benefit from the preferential tax regime there, rather than a reflection of services provided for/by Barbadian-based businesses."[89] It may legitimately be asked whether agreements with CARICOM countries are not likely to make Canada more porous in relation to tax havens. This is exactly the goal that Canada's prime minister seemed to be aiming for when he proposed in 2009 to "expand" the trade relation between Canada and Caribbean tax havens "to include services and investment."[90] Discussions between the two parties also touch on fighting crime, as defined by the Inter-American Drug Abuse Control Commission and the Inter-American Committee Against Terrorism, but the issues of financial criminality and tax evasion are not explicitly mentioned.

The stakes are high for Canada. Free-trade agreements today always include mechanisms for conflict resolution that allow a signatory country, or in some cases one of its corporations, to challenge the laws of another country as soon as it views them as a hindrance to the free market. This mechanism, enshrined in the North American Free Trade Agreement's Chapter 11, has often been used to threaten the Canadian state, which finds itself unable to regulate its economy and public activity without "distorting" the working of "free competition." And this is not even the worst of the matter – for when a tax haven signs a free-trade agreement, a corporation from a conventional state may be tempted to incorporate a subsidiary in this tax haven in order to challenge, on the basis of the tax haven's laws (or, as is usually the case, its absence of laws), the regulations of the country of origin. This may seem fantastic, but it has already occurred. An Albertan gas company, Lone Pine Resources, has launched a NAFTA Chapter 11 lawsuit against the Canadian government from its Delaware subsidiary (Delaware being a tax haven within the United States). The purpose of the lawsuit is to challenge the moratorium on fracking for shale gas imposed by the Quebec government.[91]

In a similar vein, an American citizen, Mark E. Mendel, has used a company he created in Antigua and Barbuda to challenge American laws on Internet betting and gambling. The rules he cites are those of the World Trade Organization (WTO) on international tariffs. As a perplexed *New York Times* journalist explained in 2007, "The dispute stretches back to 2003, when Mr. Mendel first persuaded officials in Antigua and Barbuda, a tiny nation in the Caribbean with a population of around 70,000, to instigate a trade complaint against the United

States, claiming its ban against Americans gambling over the Internet violated Antigua and Barbuda's rights as a member of the WTO."[92] The WTO ruled in favour of Antigua and Barbuda in 2004, both in a first decision and on appeal. Even more implausibly, Mendel then went on to claim $3.4 billion in compensation on behalf of the tax haven, and in 2013 the WTO authorized Antigua and Barbuda to compensate itself by suspending all U.S. intellectual property rights.[93]

This is the type of mechanism for settling disputes that Canada wants to include in the CARICOM free-trade agreement.[94] Looking at previous decisions gives us a sense of the kind of ruling we can expect from obscure advisers who will be given the job of settling disputes between offshore enterprises and states with social obligations. In terms of tax regimes, regulation, labour law, ecosystem protection, and professional standards, governments will continually be threatened by the fact that a company from their own jurisdiction may use a territory that does not recognize constraints of any kind to challenge any constraint.

It is clear that the proposed free-trade agreement will include a form of investor-state dispute settlement that will enable companies to challenge the power of states head on.[95] The lobbies that pressure the government to sign this kind of treaty do not care about public service. Their only concern is to eliminate as many obstacles as they can as they strive to dominate markets, and they now see the possibility of challenging laws adopted by states without even having to go through their own government.

AN IMPERIALIST APPROACH

The actual autonomy of the Caribbean countries negotiating this agreement is hard to assess. For historical reasons, Canada is seen in these jurisdictions as an occupying force. Canadian citizens have taken key positions in public administration and the banking world, while Canadian companies appropriate a market that seems to offer no resistance.

The state of Trinidad and Tobago is the largest economy in the Caribbean and is at the heart of considerations related to the real economy. It is the chief target of the projected free-trade agreement with Canada: from 1985 to the end of the 2000 decade, under CARIBCAN – an agreement to eliminate customs tariffs for Caribbean exports to

Canada – close to 80 percent of Caribbean exchanges with Canada have involved Trinidad and Tobago.[96] This is due not so much to close co-operation between the two communities as to the presence of Canadian entities that do business with each other as they take advantage of the lack of tariff barriers. "Of the total C$115 million imports from the region benefiting from CARIBCAN treatment, 79 percent comes from Trinidad and Tobago and 65 percent consists of shipments of methanol from a Canadian owned firm in Trinidad."[97] Canada is negotiating the free-trade treaty to favour the Caribbean subsidiaries of companies incorporated in Canada, especially now that Canadian firms covet the tar sand deposits on Trinidad island.[98] In 2009, France named Trinidad and Tobago as one of eleven tax havens that needed to be tackled.[99] In Canada, by contrast, Trinidad and Tobago's High Commissioner, Philip Buxo[100] – a former employee of SNC-Lavalin – was received with pomp and ceremony in 2013.[101]

Canada wields a high degree of power in Trinidad and Tobago and thus finds itself entwined with a state undermined by drug trafficking, gang violence, economic uncertainty, and the permissiveness of a corrupt oligarchy[102] for whom money laundering is simply a social reality.[103] Trinidadian investors have asserted their influence over CARICOM countries, acquiring banks, oil companies, insurance companies, agrifood companies, and airline companies in neighbouring countries.[104] An example of this expansion is CLICO, a Trinidadian conglomerate present in thirty-two countries and active in insurance, finance, real estate, agriculture, forest products, retail trade, energy, and the media. When a gigantic fraud affecting its enterprises throughout the Caribbean caused it to declare bankruptcy in 2010, the company was so large that the Trinidad and Tobago government felt obliged to bail it out.[105]

Who in fact is running the country? Trinidadians are not the only ones involved. British and American interests are present in the oil sector, while Canadians, not surprisingly, dominate the banking sector. Like Jamaica, Trinidad and Tobago became independent in 1962, carried by a strong emancipation movement, and then experienced the discreet stewardship of Canada, unobtrusive successor of the British Empire. In a clearly neo-colonial spirit, Canada today is still "actively involved in the support of good governance," providing the Trinidad and Tobago government with expert advice.[106] In its great wisdom, it may suggest that members of the Trinidadian political class (themselves often educated in Toronto)[107] to call on Canadians to manage health care, the water supply, the police force, and education – while Canadians continue, of course, to be strongly represented in the banking sector.

Canada has offered to share with Trinidad and Tobago its knowledge and scientific expertise to help it study – incarceration.[108] It has also established with Trinidad and Tobago the outline of a Technical Framework Arrangement that will "allow qualified Canadian companies to access commercial opportunities in the health sector."[109] Health issues are associated with a new market to be conquered at whatever price. In 2013, SNC-Lavalin obtained a $2.2 million contract to build the Penal Hospital in Trinidad, even though the World Bank had forbidden the company to bid on contracts that it funded because of its compromised ethical record. To reach its ends, the Quebec firm hid behind the Canadian Commercial Corporation, a Crown corporation of the government of Canada.[110]

Until they were challenged by colleagues and by the minister responsible for law enforcement in 2012, two key law enforcers in Trinidad and Tobago – the police commissioner and the deputy commissioner of the national police force – were Canadians.[111] In 2011, the level of violence in the country was such that a state of emergency was declared;[112] extreme social inequality and the oligarchy's profound corruption were certainly among the root causes of this violence but were apparently not identified as such by the authorities. Another factor was undoubtedly the socially ruinous impact of the austerity measures required by the International Monetary Fund on the basis of erroneous data.[113] Today, the Trinidad and Tobago police force receives technical assistance from Canadians in managing the Police Complaints Authority,[114] and Canadian military personnel have been active since 1970 in training Trinidad and Tobago armed forces.[115]

Canada even interferes in the judicial institutions of Trinidad and Tobago, "showing its support of the government of Trinidad and Tobago in reforming the justice sector and making crime fighting a priority."[116] Today it is providing partial funding for the placement of a prosecutor from the United Kingdom within the office of the Trinidad and Tobago attorney general in order to bring about reforms in the areas of police investigations, effective use of witnesses, and the use of technology.[117]

In another notable episode, the public works and project management sector in Trinidad and Tobago was largely taken over by Canadian investor John Calder Hart, a financial manager who became so controversial that the bankruptcy of a company he headed was the object of a commission of inquiry (the Uff Commission) in 2008. Hart was on the board of the Urban Development Corporation of Trinidad and Tobago Limited (UDeCOTT) from the time it was established in 1994 and became its executive chairman in 2006. UDeCOTT was awarded government contracts to build a large-scale "financial and commercial centre" in the capital, Port of Spain, to support "the continued regeneration of the city of San Fernando" and to ensure "the development of 13 major urban centres including Tobago."[118] Hart, a tycoon in Trinidad and Tobago, was president of the Home Mortgage Bank, Trinidad & Tobago Mortgage Finance, the National Insurance Board (NIB), and the National Insurance Property Development Company (NIPDEC).[119]

The collapse of UDeCOTT created an unprecedented financial scandal described by the Trinidadian government as a case of "historic negligence and civil fraud."[120] It was demonstrated that UDeCOTT directors consistently ignored internal monitoring reports, assigned huge contracts without tenders, and paid out large sums before the work was done or the goods delivered. Beginning in 2006, the corporation no longer even produced financial statements. Hundreds of millions of dollars were embezzled,[121] with Hart in some cases doing business with entities directed by members of his own family.[122] PricewaterhouseCoopers was manifestly indulgent to its client.[123] Afra Raymond, a profoundly knowledgeable observer of Trinidadian political life,[124] has this to say: "One thing which is clear from the Calder Hart episode is that one individual had control of a vast slice of State resources...He obviously enjoyed a tremendous level of confidence at the very highest levels of government. It is equally clear, from the Uff Report, that that confidence was woefully misplaced...Yes, that is the man who was in charge of our national savings and pensions. And yes, I will write it – He could not do such in Canada. I am saying that no single individual could properly discharge all those functions."[125] The Trinidad and Tobago minister of finance took time in his budget speech to attribute the scandal to the complete lack of regulation in the country: "Mr. Speaker, no coherent, co-ordinated planning or strategy for state enterprises exists...It is these loopholes in public accountability that resulted in the UDeCOTT scandal. This must never again happen in Trinidad and Tobago."[126] The crisis of confidence affecting the entire country led Hart to resign from his functions and leave Trinidad. He has now erased all reference to his murky past on his professional website, which focuses on his numerous alleged competencies,[127] although he claimed before the commission of inquiry that he "would not describe [him]self as an expert of anything."[128]

Another Canadian company has also derived considerable benefit from the total decay of the Trinidadian regime: Genivar, an urban planning and civil engineering firm. Not only did Genivar receive more than its share of juicy contracts with its partner of choice, UDeCOTT,[129] but it also signed many contracts with WASA, Trinidad's Water and Sewage Authority.[130] Through ignorance or cynicism, at the height of the UDeCOTT scandal, the Association of Consulting Engineers of Quebec gave Genivar and UDeCOTT a prize for revitalizing the Port of Spain seafront, asserting the prestige of a white elephant project that publicly embodied the flagrant reality of corruption.[131]

It would be naive to ask why a lively distrust of Canadians has developed on both islands. Canadians have long been everywhere,[132] and the zeal with which they manage Trinidad and Tobago's economy is a source of irritation. Bombardier, a Montreal-based multinational, offers to sell jets, while Vancouver-based Methanex extracts and exports methanol.[133] In October 2007, RBC acquired a local bank, the RBTT Financial Group, for $2.2 billion,[134] joining Scotiabank, already well entrenched,[135] and the CIBC. According to the Canadian government, "Canadian investments are concentrated in the petrochemical, oil, gas and financial sectors."[136]

▇ CANADA'S IMPERIAL GRIP ON THE CARIBBEAN

Canadian domination is not limited to Trinidad and Tobago. Throughout the British Caribbean, Canada's neo-colonial control leaves its mark in sometimes embarrassing ways. In Guyana, for example, where thirty-four Canadian mining companies are looking at promising deposits, the country's independence in terms of mining is somewhat hampered by "two Canadian educational and training institutions that are working with the Ministry of Natural Resources and the Environment and the Guyana Geology and Mines Commission to offer various courses through the Guyana Mining School and Training Centre Inc."[137]

Since 1960, Canada's Military Training Assistance Program (MTAP) has also led Canadian military personnel to oversee the armed forces of various Commonwealth countries. Canadian authorities do not even try to pretend that the goal is to support the development of the administration of poor countries. They state explicitly that "MTAP plays a key role in promoting Canadian defence and foreign policy interests worldwide among a selected group of developing non-NATO countries."[138] This means for Canada, among other things, the sale to Trinidad and Tobago of two long-range multi-mission aircraft, in accordance with an agreement signed in 2013 between Trinidad and Tobago's Ministry of National Security and the Canadian Commercial Corporation,[139] in the presence of Canadian prime minister Stephen Harper and his Trinidadian counterpart, Kamla Persad Bissessar. The audience was given many reasons to be dazzled: "In support of their shared desire to expand defence relations, the prime ministers welcomed the signature of a memorandum of understanding between the two nations to help Trinidad and Tobago take on a greater role to provide regional military capacity building training. Leaders were also pleased to announce the appointment of the first Canadian Defence Attaché accredited to Trinidad and Tobago."[140]

In the same vein, the Canadian Armed Forces supervise the technical development of the Antigua and Barbuda Defence Force.[141] In Barbados, a Canadian government website noted in 2013 that "the current and former chiefs of staff of the Barbados Defence Force are graduates of Canadian-supported military staff training colleges."[142] Canadian military personnel were also present in Jamaica until the early twenty-first century.[143] Still in the area of security, the four most senior police officers of Antigua and Barbuda were replaced by Canadians in March 2008,[144] which may remind us of previous episodes in Caribbean history: several times in the past, Ottawa has sent its army to the region to protect its economic interests, whether to Bermuda in the mid-1910s, St. Lucia from 1915 to 1919, the Bahamas, Jamaica, and again Bermuda in the 1940s, or Barbados in 1966.[145] In general, the goal has been to support regimes threatened either by foreign invasion or by the anger of their own population.

As for Canadian banks, they have created in the region a network of subsidiaries, branches, and trusts that make it impossible to ignore them. In John Grisham's novel about Caribbean tax havens, *The Firm*, all the banks in the Caribbean are Canadian. This is no accident: it is designed to ensure the plausibility of the setting, which includes "Quebecbanq" and the "Royal Bank of Montreal" in Georgetown and the "Ontario Bank" in Freeport.[146] Canadian financiers have long played a dominant role in the Caribbean,[147] to the point where the International Monetary Fund estimates that Canadian entities control 60 percent of the region's banking institutions.[148] According to *The Economist*, over $1 trillion is concentrated in the region without being related to any significant real economic activity.[149]

After the United States, the British Caribbean is the place where Canadian banks have the strongest representation.[150] Scotiabank has been the most constant representative of Canadian financial institutions in the region, with an unbroken record of maintaining institutions created in these jurisdictions.[151] Canadian financial institutions in general, however, are at home in Commonwealth countries. "Beyond language, colonial ties and shared Commonwealth membership imply similar governmental and legal structures which make for a familiar environment for banks. Indeed, the most important operations of RBC, Scotiabank, and CIBC are all located in countries where these ties are shared, namely, the Bahamas, Jamaica, Trinidad and Tobago and Barbados."[152] RBC expressed this clearly in 1965 when it was extending its operations in the Caribbean: "As an adjunct to our business in the Caribbean area, we operate trust companies in Jamaica, Trinidad, Barbados and British Guiana, and since so much of the trust business in these areas is related to and patterned after the British system, we have during the past year established The Royal Bank of Canada Trust Corporation Limited in London."[153] Present in North America, dominant in Caribbean offshore jurisdictions, and connected to the City of London, Canadian banks have established an exclusive financial triangle. Setting up in highly permissive states is also a way for the banks themselves to avoid paying taxes: in 2010, for example, the CIBC congratulated itself on having saved over $820 million in taxes thanks to its subsidiaries in tax havens.[154]

In the Caribbean, the interests of Canadian actors converge completely. As *The Economist* remarked in 2008, "Today, Canadian firms make chemicals in Trinidad and drill for natural gas offshore, mine nickel in Cuba and gold in Suriname, seek oil off Guyana and run cable television in the Bahamas and Jamaica. A tax treaty with Canada underpins offshore finance in Barbados. Several thousand migrants move north each year, mainly to Toronto."[155] In the energy sector, Canadian firms such as Canadian International Power, Emera, and Fortis are present, the first in Barbados, the second in St. Lucia, and the third in Belize and the Turks and Caicos Islands.[156]

This tentacular development also makes it possible to create sets of properties that bank secrecy makes impenetrable for any foreign investigator.

> Laddering deepens the secrecy, and the complexity. A Mexican drug dealer may have $20 million, say, in a Panama bank account. The account is not in his name but is instead under a trust set up in the Bahamas. The trustees may live in Guernsey, and the trust beneficiary could be a Wyoming corporation. Even if you can find the names of that company's directors, and even get photocopies of their passports – that gets you no closer: these directors will be professional nominees to the next rung of the ladder through a company lawyer, who is prevented by attorney-client privilege from giving out any details. Even if you break through *that* barrier you find that the corporation is held by a Turks and Caicos trust with a flee clause: the moment an enquiry is detected, the structure flits to another secrecy jurisdiction.[157]

The funds managed by Maples, the offshore law firm, pour in from New York or London without having to comply with the regulatory framework of the country they come from. This is why "the fund jurisdiction is not the place where the actions occur; that is usually in London or New York or São Paulo; not Cayman or BVI."[158] Following the "holistic" approach[159] advocated by the law firm, "ultimately, the Cayman Islands fund structure has been set up to have global appeal,"[160] also known as "universal appeal." The purity of the stratagem consists in its being usable everywhere, while social responsibility exists nowhere.

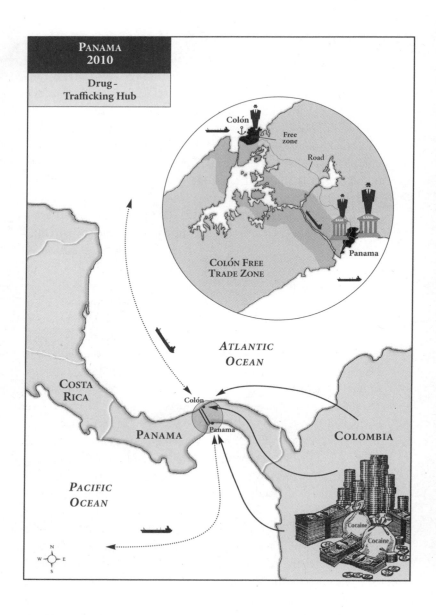

PANAMA

DRUG-TRAFFICKING HUB

In which the Canadian government signs a free-trade agreement
to the benefit of money launderers in Latin America

The best illustration of Canada's accommodating attitude to
tax havens is the free-trade agreement that Ottawa negotiated
and signed with Panama in 2010.[1] Panama is to tax havens what
a department store is to a specialized boutique. Panama is a huge
laissez-faire jurisdiction willing to compromise itself in every area
of activity. The country, with a population of almost four million
people and a local currency pegged to the American dollar, is home
to no fewer than thirty-six international banks[2] and several dozen
informal financial institutions,[3] to the point where Panama City's
Obarrio financial neighbourhood can be compared with Zurich.[4]
Over 80 percent of Panama's economy derives from its offshore
activities.[5] The country allows powerful industrial and financial mag-
nates to open anonymous accounts from a distance, to create offshore
companies, and to establish trusts and holding companies operating
in complete anonymity, since Panama will not lift bank secrecy
unless legal proceedings are already under way. As in other jurisdictions, to get Panama's co-operation, investigators must already
have the information they want to confirm; and so, in fact, Panama
guarantees impunity to all those that it welcomes with open arms.

Panama has no central bank in the usual sense of the word,[6]
and capital goes in and out without any form of supervision. The
laws on bank secrecy are based on the Swiss precedent of 1934:[7] it is
a criminal offence for a bank's agent to disclose financial information
to any foreign authority whatsoever.[8] Panamanian company law is so
lenient that it is ludicrous. Directors may reside anywhere and meet
anywhere they like in the world, not necessarily in Panama; they are

elected by the company's shareholders, but need not be shareholders themselves. A Panamanian company is not required to have its head office in Panama; all it needs is one resident agent, usually a lawyer.[9] There are no requirements as to the nationality of economic actors, and the initial outlay needed to start up a business is laughably small. In addition, "if the company has no activities within the Republic of Panama, it does not have to produce any kind of tax return or financial statement."[10] For non-resident corporations, income from sources in other countries is, of course, not taxed in any way.[11] The origins of this set of laws are less than glorious. Tax lawyer Édouard Chambost notes that the Panamanian corporation law "is based on the Delaware Corporation Law of 1927, and to keep this law as stable as possible, the Republic of Panama has not adopted any of the changes that Delaware has made to this law since 1927."[12] In Panama, a bank may be established as easily as an insurance company and, in the latter case, "the solvency ratio must be between 5 percent and 35 percent"[13] – here again there are no taxes. Finally, business corporations established under Panamanian law cannot be seized by any investigator. These provisions cause business people to chortle and brokers to proliferate. As advertised by one firm specializing in relocating assets and companies: "For Panama bank secrecy to truly be used effectively, an anonymous corporation is essential. We provide nominee directors for the corporation, so your name is not actually registered in the government's documents and therefore cannot be traced back to you in the event that your country realizes that you are holding your funds outside of the country. The corporation is controlled via bearer shares, which are registered by number and not by name, which is how you are able to control it without divulging personal information."[14] Such firms are particularly eloquent in their praise for the flexibility of Panamanian law.

Business is flourishing in Panama. Its International Banking Centre, established in 1970, held assets of over US$97 billion at the end of 2013.[15] In 2009, thirty Panamanian banks were able to dedicate themselves exclusively to offshore activities.[16] In all, there are over 120 banks in the IBC.[17] Grégoire Duhamel, a tax expert who is fond of tax havens, notes enthusiastically that "Panama's reputation as a tax haven is well deserved"[18] and observes that all banks offer numbered accounts.[19] Canadian banks are latecomers in Panama and are less present than in other Caribbean countries, but are still important institutions. According to Michel Planque, one-time head of BusinessFrance's economic mission to Central America and the Caribbean, "The Canadian Scotiabank is developing well"[20] and "is one of the six largest foreign banks in the country."[21]

At the end of the twentieth century, Panama did not yet owe its reputation throughout the world to the fact that it provided such a wide range of services. It was known, rather, for its unofficial title as the foremost country for laundering the proceeds of drug trafficking. Its free zone and free port were notorious hubs: capital circulated freely in the former and drugs in the latter. Patrice Meyzonnier, chief commissioner at the central directorate of the French investigative police, clearly believes he is stating the obvious when he describes Panama as "a narcotrafficking state and one, along with the Cayman Islands, that launders a large part of the world's dirty money."[22] Meyzonnier adds: "Panama is a crossroads between South and North, between Colombia and the United States."[23] Canada, of course, is part of this story: the Mexican-Colombian and Jamaican mafias, which are very active in Canada,[24] use Panama to transfer cocaine to the Canadian market.[25] This is what Italian mafia expert Antonio Nicaso was referring to in 1994 when he described Canada as a "Mob haven."[26]

▉ COLÓN FREE ZONE

The Colón free zone (*Zona Libre de Colón*) is at the centre of Panamanian economic activity. According to official sources, its imports and exports surpass $5 billion a year,[27] and in recent years between 2,000 and 3,000 corporations have been established in the free zone.[28] Michel Planque estimates that two-thirds of the country's total exchanges go through this area,[29] which provides companies with significant benefits: exemption from customs duties and value-added taxes, as well as various other taxes, including municipal taxes and taxes on dividends and shares; on payments made abroad; on income; on corporations; and on capital.[30] At most, companies are required to pay export duties, whose rate varies between 2.5 percent and 8.5 percent when their gains are higher than $100,000.[31]

Created in 1948 at the Atlantic entrance of the Panama Canal, the free zone is adjacent to three freight ports and container terminals. The country, in which about 8,600 ships are registered, manages the world's largest fleet of flags of convenience. By comparison, the United States registers about 3,400 vessels and China a little more than 3,700.[32] It costs $1,500 every two years to register a ship, to which derisory amounts of duties and taxes may be added, and virtually all ships are accepted. "In exchange for a few initial hassles, you are free to sail to the four corners of the world and hire seamen without having to fill out interminable papers or pay unbearable French charges."[33] In other words, thanks to Panama, anyone can ignore the laws of all other countries.[34]

The Colón zone of lawlessness "itself faces a Colombian zone without law or police enforcement."[35] In addition, a railway and a four-lane highway connect Colón to the capital, Panama City, some fifty kilometres (more than thirty miles) away. The free zone thus finds itself close to some ninety banks[36] whose word is law, and owes its success to its physical links to both maritime transportation centres and offshore finance.[37] These advantages make it the world's second hub for goods after Hong Kong.[38] The free zone's sales figures doubled between 1990 and 1995,[39] reaching $5 billion, then rose to an average of $13 billion a year between 2005 and 2010.[40] During this period, between 2,000 and 2,500 companies operated in the 500-hectare (1,200-acre) free zone,[41] which attracts 250,000 customers and visitors a year.[42]

Michel Planque, author of a handbook on investing in the region, politely describes the free zone as a "regional logistic platform for importing consumer goods and re-exporting them to Latin America and the Caribbean."[43] These "goods," when they leave Colón, are sent to more distant countries such as Canada. Unfortunately, this purely formal description is not in tune with reality. Although Planque completely accepts the free market model, even he knows that Panama has a "deficient judicial system," suffers from "political racketeering" and "corruption in the public sphere," and is an "unco-operative country in terms of taxes."[44] These appear to be well-established facts. Mladan Dinkić, governor of the National Bank of Serbia from 2000 to 2003, has stated that Slobodan Milosevic's regime channelled $6 million to Panama using accounting ploys in the import-export sector.[45] The criminal nature of the Colón economy is obvious: it is where money launderers go to launder their capital in hotels, dummy shopping centres, or fictitious rental units. Gold smuggling is a major business, and Patrice Meyzonnier also remarks that "business corporations, created through the intermediary of shady law firms, have a life span of a few hours – and you can acquire citizenship in a few hours, too."[46]

Marie-Christine Dupuis-Danon, former anti-money-laundering adviser for the United Nations Office on Drugs and Crime, describes Panama as "a key transit country" for narcotics sent from the Caribbean to North America, while in financial terms, the Colón free zone is "a regional laundering centre of the first order" when the time comes to incorporate the proceeds of this activity into the real economy.[47] Dupuis-Danon also notes that given the absence of customs duties, "authorities are not in a position to enforce regulations prevailing in the rest of the country, in particular the requirement to declare any cash entry greater than $10,000."[48]

In Panama City's Obarrio district, where the banks are located, some financial institutions are willing, in exchange for a commission, to overtly "lend" drug traffickers the money that these drug traffickers secretly bring. The terms and schedule of the "loan" are determined by the jurisdiction where the loan is authorized.[49] Panama City banks have also mastered the art of laundering assets by breaking them up into multiple postal money orders.[50] Jean-Claude Grimal, a sociologist who has written a book on globalization as it is embodied in the drug trade, explains that "Panama's dubious banks" and others known to be involved in the drug trade confer legitimacy on drug money by transferring it from one bank to another through a process, akin to going through the locks of a canal, in which higher and higher security standards apply.[51]

A number of Western drug traffickers also launder their money through Italian banks specializing in the gold trade. They buy gold ingots from these banks and immediately sell them to "investors" in Panama; the funds are then sent through legal channels to their Colombian suppliers. This system provided for the laundering of hundreds of millions of dollars in the mid-1990s.[52] Between 1985 and 1989, the Colombian Medellín cartel laundered billions of dollars by using a network of jewellery stores in the United States to transfer drug money to Uruguay. There, gold ingots "whose actual content was 90% lead" were immediately bought and resold, and the funds were deposited in Uruguay under the guise of proceeds from legal activities in the jewellery sector. Then "some of the money was sent to an account opened in Panama in a branch of a Colombian bank."[53]

These examples taken from the research carried out by Dupuis-Danon and Grimal all indicate the existence of close connections between Panama and other tax havens. "Recycling drug money often involves the planet's many tax havens... These bank havens provide traffickers with multiple benefits: absolute bank and commercial secrecy, an efficient communications network, free movement of capital, all types of transaction in any currency, freedom from taxes, technical assistance for incorporation uncomplicated by monitoring and with a minimum of formalities."[54] Many smuggling activities involve actors who transfer funds from Switzerland to Panama with the greatest of ease. Examples of this are the illicit marijuana and coffee trade organized by the Nasser family in the 1980s,[55] or, during the same period, the obscure operations carried out by Amjad Awan from Luxembourg to Panama via Switzerland and London.[56]

According to McGill University criminologist R. T. Naylor, Panama consolidated its position as a money-laundering hub in the early 1980s when political attention was focused on the Bahamas and Cayman Islands. According to Naylor, the tax agreement signed by Panama and Switzerland in the 1970s helped Panama benefit for decades – until 2011, in fact – from bank secrecy in cases of investigations launched by the United States. "Panama responded by discovering that its bank regulator did not have the legal power to make examinations."[57]

At the turn of the millennium, laundering began to be carried out more frequently in the financial sector through fraudulent stock market speculation rather than in the real economy. Criminal "investors" took control of small financial corporations and artificially caused the value of shares in companies they owned to rise by transferring them from one offshore fund to another at increased prices until traditional investors were attracted and eventually acquired expensive shares that were in fact of little value. The New York Stock Exchange took a beating in this respect.[58] Jean-Claude Grimal concludes: "This observation, shared by most experts, does not seem to lead to discussion or reflection on the part of politicians, although the financial, economic and political stakes are high."[59] Similarly, French judge Jean de Maillard believes that the gross criminal product is so large that criminal activities are, in fact, completely incorporated into the globalized economy.[60] Panama is one of the key locations observing the alliance between offshore states and organized crime.

THE CONSEQUENCES OF FREE TRADE WITH PANAMA

In signing a free-trade agreement with Panama, Canada is voluntarily opening its territory to the forces that use the Panamanian state to launder criminal funds.[61] Bill C-24, by which the Canadian Parliament ratified this agreement, is ingenuously intended to "promote, through the expansion of reciprocal trade, the harmonious development of the economic relations between Canada and the Republic of Panama." The goal is "to foster, in both countries, the advancement of economic activity" and "substantially increase investment opportunities in Canada and the Republic of Panama." The business poetry inflicted on us by the rhetoric of these treaties defines as *harmony* the "removal of barriers to trade"[62] between a state that is a drug-trafficking host and another that still presents itself as embodying the rule of law. "Barriers to trade," in this law, must be understood as including any preferential Canadian law and any handicap the Canadian government might inflict on a Panamanian so-called investor, despite all the reasons we have for believing that the goal of such investors when they knock on our door will be to launder millions of dollars generated by the narcotics trade.

The harmony cherished by Canadian lawmakers is in fact a product of cognitive dissonance. Through this free-trade agreement, Canada facilitates everything it claims elsewhere to be fighting: corruption of the political class, economic criminality, drug trafficking. Marie-Christine Dupuis-Danon makes this point, arguing that free trade facilitates the transportation of drugs. According to her, the North American Free Trade Agreement (NAFTA) has facilitated convoys of drug deliveries from Mexico to Canada via the United States: "Road transport is the method most often used, with an increasing use of commercial trucks whose border crossings are easier now that NAFTA has been signed."[63] In the case of free trade between Canada and Panama, Dupuis-Danon's writings already give us reason to anticipate that import-export companies controlled by organized crime will soon be involved in planning the transportation of drugs from Colón to various Canadian ports. As she explains, "For criminals, taking control of import-export companies provides three benefits: it gives them logistic support for potential imports of narcotics hidden among lawful goods, they can more easily bring funds back home using the same channel, and they can establish a more complex laundering system by falsifying accounting and commercial documents."[64]

Alain Delpirou and Eduardo Mackenzie, a geographer specializing in drug trafficking and a legal expert respectively, also believe that the free-trade agreement between Canada, the United States, and Mexico has favoured the contraband activities of organized crime. "In the early 1990s, the drug barons in Medellín and Cali thought that the upcoming signing of the North American Free Trade Agreement (NAFTA) between Mexico, Canada and the United States would provide them with access to a huge market in North America."[65] The authors end with the following understatement: "To tell the truth, they were not entirely wrong." NAFTA provides for "the immediate elimination of customs duties on a very wide range of products."[66] As duties and monitoring decreased and the volume of activity rose, illicit activities became easier to conceal.

OFFSHORING THE WORLD

Neo-liberals like to imply that free-trade agreements will solve, rather than fuel, problems of financial crime. Michel Planque is an example: he notices that Panama has problems of "governance" and "corruption," but in his view these occur "despite" the free-trade agreements that Panama has signed. What prejudice in favour of free trade enables him to use the word *despite*? Planque recognizes that the "corruption in the wider sense" that prevails in political circles is first and foremost "strongly rooted in business circles."[67] These are precisely the circles that are given a free hand through free-trade agreements, and their members are the investors whose position is strengthened by the Canada-Panama free-trade agreement.

Economic *globalization*, which is actually the *offshorization* of states throughout the world, facilitates money laundering in every possible way. This is the conclusion we reach after reading Jean-Claude Grimal's summary of the problem: "The development of commodity exchanges over the past few years will make [narcotics] trafficking easier. With thousands of airplanes and container ships and millions of trucks moving through the world every day, traffickers have countless possibilities. Eliminating or reducing customs controls in free-trade zones is beneficial for trafficking illegal goods. In the same way, circulation between financial markets, such as the free movement of capital from an offshore bank in a tax haven to a respectable American or Swiss bank, makes it easier to recycle drug profits and bring them into the real economy."[68]

While the Canada-Panama free-trade agreement will support tax flight from Canada by making it look like legitimate investment, it will not provide similar benefits to the Panamanian population, for Panama itself experiences tax evasion. At least $1 billion is lost to it every year through tax flight and non-payment of taxes.[69] In addition, the agreement is intended to bring about a significant reduction in customs duties, which, in a poor country like Panama, may have serious consequences: it will deprive of valuable revenue a government that is already lacking in resources and careless of its population. And finally, although this agreement is draped in environmental pretensions – the text is dotted with expressions such as "sustainable development," which, however, are not binding in any way – it will encourage Canadian mining companies to carry out controversial and highly polluting projects, including open-pit mining projects such as the Molejón gold mine operated by Petaquilla Minerals.[70]

THE DEAFNESS OF CANADIAN MEMBERS OF PARLIAMENT

Under the Canada-Panama free-trade agreement, Panamanian corporations established in Canada will be in a position to shape Canadian laws. Chapters 9 and 10 of the agreement reproduce substantial elements of NAFTA's oft-criticized Chapter 11, which allows a company to sue a government if the government's regulations supposedly create barriers to trade. According to Todd Tucker of Public Citizen, who testified in front of the Canadian Parliament's Standing Committee on International Trade on November 17, 2010, "there are hundreds of thousands of U.S., Chinese, Cayman, and even Canadian corporations that can attack Canadian regulations by using aggressive nationality planning through their Panamanian subsidiaries."[71] Ben Beachy, research director for Public Citizen's Global Trade Watch, offered similar testimony when he appeared before a Canadian Senate committee on December 6, 2012: "The Canada-Panama Trade Agreement would make it more difficult for Canadian policymakers to curb Panama-based tax evasion. Should Canada, for example, try to limit Canadian firms from transferring money to Panama-based subsidiaries deemed to be shell corporations established for tax evasion, the policy could be challenged as a violation of Article 9.10 of the pact, which says, 'Each party shall permit transfers related to a covered investment to be made freely and without delay into and out of its territory.'"[72] There are already precedents for this under NAFTA, such as the case of Lone Pine, the Alberta natural gas company that has gone through its Delaware subsidiary to challenge Quebec's ban on shale gas fracking under NAFTA's Chapter 11.[73]

Even the United States, closely connected to Panama throughout its history, blows hot and cold in relation to the country. U.S. strategic interests, colossal in scale, sometimes lead to decisions that are appalling even in fiscal terms. "In 2003, in partnership with the World Bank's International Finance Corporation, the Panamanian government planned to make the American Howard military base into a special economic zone with high-tech telecommunications and logistics facilities. Tax breaks are to be granted to companies that settle there."[74] In 2011, however, the United States obtained for its affairs a complete and definitive elimination of Panamanian bank secrecy. "The 2011 agreement between the U.S. and Panama effectively gives the U.S. government carte blanche over any information it wants from Panamanian bank accounts. The agreement authorizes 'fishing expeditions,' and it requires Panamanian authorities to cooperate with U.S. investigations even when the charges are not criminal in nature or violate Panamanian law."[75]

That same year, Canada ratified its free-trade agreement with Panama.

UNDER SIEGE

A SYSTEM OF VOLUNTARY BLINDNESS

In which the fight against tax havens is found
to be rooted in the public conscience

Not only has Canada been a pioneer in creating Caribbean tax havens, but it is also now in the process of becoming an object manipulated by its own creatures. Despite the problem's astonishing nature and massive scale, until recently dead silence has been the rule as to the facts of the case. Ministers and MPs, if they are aware of the issue, have rarely mentioned it, and government departments "qualified" to deal with the matter have remained myopic. Few "experts" have viewed it in any other terms than the threadbare clichés of liberal thought, and it has taken years for a small number of intellectuals and journalists to develop an interest in it. Today, at last, the population is in a position to address this issue in a straightforward way. Why has it taken so long?

▨ BEFUDDLED MINISTRIES

Although tax havens have been receiving tax evaders' money for decades, governments in Canada have not even attempted to calculate the cost to the public purse. While government departments have ways of assessing tax evasion, these methods do not allow them to look at tax havens. "Tax Evasion in Quebec,"[1] the 2005 issue of a periodical published by the Quebec Ministry of Finance, is a perfect illustration of the state's failure to choose theoretical tools that would enable it to deal with the offshore problem. When the ministry scrutinizes the underground economy, abusive tax deduction claims, or taxpayers' illicit operations, its methods lead it to focus exclusively on small and medium-sized actors.

The literature favoured by the Quebec ministry is often produced by researchers working for the federal Department of Finance, federal agencies such as Statistics Canada, or associations of economists, law-yers, accountants, and other tax professionals, some of which receive corporate funding.[2] And since tax havens were taboo for many years in Ottawa as well as Quebec, the Quebec ministry's strategies to fight tax fraud have been based on a list of stereotyped targets such as local industry, small construction sites, or small restaurant owners. In the literature consulted by officials, tax fraud is viewed as identical to low-level cheating and is confined to something known as the "underground economy." However, this underground economy is only one aspect of the far wider issue of tax evasion. Relying exclusively on this concept, the ministry reverses the relationship between the parts and the whole: it seems to believe that tax evasion is a subcategory of the underground economy rather than vice versa. Restricting itself to data arising from transactions within the domestic economy, it shows no interest in more ambitious methods that would produce wider results.[3]

The Quebec ministry's system is also at fault when it assesses the losses to the treasury caused by tax fraud. The indicator on which it relies is the GDP (gross domestic product), but the only kind of fraud revealed by this indicator is small-scale fraud involving "goods and services sold on the markets"[4] within the domestic economy.[5] In other words, the unrecorded economy approach ignores manipu-lations carried out abroad, focusing only on the domestic market. According to Statistics Canada analyst Gylliane Gervais, quoted in the Quebec ministry study, it is therefore useless to rely on GDP data to assess tax evasion as a whole. As she explains, the purpose of her study is exclusively to ascertain "whether or not particular trans-actions are captured in GDP, and if any are missing, how much they can possibly amount to"[6] – only these missing transactions constitute the underground economy, defined for Gervais's purposes as "*legal economic production hidden from the authorities in order to avoid taxes and regulations.*"[7] But "*a measure of the size of the underground economy, however defined, is not a comprehensive measurement of tax evasion* and should never be interpreted as such."[8] The GDP is strictly an assessment of the value of domestic transactions according to the econometric considerations prevailing in a market economy.[9] The Quebec ministry, however, chooses to use GDP data to assess tax evasion, even though its own sources tell it not to do so.

One reason why it is so hazardous to attempt to speculate on the social costs related to tax evasion on the basis of GDP estimates is that these estimates fail to include many crucial transactions, including – surprise, surprise! – those carried out either by shareholders or by multinational corporations: "Capital gains are another type of income which is taxable, but outside the scope of GDP because they do not arise out of current production. Undeclared capital gains would come under the scrutiny of the tax authorities, but they are not part of underground production."[10] Gervais also states that "conceptual differences preclude a comparison of 'national accounts' profits and 'taxation' profits, themselves different from 'book' profits, especially for the financial sector."[11] In other words, only the "underground economy" – that is, the sale of goods and services in the domestic market "on which taxes have purposely not been paid"[12] – is included in GDP estimates.

The methodology involving the use of GDP data is blind to a wide range of accounting operations that ought to be of interest to tax authorities. Subordinating the huge issue of tax evasion to the small issue of the underground economy, the government does not attempt, for example, to calculate how much it loses by allowing the practice of transfer pricing. As Gervais remarks, "Transfer pricing is legal and does not constitute an instance of underground production."[13] She confirms that it is not part of Statistics Canada's job to study such operations,[14] and it would therefore be a mistake to confuse *underground economy* and *tax evasion*. Gervais puts things in perspective when she explains that it is "misleading to employ the two expressions interchangeably. If all underground (and illegal) production entails tax evasion in one form or another, tax evasion is not limited to domestic economic production. Capital gains, income earned abroad and cross-border purchases which are undeclared have nothing to do with the underground 'economy.'"[15] These funds account for a significant share of tax evasion, and a number of experts from the federal government and other institutions continue to assert this view.[16]

▪ STATISTICS AND CLASS CONSCIOUSNESS

The methodological weaknesses leading tax authorities to carry out social profiling with an exclusive focus on petty cheaters[17] give rise to a number of problems. Since officials can only grasp categories to which their theoretical model is responsive, they pay most attention to the artisans and small business owners whom they see as having a propensity to fraud.[18]

Meanwhile, anyone practising fraud on a large scale is automatically proven innocent by the government's preferred theoretical models. Tax experts David Giles and Lindsay Tedds, for example, exclude large corporations from their study of tax fraud as a matter of principle. According to their strictly limited legal point of view, these firms "are not usually 'evading' taxes in the sense of failing to meet their legal obligations; they are simply seeking, rationally and within the law, to minimize taxes as a cost of doing business."[19] For Giles and Tedds, the idea that "'big corporations evade taxes'" is a cliché, to be handled with scare quotes: when the common people take it up, this simply shows their ignorance of the intricacies of the law. Whatever is done by large corporations is not part of the underground economy as theoretically defined, and arguing about their tax strategies is a matter of legal quibbling.[20] The issue of tax havens is not so much censored by the government's theoretical model as reduced without further analysis to the level of an indisputable economic "fact." The use of tax havens by corporations is not a problem, precisely because the government has legalized this use even though it clearly violates the spirit of the law. "Corporations may minimize their profits for tax purposes, but normally do so by using the tax laws to their best advantage: the situation here is one of tax avoidance rather than tax evasion."[21] For Gylliane Gervais, current laws enable corporations and the wealthy to avoid illegality: privileged actors form a class that is in a position to stay clear of low-level trickery.

The stereotype that fraud is practised only by small businesses, an idea well rooted in conventional thinking on tax evasion,[22] has come to be endorsed by researchers. When Gylliane Gervais focuses on a problem, she begins by excluding major corporations: "Let us consider the example of household furniture retailing and assume for simplicity that there is no wholesale furniture retailing."[23] This is quite a simplification. The reality principle would require us to consider the fact that wholesale merchants do exist – at this point, they might even be exercising a quasi-monopoly. The government's restricted thinking enables it to pay attention to small retailers and ignore everyone else. Gervais even specifies that large corporations do not practise this type of fraud because it would be impossible for them to coordinate, on a large scale, the minor concealments (skimming) carried out by small businesses[24] – as if the methods of multinationals had to resemble those of petty crooks. Since Statistics Canada does not have access to the audits conducted by tax authorities,[25] Gervais later simply reverts to the issue of the GST that is not remitted by small retailers.

The government's methodological premises are designed to confirm its less-than-convincing intellectual position. The ministry acknowledges that it tries to detect tax fraud by targeting categories of taxpayers not according to their ability to commit fraud, but according to the number of tax dodgers caught ... by the use of these targeting methods. On the basis of this circular reasoning, sociological profiles are established.[26] Because the ministry has not found evidence of a certain number of offences committed by large corporations or high-level financiers, it excludes them from its field of vision and priorities, using the following charmingly ingenuous piece of reasoning: "large businesses are proportionally less likely to conceal income than small ones are."[27] For the government, the theoretical definition of tax evasion is derived from the (highly relative) efficiency of its methods of recovery.[28]

■ "ABUSIVE TAX PLANNING," OR THE TRIUMPH OF EUPHEMISM

The Quebec government showed its mettle in 2009. In January, it produced a timid working paper; in October 2009 and February 2010, this was followed by two bulletins from the finance ministry dealing with "aggressive tax planning." The two bulletins described minimal requirements for information disclosure,[29] while the working paper presented thoughts on the way some taxpayers, including businesses, comply with the letter but abuse the spirit of the law.[30] The ministry was even daring enough to mention extraterritorial operations: "This need among businesses [to control their tax costs] in turn fostered the expansion of firms of tax intermediaries – lawyers, accountants, investment banks, in particular – and the development among the latter of an advanced knowledge of various tax regimes as well as sophisticated expertise for integrated management of their clients' tax situation on a global basis."[31] The document also stated that tax consulting services fuel "the appetite of taxpayers to further reduce their tax costs" and foster the development of abusive tax planning.[32] Although the ministry's experts do not go any further in analyzing the flight of money toward tax havens, their document does open the possibility of considering not only illegal tax evasion but also illegitimate tax avoidance, and looking for ways of adopting legislative and legal measures to penalize it. Suddenly, wealthy or powerful actors are targeted – although with far less sociological detail than when hairdressers, craftspeople, self-employed people, or restaurant owners are under discussion. "Large businesses" are mentioned, though once again the ministry suspects them only of carrying out manoeuvres resembling the simple lies of small-time cheaters, since this is the only type of fraud of which it is aware.[33] Nor do Quebec tax authorities seem interested in taking a closer look at corporate executives who receive shares in lieu of salary and are thus able to avoid taxes on half their income.[34] The ministry's insignificant goals are a true reflection of its narrow mindset: "these amendments on Quebec's public finances" are expected to bring in "tens of millions of dollars."[35] Quebec's tax recovery goals for Revenu Québec have steadily increased in recent years, from $1,669 million in 2006–2007 to $3,866 million in 2013–2014.[36] These anticipated recoveries are essentially concentrated in the category of known tax cheaters; that is, the construction industry, the restaurant industry, and tobacco sales.[37] And in fact, of the $403 million actually recovered in the first quarter of 2013, only $86 million was related to money that had been moved outside the country.[38] If a mere tightening of controls over a few sectors of the shadow economy leads to such results, we can only imagine how much money the tax revenue agency might recover by working harder to fight abusive tax planning and the use of tax havens.

However, the ministry appears seriously inhibited when the time comes to locate the problem at the extraterritorial level. In official circles, the term *aggressive fiscal planning* serves to attenuate criticism of tax frauds carried out by rich people, while *shadow economy* or *underground economy* are words for the illicit activities of poor people. The use of hackneyed turns of speech is a way of not saying anything harsh about privileged groups that benefit from tax havens or about the accommodating jurisdictions themselves. When the Quebec ministry, for example, decides to tackle the issue of fraud carried out through trust funds, it appears to be interested solely in bookkeeping tactics used at the national level. Thus, bizarrely, its 2009 working document focuses on "interprovincial ATP [aggressive tax planning] scheme[s],"[39] even though the problem of tax losses involving tax havens and family trusts or income trusts was already making headlines in 2006.[40] Only in 2013 did the Quebec government timidly dare to bring up tax havens as part of an advertising campaign[41] in which, like the federal government,[42] it finally mentioned the possibility of tighter monitoring of individuals making fraudulent use of them.[43]

IDEOLOGICAL UNDERPINNINGS

Many of the authors on which the Quebec Ministry of Finance relies are in fact completely opposed to the principle of using taxation to redistribute wealth. For example, three economists from the University of Alberta's Faculty of Business, Rolf Mirus, Roger S. Smith, and Vladimir Karoleff, suggest that Canada's "high tax rates," its "excessive and improper regulation," and the notorious incompetence of its "inefficient" government explain, although they may not justify, the underground economy.[44] According to them, "It is natural that individuals should wish to escape, and have a route of escape, from these 'oppressions.'"[45]

In a similar vein, an article by two economists, Friedrich Schneider and Dominik Enste, is essentially an argument against the flaws of the social security state and the tax burden that it implies – two factors that they see as directly causing the existence of the shadow economy. The authors mock collectivities that use punitive measures to try to stem the universal tide of tax evasion, instead of carrying out tax and social security reforms that would improve "the dynamics of the official economy."[46] In other words, studying the shadow economy is an opportunity to advance the idea that the taxes imposed on an "overburdened" population must be reduced.[47] Schneider and Enste produce a list of other factors that have contributed to the rise of the shadow economy, including social programs such as welfare or unemployment insurance that fail to provide incentives that would make beneficiaries work.[48] More relevantly, the authors note that the shadow economy makes the state's official indicators unreliable (on phenomena such as unemployment, the labour force, income, consumption, etc.) and that it discredits government policies.[49] They also identify political corruption as one of the criteria by which the shadow economy can be recognized.[50]

In a study also quoted by the Quebec ministry, Don Drummond and his colleagues from the federal Department of Finance use a more moderate tone, but they too mention rising taxes and quote a survey carried out by the *Financial Post* in 1994 indicating that Canadians take a critical view of a government believed to be "wasting resources."[51]

A document on the underground economy produced by the Quebec finance ministry in 1996 provides a timid answer to these ideological clichés while simultaneously treating them as credible, or even convincing, arguments.[52] The ministry's analysts grant that individuals and businesses may think that taxes are too high, public funds are poorly managed and collective agreements with unionized workers are too inflexible,[53] and that this leads them to accept tax evasion as a normal phenomenon.[54] The writers then limply recall the reasons justifying the existence of taxes and indicate that tax evasion prevents fiscal institutions from working properly and threatens their integrity. They delicately bring up the fact that the government does not always have "sufficient leeway" to reduce taxes, and that, in order to "provide the public with high quality services,"[55] the government must have tax revenues. They point out that the underground economy, which, as defined in 1996, includes unreported and criminal economic activities, has noxious effects: it leads to the coexistence of two price systems in the economy,[56] penalizes compliant individuals and businesses,[57] and provides businesses that practise tax fraud with an unfair competitive advantage.[58] From the point of view of public institutions, the underground economy also "undermines the credibility of the taxation system" and "encourages organized crime-related activity,"[59] in addition, of course, to causing losses of revenue for the government.[60] Unreported activities are said to damage the "bond of trust" between taxpayers and the government, jeopardizing a system based on self-assessment by the taxpayer.[61] An increase in fraud might even lead the government to become more coercive.[62] All in all, these government statements are a reminder that in order to work properly, a "liberal" economy based on the "free market" must still be supervised and regulated by an outside party – that is, the state.

This is as far as the ministry is willing to go.[63] It acts as if less orthodox studies did not exist, even though some have been highly visible. In 2005, for example, while the ministry was working on its major document on tax evasion, Quebec media were discussing a book called *Ces riches qui ne paient pas d'impôts*[64] (a title that translates as "Rich People Who Don't Pay Taxes"). This 2004 book by Harvard-trained tax specialist Brigitte Alepin challenges the basic assumptions of the orthodox approach. Alepin compiles examples of fraud, disguised fraud, legalized misdeeds, and tax avoidance contrary to the spirit of the law, all carried out by members of Canada's wealthy or ruling classes. The book addresses a number of exemplary, and often notorious, cases. Questioning the idea that tax fraud is chiefly associated with low-level cheating, Alepin focuses on the powerful classes: wealthy individuals, large businesses, and multinational corporations. Her book investigates the part played by this group in tax fraud, analyzing the obvious complicity of Canadian federal and provincial tax authorities, the co-operation displayed by lawmakers, and the indulgence of the judiciary with regard to this social category.[65] Alepin also illuminates other practices that public institutions ought to be monitoring: abusive use of charitable foundations (the Chagnon family is a notorious example)[66] or family foundations (the Bronfmans),[67] use of nominees as fronts (as in the Cinar affair),[68] and offshore operations.[69] Fortunately, Alepin has not been subjected to the kind of legal threat or lawsuit that is often brought by political actors intent on defending their fragile good name; others have not been as lucky.[70]

Other critical sources were available to the ministry on the issue of tax evasion in 2005. A year before the ministry published its study, McGill-Queen's University Press issued a new edition of a scholarly work by an internationally recognized McGill University criminologist. R. T. Naylor's voluminous *Wages of Crime* deals with the connections between international criminal finance and traffickers of the informal domestic market. The book's subtitle, *Black Markets, Illegal Finance, and the Underworld Economy*, indicated its relevance to issues of tax evasion.[71] Also appearing in 2004 was

Paul Martin et compagnies, our critical examination of tax havens in connection with the prime minister of Canada (translated in 2006 under the title *Paul Martin and Companies*).[72]

◼ A CORRUPT TAX COLLECTION AGENCY

There are other problems. For one thing, there is every reason to believe that the Canada Revenue Agency (CRA) itself faces the gangrene of corruption. Its Montreal offices appear to have been infiltrated by the mafia, and a number of businesses seem to have benefited from inside help in developing detailed plans for tax evasion without having to worry about inconveniently strict audits. A few incidents from this ongoing saga: according to an RCMP investigation undertaken in 2007 and widened in 2011, two CRA employees appear to have helped businesses send $1.7 million to tax havens.[73] In 2009, another case of alleged fraud involved construction companies belonging to the notorious Tony Accurso; CRA employees, of whom nine were later investigated, appear to have enabled these companies to reduce their taxable income by $4.5 million.[74] In 2007, under mysterious circumstances, Canadian tax authorities sent a cheque for close to $382,000 to Nick Rizzuto, a central figure of the Montreal mafia – this at a time when Rizzuto actually owed $1.5 million in back taxes.[75] Other sordid tales of a more petty nature have regularly been covered by the media over the past several years. An auditor ensures a lax audit in exchange for home renovations;[76] another demands a bribe from a restaurant owner.[77] In this context, there is perhaps nothing terribly surprising about the federal government's announcement, in 2013, that "it ha[d] convicted just 44 individuals of offshore tax cheating since 2006."[78]

A glance at Quebec tax authorities is hardly more inspiring. In October 2013, Revenu Québec fired Benoît Roberge, a former Montreal police officer who had been hired in March of the same year to head the agency's intelligence unit. Roberge was fired because he had been arrested on charges of selling information to criminal Hells Angels biker groups.[79] Since the Quebec Ministry of Revenue became an agency in 2011, a surprising number of positions have been filled by police officers in a professional body that should theoretically include more tax experts than representatives of law enforcement agencies. Police officers have been appointed to key positions: Yves Trudel, formerly of the Sûreté du Québec, was suddenly promoted to senior director of investigations and inspections;[80] Florent Gagné, who directed the Sûreté du Québec between 1998 and 2003, today chairs Revenu Québec's board of directors.[81] In 2012, the Quebec civil servants' union (SFPQ) deplored the new agency's "tense working climate" and "dubious hiring processes" that were sometimes akin to nepotism.[82] While the agency denies these allegations, the police presence in the institution is a matter of concern. In doing their job, police officers tend to develop connections with government representatives that are not always conducive to detailed probes. In any case, the climate at the agency worsened when members of the board eliminated jobs in order to balance the budget, shortly after having voted themselves bonuses of slightly over $1 million in 2011–2012.[83]

LOBBYISTS AND POWER

Canada's tax policies will also, in all likelihood, be affected for many years to come by the revolving door between political positions and banks. In 2006, for example, a former minister of the environment, Jim Prentice, became executive vice-president of the Canadian Imperial Bank of Commerce (CIBC). Michael Fortier, minister of international trade in 2008, was hired by the Royal Bank of Canada (RBC) in 2010 as vice-president of the board of RBC Capital Markets; before his appointment to the federal Cabinet, he had worked on Wall Street for Morgan Stanley and Credit Suisse. A Conservative MP, Andrew Saxton, is also a former employee of Credit Suisse. As branch director in the 1990s, he authorized "the transfer of $200,000 to Switzerland by a Canadian client so that the client might avoid paying income tax in Canada."[84] Tim O'Neill, chief economist and vice-president of the Bank of Montreal, is a close adviser of public policymakers and was hired by Ottawa to direct a review of the country's economic forecasting methods. In Quebec, financiers such as the Bank of Montreal's Jacques Ménard or Claude Castonguay, long-time president of the Laurentian Bank of Canada, were invited in the first decade of the twenty-first century to chair public commissions on health care issues.[85] And so on. The list, in fact, is endless.

Finance ministries prefer the ritualized stories of their designated experts to even the mildest criticism from independent thinkers. In Ottawa, the Finance Department has chosen to be supervised by the banking and industry lobby through the Advisory Panel on Canada's System of International Taxation[86] – a panel whose lack of objectivity was denounced by tax experts Brian Arnold and André Lareau as they asserted the independence of their profession.[87] R. T. Naylor mentions in passing, as an obvious fact, that banks are "the strongest business lobby in Canada."[88] History reminds us that banks and public policymakers have been acting in tandem for a very long time: in 1956, for example, the Bank of Nova Scotia's annual report described the bank's co-operation in the British Caribbean with the Canadian government's External Trade Service, representatives of provincial governments, railway companies, and local businessmen.[89]

In Quebec, when the finance minister, Alain Paquet, decided in 2012 to provide $350,000 in funding for a Centre of Expertise on Fighting Financial Crime, he asked Professor Messaoud Abda of the Faculty of Administration at the Université de Sherbrooke to direct the project[90]...in partnership with the CIBC Research Chair on Financial Integrity.[91] The CIBC appears to have been involved in many controversial affairs related to offshore management. According to economist Thierry Godefroy and legal expert Pierre Lascoumes, "The Canadian Imperial Bank of Commerce is known as the bank of many African dignitaries."[92] François-Xavier Verschave describes it as "the nefarious CIBC, favourite bank of African oil dictators,"[93] and it has often been mentioned by Verschave's highly trustworthy *Lettre du continent* in connection with unsavoury affairs.[94] In 1997, for example, the CIBC handled the transfer of $22 million from Geneva to the British Virgin Islands on behalf of Kourtas, a firm belonging at the time to Gabonese dictator Omar Bongo.[95]

The CIBC also played a key role in 1980s tax fraud trials held in the United States. In one such case, the U.S. Internal Revenue Service (IRS) argued that the CIBC had hurried to the rescue of a bank serving organized crime that was under pressure in the Bahamas in the 1970s.[96] Located in the Bahamas but directed from Chicago and Miami by corporate lawyers with ties to organized crime, the Castle Bank was involved in drug smuggling, financial fraud, forgery and use of forged documents, and financial operations to facilitate tax evasion.[97] When American tax authorities began to scrutinize the Castle Bank in 1972,[98] at a time when the Bahamas was contemplating independence, the institution made plans to duplicate its structures in the neighbouring Cayman Islands, ensuring it could move all its assets there at a moment's notice. The CIBC's contribution was to safeguard the Castle Bank's records.[99] The Castle Bank was later hunted down by the IRS when it enabled the producers of the highly successful movie *One Flew Over the Cuckoo's Nest* to hide the film's profits from tax authorities.[100] According to Alan Block, the CIBC "took over many Castle accounts when Castle had to fade from the Bahamian and the Caymanian scenes."[101] In the case presented by the IRS to a Colorado court, the Castle Bank and the CIBC are depicted as Siamese twins, and their joint manoeuvres are viewed as a tax evasion plan.[102] However, IRS legal proceedings against Castle were dropped under pressure from the CIA, which is thought to have used the Castle Bank as part of its anti-Castro operations.[103]

Closer to home, Échec aux paradis fiscaux, a Quebec anti-tax haven collective that brings together grassroots organizations and labour unions, has shown on the basis of CIBC annual reports that the bank's presence in accommodating jurisdictions enabled it to avoid $1.4 billion in taxes in Canada between 2007 and 2011; none of this was illegal.[104] Of interest to Quebecers is the fact that Charles Sirois, chairman of the CIBC board, is one of the founders of a right-wing provincial political party, the Coalition Avenir Québec (CAQ).

The accommodating jurisdictions in which the CIBC has dealings include the Bahamas, Barbados, the Cayman Islands, Jamaica, and Trinidad and Tobago. Perhaps we may hope that the CIBC Research Chair, as a partner of the Université de Sherbrooke's Centre of Expertise on Fighting Financial Crime, will provide it with empirical data on financial criminality to help the Centre "popularize Quebec's expertise in fighting financial criminality" and "increase the level of public confidence in Quebec institutions."[105]

▪ UNIVERSITY INC.: ADVISERS TO THE PRINCE

Professor Messaoud Abda's centre focusing on financial crime provides the state with an "expertise" that is undermined by a number of unsavoury allegiances. At the "annual colloquium on the prevention of financial fraud," organized by Professor Abda with one of his colleagues on March 23, 2012, at the Université de Sherbrooke,[106] the president of the Enterprise Center for Investment Training and Ethics, Louis L. Straney, explained to the audience that the causes of financial crime are chiefly "tribal." According to Straney, in many ghettoized communities, "tribes" of small investors tend to trust financial representatives strictly because they belong to the same clan, instead of turning to honest professional brokers that will sell them triple-A financial products (securities backed by subprime mortgages? Enron shares?). Straney provided a jumbled enumeration of swindlers from "ethnic" minorities, including Eddie Long and Ephrem Taylor II from Atlanta's New Birth Missionary Church, Weizhen Tang from Toronto's Chinese community, Henry Jones as a representative of born-again Christians, Salim Damji from British Columbia's Ismaili community, and Ronald Randolph, a member of the Afro-American community. Straney also included, in his "tribal" category, Earl Jones of the Montreal Anglophone community of Notre-Dame-de-Grâce, and Bernard Madoff, a member of New York's Fifth Avenue Synagogue "tribe." In this last, ludicrous example, the "tribal" factor is supposed to explain the influence of a man who was president of one of the largest stock exchanges in the world (NASDAQ) and had access to European business circles through his Luxembourg tax haven connections. The fact that such drivel can be presented in an academic setting demonstrates the intellectual bankruptcy of academics who have taken on the job of supporting our society's financial ruling class.

Tax experts provided most of the substance throughout the colloquium, since accountants and auditors had shown up for the purpose of showing their organizations' websites. The tax experts' presentations generally focused on ways for businesses to avoid harbouring agents likely to abuse them by committing fraud. "More than 75% of fraudulent activities involve employees,"[107] to quote the consulting firm associated with Michel Picard, a former professor at the Sherbrooke centre on fighting financial crime. An economic criminal is necessarily a dishonest employee, client, or financial representative; the organization itself would appear to be ontologically virtuous. Among colloquium participants, some presented themselves as the immune system of an economic order that does not pose any kind of problem in itself. Tax havens were mentioned by only one person, Professor Abda, the man in charge of the Centre of Expertise on Fighting Financial Crime. Abda's motto would appear to be "If you can't beat 'em, join 'em." His first premise was clearly ideological: capital needs "oxygen"; that is, it needs to be released from taxes and, in fact, from any constraint. His second premise was that money leaving Canada merely goes through the revolving door of tax havens before returning to Canada in a defiscalized state. He used the image of water going through the filter of a swimming pool: according to him, offshore banks are simply the pump that makes the water move.[108] Abda's proposed solution is to create, within Canada, a circuit that would allow financial capital to bypass taxes – that is, to establish in Canada an inner channel fulfilling the functions of a tax haven, as Delaware does in the United States. Since the world is a well-organized place, corporations will then have more capital available to them and will certainly create jobs.

The professor's smug theorizing collapses as soon as it is subject to analysis. Capital is already receiving plenty of oxygen; in fact, it is currently on nitrox. A study by sociologist Éric Pineault shows that in 2009, the liquid assets of major Canadian corporations amounted to five times the Quebec government's budget: $400 billion was stashed in corporate bank accounts, of which about one-third was held in foreign exchange. This is the famous capital that business is supposed to "need" in order to be able to "invest."[109] According to a Statistics Canada estimate, corporations had a cash hoard of $630 billion in the first quarter of 2014.[110] Corporations can access these reserve funds at any time to invest in the real economy, and their reserves have kept on growing as the Harper government has kept on reducing taxes on corporate capital.

Another argument against Professor Abda's rhetoric: capital invested offshore does not necessarily return in the same form. While the monetary mass might remain the same, nothing indicates that the same amounts are leaving and entering the country and that their time on the tax haven merry-go-round has no effect other than to defiscalize them. Abda, who is very well acquainted with the Swiss banking sector, actually cites a number of cases in which businesses use offshore trusts and foundations to conduct delicate operations that could not easily be carried out in conventional states.[111]

Academic experts play a useful role in blocking reasonable proposals to improve public finances. For example, as economic crisis follows on economic crisis and austerity budgets repeatedly call for user fees for public services, it might seem imperative to tax billionaires in a rational manner. Against this option, liberal ideology presents what it views as an unanswerable argument, claiming that rich people would choose exile if we were collectively hateful enough to ask them to pay their share. This is a persistent myth, recently expounded in Quebec by lawyer Paul Ryan. His book *Quand le fisc attaque,*[112] published in 2012, repeatedly warns that "it would be hard to ask the rich for more."[113] For him, "rich people" are taxpayers earning over $100,000 or $150,000 a year; other tax brackets beyond this limit would appear to be inconceivable. Academic writings are available to buttress Ryan's dubious assertions. A few years earlier, Luc Godbout from the Faculty of Administration of Université de Sherbrooke, along with two other academics, Pierre Fortin and Suzie Saint-Cerny, had argued that businesses today are paying their share of taxes in Quebec, even claiming that any argument to the contrary can be reduced to "myth" or "popular belief." These academic experts added that the corporate contribution cannot be assessed solely on the basis of tax rates: we should also take into consideration how benefits are defined and the evolution of tax deductions.

Jim Stanford is an economist who actually looked at the figures instead of just saying things like "it's more complicated than it looks." His conclusion is that tax deduction programs, and especially federal ones, have been structured for decades to benefit business: "Due to the impact of various deductions and loopholes, the effective tax actually paid by corporations ... is almost always lower than the statutory rate."[114] The picture painted by Godbout, Fortin, and Saint-Cerny is also highly adapted to the needs of corporate capital in that it makes no distinction between businesses according to size: a small company producing artisanal cheeses in Quebec's Beauce region is sociologically identical to a multinational pharmaceutical company. In addition, the only data presented are GDP figures, as if this were the only possible frame of reference.[115]

Marco Van Hess, a corporate income tax inspector in Belgium, has dedicated an entire book to taking these clichés apart.[116] At a time when states clearly need to get things back on an even keel, the alleged exile of wealthy individuals is often blown out of all proportion in relation to actual sociological data. Apostrophizing the rich, Van Hess highlights the economic potential of taxing large fortunes. "You already have a manor at Uccle, a villa at Zoutre, a chalet at Grans-Montana, a Maserati and a Porsche Cayenne in your garage, a mistress, and a yacht in Cannes. As a consumer, you have reached your horizon: your income, from now on, can only accrue in the form of accumulated capital. I'm sorry to tell you this so bluntly, but the fact is, you are living below your means ... Let us tax your assets. Your mountain of capital will be slightly reduced and we will be able to create thousands of jobs in health care, teaching, and social services."[117] These are exactly the reasons why income tax in the United States, between 1941 and 1964, was set at 91 percent for the wealthiest Americans.

Today, the idea that it is "populist" to promise to increase taxes paid by the rich is increasingly discredited.[118] Unsurprisingly, popular surveys are in favour of such measures,[119] but the people are not alone: even the highly conservative International Monetary Fund (IMF) believes that the Canadian government could increase the maximum tax rate of high-income Canadians by as much as 15 percent without causing capital flight.[120]

CHRONIC INCOMPETENCE

In the current ideological context, Canadian governments are at a loss when it comes to fighting a phenomenon that has become unmanageable. In the fall of 2013, the *Journal de Montréal* demonstrated for the umpteenth time how easy it is to open a bank account in Belize and enjoy tax-free assets while residing in Canada. In response, Nicolas Marceau, the Quebec minister of finance, had nothing better to say than: "I'm very surprised."[121] Investors probably do not find the process quite so mysterious. There is plenty of information available online, including on the *Canada-Offshore* website if you happen to be interested in Belize.[122]

But ministers may be better off pretending to be halfwits. The federal minister of national revenue, Jean-Pierre Blackburn, was forced to leave the ministry in January 2010, shortly after he had taken a close interest in the affairs of the Royal Bank of Canada in Liechtenstein. The bank was said to have helped 106 wealthy Canadians avoid taxes by depositing as much as $100 million in Liechtenstein. Although the allegation was partly corroborated by an investigation carried out by the Canada Revenue Agency, no legal action was taken. Federal authorities were satisfied with $6 million,[123] and Blackburn was relegated to the Department of Veterans Affairs.

The many treaties that Canada has signed with tax havens make it easy for taxpayers to avoid paying taxes. Canadian authorities have gone forward with these agreements without taking any steps to guard against the highly predictable abuses that were bound to follow. The federal Department of Finance writes ingenuously in 2013: "In the aggregate statistics on FDI [foreign direct investment], it is difficult to distinguish indirect investment through intermediaries from direct investment, and even more difficult to separately identify cases involving indirect investment for tax planning purposes. Moreover, the use of intermediaries may involve tax planning other than treaty shopping. For example, intermediaries in low tax jurisdictions (or jurisdictions with preferential regimes) may be used to reduce or defer taxation in the country in which the ultimate beneficial owner is resident and not the source country."[124] Has the government just realized this? Is it only now discovering tax havens? There are countries whose direct investments into Canada are greater "than the economic linkages suggested by the trade partner rank would warrant." Luxembourg, for example, "ranks only 72 on the trade partner rank, but number seven in terms of the source of investment in FDI stocks in Canada." The top ten investor countries also include the Netherlands and Switzerland, suggesting "that they play a role in conduit investments, although not all investments undertaken through multiple countries are driven by treaty shopping."[125]

Given the legal categories into which policymakers choose to lock themselves, obvious facts never constitute the evidence required to punish tax dodgers. "A country with a high ranking in terms of inbound FDI stocks in Canada, even when paired with a low ranking on economic linkages demonstrated by trade partner rank, does not demonstrate the existence of treaty shopping." As a consequence, tax authorities have few alternatives other than to try and gain time. They may, for example, organize a consultation to ask the population if they should review all the tax treaties that they have unfortunately signed with so many countries – "a difficult task given that these countries may not wish to re-negotiate," as the federal Department of Finance explains. They may also wonder if they should rewrite national laws, which "may produce less certain outcomes in some cases... and, accordingly, may expose businesses to some compliance risks."[126]

In fact, Ottawa is simply pretending to tackle tax havens. Tax experts organizing the delocalization of firms and assets toward sunnier climes shrug their shoulders when faced with this kind of consultation project. Law firms such as Osler think that the government has no legal basis other than "anecdotal and (indirect) empirical evidence"[127] to justify the assertion that taxpayers are making improper use of tax treaties to evade taxes. McCarthy Tétrault pointed out in 2009 that "the current state of the law in Canada remains quite favourable for transactions structured to efficiently utilize Canada's array of bilateral tax treaties."[128] These are treaties signed by the government to facilitate tax avoidance, and which it refuses to touch.

CANADIAN NATIONALISM: THE SHORT-SIGHTEDNESS OF CRITICAL INTELLECTUALS

Another awkward question comes to mind. How is it that Canadian universities have not yet produced a critical analysis of Canada's historic role in the shaping of Caribbean islands as offshore territories? Or, more specifically, how is it that Canadian intellectuals with a background in political economy and the critical tradition have not noticed the troubling nature of Canadian influence in the Caribbean as exerted by MPs, banks, development agencies, and experts of all shades and stripes? Apart from a handful of historians, criminologists, and tax experts (such as Christopher Armstrong and H. V. Nelles, Brian Arnold, Donald Brean, Gregory Marchildon, James D. Frost, André Lareau, and R. T. Naylor), we look in vain for academic analyses today that scrutinize Canadian responsibility in transforming the Bahamas, Barbados, the Cayman Islands, Jamaica, and Trinidad and Tobago into tax havens, and in establishing suspect partnerships with jurisdictions such as Bermuda and Panama.

Even when they have information that ought to lead them in this direction, Canada's "critical" intellectuals do not feel that this is their responsibility, often because they are not able to imagine the overly obliging nature of the Canadian state. The problem is not that they are blind to the involvement of foreign states in Caribbean development; rather, they suffer from a specific form of blindness to Canada's agency. Canada's political culture is the issue here, including, first and foremost, the political culture of its left-wing academics. A critique of their own state seems to be beyond their capacity.

The work of Kari Polanyi Levitt illustrates this problem. Levitt, the daughter of Austrian economist Karl Polanyi, is today emerita professor of economics at McGill University. A specialist of Canada and the Caribbean, she has made herself known throughout her career, beginning in the 1960s, as an active figure among English Canadian radical academics. Along with Mel Watkins, whom she met when she was a graduate student at the University of Toronto, she was a member of the Waffle group, the radical wing of the New Democratic Party (NDP) that agitated for an "independent and socialist Canada," free from the domination of American imperialism.[129] At the time, she was considered so radical that the NDP expelled her in 1972. With the support of philosopher Charles Taylor, Levitt then published a book that created a stir, *Silent Surrender*, in which she argued that American multinationals threatened to fragment Canada by promoting north-south rather than east-west continental trade.[130] She called this dominant economic system the "new mercantilism," alluding to the eighteenth-century colonial system in which metropolitan companies benefited from protected markets in the colonies. Of course, according to economic indicators, Canada was a wealthy country profiting from its close ties to the American giant. However, Levitt argued that a country's degree of development cannot be measured in economic statistics. Rather, it must be assessed in terms of its ability to innovate and show initiative and in terms of its sovereignty in the use of its natural resources. From this point of view, Levitt believed that Canada was constrained by the power of foreign multinationals active within its borders.[131]

Caribbean students at McGill saw analogies between the Caribbean and Canada and were inspired by Levitt as both intellectuals and activists. Levitt became interested in Jamaica's accession to independence, among other Caribbean issues, and undertook an in-depth study of Caribbean economic and political development. Her commitment to Caribbean emancipation led her to collaborate with critical intellectuals and actors from the region, including, in particular, Lloyd Best. In the early 1970s, Levitt worked on a system of national accounts for the government of Trinidad and Tobago,[132] then spent many years teaching economics in Jamaica. In the context of the "hopes and dreams" born of decolonization,[133] Levitt committed herself intellectually, politically, and professionally to the Caribbean, with which she came to identify closely.

Despite her works of critical analysis on the one hand, and her political activism in Canada on the other, throughout her long and rich involvement with the Caribbean, Levitt has had nothing to say about Canada's imperialist role in the banking sector and in shaping the Caribbean into a group of international financial centres. What is the reason for this short-sightedness?

During the period in the mid-1960s when she was studying American multinationals' domination of Canada, Levitt was working with Lloyd Best on what she calls "models" of the Caribbean's specific economic development, from plantation slavery and its subsequent avatars – local production and craft work, then the economic ascendancy of large industrial corporations – to a hoped-for definitive exit from this system.[134] Even summarily exposed, her theses on the Caribbean have obvious affinities with her theses on Canada: the same long-term dependence on eighteenth-century mercantilism, a system that created an economy based on exporting cheap natural resources to the metropolis and shaped subsequent development; the same timid attempts to develop the domestic economy in the last third of the nineteenth century – attempts that, although they were still based on export of natural resources, involved taking control of the national economy; and, especially, the same ascendancy of multinational corporations (American and British) as part of the domination of the new mercantilism that developed from the 1950s on. When Levitt writes in 1996 that the Caribbean is suffering from the fact that multinationals control market access, licences, technology, and patents,[135] we recognize the features of a system whose impact on the Canadian economy she was denouncing thirty years earlier. Finally, the last stage, in which the Caribbean will exit at last from its long dependency on mercantilism, is practically identical – except for the radical rhetoric – to Levitt's political positions in Canada in the 1960s.[136] True, Canada never had large-scale slave plantations or the authoritarian regimes with which they were associated in the Caribbean, and Levitt does discuss this issue. However, to her it seems indisputable that within the world capitalist system, the Canadian and Caribbean economies are similarly dominated.[137] Are they not both colonial countries locked into a staples economy, to use the term coined by historian Harold Innis in the 1920s?[138] The global capitalist system developing after the Second World War placed Canada and the Caribbean in the same position as *colonies* of a regime dominated by multinationals, and these multinationals, of course, were essentially American.[139]

Defining Canada purely as a victim, Levitt never emerged from her comparatist bias: everywhere the same causes would necessarily lead to the same consequences, in Canada as in the Caribbean. Located geographically on the same front line as Caribbean countries held by the United States in an iron grasp,[140] Canada is the last country that Levitt suspects of playing an imperialist role in Caribbean countries, whether in the banking sector or in any other field. Canada, by definition good and subservient, cannot be among the oppressors. Nor does Levitt's discourse on what she calls the "globalization agenda,"[141] coming after her postcolonial approach of the 1960s and 1970s, favour any greater awareness of Canada's formidable presence in the Caribbean. Her lucid and courageous critique of debt programs for countries in the South – programs that were defended, beginning in the 1980s, by prominent American academics and think tanks as well as the World Bank and the IMF[142] – do not make her assessment of Canada's role any more accurate. Faithful to her perspective, she never includes the Canadian state in operational categories such as "dominant multinationals," the World Bank, or the IMF. It does not seem even to cross her mind that the word *Canadian* might apply to some of the actors at the top of the economic pyramid established during this period of globalization, actors consisting of 40,000 multinationals and their 250,000 foreign affiliates.[143] Is this ignorance, or a refusal to see? According to Levitt, the measures imposed on

Caribbean countries by international financial institutions serve American interests first and foremost, and secondarily the interests of America's British and European allies.[144]

For Levitt, the transformations and adjustments characterizing Caribbean economies since the 1980s have been instigated by the United States acting through the IMF and the World Bank. American government policy since 1982 has been the sole force shaping the policies of these institutions, policies that require the reimbursement of debts contracted in the United States.[145] From this point of view, the North American Free Trade Agreement (NAFTA) signed by Canada, the United States, and Mexico in 1994 is strictly an illustration of Canada's presence among countries subject to the logic of American imperial rule.[146]

Pursuing her argument, Levitt believes that Canada, which cannot be seen as a key player in the system that she denounces, is, to the contrary, the bearer of solutions for the Caribbean. She hopes that a decision announced by the Canadian International Development Agency (CIDA) to write off Jamaica's debt may be the prelude to a strong commitment on the part of the Canadian government to speak on behalf of the Caribbean to the "Washington-based agencies," meaning the IMF and the World Bank.[147] Strangely, when describing the "strong ties" between Canada and Jamaica, she reproduces the clichés of an official brochure:

> Jamaica is the most important country in Canada's development assistance program in all of Latin America and the Caribbean, and Canadian International Development Agency (CIDA) expenditures on Jamaica are larger than on any other country in the region. Canada has strong ties with Jamaica and enjoys the goodwill of Jamaicans. The ties are largely "people-ties" – the result of generations of Jamaicans who have made their home in Canada, and tens of thousands of Canadians who have visited Jamaica as tourists.[148]

While it is impossible for her not to see the domination of Canadian financial institutions, such as Scotiabank or the Royal Bank of Canada, in cities in which she spends time such as Kingston or Port of Spain, Levitt manages to make them into symbols of – Canadian commitment to the development of the Caribbean! The same denial comes into play when she looks at the role of Alcan in Jamaica. Of course, nothing in the behaviour of this multinational sets it apart from its American counterparts, but Levitt in 2012 stubbornly persists in viewing it as a company that, had it not been bought by Rio Tinto, would have been in the vanguard of a possible Canadian response to American domination in the countries of the South.[149]

If she had pursued her work in a more critical frame of mind, Levitt would have seen the very un-tourist-like demeanour of the Canadian state, its agencies, and the private institutions with which it is associated in the Caribbean. The genesis of the transformation of Caribbean territories into tax havens, already described by law professor Daniel Jay Baum in 1974 in *The Banks of Canada in the Commonwealth Caribbean: Economic Nationalism and Multinational Enterprises of a Medium Power*,[150] would have been clear to her, and she would have appreciated to what extent Canada, far from embodying some kind of potential protection against the IMF and the World Bank in the region, is in fact their enthusiastic agent. She might even have seen that Canadian multinationals participate in the domination of the Caribbean economy.[151]

TAX HAVENS: A FORM OF DEVELOPMENT?

While radical critics such as Levitt fail to see Canada's role in a global system that maintains the Caribbean economy in a subservient position, a number of liberal-minded thinkers entertain the delusion that becoming a tax haven is a form of *development* for poor countries.[152] Yet today, the offshorization of small states is known to be a curse. In almost every case, populations in the South become poorer when their state transforms tax systems and investment rules to suit the needs of corporate capital. As their personal situation deteriorates, island populations see billions flying around above their heads. Customs duties and property values go up. The sudden development of the bank sector may put an end to maritime activities, throwing thousands of seamen into idleness.[153] This does not prevent the usual tax experts from providing extraordinary levels of nuance as they argue, for example, that it is not "perfectly clear" that "pension fund investments in tax havens are scandalous," since "the phenomenon of tax havens is the emergence of fiscal competition between every country in the world" in which "poor countries exhibit the only advantage they have compared to developed countries: a more generous tax system."[154] The truth, however, is apparent to anyone who chooses to look for it: policymakers in the South, obsessed with attracting tax tourists, have turned away from their social mission, and the potential for corruption is extraordinary.

In short, although it is obvious to democrats that the offshore phenomenon is antagonistic to principles that Western states based on the rule of law claim to defend, the exalted defenders of middle-of-the-road positions, and other fanatics of moderation, soften their criticisms in order to keep the favour of the classes providing them with symbolic capital.

PROPOSED TECHNICAL SOLUTIONS

Fortunately, not all science is subservient. Many writers specializing in accounting techniques have put forward strong proposals that could lead us out of the swamp. Technical solutions do exist. They are neither revolutionary nor entirely satisfactory, but they embody a genuine possibility of doing things differently. The problem is that we do not have political representatives or – especially – a financial and industrial class willing to deal with the problem. What are these solutions?

- **Define tax havens as a political problem caused by the over-obligingness of states.** Brian Arnold concludes his long study of international taxation with a justified denunciation of the network of tax havens in which Canada is seamlessly incorporated. "Tax havens enable Canadian taxpayers to avoid and evade Canadian tax in a wide variety of ways. Leaving tax evasion aside, if Canadian residents could not shift incomes to tax havens or non-residents could not invest in Canada through tax havens, the international tax rules could be considerably simpler. Assuming a Canadian corporate tax rate of approximately 35 percent, multinational corporations have a powerful incentive to shift income out of the Canadian tax system if the diverted income is not taxable, or is taxable at a low rate in a tax haven."[155] Arnold states bluntly that "the current links between the foreign affiliate rules and Canada's tax treaties should be eliminated."[156]

To put an end to the noxious effects of tax havens, it would first be necessary to abolish all of the Canadian laws and regulations that encourage the use of offshore advantages. This would include repealing the double taxation agreement signed with Barbados in 1980, as well as all the treaties involving exchange of tax information that Canada is now signing with tax havens in order to make them more easily accessible to our country's financial establishment.[157] According to some, it may already be too late to do this.[158] To do so, on a practical level it would also be necessary to make a clean sweep of Canadian laws that grant the status of non-resident taxpayer to entities registered in an accommodating jurisdiction in which they have no tangible activity.[159] It would also make sense to eliminate the principle of tax-exempt status for earnings registered abroad as dividends when these earnings are transferred to Canada.[160]

- **Deal with Caribbean jurisdictions that Canada has reduced to the status of vassal states by consolidating taxed earnings.** Among the "more important" tax havens identified by tax expert Donald Brean are three that Canadians were instrumental in creating: the Bahamas, Barbados, and the Cayman Islands.[161] "There can be no doubt of the role of tax havens in modern corporate tax planning," as Brean was already emphasizing in 1984.[162] Tax havens are a systemic problem that cannot be framed solely in relation to "individuals." "Tax problems are created by tax systems,"[163] especially since our tax system presents itself as a joust based on the art of violating the spirit of the law while complying with the letter. Where taxation is concerned, Brean claims that there can be no "extraordinary compliance" by corporations.[164] In a game like this, corporations are almost sure to win, especially since they alone have the means to exploit the hermeneutic possibilities of abstruse legal texts in a courtroom.[165] And the game will continue as long as taxes are fragmented between entities belonging to a single group that can spread its fiscal obligations from Barbados to Luxembourg, while presenting its assets to shareholders in a single consolidated balance sheet.[166]

CONCLUSION – NOW: UNDER SIEGE

- **Keep an eye on our governments as they toy with the offshore temptation.** Quebec has been flirting for some time with the idea of making itself into a partly deregulated jurisdiction, and has sought out experts to reinforce this position. In the early 2010s, the minister of finance, Monique Jérôme-Forget, toyed with the idea of making Quebec into a "Northern Delaware" for speculators, or maybe even swindlers. In 2010, Georges Lebel, professor of law at the Université du Québec à Montréal, dug up a consultation document annexed to the previous year's Business Corporations Act, in which it was suggested that Quebec could become a regulatory haven protecting corporate directors from shareholders. As in any self-respecting permissive jurisdiction, the law would have been used to neutralize itself: the idea was literally "to insert in the law a clause absolving directors who failed to meet their obligations with regard to caution and diligence, so that shareholders and creditors could not sue for damages."[167] While the ministry was clearly aware that this transformation of the Quebec legal system would harm small investors, it believed that such a strategy of the regulatory lowest bidder would convince companies from the rest of Canada and the United States to come to Quebec. The project was being debated within the Ministry of Finance at the very moment when Quebec was experiencing the impact of massive financial fraud schemes carried out by Vincent Lacroix and Earl Jones.

- **Legislate to ensure that the state taxes earnings where an activity actually takes place and not in the location where earnings have been circumstantially recorded.** André Lareau, professor of tax law at Université Laval, suggests that an entity's legal residence be determined by the location of the person "who is most likely to reap the benefits of the operation."[168] Arnaud Mary, who coauthored the suggestion, links it to a ruling by Justice Woods of the Tax Court of Canada, identifying Canada as the place where the beneficiary of a trust registered in Barbados should be taxed.

- **Develop laws to fight tax evasion strategies even when they comply with the letter of the law.** Professor Jean-Pierre Vidal of Hautes études commerciales (HEC) Montréal suggests that laws be worded so that earnings registered in tax havens can be taxed, whether or not abusive manoeuvres are legal in the sense that they formally comply with the law. To apply such a principle, the courts must be able to look not at the intentions of presumed tax dodgers but at the fiscal consequences of their operations.[169] The formal definition of the expression "aggressive tax planning" includes any operation that transfers funds between entities belonging to the same group and that leads to a tax advantage. Aggressive tax planning is "a plan involving at least two jurisdictions, that complies with tax law clauses, and that leads to at least one physical person receiving a net after-tax accrual of wealth (either real or potential) superior to what this person would have obtained in the absence of all the entities interposed between the person and the source of increased wealth."[170] Vidal then takes aim, not at those who are "getting a free ride," but at states tending to give in to the "perverse objective" of "attracting" those who "want to reduce their tax payments without acting illegally." He cites, in the first place, three creatures of the Canadian establishment: the Bahamas, Barbados, and the Cayman Islands. Applying this principle would make it possible to abolish advantages that appear unwarranted, whatever the initial or sincere motives behind the operation.[171] This proposal is similar to one put forward by Gilles Larin and Robert Duong.[172]

- **Demand that banks provide access to all the information they hold throughout the world.** This would mean reproducing in Canada the United States' new banking law, FATCA (Foreign Account Tax Compliance Act), enacted in 2010. The law creates an automatic mechanism for exchange of information between U.S. tax authorities and any institution directly or indirectly involved in handling foreign accounts belonging to American taxpayers.

- **Coordinate tax laws with social policies and ecosystem protection standards.** According to Brigitte Alepin, tax advantages granted to charitable foundations that are generous only to those who control them should be radically reviewed. She also argues that tax measures should support ecological practices compatible with transformative environmental policies adapted to the realities of the twenty-first century.[173]

- **Avoid the trap of replacing a political debate with an argument about legal issues.** This is the position taken in this book. A legal debate is one that focuses solely on efforts to prevent tax swindles – which means that as soon as the government makes a tax avoidance strategy legal, there is no longer anything to discuss. The focus on legal issues helps justify the tax policies of the federal government as it legalizes stratagems that harm the common good and supports companies and wealthy individuals that are actively seeking to cheat on their tax payments.

MAPPING THE OLIGARCHS

For oligarchs, using tax havens is now part of everyday life, and very few people in power are willing to challenge their lifestyle in this respect.[174] For this reason, nothing is ever done, no matter how much politicians express their passion for "good governance" or make statements about their principles.

In her obsequious studies of Canadian fortunes, financial journalist Diane Francis provides individual snapshots of Canadians active in tax havens:

- *The Irvings.* "New Brunswick is a company town owned by the Irving family... But technically, ownership is held in a series of trusts in Bermuda."[175]

- *Harold Siebens* "sold his 34 percent of Siebens Oil to Dome for $120 million in 1978 and immediately became a permanent resident of the Bahamas."[176]

- *John MacBain* "lives luxuriously, and relatively tax-free, in Geneva, Switzerland, giving away money around the world out of proceeds from a business empire he created in 20 countries."[177]

- *Alex Shnaider* "is the chairman of the Midland Group of companies, which employs 40,000 people and owns real estate, agri-food businesses, chemical works, and two of the world's biggest steel mills... This conglomerate, co-owned with partner Eduard Shifrin, has offices in Moscow, Kiev, Toronto, and the Channel Islands."[178]

- *Michael Lee-Chin* "owns about 70 percent of one of Jamaica's largest financial institutions, the National Commercial Bank... He also owns Total Finance (now called AIC Financial Ltd. [Trinidad]) in Trinidad and Tobago and Columbus Communications in Barbados."[179]

- *Frank Stronach.* "Today, however, he is clearly a globalist living in a tax haven and now hoping to conquer Russia, then Asia."[180]

- *Mike DeGroote* "left Canada in 1990 for Bermuda to retire and get out from under Canada's excessive taxation rates and government inefficiencies."[181]

- *David Gilmour.* His financial partner, Peter Munk, asserts that he "went to the Bahamas. He said his family had paid high taxes in Canada for five generations and he was sick of it."[182] In another priceless remark, the man who cofounded Barrick Gold (with the help of arms dealer Adnan Khashoggi) suggests that Switzerland, the quintessential tax haven, has the ability to accumulate capital simply because of its financial virtue – as if its capital were self-generated.[183]

These capital holders and highly influential lobbyists have been working for years to make Canada itself into an offshore sieve. This was already apparent in a speech given in 1963 by the president of the Royal

Bank, Earle McLaughlin, to the yearly general meeting of shareholders. McLaughlin remarked with great subtlety: "For example, let us take taxation and fiscal policy. This is a tempting field for gimmicks; that is, for ingenious devices using a tax carrot or tax stick to induce businessmen or investors to do what they otherwise would not do. Few of us are immune to the subtle wiles of the tax gimmick as a device for solving immediate problems. I do not pretend I have been immune myself. However, recent experience both in Canada and in the United States has underlined the inherent dangers of this device."[184] The worst of these dangers is the risk of a "retaliation abroad" that would be caused by the mysterious "gimmicks" used to bypass taxes, an effect that might lead to "higher costs to foreign-owned subsidiaries."[185] (Customs have changed since 1963; wealthy Canadians are now likely to boast about their offshore holdings.) As the RBC prepared to invest massive sums in tax havens, McLaughlin warned hia audience that "tax gimmicks cannot be relied on to foster investment by Canadians in their own industrial expansion... or to increase the attractiveness of home sources of capital."[186] The bank asked the Canadian government to remove "tax dis-incentives which now inhibit investment by Canadians in Canadian industry or, in general, prevent the mobilization of investment funds in a freely working national and international capital market."[187] This barely veiled threat to the Canadian state inaugurated a type of rhetoric that was to prove long-lived: taxes, though they are imposed by states governed by the rule of law, are responsible for the creation of tax havens. If Canada itself becomes a tax haven – which should not take more than a few decades if current trends continue – there will be no more movement of capital investments toward tax havens.

According to Diane Francis, "Canada's high business taxes contribute to the country's continuing brain drain," and she deplores in her book the "overtaxation" that afflicts the Canadian ruling class,[188] especially the capital gains tax introduced in 1972.[189] However, neither Francis nor the (a)social actors she so abundantly quotes ever refer to the benefits that investors reap from the Canadian institutions for the common good – benefits, funded by taxes, that make their investments profitable, such as Canada's well-maintained roads, its airport and port infrastructures, its custom-trained population, its adapted labour force, its dangerously effective security system, its liberal judiciary defending the principle of unlimited wealth accumulation in the name of justice, its multiple support and subsidy programs for corporations, its administration of a scholarship system, its central bank, and its network of embassies and commercial offices throughout the world.

Populations suffer from the massive capital outflows provoked by the indulgence of our governments. Right in the middle of an episode of budget cuts, the Quebec government of Pauline Marois funded job creation by business to the tune of $2 billion (Ubisoft, Lassonde, etc.), while Hydro-Québec, whose board was directed at the time by multimillionaire businessman Pierre-Karl Péladeau, offered corporations hydroelectric surpluses at a discount. Meanwhile, not only are public services deteriorating in terms of quality, but they are more and more often associated with user fees.[190]

This illustrates the vicious circle in which we are currently trapped: states and other institutions created for the common good are themselves establishing the economic infrastructures enabling businesses and assets to move to tax havens created by their own wealthy citizens. The money accumulated in these outlaws' dens moves around without any legal, fiscal, political, or regulatory constraint, as states encourage the emergence of a class of privileged property owners who are then courted by these same states offering new political and fiscal incentives. As French magistrate Jean de Maillard remarks, it is assumed that "everything that enters into the process of economic and financial globalization should, by its very nature, be excluded from the reach of any law except those guaranteeing freedom of exchange. The problem is that this exclusion is neither possible nor desirable, even though protagonists are relentless in their attempts to establish some kind of legal immunity for their schemes."[191] In short, the framework of capitalist globalization makes it possible for powerful people to bypass the constitutional principles that are the foundation of states, and Canada in this sense is actively pursuing its own destruction.

ACCOMMODATING JURISDICTIONS: AN INDEFENSIBLE REALITY

The political issues associated with taxation and tax havens raise questions that people are forced to consider every day. At times in history, populations have taken on political responsibilities that cannot be delegated to a small number of technicians and ideologues serving established powers. Revolutions and sporadic acts of resistance arise to influence how a society's collective surplus is handled. The Occupy movement, Idle No More, the recurrence of political springtimes tell us we are now experiencing such a moment.[192] At the political level, this struggle is the equivalent of the issue of climate change at the ecological level.

In this case, the media that we have so often criticized have played a key role, as was apparent in April 2013 when the International Consortium of Investigative Journalists (ICIJ) dropped its bombshell by releasing, in each country where it had members, information about accounts held in tax havens. At that point, three things became clear:

1. Tax havens are a worldwide issue and must be considered as such. In dealing with offshore affairs, there is little point in focusing on any single country or attempting to isolate any one territory from a state of generalized gangrene.

2. Only a small part of the ICIJ's 2.5 million records have today been analyzed and made available on the Internet, and this small part embodies only a tiny proportion of the offshore operations carried out year after year. However, financiers are now experiencing doubt. Bank secrecy is no longer watertight. Computer experts angry with their employers or horrified by the decadent banking culture in which they find themselves, have released data on offshore clienteles. These leaks, initially isolated and coming from Switzerland[193] or Liechtenstein,[194] were followed by the ICIJ's stunning "Offshore Leaks" operation, and there will be others. The random nature of such revelations means that bank secrecy, throughout the world, is no longer a certainty.

3. Now that the offshore question is publicly framed in international terms, states can no longer justify their inaction by claiming they cannot act alone. The ambitious declaration made at the G20 summit in 2013 is an irreversible step toward intergovernmental co-operation.

However, international co-operation will not take place unless close connections are established at home between contributions to the common fund and ensuing decisions. Shall we buy fighter planes or pay for public services? A serious political debate will not be possible until we oppose the reactionary rhetoric that sees taxes as money "given" to the government as if it were some kind of mafia.[195]

In Canada, as elsewhere, groups have been formed as part of an international movement, initiated by the London-based Tax Justice Network, to oppose tax havens. This is only a first step. We hope that soon there will be no need for organizations specifically dedicated to tax havens, because the issue will have been appropriated by all groups within society. Nurses, physicians, advocates of the social security state, students, professors, artists, and advocates of co-operative and local economic development will be thinking about the fact that citizens' public institutions are destroyed by tax havens. Here, as elsewhere, the people will learn to re-establish institutions in their own likeness.

■ NOTES

INTRODUCTION

1   Zach Dubinsky, Harvey Cashore, Frédéric Zalac, and Alex Shprintsen, "Massive Data Leak Exposes Offshore Financial Secrets," CBC News, April 4, 2013. See also the interactive maps on the CBC News website.

2   A TV documentary by Valentine Oberti and Wandrille Lanos, "Ces milliards de l'évasion fiscale," broadcast June 11, 2013, on the France 2 TV network as part of the *Cash Investigation* program, is one of several sources of information on this story. A summary of the Falciani affair is provided by Doreen Carvajal and Raphael Minder, "A Whistle-Blower Who Can Name Names of Swiss Bank Account Holders," *New York Times*, August 8, 2013.

3   Mike Esterl, Glenn R. Simpson, and David Crawford, "Stolen Data Spur Tax Probes," *Wall Street Journal*, February 19, 2008, A4; "The Liechtenstein Affair: German Banks Suspected of Helping Clients Evade Taxes," *Spiegel Online International*, February 21, 2008.

4   Anne Michel, "Les grandes banques sommées de traquer les évadés fiscaux américains," *Le Monde* (Paris), April 4, 2012 [our translation]. Enacted March 18, 2010, FATCA added section 6038D of the Internal Revenue Code to require the reporting of any interest in foreign financial assets over $50,000 for taxable years beginning after the date of enactment (26 U.S. Code, section 6038D: Information with respect to foreign financial assets).

5   Julien Ponthus, "Vers un procureur national pour lutter contre la fraude fiscale," Reuters, May 7, 2013.

6   "Le patrimoine des élus et des ministres sera contrôlé," *Le Figaro* (Paris), April 10, 2013.

7   David Milliken, "British Overseas Territories Sign Deal to Curb Tax Evasion," Reuters, May 2, 2013.

8   Fourteen countries were the top recipients of a total of $711.6 billion in Canadian foreign direct investment in 2012, of which $155 billion (nearly 22 percent) went to seven tax havens (in order): Barbados, the Cayman Islands, Luxembourg, Ireland, Bermuda, the Netherlands, and Hong Kong ("Foreign Direct Investment Positions at Year-End," Statistics Canada, May 9, 2013).

9   "Combating International Tax Evasion and Aggressive Tax Avoidance," in *Economic Action Plan 2013*, Government of Canada website, March 21, 2013. See also "Informant Leads Program," CRA website, January 15, 2014; François Normand, "Ottawa s'en prend à l'évasion fiscale," *Les Affaires.com*, March 21, 2013; Alain Deneault, "Lutte contre l'évasion fiscale d'Ottawa: l'effet d'optique," *Le Devoir* (Montreal), March 23, 2013.

10 Canadian Press, "Offshore Tax Havens Leak: Ottawa Threatens to Use Courts in Bid to Get CBC Tax Evasion List," *Huffington Post*, April 9, 2013.

11 Madhavi Acharya-Tom Yew, "Federal Budget 2013: Tax Loopholes, Hidden Offshore Money Targeted," *Toronto Star*, March 21, 2013.

12 CRA, "Harper Government Announces New Measures to Crack Down on International Tax Evasion and Aggressive Tax Avoidance," news release, May 8, 2013.

13 "Outlook for Budgetary Revenues: The Revenue Outlook," Table 4.2.5, *Economic Action Plan 2013*, Government of Canada website, March 21, 2013, 289.

14 "Agreement Between the Government of Canada and the Government of Bermuda Under Entrustment from the Government of the United Kingdom of Great Britain and Northern Ireland on the Exchange of Information with Respect to Taxes," Department of Finance Canada, signed on June 14, 2010, and in force on July 1, 2011.

15 "Foreign Direct Investment Positions at Year-End," Statistics Canada, May 9, 2013.

16 Department of Finance Canada, "Minister of Finance to Strengthen Economic Bonds Between Canada and Bermuda," news release, April 11, 2013.

17 Mike Godfrey, "Canada's Flaherty Promotes Trade in Bermuda," *Tax-News.com* (Washington, DC), April 15, 2013.

18 Alain Deneault, *Offshore: Tax Havens and the Rule of Global Crime*, tr. from the French by George Holoch (New York: New Press, 2011 [2010]).

19 Raymond W. Baker, *Capitalism's Achilles Heel: Dirty Money and How to Renew the Free-Market System* (Hoboken, NJ: Wiley, 2005), 192.

20 Alex Doulis, *My Blue Haven* (Etobicoke, ON: Uphill, 1997; reissued in 2001), 76.

21 Alain Supiot, *L'esprit de Philadelphie. La justice sociale face au marché global* (Paris: Seuil, 2010), 68.

22 Marie-Christine Dupuis-Danon, *Finance criminelle. Comment le crime organisé blanchit l'argent sale* (Paris: Presses universitaires de France, 2004 [1998]), 6–7 [our translation; emphasis in the original].

23 Patrick Rassat, Thierry Lamorlette, and Thibault Camelli, *Stratégies fiscales internationales* (Paris: Maxima, 2010), 198 [our translation].

24 Gordon's exact words are "a country is a tax haven if it looks like one and if it is considered to be one by those who care" (R. A. Gordon, *Tax Havens and Their Use by U.S. Taxpayers: An Overview* [Washington, DC: IRS, 1981], 14).

25 Édouard Chambost, "Canada," in *Guide mondial des secrets bancaires* (Paris: Seuil, 1980), 113–17.

26 Throughout this book, the expression "British Caribbean" refers to the islands that were known as the British West Indies during the colonial period. The wider Caribbean region is the region as defined in the Cartagena Convention (Convention for the Protection and Development of the Marine Environment of the Wider Caribbean Region), covering the Gulf of Mexico and the area of the Atlantic Ocean that includes the Bahamas, the Lesser Antilles (such as Antigua and Barbuda, Barbados, St. Vincent and the Grenadines, and Trinidad and Tobago), and the Greater Antilles (Cuba, Puerto Rico, Jamaica, and Haiti and the Dominican Republic on the island of Hispaniola). The Caribbean region also includes states bordering on the Caribbean Sea such as Belize and Panama.

27 Mario Possamai, *Money on the Run: Canada and How the World's Dirty Profits Are Laundered* (Toronto: Viking, 1992).

28 Ibid., 9.

29 Ibid., 8.

30 Ibid., 15; Bernard Berossa with Agathe Duparc, *La Justice, les affaires, la corruption* (Paris: Fayard, 2009), 190.

31 Possamai, *Money on the Run*, 15.

32 Ibid., 1.

33 Ibid., 16.

34 Ibid., 17.

35 Ibid., 20.

36 Ibid., 18.

37 Ibid., 22. See also Frederic Dannen, "Life-Styles of the Rich and Infamous," *Vanity Fair* (April 1992), 78.

38 Possamai, *Money on the Run*, 20–21.

39 Ibid., 118–19 (illustration).

40 Ibid., 19.

41 Ibid., 1.

42 Ibid., 14.

43 Ibid., 23.

THE DOMINION OF CANADA

1 "Un scandale financier qu'on cherche à étouffer: comment on draine l'épargne française," *L'Humanité* (Paris), October 16, 1913 [our translation].

2 Ibid. [our translation]. Information on the Barcelona Traction affair is provided by Christopher Armstrong and H. V. Nelles, *Southern Exposure: Canadian Promoters in Latin America and the Caribbean 1896–1930* (Toronto: University of Toronto Press, 1988), 163–68; Jean-Marc Delaunay, *Méfiance cordiale: les relations franco-espagnoles de la fin du XIXᵉ siècle à la Première Guerre mondiale, 3* vol., *Les relations économiques* (Paris: L'Harmattan, 2010), 3:428–40; Peter Hertner and H. V. Nelles, "Contrasting Styles of Foreign Investment: A Comparison of the Entrepreneurship, Technology and Finance of German and Canadian Enterprises in Barcelona Electrification," *Revue économique* 58, no. 1 (2007): 191–214.

3 "L'affaire de la 'Barcelona Traction,'" *L'Humanité* (Paris), November 1, 1913 [our translation]. The injured bondholders were dismissed by the court in December 1913 (Delaunay, *Méfiance cordiale*, 3:433–34). See also "Un scandale financier qu'on veut étouffer. Y réussira-t-on?," *L'Humanité* (Paris), October 21, 1913.

4 Jean-François Couvrat and Nicolas Pless, *La face cachée de l'économie mondiale* (Paris: Hatier, 1981), 23 [our translation].

5 Jean-Claude Grimal, *Drogue : L'autre mondialisation* (Paris: Gallimard, 2000), 173.

6 Peter Gillespie, "The Trouble With Tax Havens: Whose Shelter? Whose Storm?," in Richard Swift (ed.), *The Great Revenue Robbery: How to Stop the Tax Cut Scam and Save Canada* (Toronto: Between the Lines, 2013), 55.

7 At the time of its incorporation, the Bank of Montreal's Articles of Association – surprisingly lax in this respect compared to those of American banks – allowed it to be directed by foreigners. (In the United States, not only were non-citizens forbidden to administer a bank, but the foreign shareholders of the First Bank of the United States were not even allowed to vote.) Only in 1822 were Bank of Montreal directors required, by the institution's charter, to be British subjects. According to the bank's official historian, Merrill Denison, citizenship qualifications were probably dropped in order "to make possible representation of the heavy American stock interest that may already have been secured" (Robert C. H. Sweeny, "Banking as Class Action: Social and National Struggles in the History of Canadian Banking," in Alice Teichova, Ginette Kurgan-Van Hentenryk, and Dieter Ziegler [eds.], *Banking, Trade, and Industry: Europe, America, and Asia from the Thirteenth to the Twentieth Century* [Cambridge: Cambridge UP, 1997], 318–19; Bernard Élie, *L'internationalisation des banques et autonomie nationale au Canada* [doctoral thesis in economics, Université Paris 1 Panthéon-Sorbonne, 1986], 113–14; Merrill Denison, *Canada's First Bank: A History of the Bank of Montreal,* 2 vol. [Montreal and Toronto: McClelland and Stewart, 1967], 1:83 and 2:100; Lance E. Davis and Robert E. Gallman, *Evolving Financial Markets and International Capital Flows: Britain, the Americas, and Australia, 1865–1914* [Cambridge: Cambridge UP, 2001], 406).

8   Sweeny, "Banking as Class Action," 319.

9   R. T. Naylor, *The History of Canadian Business, 1867–1914* (Montreal, New York, and London: Black Rose Books, 2006 [1975]), 1:74–76. See also Duncan McDowall, *Quick to the Frontier: Canada's Royal Bank* (Toronto: McClelland and Stewart, 1993), 60: "Pragmatic reform of legislative constraints on Canadian banking was from the outset the product of the informal, consensual relationship of Canadian bankers and politicians." In 1913, Edmund Walker of the Canadian Bank of Commerce "could openly boast that every major change in banking legislation since the first Bank Act had been initiated by the bankers themselves" (Naylor, *The History of Canadian Business,* 1:76).

10 Armstrong and Nelles, *Southern Exposure,* 4–9.

11 "If one visits a meeting of the American Bankers' Association, nothing strikes one so much as the fact that it is practically a great convention; hundreds and sometimes thousands of bankers attend... On the other hand... the interest of banking in Canada, of our 36 banks with five or six hundred branches is represented by 40 or 50 men, and practically by the 15 or 16 members of the Executive Council [of the Bankers' Association]... The consensus of opinion of the bankers of Canada upon any public question can be arrived at without difficulty. We have the great advantage of knowing without coming together, from the fact that we are acquainted with each other, and have often met to discuss subjects, what is the thought upon a public question. For that reason we exercise in this country a force that seems to be out of all proportion to our numbers" (Sir Edmund Walker, president of the Canadian Bank of Commerce, 1901, quoted in Naylor, *The History of Canadian Business,* 1:77).

12 Jacob Viner, *Canada's Balance of International Indebtedness, 1900–1913* (Toronto: McClelland and Stewart, 1975 [1924]), 89–94. In 1909, the net value of loans made by Canadian banks abroad (especially in the United States) reached a peak of close to $90 million. The net value of foreign loans is calculated by subtracting the value of foreign deposits (Naylor, *The History of Canadian Business,* 2:240 and 2:246).

13 Ranald C. Michie, "The Canadian Securities Market, 1850–1914," *Business History Review* 62, no. 1 (1988): 49.

14 Karl Marx, *Capital,* Book III, chapter 15, section 3 (New York: International, 1967), 256.

15 McDowall, *Quick to the Frontier,* 167; see also Neil C. Quigley, "The Bank of Nova Scotia in the Caribbean, 1889–1940: The Establishment of an International Branch Banking Network," *Business History Review* 63, no. 4 (1989): 803–4.

16 In fact, American banks were not allowed to have branches even in the United States, except in a few states (Pierre-Bruno Ruffini, *Les Banques multinationales. De la multinationalisation des banques au système bancaire transnational* [Paris: Presses universitaires de France, 1983], 74; Benjamin J. Klebaner, *American Commercial Banking: A History* [Boston: Twayne, 1990], 70–71; Mira Wilkins, *The History of Foreign Investment in the United States, 1914–1945* [Cambridge, MA: Harvard UP, 1989], 107; Harold van B. Cleveland and Thomas F. Huertas, *Citibank, 1812–1970* [Cambridge, MA: Harvard UP, 1985], 43; Quigley, "The Bank of Nova Scotia in the Caribbean," 804). After 1913, American banks with capital and reserves of more than $1 million were allowed to open foreign branches (Élie, *L'internationalisation des banques et autonomie nationale au Canada,* 87). Starting in 1914, they began to open branches in the Caribbean, but Canadian banks were already well-established in the region and continued to outperform them (Quigley, "The Bank of Nova Scotia in the Caribbean," 797).

17   Naylor, *The History of Canadian Business*, 2:226; Wilkins, *The History of Foreign Investment in the United States, 1914–1945*, 107; Mira Wilkins, "Banks over Borders: Some Evidence from Their Pre-1914 History," in Geoffrey Jones (ed.), *Banks as Multinationals* (London and New York: Routledge, 1990), 235, 238; Benjamin J. Klebaner, *American Commercial Banking*, 77.

18   "Canadian Banks in New York," *Monetary Times* (Toronto), December 4, 1874; reproduced in E. P. Neufeld (ed.), *Money and Banking in Canada: Historical Documents and Commentary* (Toronto: McClelland and Stewart, 1964), 167–69.

19   Armstrong and Nelles, *Southern Exposure*, 16–17.

20   Ibid., 23.

21   Mira Wilkins, *The History of Foreign Investment in the United States, 1914–1945* (Cambridge, MA: Harvard UP, 2004), 5. According to Wilkins, in 1914, foreign capital invested in Canada totalled $3.7 billion (ibid.). According to Jacob Viner, in 1900, the value of foreign capital invested in Canada reached $1.2 billion; over 80 percent of this capital came from the United Kingdom (Viner, *Canada's Balance of International Indebtedness*, 99). In 1914, British investments in Canada had reached almost $3 billion (Naylor, *The History of Canadian Business*, 1:230).

22   Mira Wilkins estimates that in 1914, these investments in the United States were worth US$275 million. She is surprised that a country as small as Canada should be one of the top five countries investing in the United States during this period (Wilkins, *The History of Foreign Investment in the United States, 1914–1945*, 9). See also Kees van der Pijl, *The Making of an Atlantic Ruling Class* (London and New York: Verso, 2012 [1984]), 40; Quigley, "The Bank of Nova Scotia in the Caribbean, 1889–1940," 798; Armstrong and Nelles, *Southern Exposure*, xi; Naylor, *The History of Canadian Business*, 2:223–25, 2:240, 2:266–67; Élie, *L'internationalisation des banques et autonomie nationale au Canada*, 86; D. L. C. Galles, "The Bank of Nova Scotia in Minneapolis, 1885–1892," *Minnesota History* 42, no. 7 (1971): 269. According to Michael Kaufman, "There was a continuous investment south of the border at the same time as Canada relied on large capital imports from the U.K. and U.S." (Kaufman, "The Internationalization of Canadian Bank Capital [With a Look at Bank Activity in the Caribbean and Central America]," *Journal of Canadian Studies* 19, no. 4 [1984]: 63–64).

23   Naylor, *The History of Canadian Business*, 2:240.

24   Victor Ross, *A History of the Canadian Bank of Commerce* (Toronto: Oxford UP, 1922), 2:63–65.

25   D. L. C. Galles, "The Bank of Nova Scotia in Minneapolis," 273; Joseph Schull and J. Douglas Gibson, *The Scotiabank Story: A History of the Bank of Nova Scotia, 1832–1982* (Toronto: Macmillan of Canada, 1982), 68. In Chicago and New York, in the 1870s, Canadian banks were able to avoid all or part of the taxes paid by American banks (E. P. Neufeld, *The Financial System of Canada: Its Growth and Development* [Toronto: Macmillan of Canada, 1972], 124–25; F. Cyril James, *The Growth of Chicago Banks* [New York: Harper, 1938], 500). Canadian banks also used their agencies and branches in the United States to escape the restrictions of Canadian laws. By 1859, for example, the Bank of Montreal knew that it could get better returns on call loans and short-term loans in New York than in Canada, where it was "prohibited by law from charging more than six per cent for ninety-day loans" (Denison, *Canada's First Bank*, 2:101; Wilkins, *The History of Foreign Investment in the United States, 1914–1945*, 99). As a consequence, the bank was heavily involved in this market. RBC, Scotiabank, and CIBC also favoured investments in New York such as call loans and short-term loans,

to which they dedicated ever-increasing amounts of money in the first decades of the twentieth century, to the detriment of comparable loans in Canada (Benjamin Haggott Beckhart, "The Banking System of Canada," in Henry Willis Parker and B. H. Beckhart [eds.], *Foreign Banking Systems* [New York: Henry Holt, 1929], 416–17; see also Naylor, *The History of Canadian Business*, 1:217, for the period between 1901 and 1913). Between 1900 and 1925, the amount of call loans and short-term loans made in New York by the four major Canadian banks (Bank of Montreal, RBC, CIBC, and Scotiabank) increased from $50 million to $240 million (Beckhart, "The Banking System of Canada," 417). According to Ranald C. Michie, in the early twentieth century the Bank of Montreal refused to make call loans in Canada; Canadian borrowers who wanted this type of loan had to make their request to the bank's New York agency (Michie, "The Canadian Securities Market," 52–54). The banks claimed that New York was the ideal place to invest Canadian reserves because call loans and short-term loans were liquid and Canadian creditors were thus protected from the vagaries of the international financial system. This protection was actually bogus, as was demonstrated in 1902 and again in 1907 when Canadian banks demanded the immediate reimbursement of loans in Canada in order to compensate for fluctuations of the American market (Naylor, *The History of Canadian Business*, 1:218). As for liquidity, in fact banks could not always immediately obtain reimbursement of call loans, as Beckhart acknowledges in a footnote (Beckhart, "The Banking System of Canada," 416).

26   Canada's chief railway companies, the Grand Trunk, the Canadian Pacific, and later the Canadian Northern, were financed by British capital (Andrew Dilley, *Australia, Canada, and the City of London, c. 1896–1914* [Houndmills, UK: Palgrave Macmillan, 2012], 57–60; Élie, *L'internationalisation des banques et autonomie nationale au Canada*, 50–55). The first railway company to operate on a national scale in Canada, the Grand Trunk, raised money in Britain thanks to the connection between the Bank of Montreal and two major London financial houses, Baring Brothers and Glyn, Mills & Co. (Élie, *L'internationalisation des banques et autonomie nationale au Canada*, 50–55).

27   Élie, *L'internationalisation des banques et autonomie nationale au Canada*, 51 [our translation]. Around the same time (1865), the Bank of Montreal established ties with three British colonial banks to carry out its activities in other countries: the Oriental Bank (for the Far East, India, and China), the National Bank of Scotland (for Ireland), and the Colonial Bank (for the British West Indies).

28   Ibid. [our translation]. See also Jacob Viner, *Canada's Balance of International Indebtedness*, 118. These British investments represented colossal amounts, for in the decade before the First World War, Canada became the largest borrower of British capital in the world, surpassing even the United States and receiving as much as a third of the sums loaned by Great Britain abroad (Gregory P. Marchildon, *Profits and Politics: Beaverbrook and the Gilded Age of Canadian Finance* [Toronto: University of Toronto Press, 1996], 63–64).

29   Armstrong and Nelles, *Southern Exposure*, 8.

30   George Stephen (Lord Mount Stephen) and his cousin Donald Smith (Lord Strathcona) are striking examples of this career path. Born in Scotland, they both made a fortune as part of major Canadian companies (Canadian Pacific Railway or Hudson's Bay Company). Having become millionaires, they personally invested huge sums in the United States, particularly in railways. Both spent the last years of their life in Great Britain. An eminent American historian, Mira Wilkins, finds herself unable to say if they are British or Canadian (Wilkins, *The History of Foreign Investment in the United States, 1914–1945*, 173, 213–15, 716n117, 741n210). Max

Aitken is a similar case. Born in Canada where dubious financial transactions allowed him to accumulate great wealth (Marchildon, *Profits and Politics*, 5), he moved to London where he was raised to the peerage and became a British press tycoon under the name of Lord Beaverbrook.

31   Robert Sweeny describes the impact of the early actions of banks located in British North America such as the Bank of Montreal: "The systematic redirection out of British North America of the best commercial paper, while benefiting bank share-holders, certainly reduced the capacity and facility with which colonial producers could meet their international obligations. So these bank profits were achieved at the expense of expanding production in the garment and metal trades. Ahistorical, neo-liberal, advocates of free trade will find little to object to here," but people at the time did object (Sweeny, "Banking as Class Action," 320).

32   "Canadian Trade with the Caribbean," *Monthly Review* (Toronto), Scotiabank, October 1955.

33   Victor Ross, *A History of the Canadian Bank of Commerce*, 1:93–94; C. V. Callender, *The Development of the Capital Market Institutions of Jamaica* (Kingston: Institute of Social and Economic Research, University of the West Indies, 1965), 42.

34   Ross, *A History of the Canadian Bank of Commerce*, 1:25–26, 1:42–44; Naylor, *The History of Canadian Business*, 1:163–64; Diane M. Barker and D. A. Suth-erland, "Enos Collins," *Dictionary of Canadian Biography*, vol. 10, *1871–1880* (Quebec and Toronto: Université Laval and University of Toronto, 1972) (available at *biographi.ca*).

35   Schull and Gibson, *The Scotiabank Story*, 70–71.

36   McDowall, *Quick to the Frontier*, 169–72.

37   James D. Frost, *Merchant Princes: Halifax's First Family of Finance, Ships, and Steel* (Toronto: James Lorimer, 2003), 226. The Union Bank was acquired by RBC in 1910.

38   A. St. L. Trigge, *A History of the Canadian Bank of Commerce, 1919–1930* (Toronto: Canadian Bank of Commerce, 1934), 3:12.

39   Quigley, "The Bank of Nova Scotia in the Caribbean," 799.

40   Ibid., 808–12; James D. Frost, "The 'Nationalisation' of the Bank of Nova Scotia, 1880–1910," *Acadiensis* 12, no. 2 (1982): 13; Callender, *The Development of the Capital Market Institutions of Jamaica*, 45.

41   Quigley, "The Bank of Nova Scotia in the Caribbean," 808–12.

42   McDowall, *Quick to the Frontier*, 172; Daniel Jay Baum, *The Banks of Canada in the Commonwealth Caribbean: Economic Nationalism and Multinational Enterprises of a Medium Power* (New York: Praeger, 1974), 21; Peter James Hudson, "Imperial Designs: The Royal Bank of Canada in the Caribbean," *Race and Class* 52, no. 1 (July 2010): 38.

43   Baum, *The Banks of Canada in the Commonwealth Caribbean*, 21; Hudson, "Imperial Designs," 38.

44   In addition to its 1837 agreement with the Halifax Banking Company, the Colonial Bank had signed a partnership agreement with the Bank of Montreal in 1865 (Élie, *L'internationalisation des banques et autonomie nationale au Canada*, 51). In the early twentieth century, the Colonial Bank's connections with Canadian banks were the object of persistent rumours (A. S. J. Baster, *The Imperial Banks* [London: P. S. King, 1929], 236). The Royal Bank was thinking of buying it in 1911 (ibid., 236; Kathleen E. A. Monteith, *Depression to Decolonization: Barclays Bank (DCO) in the West Indies, 1926–1962* [Kingston: University of West Indies Press,

2008], 288n26; Callender, *The Development of the Capital Market Institutions of Jamaica*, 49). British-Canadian financier Max Aitken was the main shareholder of the Colonial Bank from 1911 to 1918 (Katherine V. Bligh and Christine Shaw, "William Maxwell Aitken," in David J. Jeremy [ed.], *Dictionary of Business Biography* [London: Butterworths, 1984], 1:24). From 1920 to 1933, the Bank of Montreal was a major shareholder of the Colonial Bank (Geoffrey Jones, *British Multinational Banking, 1830–1990* [Oxford: Clarendon, 1993], 149) and of the Barclays (DCO) bank created when the Colonial Bank merged with two other British overseas banks (Élie, *L'internationalisation des banques et autonomie nationale au Canada*, 148; Monteith, *Depression to Decolonization*, 27). The Bank of Montreal's interest in the Colonial Bank was "substantial" (James Darroch, *Canadian Banks and Global Competitiveness* [Montreal: McGill-Queen's UP, 1994], 43; Jones, *British Multinational Banking*, 149; Monteith, *Depression to Decolonization*, 289n55; Bernard Élie, *Le régime monétaire canadien. Institutions, théories et politiques* [Montreal: Presses de l'Université de Montréal, 2002 (1998)], 131, 134). The board of directors of Barclays (DCO) included a representative of the Bank of Montreal (Baster, *The Imperial Banks*, 236, 240). In 1928, Barclays (DCO) established a Canadian subsidiary, Barclays (Canada) Ltd., to finance trade between Canada and the Caribbean (Monteith, *Depression to Decolonization*, 66). This subsidiary, which existed until 1956, had as its first president Robert Borden, former prime minister of Canada and director of Scotiabank (Baster, *The Imperial Banks*, 242).

45   McDowall, *Quick to the Frontier*, 167 and 176.

46   Ibid., 177–78, 188, 193; Quigley, "The Bank of Nova Scotia in the Caribbean," 800, 814–15, 825–26. See also Stephen J. Randall and Graeme S. Mount, *The Caribbean Basin: An International History* (London and New York: Routledge, 1998), 96. The word *ruthless* is from Quigley (ibid., 826). The Platt Amendment (1903) "stipulated the conditions for U.S. intervention in Cuban affairs and permitted the United States to lease or buy lands for the purpose of establishing naval bases (the main one was Guantánamo Bay) and coaling stations in Cuba" (available at *ourdocuments.gov*).

47   McDowall, *Quick to the Frontier*, 188.

48   Ibid., 188, 192–93.

49   Should we perhaps view the Royal Bank as a "Russian" institution? In 1918, it opened a branch in Vladivostok, Siberia, occupied at the time by White Army and Allied troops. In 1919, the branch received a threatening telegram, signed by Lenin and Trotsky, announcing the imminent arrival of the Red Army. The bankers fled; a "Soviet" identity was presumably impossible (ibid., 194–95).

50   Howard Zinn, *A People's History of the United States, 1492 – Present* (New York: HarperCollins, 2005), 310.

51   McDowall, *Quick to the Frontier*, 170.

52   Ibid., 171, 174.

53   Ibid., 171–72, 179.

54   Ibid., 182.

55   Quigley, "The Bank of Nova Scotia in the Caribbean," 808–12.

56   McDowall, *Quick to the Frontier*, 179.

57   Ibid., 84, 179, 182.

58   Juan C. Santamarina, "The Cuba Company and the Expansion of American Business in Cuba, 1898–1915," *Business History Review* 74, no. 1 (2000): 42.

59   Armstrong and Nelles, *Southern Exposure*, 37.

60   Santamarina, "The Cuba Company and the Expansion of American Business in Cuba," 42–43.

61   McDowall, *Quick to the Frontier,* 179, 185; Marchildon, *Profits and Politics,* 55.

62   R. T. Naylor, *Canada in the European Age, 1453–1919* (Montreal: McGill-Queen's UP, 2006 [1987]), 484; J. C. M. Ogelsby, *Gringos from the Far North: Essays in the History of Canadian-Latin American Relations, 1866–1968* (Toronto: Macmillan of Canada, 1976), 113; Valerie Knowles, *From Telegrapher to Titan: The Life of William C. Van Horne* (Toronto: Dundurn, 2004), 348–50. The word *unreasonable* is from Knowles, 350.

63   McDowall, *Quick to the Frontier,* 187–88.

64   Ibid., 198–99. In Colombia and Venezuela, the bank's presence was related to the presence of oil companies, including the International Petroleum Company (IPC), a Canadian subsidiary of Standard Oil of New Jersey: in Colombia, a few Royal Bank senior executives, including its president, Herbert Holt, established a company that built a pipeline to carry IPC oil to the sea (Ogelsby, *Gringos from the Far North,* 93–97, 99, 115, 118n37; McDowall, *Quick to the Frontier,* 199).

65   Élie, *L'internationalisation des banques et autonomie nationale au Canada,* 105–6. The Royal Bank had more foreign branches than all the other Canadian banks combined (115 out of a total of 201 in 1921). However, the Bank of Montreal, with only 15 foreign branches, generated financial transactions equal in value to those of the Royal Bank. In 1908, the Bank of Montreal controlled two-thirds of Mexico's foreign exchange market from a single branch in Mexico City (ibid., 73–74).

66   American banks started to expand in the region after 1914. However, Canadian banks still surpassed them in terms of commercial services throughout the 1920s and 1930s; they had more branches than American banks in all of the islands except Haiti (Quigley, "The Bank of Nova Scotia in the Caribbean," 797, 800–801). In Cuba and in South America, the Royal Bank felt that it had only one serious competitor, the National City Bank of New York (McDowall, *Quick to the Frontier,* 188). In the British West Indies, only the British Colonial Bank surpassed the Canadian banks, but the Canadian banks were strong enough to threaten its supremacy, especially in Jamaica (Jones, *British Multinational Banking,* 200; Monteith, *Depression to Decolonization*).

67   Collusion between Canadian banks and the Colonial Bank, known as Barclays (DCO) after 1926, has been analyzed by historian Kathleen Monteith through the archives of the British bank. Monteith examined the correspondence between Caribbean branches and the London head office as well as the journal of one of the bank's directors (Monteith, *Depression to Decolonization,* 54–74). Later, in 1973, the eight multinational banks active in Jamaica created a bankers' association, demonstrating what Maurice Odle describes as the "irrepressible urge of multinationals to collude via informal agreements (in situations where formal interbank agreements are not allowed) and to suppress remaining areas of competition" (Maurice Odle, *Multinational Banks and Underdevelopment* [New York: Pergamon, 1981], 93–94).

68   McDowall, *Quick to the Frontier,* 174.

69   Quigley, "The Bank of Nova Scotia in the Caribbean," 809–10.

70   Trigge, *A History of the Canadian Bank of Commerce, 1919–1930,* 3:460–63; Schull and Gibson, *The Scotiabank Story,* 225; S. Sarpkaya, *The Banker and Society* (Montreal: Institute of Canadian Bankers, 1968); Monteith, *Depression to Decolonization,* 60.

71   Bank of Jamaica, "History of Our Currency," *boj.org.jm*; Callender, *The Development of the Capital Market Institutions of Jamaica,* 72–76, 161–62. In 1933, RBC

banknotes circulating in the British West Indies were worth close to £240,000 (Monteith, *Depression to Decolonization*, 60).

72 In the United States, the activities of foreign banks were strictly regulated: "Foreign banks ... had to structure their business so as to conform with the rules in this highly regulated sector; both the government-imposed restrictions that were general to domestic and foreign participants and those that were specific to foreign investors had pronounced impact on the type, size, and most particularly, forms of banking operations" (Wilkins, *The History of Foreign Investment in the United States, 1914–1945*, 110). These regulations became even more restrictive in the early 1920s.

73 Monteith, *Depression to Decolonization*, 126–27.

74 Baum, *The Banks of Canada in the Commonwealth Caribbean*, 42.

75 Ibid., 29.

76 Ibid., 30.

77 Ibid., 31.

78 Ogelsby, *Gringos from the Far North*, 99.

79 Ibid., 109.

80 Ibid., 110.

81 Quigley, "The Bank of Nova Scotia in the Caribbean," 826.

82 Randall and Mount, *The Caribbean Basin: An International History*, 96.

83 Hudson, "Imperial Designs," 42.

84 Ibid., 34.

85 Ibid., 33–35. The Royal Bank's official historian is completely silent on all such episodes (McDowall, *Quick to the Frontier*).

86 Yves Engler, *The Black Book on Canadian Foreign Policy* (Black Point, NS, and Vancouver: Fernwood and RED, 2009), 16.

87 Ibid., 7–8.

88 For the Caribbean: Naylor, *The History of Canadian Business*, 2:255. In the Maritimes, James Frost has shown that until the 1880s, the Bank of Nova Scotia was lending money to regionally based companies, including manufacturing concerns. By 1900, however, even though nearly half the deposits collected by the bank still came from the Maritimes, the region only accounted for one-third of its loans, and "more than $5.3 million of 'surplus' capital was leaving the region for employment elsewhere." By 1910, "an enormous sum of capital was being drained away from the Maritimes by the Bank of Nova Scotia" (Frost, "The 'Nationalisation' of the Bank of Nova Scotia," 15 and 29). The bank began to favour foreign investment in the 1880s. It started by investing in American railway securities, which accounted for 85 percent of its profits in 1885. It also opened branches in Minneapolis, Jamaica, and Chicago. In 1893, after the opening of the Chicago branch, the bank's general director sent a memo to his Halifax agents, deploring the excessive amounts of money loaned in the Maritimes: "All this money has had to be brought here from Chicago where it might have been getting 10 per cent or more" (ibid., 16). Quigley, Drummond, and Evans, who disagree with the idea that the bank was (necessarily) discriminating against Maritime borrowers, or that capital exodus (necessarily) harmed the Maritime economy, acknowledge that money was leaving the Maritimes: "in terms of both the banking and savings bank systems there is little doubt that the Maritimes had net claims on the financial system in this period, or that through a variety of channels significant amounts of funds from the Maritimes found higher

returns outside the region than were available locally" (Neil C. Quigley, Ian M. Drummond, and Lewis T. Evans, "Regional Transfers of Funds through the Canadian Banking System and Maritime Economic Development, 1895–1935," in Kris Inwood [ed.], *Farm, Factory, and Fortune: New Studies in the Economic History of the Maritime Provinces* [Fredericton: Acadiensis, 1993], 248–50). According to Frost, there are two reasons for the change in the bank's orientations in the mid-1880s: first, the bankers' confidence in the Maritime economy had been profoundly undermined by the 1880s recession; second, they glimpsed "the prospect of enormous profits to be made elsewhere" (Frost, "The 'Nationalisation' of the Bank of Nova Scotia," 15). This does not mean that no profit was possible in the Maritimes, but only that they expected greater profits somewhere else.

89   Naylor, *The History of Canadian Business*, 2:255.

90   Quigley, "The Bank of Nova Scotia in the Caribbean," 828–30, 837.

91   Kaufman, "The Internationalization of Canadian Bank Capital," 74; Odle, *Multinational Banks and Underdevelopment*, 80–81. According to C. V. Callender, in 1965, "the commercial banks mobilised the savings of the Jamaican residents, utilised a portion to provide a base for short-term credit to the commercial and agricultural sectors, and to a lesser extent the industrial sector, and invested the remainder in suitable securities outside Jamaica" (Callender, *The Development of the Capital Market Institutions of Jamaica*, 162). In 1984, Michael Kaufman found that the only major loans made by Canadian banks to support Jamaican agriculture were granted in the 1970s; these loans appeared to have been channelled to marijuana production (Kaufman, "The Internationalization of Canadian Bank Capital," 74).

92   Baum, *The Banks of Canada in the Commonwealth Caribbean*, 5–6.

93   Monteith, *Depression to Decolonization*, 99, 101.

94   Odle notes that in poor countries, borrowers are required to have "safe assets": the bank feels that exemplary caution is required. In rich countries, as a lender, it is entitled to make choices that are "rather more risky and sometimes profligate" (Odle, *Multinational Banks and Underdevelopment*, 6–7).

95   Kaufman, "The Internationalization of Canadian Bank Capital," 64, 72–73; Naylor, *The History of Canadian Business*, 2:255.

96   Quigley explains that for the managers of a multinational bank, there is no reason to care about the balance between deposits and loans in a given region: profitability is the only issue. "Setting aside exchange risk, the balance between deposits and loans on different islands of the Caribbean was of no more concern to the general manager of the Bank of Nova Scotia than was a similar imbalance between individual regions in Canada: he simply attempted to ensure that loans were allocated (and thus reserves used) in the most profitable possible way" (Quigley, "The Bank of Nova Scotia in the Caribbean," 837).

97   "Lending activity was mainly confined to the United Fruit Company, loans did not keep pace with deposits, increasing from $155,040 to $865,277, and as a result Jamaica became an area of surplus savings" (Frost, "The 'Nationalisation' of the Bank of Nova Scotia," 24).

98   Naylor, *The History of Canadian Business*, 2:255.

99   Quigley, "The Bank of Nova Scotia in the Caribbean," 831–37.

100   Élie, *L'internationalisation des banques et autonomie nationale au Canada*, 100, 105–6.

101   Ibid., 106–7; Élie, *Le régime monétaire canadien*, 131.

102   Quigley, "The Bank of Nova Scotia in the Caribbean," 800–801.

103 Ogelsby, *Gringos from the Far North*, 108–9.

104 Ibid., 101–2.

105 Armstrong and Nelles, *Southern Exposure*, 283–84.

106 See, for example, ibid., 277–78; Ranald C. Michie, "Dunn, Fischer, and Company in the City of London, 1906–14," *Business History* 30, no. 2 (1988): 205; Naylor, *The History of Canadian Business*, 2:264; Ogelsby, *Gringos from the Far North*, 92–93.

107 Armstrong and Nelles, *Southern Exposure*, 286.

108 Gregory P. Marchildon, "A New View of Canadian Business History," *Business History* 32, no. 3 (July 1990): 165: "Concessionary agreements negotiated by a coterie of lawyer-promoters protected profits and excluded competitors. Aside from revolution, which could and did occur, and the problems of currency convertibility which affected the purchase price of North American and European equipment as well as the outflow of dividends and bond interest, the profitability of such operations was remarkable."

109 Armstrong and Nelles, *Southern Exposure*, 34, 38, and 108; Élie, *L'internationalisation des banques et autonomie nationale au Canada*, 77; Christopher Armstrong, "Making a Market: Selling Securities in Atlantic Canada before World War I," *Canadian Journal of Economics* 13, no. 3 (August 1980): 440.

110 This list, which does not pretend to be complete, is based on Armstrong and Nelles, *Southern Exposure*, 252, 253, and 271. The Barcelona company was the one involved in the financial scandal denounced by *L'Humanité* in 1913.

111 Marchildon, "A New View of Canadian Business History," 165.

112 These entrepreneurs included five men associated with the construction of Canadian railways: William Mackenzie, Donald Mann, William Van Horne, James Ross, and Herbert Holt.

113 First and foremost among the new financiers were Max Aitken and his mentor, John Stairs, but also B. F. Pearson, C. Cahan, James Dunn, Arthur Nesbitt, and Garnet Grant (Michie, "Dunn, Fischer, and Company in the City of London," 70–71, 76; Gregory P. Marchildon, "John F. Stairs, Max Aitken, and the Scotia Group: Finance Capitalism and Industrial Decline in the Maritimes, 1890–1914," in Kris Inwood [ed.], *Farm, Factory, and Fortune*, 197–218; Marchildon, *Profits and Politics*, 36).

114 Marchildon, "A New View of Canadian Business History," 165.

115 Gregory P. Marchildon, "British Investment Banking and Industrial Decline before the Great War: A Case Study of Capital Outflow to Canadian Industry," *Business History* 33, no. 3 (July 1991): 84–89; Gregory P. Marchildon, "'Hands Across the Water': Canadian Industrial Financiers in the City of London, 1905–1920," *Business History* 34, no. 3 (July 1992): 71.

116 In Canada, banks and insurance companies were strictly regulated, and trusts, while not subject to strict constraints, were prevented by common law from engaging in speculative activities; but investment banks (known as "investment houses," "trust companies," "securities corporations," "bond dealers," etc.), involved in promoting and subscribing newly issued securities, were practically unregulated (Marchildon, *Profits and Politics*, 36). Security financing was much less regulated in Canada than in Great Britain or Germany in the early twentieth century (Gregory P. Marchildon, "Canadian Multinationals and International Finance, Past and Present," *Business History* 34, no. 3 [July 1992]: 12; Gregory P. Marchildon, "The Role of Lawyers in Corporate Promotion and Management: A Canadian Case Study and Theoretical Speculations," *Business and Economic History*, 2nd series, 19 [1990]: 200).

117 Armstrong and Nelles, *Southern Exposure*, 25–33; Christopher Armstrong and H. V. Nelles, "A Curious Capital Flow: Canadian Investment in Mexico, 1902–1910," *Business History Review* 58, no. 2 (1984): 189–90.

118 In North America, "an important minority of lawyers chose to become the handmaidens of big business" (Marchildon, "The Role of Lawyers in Corporate Promotion and Management," 199–200).

119 Robert G. Gordon, "A Perspective from the United States," in Carol Wilton (ed.), *Beyond the Law: Lawyers and Business in Canada, 1830 to 1930, Essays in the History of Canadian Law* (Toronto and Vancouver: The Osgoode Society/ Butterworths, 1990), 4:431.

120 Marchildon, "The Role of Lawyers in Corporate Promotion and Management," 199.

121 Ibid., 194. See also Gregory P. Marchildon, "International Corporate Law from a Maritime Base: The Halifax Firm of Harris, Henry, and Cahan," in Carol Wilton (ed.), *Beyond the Law*, 201–34.

122 Theodore Regehr, "Zebulon Aiton Lash," and Duncan McDowall, "Frederick Stark Pearson," both in *Dictionary of Canadian Biography*, vol. 14, *1911–1920* (Quebec City and Toronto: Université Laval and University of Toronto, 1972) (available at *biographi.ca*).

123 Armstrong and Nelles, *Southern Exposure*, 277. The authors add: "The vernacular word for the streetcars in Brazil – *bondes* – symbolized this irritating debt to Canada."

124 "It was known, pejoratively, as the 'Canadian octopus' because its tentacles extended through all of [Rio de Janeiro's] urban space" (Amara Silva de Souza Rocha, "Luzes da ribalta," *Revista de História da Biblioteca Nacional* (Rio de Janeiro), 2007 [our translation]). Established in 1912 through the merger of two Canadian companies founded in 1899 and 1904, the "octopus" at its peak around 1946 was the largest Canadian company abroad with assets of close to $500 million. The company owned the streetcars of São Paulo and Rio de Janeiro, but more importantly, it provided over half Brazil's electricity and three-quarters of the country's telephone services (Duncan McDowall, *The Light: Brazilian Traction, Light, and Power Company Limited, 1899–1945* [Toronto: University of Toronto Press, 1988]; Ogelsby, *Gringos from the Far North*, 129; Marchildon, "A New View of Canadian Business History," 164). After 1979, the company (known as Brascan since 1969) continued to hold significant assets in Brazil but was no longer the owner of public utilities. The holding company has survived into the twenty-first century under the name of Brookfield Asset Management (Shirley Won, "What's In a Name? Plenty If It's Brascan," *Globe and Mail* [Toronto], September 16, 2005).

125 McDowall, *The Light*, 51–52.

126 Ibid., 52; Marchildon, *Profits and Politics*, 41.

127 McDowall, *The Light*, 52. In Camagüey, for example, ordinary shares valued at $700,000 were distributed free of charge to promoters and subscribers (who were often the same people). Brokers, as well as two Royal Bank managers who had acted as intermediaries, also received a small part of the bonus stock (Marchildon, *Profits and Politics*, 70–71).

128 A Canadian consortium that wanted a monopoly on electric tramway services in Birmingham, England, learned that English company law did not allow insiders to receive important blocks of free shares. Canadian law did not include any prohibition of this kind (Armstrong and Nelles, *Southern Exposure*, 31).

129 Ibid., 29–33. The "Canadian octopus," for example, was initially "an overcapitalised vehicle for promoters' profits" (Marchildon, "A New View of Canadian Business History," 164). At the time the company was created in 1912 through the merger

of the São Paulo and Rio de Janeiro companies, its president, William Mackenzie, and his acolyte F. S. Pearson pocketed millions of dollars by diluting the capital of both companies (Charles A. Gauld, *The Last Titan: Percival Farquhar, American Entrepreneur in Latin America* [Stanford and Felton: California Institute of International Studies and Glenwood, 1972], 82; McDowall, "Frederick Stark Pearson"). Overcapitalization did not only occur in the South; Montreal streetcars, for example, were the object of the same kind of operation in 1911 (Jean-Pierre Dagenais, *Ironie du char. Un essai sur l'automobile et la crise des transports à Montréal* [Montreal: J. P. Dagenais, 1982]).

130   Marchildon, *Profits and Politics*, 5. The criminal flavour of Aitken's deals is confirmed by Katherine V. Bligh and Christine Shaw; according to them, Aitken's decision to settle permanently in London in 1910 was partly motivated by a desire to flee his lawyer, Charles Hazlitt Cahan (future Secretary of State in the Conservative government of R. B. Bennett from 1930 to 1935), who was blackmailing him about his dubious operations in the merger of Canadian cement companies. Aitken was now *persona non grata* in Canada and never again intervened in Canadian public life, even though, for the rest of his life, the greatest part of his income came from Canada (Bligh and Shaw, "William Maxwell Aitken," 23–24).

Aitken's career began in Nova Scotia, where he sold Trinidad Electric securities to small investors (Marchildon, *Profits and Politics*, 34); Trinidad Electric was a company established in Halifax in 1900 to manage Port of Spain's trolleys and electric power plant. Aitken then became the driving force behind the Royal Securities Corporation, a Halifax investment company that moved to Montreal in 1906; the firm mobilized capital to establish Canadian utilities in the Caribbean or to carry out mergers of Canadian producers of cement, rolling stock, or steel. (The three largest mergers carried out in Canada at the time, involving Canada Cement, Canadian Car and Foundry, and the Steel Company of Canada, were the work of Aitken in 1909–1910 [Marchildon, "'Hands Across the Water'," 85–86].) Aitken's business deals in Canada made him a millionaire by the age of thirty; this outcome is certainly related to the overcapitalization characteristic of most of the companies he set up. In Canada, Aitken recruited and trained financiers who later became mythical figures in Canadian economic history: Izaak Walton Killam, Arthur Nesbitt, and Ward Pitfield.

In Great Britain, Aitken was elected to Parliament, was made a peer under the name of Lord Beaverbrook, was appointed Minister of Information during the First World War, and became a British press tycoon (ibid., 85–89). With Churchill, he was one of the major representatives of the fraction of the British ruling class that was favourable both to the unity of Great Britain and North America and to the preservation of the British Empire in the face of American hegemony (Van der Pijl, *The Making of an Atlantic Ruling Class*, 37).

In the final analysis, this transatlantic career seems utterly Canadian, and Aitken-Beaverbrook's worthy successor today would appear to be the millionaire Conrad Black, a Canadian who became a press tycoon, was raised to the peerage in Great Britain as Baron Black of Crossharbour, and was jailed for financial fraud in the United States in 2007.

131   Michie, "Dunn, Fischer and Company in the City of London"; Marchildon, "'Hands Across the Water'"; Dilley, *Australia, Canada, and the City of London*, 56, 62–63, 183. Canada's upper class was joined to the City by a complex web of interconnected relations (Dilley, *Australia, Canada, and the City of London*, 56). "The range of channels through which capital flowed to Canada was striking, as was their fluidity" (ibid., 62–63). Canadian investment houses in London included Dunn Fischer (James Dunn), Dominion Securities (E. R. Wood), Royal Securities Corporation

(Max Aitken), Wood Gundy, Canada Securities Corporation (Rodolphe Forget, the one and only French Canadian of the lot), C. Meredith and Company (associated with the Bank of Montreal), Dominion Bond (Garnet Grant), the Investment Trust Company (Arthur Nesbitt), and the Greenshields, O'Hara, Mackay, and R. S. Meredith firms (Marchildon, "'Hands Across the Water,'" 69–70). These companies complemented more majestic channels: the Bank of Montreal and the Canadian Bank of Commerce (Dilley, *Australia, Canada, and the City of London*, 62–63, 183). The future CIBC had opened a branch in London in 1901 (Michie, "Dunn, Fischer, and Company in the City of London," 197; Ross, *A History of the Canadian Bank of Commerce*, 2:213). The major Canadian investment houses established in the early twentieth century were later bought by the chartered banks: this is the origin of contemporary institutions such as RBC Dominion Securities, CIBC Wood Gundy, and BMO Nesbitt Burns (Marchildon, "'Hands Across the Water,'" 90n3).

132   One effect of these techniques was to blur the distinctions between the primary and the secondary market; that is, the initial offering of shares and the sale of already-issued shares (Michie, "Dunn, Fischer and Company in the City of London," 212).

133   Marchildon, "A New View of Canadian Business History," 163; Michie, "The Canadian Securities Market," 43; Armstrong and Nelles, *Southern Exposure*, 249; Élie, *L'internationalisation des banques et autonomie nationale au Canada*, 78–79. Christopher Armstrong and H. V. Nelles summarize the situation in Mexico: "British and Canadian capital was routed through Canadian companies to buy largely American equipment for operations in Mexico" (Armstrong and Nelles, "A Curious Capital Flow," 199).

134   "British and European investors gradually replaced the initial Canadian holders of the stocks and bonds of Latin American utilities, and the market in many of them switched to other centers, such as London, Paris, and, especially, Brussels, which was the leading center for tramway undertakings in the world" (Michie, "The Canadian Securities Market," 43). In the mid-1920s, even though their head office was still located in Toronto, the "Canadian" utility companies of Barcelona, Mexico, and Brazil belonged to SOFINA, a conglomerate based in Belgium (Armstrong and Nelles, *Southern Exposure*, 271).

135   Ibid., 282.

136   Marchildon, *Profits and Politics*, 287n7.

137   When Christopher Armstrong and H. V. Nelles published *Southern Exposure* in 1988, Mexican administrators of the Mexican Light and Power Company, which had been nationalized many years previously, were still travelling to Toronto every February to carry out legal rites required to maintain the corporation's existence (Armstrong and Nelles, *Southern Exposure*, 291–92). Today, in many cases, the addresses of convenience have disappeared, but Toronto law firms no doubt still hold the archives of the Mexico Tramways Company and Mexican Light and Power (McDowall, "Frederick Stark Pearson").

138   Armstrong and Nelles, *Southern Exposure*, 271 and 277.

139   The Bank of Montreal and the Canadian Bank of Commerce withdrew from Mexico; the Bank of Montreal gave up its participation in Barclays (DCO); the Royal Bank closed 34 branches in the Caribbean. Only the Bank of Nova Scotia retained a certain vigour, though it too closed a number of branches (Élie, *L'internationalisation des banques et autonomie nationale au Canada*, 148–49).

140   In Jamaica, for example, there were four commercial banks in 1945 of which three were the usual Canadian financial institutions found in the Caribbean: Scotiabank, RBC, and CIBC. The fourth institution was the British bank, Barclays (DCO). There were no American banks in Jamaica until the arrival of the First

National City Bank of New York in 1961 (Callender, *The Development of the Capital Market Institutions of Jamaica*, 95).

141 Frost, "The 'Nationalisation' of the Bank of Nova Scotia," 29.

142 Marchildon, "John F. Stairs, Max Aitken and the Scotia Group," 218.

143 Marchildon, "Canadian Multinationals and International Finance," 5. The three European countries were the United Kingdom, France, and the Federal Republic of Germany.

144 Ronen Palan, "International Financial Centers: The British-Empire, City-States, and Commercially Oriented Politics," Tel Aviv, *Theoretical Inquiries in Law* 11, no. 1 (January 2010): 160–62; Ronen Palan and Jamie Stern-Weiner, "Britain's Second Empire," *New Left Project*, no. 17 (August 2012).

145 Christian Chavagneux and Ronen Palan, *Les paradis fiscaux* (Paris: La Découverte, 2012), 42 [our translation].

146 Ibid., 41–42.

147 The Caribbean jurisdictions were not subject to the same legal constraints as the Channel Islands and belonged to the same time zone as New York (Ronen Palan, "International Financial Centers," 170–71).

▩ JAMAICA

1 Bank of Nova Scotia, 1953 annual report, 33.

2 Duncan McDowall, *Quick to the Frontier: Canada's Royal Bank* (Toronto: McClelland and Stewart, 199), 196.

3 Daniel Jay Baum, *The Banks of Canada in the Commonwealth Caribbean: Economic Nationalism and Multinational Enterprises of a Medium Power* (New York: Praeger, 1974), 22.

4 Kathleen E. A. Monteith, *Depression to Decolonization: Barclays Bank (DCO) in the West Indies, 1926–1962* (Kingston: University of West Indies Press, 2008); C. V. Callender, *The Development of the Capital Market Institutions of Jamaica* (Kingston: Institute of Social and Economic Research, University of the West Indies, 1965), 95.

5 Duncan McDowall, *Quick to the Frontier: Canada's Royal Bank* (Toronto: McClelland and Stewart, 1993) 173.

6 These are the words of Towers's biographer Douglas H. Fullerton in *Graham Towers and His Times* (Toronto: McClelland and Stewart, 1986), 286.

7 Baum, *The Banks of Canada in the Commonwealth Caribbean*, 32n42. Baum's endnote refers to Ministry Paper no. 6 (M.P. no. C2729/88), Government of Jamaica, March 9, 1960.

8 Callender, *The Development of the Capital Market Institutions of Jamaica*, 148.

9 Graham F. Towers, *The Financial System and Institutions of Jamaica* (Kingston: Government Printer, 1958 [April 20, 1956]).

10 Ibid., 19–20, section 67–68.

11 Ibid., 18, section 64; 21, section 3.

12 Ibid., 1, section 3.

13 Ibid., 7, section 27.

14 The two measures are the *Industrial Incentives Law* and the *Export Industry Encouragement Law*, both described by Wayne Thirsk, "Jamaican Tax Incentives," in Roy Bahl (ed.), *The Jamaican Tax Reform* (Cambridge: Lincoln Institute of Land Policy, 1991), 702. This article includes elements from another

paper by the same author, "Jamaican Tax Incentives," published as part of the *Jamaican Tax Structure Examination Project*, Staff Paper no. 9, Metropolitan Studies Program and Board of Revenue, Government of Jamaica, The Maxwell School, Syracuse University, August 1984.

15   V. L. Arnett, "Ministry Paper no. 11: Assurance Re-Amendment of International Business Companies (Exemption from Income Tax) Law no. 36 of 1956," March 6, 1962. Through this document, the Minister was attempting to make the clauses of the law even more explicit.

16   André Beauchamp, *Guide mondial des paradis fiscaux* (Ville Mont-Royal, QC: Éditions Le Nordais, 1982 [Paris: Grasset et Fasquelle, 1981]), 44.

17   Yves Engler, *The Black Book on Canadian Foreign Policy* (Black Point, NS, and Vancouver: Fernwood and RED, 2009), 9.

18   Carlton E. Davis, *Jamaica in the World Aluminium Industry*, vol. II, *Bauxite Levy Negotiations, 1974–1978* (Kingston: Jamaica Bauxite Institute, 1995), 3 and 15.

19   He remained on the RBC Board until 1966 (Fullerton, *Graham Towers and His Times*, 285).

20   RBC, 1963 annual report, 20.

21   RBC, 1964 annual report, 20 and 51. This report is a far cry from the RBC's annual reports before 1956, which dealt chiefly with the textile industry and food staples and focused on the price of commodities rather than tax benefits.

22   Bank of Nova Scotia, 1961 annual report, 28.

23   Bank of Nova Scotia, 1966 annual report, 19, and 1967 annual report, 17 and 20. During this period, the Bank of Nova Scotia's policy was to open offices in new offshore jurisdictions such as Beirut, Rotterdam, or Dublin (Bank of Nova Scotia, 1966 annual report, 20).

24   Bank of Nova Scotia, 1966 annual report, 19.

25   Canadian banks in Jamaica today include CIBC, Scotiabank, and the National Commercial Bank, whose majority shareholder is the AIC group. ("Canadian Banks – Jamaica, Barbados, Cayman Islands, Turks and Caicos Islands," Canadian Trade Commissioner Service, June 2014).

26   Callender, *The Development of the Capital Market Institutions of Jamaica*, 160, 166.

27   Kathleen E. A. Monteith, *Depression to Decolonization: Barclays Bank (DCO) in the West Indies, 1926–1962* (Kingston: University of the West Indies Press, 2008), 126–27.

28   Michael Kaufman, "The Internationalization of Canadian Bank Capital (With a Look at Bank Activity in the Caribbean and Central America)," *Journal of Canadian Studies* 19, no. 4 (Winter 1984–85): 72.

29   Callender, *The Development of the Capital Market Institutions of Jamaica*, 90–91.

30   Ibid.

31   Neil C. Quigley, "The Bank of Nova Scotia in the Caribbean, 1889–1940: The Establishment of an International Branch Banking Network," *Business History Review* 63, no. 4 (1989): 835–37. Quigley explains that from the bank's accounting perspective, Jamaica was just one element of its international system.

32   "Five years after Towers' report, Jamaica set up a central bank. The performance of the Jamaican economy since, and the inflation, unemployment, and unrest that ensued hardly suggest that central banks are an unmixed blessing or a universal panacea" (Fullerton, *Graham Towers and His Times*, 287).

33 These import substitution measures produced real results: between 1971 and 1978, fifty-eight new firms were created to answer Jamaican domestic demand while only fifteen were launched with a strictly export orientation (Thirsk, "Jamaican Tax Incentives," 702, 706). Companies supplying the domestic market benefited from the Industrial Incentives Law while exporting companies developed under the Export Industry Encouragement Law.

34 Russell Banks, *The Book of Jamaica* (New York: HarperPerennial, 1996 [1980]), 89.

35 Édouard Chambost, *Guide Chambost des paradis fiscaux*, 8th ed. (Lausanne: Favre, 2005 [1980]), 556–57; Beauchamp, *Guide mondial des paradis fiscaux*, 44. For more on the theme of black humour and ordinary racism in tax haven guides, see Alain Deneault, "Esthétique coloniale, paradis fiscaux et vahinés ..." in Pascal Blanchard and Nicolas Bancel (ed.), *Culture post-coloniale 1961–2006* (Paris: Autrement, 2006), 134–43; Alain Deneault, "Les symboles coloniaux au service de l'humour noir 'offshore': l'île dans la 'littérature' du fiscaliste Édouard Chambost," in Catherine Coquio (ed.), *Retours du colonial? Disculpation et réhabilitation de l'histoire coloniale* (Nantes : Éditions L'Atalante, 2008), 239–58.

36 Chambost, *Guide Chambost des paradis fiscaux*, 556–57.

37 Beauchamp, *Guide mondial des paradis fiscaux*, 44.

38 Ibid., 57.

39 Duncan C. Campbell, *Global Mission: The Story of Alcan* (Don Mills: Ontario Publishing, 1985), 2:252.

40 In fact, the Jamaican government set the standard price per ton at US$3.85, but only half of this amount was set to vary according to the price of aluminum. As a result, the actual overall rate was US$2.30 (Robert Conrad, *Bauxite Taxation in Jamaica*, Staff Paper no. 5, Metropolitan Studies Program, The Maxwell School, Syracuse University and Board of Revenue, Government of Jamaica, February 1984, 6–7).

41 Romain Cruse, "Politiques de la fragmentation urbaine et violence. L'exemple de Kingston, Jamaïque," *Cybergeo – Revue européenne de géographie* 511 (2010): section 28.

42 Conrad, *Bauxite Taxation in Jamaica*, 6.

43 Ibid., 7.

44 Ibid., 6–7.

45 Damien Millet and François Mauger, *La Jamaïque dans l'étau du FMI. La dette expliquée aux amateurs de reggae, aux fumeurs de joints et aux autres* (Paris: L'esprit frappeur/Comité pour l'annulation de la dette du tiers-monde [CADTM], 2004), 19.

46 Campbell, *Global Mission*, 223.

47 Ibid., 309.

48 Ibid., 310.

49 Ibid., 232.

50 Ibid., 260.

51 Ibid., 273–74.

52 Ibid., 239.

53 Among other criteria, the law drafted by Alcan with Jamaican officials favoured companies incorporated under Jamaican law, even if they were established with foreign capital. This explains why Alcan always operated through companies directly incorporated in Jamaica, such as Jamaica Bauxites. From the beginning, Alcan mastered the subtleties of the system; meanwhile, "Since they had taxation arguments

for remaining as branch operations, the American companies in Jamaica would not follow this incorporation route for some years" (Campbell, *Global Mission*, 261).

54 Ibid., 241–42.

55 Davis, *Bauxite Levy Negotiations*, 17–18.

56 Ibid., 264ff. Beginning in 1957, companies no longer needed to own land in order in to obtain a mining lease (Davis, *Bauxite Levy Negotiations*, 8).

57 Campbell, *Global Mission*, 260.

58 Ibid., 261.

59 The Jamaican government's credibility on the Jamaicanization issue was weakened by the fact that members of the National Bauxite Commission and the negotiating team representing the government, such as Mayer Matalon and Patrick Rousseau, were also businessmen interested in investing in this sector of activity (Davis, *Bauxite Levy Negotiations*, 13).

60 Campbell, *Global Mission*, 261ff; Davis, *Bauxite Levy Negotiations*, 102.

61 Campbell, *Global Mission*, 257.

62 Vijay Prashad, *The Darker Nations: A People's History of the Third World* (New York: New Press, 2008), xv.

63 Founding members were Australia, Guinea, Guyana, Jamaica, Sierra Leone, Surinam, and Yugoslavia; Ghana, Haiti, Indonesia, and the Dominican Republic joined a few years later. The organization was weakened by the fact that Brazil was not a member. Many organizations of this kind were created by Caribbean jurisdictions during this period.

64 Campbell, *Global Mission*, 275.

65 The new tax was "a production tax on bauxite mined…at a rate of 7.5 percent of the price of aluminum ingot…the production tax would be about US$11 per tonne (US$9.98 per ton) of bauxite mined. This would be in addition to existing mining royalties at J50 cents per tonne" (Campbell, *Global Mission*, 278).

66 Marie-Claude Céleste, "La solidarité de l'Association des pays exportateurs de bauxite à l'épreuve," *Le Monde diplomatique*, November 1971, 8 [our translation], quoted in Bonnie K. Campbell, *Les enjeux de la bauxite. La Guinée face aux multinationales de l'aluminium* (Montreal and Geneva : Presses de l'Université de Montréal and Institut universitaire des hautes études internationales, 1983), 41.

67 The tax rate of 7.5 percent in 1974 rose to 8 percent in 1975–1976 and 8.5 percent in 1976–1977 (Campbell, *Global Mission*, 278). See also Millet and Mauger, *La Jamaïque dans l'étau du FMI*, 19–20; Fred Célimène and Romain Cruse, *La Jamaïque: les raisons d'un naufrage* (Paris: Publibook [presented under the imprint of the Presses de l'Université des Antilles et de la Guyane], 2012).

68 Campbell, *Global Mission*, 282–83; Prashad, *The Darker Nations*, 227.

69 Millet and Mauger, *La Jamaïque dans l'étau du FMI*, 24; Campbell, *Global Mission*, 283.

70 The company claimed reserves of 340 million tons of ore and, according to a 1974 assessment, was extracting 2.43 million long dry tons a year (Davis, *Bauxite Levy Negotiations*, 76 and 111). (A long dry ton is a measurement applied to bauxite: it means 1.016 metric tonnes of material dried at 100°C to 105°C (ibid., viii).

71 Ibid., 202.

72 Campbell, *Global Mission*, 274. "Mismanagement" and "ill-advised theorizing" are quotes from *The Economist*.

73 Ibid., 281.

74 Ibid., 278.

75 Ibid., 259, 278–79.

76 Ibid., 276.

77 Ibid., 281.

78 Ibid., 281.

79 Ibid., 281–82.

80 Millet and Mauger, *La Jamaïque dans l'étau du FMI*, 24 [our translation].

81 Campbell, *Les enjeux de la bauxite*, 41–42.

82 Davis, *Bauxite Levy Negotiations*, 298.

83 Prashad, *The Darker Nations*, 227; Millet and Mauger, *La Jamaïque dans l'étau du FMI*, 20; Conrad, *Bauxite Taxation in Jamaica*, 7; James Wozny, "The Taxation of Corporate Source Income in Jamaica," in Bahl (ed.), *The Jamaican Tax Reform*, 265–323.

84 Davis, *Bauxite Levy Negotiations*, 298.

85 Julien Arnoult, "Un vent républicain souffle en Jamaïque," in Alexis Bautzmann, *Atlas géopolitique mondial* (Paris: Argos, 2013), 131.

86 Campbell, *Global Mission*, 285–86.

87 Cruse, "Politiques de la fragmentation urbaine et violence."

88 Célimène and Cruse, *La Jamaïque: les raisons d'un naufrage*, 144.

89 Banks, *The Book of Jamaica*, 297.

90 Thirsk, "Jamaican Tax Incentives," 706; M. L. Ayub, *Made in Jamaica* (Baltimore: Johns Hopkins UP, 1981).

91 Ibid.

92 Thirsk, "Jamaican Tax Incentives," 704 [emphasis in the original].

93 Ibid., 706.

94 Millet and Mauger, *La Jamaïque dans l'étau du FMI*, 41–49.

95 Ibid., 40–49.

96 Ibid., 56.

97 Ibid., 70 [our translation].

98 "IMF Executive Directors and Voting Power," IMF (Washington, DC), February 8, 2015.

99 Millet and Mauger, *La Jamaïque dans l'étau du FMI*, 34.

100 Traditional debt forgiveness is a way of saving states from complete bankruptcy so that they can keep on with the cyclical process of paying their debts. The machinery of indebtedness for the benefit of capital holders is thus kept going. The South funds Northern financial institutions – and not the other way round.

101 Alicia Dunkley, "It's Not Enough! Offshore Business Legislation Passes Despite Opposition Warnings," *Jamaica Observer* (Kingston), March 6, 2011.

102 Millet and Mauger, *La Jamaïque dans l'étau du FMI*, 53 [our translation].

103 Ibid. [our translation].

104 Angela Shah, "Free-Trade Zones Attract Criminals," *New York Times,* November 10, 2010.

105 Stephanie Black, *Life and Debt*, documentary film (United States: Tuff Gong Pictures, 2001), 86 minutes; on the island's chronic state of indebtedness, William Karel, *Jamaïque/FMI : mourir à crédit*, documentary film (France: Arte, 1996), 84 minutes.

106 Wozny, "The Taxation of Corporate Source Income in Jamaica," 302.

107 Ibid.

108 Ibid.

109 Arnoult, "Un vent républicain souffle en Jamaïque."

THE BAHAMAS

1 Alan Block, *Masters of Paradise: Organized Crime and the Internal Revenue Service in The Bahamas* (New Brunswick, NJ: Transaction, 1991), 6.

2 Robert Blakey, Ronald Goldstock, and Charles Rogovin, *Rackets Bureaux: Investigation and Prosecution of Organized Crime* (Washington: National Institute of Law Enforcement and Criminal Justice, Law Enforcement Assistance Administration, U.S. Dept. of Justice, March 1978), 4, quoted in Block, *Masters of Paradise*, 5.

3 Office of Administrative Law, Casino Control Commission, State of New Jersey, *In the Matter of the Application of Resorts International Hotel, Inc. for a Casino License*, 10 NJAR 244 (November 22, 1979), 266. On the American mafia in Cuba, see Enrique Cirules, *The Mafia in Havana: A Caribbean Mob Story* (Melbourne: Ocean Press, 2004).

4 Jean-François Couvrat and Nicolas Pless, *La face cachée de l'économie mondiale* (Paris: Hatier, 1988), 191 [our translation].

5 Block, *Masters of Paradise*, 74; Alain Vernay, *Les paradis fiscaux* (Paris: Seuil, 1968), 165. "Bay Street" here is Nassau's main street (and not the main street of Toronto's financial district).

6 "Stafford Sands," *Bahamasb2b* website; Block, *Masters of Paradise*, 31.

7 Block, *Masters of Paradise*, 29.

8 Ibid., 31. Casinos at the time were illegal and were tolerated only if the owner benefited from some kind of protection; for example, the protection offered by Kenneth Salomon, a member of the local financial establishment. This establishment included many direct descendants of pirates, shipwreckers (Vernay, *Les paradis fiscaux*, 165) and merchants who had run the blockade to sell arms to the Confederate States during the American Civil War (Richard Oulahan and William Lambert, "The Scandal in the Bahamas," *Life* magazine, February 3, 1967, reproduced in Jim Baker, *Bahamian Fragments: Bits and Pieces from the History of the Bahamas* (*JabezCorner.com*).

9 "An Informal History of the Grand Bahama Port Authority, 1955–1985," in Jim Baker, *Bahamian Fragments: Bits and Pieces from the History of the Bahamas*.

10 Block, *Masters of Paradise*, 27.

11 Ibid., 28; Vernay, *Les paradis fiscaux*, 158; Craig Wolff, "Wallace Groves Is Dead at 86: Developer of Resort in Bahamas," *New York Times*, February 1, 1988. For details of this affair, see "Investment Trusts and Investment Companies: Letter from the Acting Chairman of the Securities and Exchange Commission Transmitting, Pursuant to Law, a Report on Abuses and Deficiencies in the Organization and Operation of Investment Trusts and Investment Companies" (Washington, DC: U.S. Government Printing Office, 1940 [May 3, 1939]).

12 Office of Administrative Law, Casino Control Commission, State of New Jersey, *In the Matter of the Application of Resorts International Hotel, Inc. for a Casino License*, 264–65; Block, *Masters of Paradise*, 28.

13 Ed Reid, "Bahamas Hoodlum Sea," chapter 7 of *The Anatomy of Organized Crime: The Grim Reapers* (Washington, DC: Henry Regnery Company, 1969), 106, in Jim

Baker, *Bahamian Fragments: Bits and Pieces from the History of the Bahamas*; Block, *Masters of Paradise*, 28. Sands's support, which implied the support of the Nassau government, restored Groves's prestige in the eyes of powerful outside financiers attracted by the new economic model. As the chief shareholder of a major hotel company remarked, the fact of being accepted by Nassau rehabilitated Groves as a business partner (Office of Administrative Law, Casino Control Commission, State of New Jersey, *In the Matter of the Application of Resorts International Hotel, Inc. for a Casino License*, 264).

14 Block, *Masters of Paradise*, 27–29.

15 Ibid., 28. The text of the Hawksbill Creek, Grand Bahama (Deep Water Harbour and Industrial Area) Act, Statute Law of the Bahamas 2001, chapter 261, can be found online.

16 Bill Davidson, "The Mafia: Shadow of Evil on an Island in the Sun," *Saturday Evening Post* 204, no. 4 (February 25, 1967): 27–37, in Jim Baker, *Bahamian Fragments: Bits and Pieces from the History of the Bahamas*, 4.

17 Block, *Masters of Paradise*, 29–30.

18 Vernay, *Les paradis fiscaux*, 159.

19 Ibid. [our translation].

20 Bill Davidson, "The Mafia: Shadow of Evil on an Island in the Sun," 4; Block, *Masters of Paradise*, 28–30.

21 Block, *Masters of Paradise*, 30.

22 Ibid., 33.

23 Ibid., 31–32.

24 Ibid., 11.

25 Ibid., 28.

26 Ibid., 34.

27 Ibid., 34, 36.

28 Ibid., 39, referring to the two corporations Lorado of Bahamas Ltd. and Canadian Dyno Mines Ltd.

29 Vernay, *Les paradis fiscaux*, 161.

30 *Hearings: Organized Crime, Stolen Securities* (Washington, DC: Permanent Subcommittee on Investigations, United States Senate, July 28, 1971), 857, quoted in Block, *Masters of Paradise*, 36 and 53n12. See also David McClintick, *Indecent Exposure: A True Story of Hollywood and Wall Street* (New York: Dell, 1983), 88; Hank Messick, *Syndicate Abroad* (New York: Macmillan, 1969), 64.

31 Vernay, *Les paradis fiscaux*, 161 [our translation].

32 Quoted in Mario Possamai, *Money on the Run: Canada and How the World's Dirty Profits Are Laundered* (Toronto: Viking, 1992), 107. See also Block, *Masters of Paradise*, 34, 36.

33 Possamai, *Money on the Run*, vii–x.

34 Ibid., 107.

35 Block, *Masters of Paradise*, 43.

36 Ibid., 34.

37 Ibid., 39–40.

38 Chesler held ownership in his own name, while Groves's ownership was indirect: his wife, Georgette, was formally listed among the owners (Office of Administrative

Law, Casino Control Commission, State of New Jersey, *In the Matter of the Application of Resorts International Hotel, Inc. for a Casino License*, 266).

39 Block, *Masters of Paradise*, 41, 64.

40 Ibid., 40; Monroe W. Karmin and Stanley Penn, "Las Vegas East," *Wall Street Journal*, October 5, 1966, in Jim Baker, *Bahamian Fragments: Bits and Pieces from the History of the Bahamas*, 2.

41 Block, *Masters of Paradise*, 40.

42 Ibid., 42.

43 Vernay, *Les paradis fiscaux*, 162n [our translation]. Sands himself admitted that he was offered $1 million in 1960 for exclusive gambling rights on the islands; he claimed to have indignantly rejected the offer (Oulahan and Lambert, *Life* magazine, February 3, 1967). Later, after gambling had been legalized in the Bahamas, he was paid at least $1.8 million. Sands justified these payments to Alain Vernay by saying that dedicated citizens who were willing to hold political office in the Bahamas did not receive any salary from the Bahamian government (Vernay, *Les paradis fiscaux*, 172).

44 Block, *Masters of Paradise*, 41.

45 Ibid., 45.

46 Ibid., 40.

47 Vernay, *Les paradis fiscaux*, 156.

48 Block, *Masters of Paradise*, 34, 38.

49 Peter Gillespie, "The Trouble With Tax Havens: Whose Shelter? Whose Storm?," in Richard Swift (ed.), *The Great Revenue Robbery: How to Stop the Tax Cut Scam and Save Canada* (Toronto: Between the Lines, 2013), 55.

50 Block, *Masters of Paradise*, 10–11.

51 "The RCMP reported that Mob money was being invested in every kind of business in Toronto, from hotels, restaurants, and shopping plazas to real estate" (Peter Gillespie, "The Trouble with Tax Havens," 56). Gillespie's source is Margaret Baere and Stephen Schneider, *Money Laundering in Canada* (Toronto: University of Toronto Press, 2007).

52 Born in Poland under Russian rule, Maier Suchowljansky (alias Meyer Lansky) is known for his partnership with the pioneer of Las Vegas, Bugsy Siegel. However, Lansky's chief contribution to the history of international gangsterism was his work as treasurer of the National Crime Syndicate, a confederation of Jewish and Italian organized crime groups founded in 1929. Troubled by Al Capone's conviction for tax fraud and Prohibition violation in 1931, Lansky was one of the first in the criminal world to develop ways of eluding U.S. tax rules. Taking advantage of Switzerland's 1934 law on bank secrecy, he transferred his illegal casino earnings to an anonymous Swiss bank account. The "loan-back" technique was a completely safe money-laundering tactic: Lansky could get the money back into the United States as a loan on which he paid interest that he could then deduct from his taxable income. According to criminologist R. T. Naylor, "the flourishing activities of the Lansky-Luciano mob, and the subsequent necessity for sophisticated methods of hiding and directing the flow of cash, proved to be the mother of offshore invention" (Naylor, *Hot Money and the Politics of Debt* [Montreal: McGill-Queen's UP, 2004 (1987)], 21). As Prohibition came to an end, Lansky invested in gaming in places such as New Orleans and Miami. In 1938, Cuban president Batista invited him to revitalize Cuban gambling venues, where Lansky was able to recycle illegal money far from the prying eyes of the IRS. After the 1959 revolution in Cuba,

Lansky looked to the Bahamas, another location close to Miami. Lansky is the basis for Hyman Roth, the character played by Lee Strasberg in the second film (1974) of Francis Ford Coppola's *Godfather* trilogy. In this film, Roth makes a statement that is a direct quote from Lansky: "We're bigger than U.S. Steel!" (Nicholas Shaxson, *Treasure Islands: Tax Havens and the Men Who Stole the World* [London: Bodley Head, 2011], 104; Jean-François Couvrat and Nicolas Pless, *La face cachée de l'économie mondiale*, 192; Cirules's appendix on "The Luxury Hotels of Havana" in *The Mafia in Havana*, 148–55).

53   Block, *Masters of Paradise*, 36–37.

54   Ibid., 37, 39.

55   Ibid., 51.

56   Ibid., 84–85.

57   Ibid., 43.

58   Ibid., 48.

59   Ibid.

60   Federal Bureau of Narcotics, "Translation of report, in Re: Meyer Lansky," Letter 1395, December 11, 1962; Interpol Weisbaden Bundeskriminalamt, "Investigation Reports submitted by the Landeskrimininalamt Hamburg and Kiel, Re: Joseph Nesline," variously dated in 1977, 1978, and 1979, cited in Block, *Masters of Paradise*, 48–49.

61   Possamai, *Money on the Run*, 107–8.

62   Block, *Masters of Paradise*, 43–44.

63   Ibid., 44.

64   Ibid., 43.

65   Ibid., 43–44.

66   Ibid., 71.

67   Ibid., 150–51.

68   Arthur Herzog, *Vesco: From Wall Street to Castro's Cuba: The Rise, Fall, and Exile of the King of White-Collar Crime ... A Fascinating Story of Big Money, High Living, and Financial Trickery* (Lincoln, NB: Authors Choice, 2003), quoted in electronpress.com.

69   Block, *Masters of Paradise*, 135.

70   Naylor, *Hot Money*, 40.

71   Jean-François Couvrat and Nicolas Pless, *La face cachée de l'économie mondiale*, 168.

72   Naylor, *Hot Money*, 40–41.

73   Block, *Masters of Paradise*, 13 and 153. In addition, "a nephew of President Nixon, Donald A. Nixon, [was] an employee of Vesco" (according to a diplomatic cable sent by the U.S. Secretary of State on November 26, 1973, made available by Wikileaks.

74   Naylor, *Hot Money*, 40.

75   Diplomatic cable of the U.S. Secretary of State, November 26, 1973, made available by Wikileaks.

76   *Staff Study of the Frank Petroff Case*, Permanent Subcommittee on Investigation, Washington, DC, U.S. Senate, 1975, quoted in Block, *Masters of Paradise*, 146.

77   Block, *Masters of Paradise*, 147.

78   Ibid., 147–48.

79   Naylor, *Hot Money*, 300.

80   *New York Times*, November 24, 1982, and October 17, 1983, and *Wall Street Journal*, March 8 and March 31, 1983, quoted in Naylor, *Hot Money*, 301 and 494n13.

81   Charlotte Hays, *The Fortune Hunters: Dazzling Women and the Men They Married* (New York: St. Martin's, 2007), 27.

82   Marilyn James, "A Biography of Daniel K. Ludwig," *Executive Intelligence Review* 8, no. 49 (December 22, 1981); Vernay, *Les paradis fiscaux*, 159.

83   Block, *Masters of Paradise*, 32.

84   Ibid.

85   Ibid., 33.

86   Vernay, *Les paradis fiscaux*, 159n4.

87   Bill Davidson, "The Mafia: Shadow of Evil on an Island in the Sun," quoted in Block, *Masters of Paradise*, 75.

88   Ibid., 13–14.

89   Ibid., 10.

90   Ibid., 6.

91   Judgment given in 1972 in the case of RBC and the British tax authorities (Internal Revenue Commissioners, IRC), quoted in Édouard Chambost, *Guide mondial des secrets bancaires* (Paris: Seuil, 1980), 103.

92   Vernay, *Les paradis fiscaux*, 178 [our translation].

93   Ibid., 168 [our translation].

94   Ibid., 151.

95   Block, *Masters of Paradise*, 51–52.

96   Ibid., 65.

97   Ibid., 52.

98   Ibid., 71, 141 and 157n24.

99   Vernay, *Les paradis fiscaux*, 163 [our translation].

100 Ibid., based on articles in *Life* magazine, September 1 and September 8, 1967.

101 Ibid., 164.

102 Ibid.

103 William Brittain-Catlin, *Offshore: The Dark Side of the Black Economy* (New York: Farrar, Straus, and Giroux, 2005), 154.

104 Vernay, *Les paradis fiscaux*, 164 [our translation].

105 Ibid., 172 [our translation].

106 Block, *Masters of Paradise*, 50.

107 Ibid., 51.

108 RBC, 1965 annual report, 3 and 10, and 1966 annual report, 3. Alain Vernay discusses Sands's twofold role in *Les paradis fiscaux*, 166. The subject is also mentioned by Michael Craton and Gail Saunders in *Islanders in the Stream: A History of the Bahamian People*, vol. 2, *From the Ending of Slavery to the Twenty-First Century* (Athens: University of Georgia Press, 1996), 342.

109 Vernay, *Les paradis fiscaux*, 166.

110 Ibid.

111 "Stafford Sands," *Bahamasb2b* website.

112 Vernay, *Les paradis fiscaux*, 166 [our translation].

113 Ibid., 171 [our translation]. This was the view of Sands's political opponent, Pindling.

114 Ibid., 167 [our translation].

115 Ibid., 168 [our translation].

116 Michael Kaufman, "The Internationalization of Canadian Bank Capital (with a Look at Bank Activity in the Caribbean and Central America)," *Journal of Canadian Studies* 19, no. 4 (Winter 1984–1985): 76.

117 RBC, 1963 annual report, 20–21.

118 Ibid., 20–21.

119 RBC, 1964 annual report, 20, 51. Through one of these branches, the Royal Bank in 1966 acquired a share in a Lebanese bank, the Banque des activités économiques, enabling it to enter the Middle East (RBC, 1966 annual report, 21). Lebanon itself was viewed at the time as a tax haven (Vernay, *Les paradis fiscaux*, 93–120).

120 RBC, 1965 annual report, 21.

121 Block, *Masters of Paradise*, 94.

122 Vernay, *Les paradis fiscaux*, 156 [our translation].

123 Block, *Masters of Paradise*, 68.

124 Ibid.

125 Ibid.; Vernay, *Les paradis fiscaux*, 156.

126 Block, *Masters of Paradise*, 81ff.

127 RBC, 1965 annual report, 21.

128 Ibid., 35.

129 The RBC's branch on the tiny island of Bimini, described at the time as a "hot dog stand" because its business volume was so small, suddenly transferred $544,360 in cash to the Bahamas' central bank in 1977, then over $12 million in 1982. "The central bank could not establish that these amounts had come 'from any ordinary business transaction', especially since Bimini was a relatively poor island of just two thousand people" (Possamai, *Money on the Run*, 109). The $12 million was "a sum that the central monetary authority of the Bahamas believed could have originated only from drug deals" (Naylor, *Hot Money*, 300). Mario Possamai's guess is that it came from cocaine trafficking in the United States. The situation was serious enough for central bank administrators to think it required urgent action.

130 Rod McQueen, *The Moneyspinners: An Intimate Portrait of the Men Who Run Canada's Banks* (Toronto: Macmillan of Canada, 1983), 20.

131 Block, *Masters of Paradise*, 68. The New Jersey agency regulating gambling noted the presence of the Bank of Nova Scotia in the vague conglomeration surrounding the project (Office of Administrative Law, Casino Control Commission, State of New Jersey, *In the Matter of the Application of Resorts International Hotel, Inc. for a Casino License*, 265, 287).

132 Bank of Nova Scotia, 1960 annual report, 15.

133 Ibid.

134 Block, *Masters of Paradise*, 122.

135 Office of Administrative Law, Casino Control Commission, State of New Jersey, *In the Matter of the Application of Resorts International Hotel, Inc. for a Casino License*, 287.

136 Naylor, *Hot Money*, 301.

137 Ibid., 299.

138 Ibid.

139 "Crime and Secrecy: The Use of Offshore Banks and Companies" (staff study by the U.S. Senate Permanent Subcommittee on Investigations, February 1983), 99, quoted in Possamai, *Money on the Run*, 110.

140 Naylor, *Hot Money*, 301.

141 Ibid., 301–2.

142 Possamai, *Money on the Run*, 110–11 and 114.

143 Ibid., 101.

144 Ibid.

145 Patrice Meyzonnier, *Trafics et crimes en Amérique centrale et dans les Caraïbes* (Paris: Presses universitaires de France, 1999), 90 [our translation].

146 Jean-François Couvrat and Nicolas Pless, *La face cachée de l'économie mondiale*, 84.

147 Possamai, *Money on the Run*, 104.

148 This kind of information on deposits in Bahamian accounts is extremely rare. In this case, the information is available because Lehder was arrested in Colombia in 1987, extradited to the United States, and convicted in 1988 – a highly unusual occurrence (Possamai, *Money on the Run*, 102–3).

149 Possamai, *Money on the Run*, 103.

150 Meyzonnier, *Trafics et crimes en Amérique centrale et dans les Caraïbes*, 90.

151 Naylor, *Hot Money*, 306.

152 Ibid., 301–2.

153 Possamai, *Money on the Run*, 112.

154 Ibid., 112–13.

155 Naylor, *Hot Money*, 302.

156 Possamai, *Money on the Run*, 112–13.

157 Cedric Ritchie, "Banks Must Balance Two Basic But Conflicting Responsibilities," *Toronto Star*, February 3, 1986, quoted in ibid., 111.

158 Possamai, *Money on the Run*, 114.

159 Ibid., 111–12.

160 "Fleming, The Hon. Donald Methuen," Members of the House of Commons, *PARLINFO* website.

161 "30 septembre 1961, Début des travaux de l'Organisation de coopération et de développement économiques," *Perspective Monde* (Université de Sherbrooke) website.

162 Chambost, *Guide mondial des secrets bancaires*, 221; "Donald Fleming Dies; Ex-Canadian Official," *New York Times*, January 3, 1987.

163 "Fleming, The Hon. Donald Methuen," *PARLINFO* website.

164 Bank of Nova Scotia, 1968 annual report, 51.

165 Donald M. Fleming, *So Very Near: The Political Memoirs of the Honourable Donald M. Fleming*, vol. 2, *The Summit Years* (Toronto: McClelland and Stewart, 1985), 677.

166 Ibid., 680.

167 Ibid., 685.

168 Chambost, *Guide mondial des secrets bancaires*, 221 [our translation].

169 Fleming, *The Summit Years*, 681.

170 Ibid., 678.

171 Ibid., 681.

172 Brittain-Catlin, *Offshore*, 154.

173 Chambost, *Guide mondial des secrets bancaires*, 221 [our translation].

174 Donald M. Fleming, "The Bahamas (Tax) Paradise," *The Tax Executive* (Washington, DC), no. 96 (1975–1976).

175 Possamai, *Money on the Run*, 106.

176 Naylor, *Hot Money*, 300.

177 Ibid., 194, 299, and 304.

178 Ibid., 494n10.

179 Ibid., 300.

180 Vernay, *Les paradis fiscaux*, 172 [our translation].

181 Ibid., 173 [our translation].

182 Ovid Demaris, *Dirty Business: The Corporate-Political Money-Power Game* (New York: Harper's Magazine Press, 1974), 114.

183 Vernay, *Les paradis fiscaux*, 168.

184 Meyzonnier, *Trafics et crimes en Amérique centrale et dans les Caraïbes*, 89–90 [our translation].

185 Bank of Nova Scotia, 1968 annual report, 13.

186 Ibid.

187 Naylor, *Hot Money*, 298.

188 Ibid.

189 All three quotations are from Vernay, *Les paradis fiscaux*, 154 [our translation].

190 Vernay, *Les paradis fiscaux*, 157.

191 Block, *Masters of Paradise*, 141.

192 "Sir Harry Oakes," *Discover Our History: History Notes*, Niagara Falls History Museum website.

193 Vernay, *Les paradis fiscaux*, 157n [our translation].

194 Ibid. [our translation].

195 Ibid.

196 Ibid. This rule is known today as the "183-day rule" in Canadian law: "If you sojourned in Canada for 183 days or more (the 183-day rule) in the tax year, do **not** have significant residential ties with Canada, **and** are **not** considered a resident of another country under the terms of a tax treaty between Canada and that country, you may be considered a deemed resident of Canada" ("Non-Resident of Canada," Canada Revenue Agency website, January 6, 2015 [bold type in original]).

197 Diane Francis, *Controlling Interest: Who Owns Canada?* (Toronto: Macmillan of Canada, 1986), 269.

198 Diane Francis, *Who Owns Canada Now? Old Money, New Money, and the Future of Canadian Business* (Toronto: HarperCollins, 2008), 193.

199 Marc Pigeon, "Misère de millionaire," *Le Journal de Montréal*, April 8, 2010; Alain Deneault, "Un Québec offshore? La tentation du paradis fiscal," in Miriam Fahmy (ed.), *L'État du Québec 2011* (Montreal: Boréal, 2011), 120, reprinted in Alain Deneault, *Faire l'économie de la haine* (Montreal : Écosociété, 2011), 45.

200 Ralph Deans, "History and Success – Financial Services Evolution," *The Bahamas Investor* (Nassau), July 2009.

201 Ronen Palan, "International Financial Centers: The British-Empire, City-States, and Commercially Oriented Politics," *Theoretical Inquiries in Law* 11, no. 1 (January

2010): 170; Henry Morgenthau Jr., "My Dear Mr. President," May 21, 1937, File: Taxes, Box 166, President's Secretary's File, FDR Library, *taxhistory.org*.

202 Agence France-Presse, "Profession: courtier en îles privées," *Le Journal de Montréal*, August 2, 2010.

203 Possamai, *Money on the Run*, 116–17.

204 "Scotiabank in the Bahamas," Bank of Nova Scotia website.

205 Geoffrey Jones, *British Multinational Banking, 1830–1990* (Oxford: Clarendon, 1993), 266–68; Kaufman, "The Internationalization of Canadian Bank Capital," 72; Daniel Jay Baum, *The Banks of Canada in the Commonwealth Caribbean: Economic Nationalism and Multinational Enterprises of a Medium Power* (New York: Praeger, 1974), 23.

206 Joseph Schull and J. Douglas Gibson, *The Scotiabank Story: A History of the Bank of Nova Scotia, 1832–1982* (Toronto: Macmillan of Canada, 1982), 216. See also Ralph Deans, "History and Success – Financial Services Evolution," *The Bahamas Investor* (Nassau), July 2009.

207 "CIBC's History in the Caribbean," FirstCaribbean International Bank website.

208 James Ball, "IRS Targets FirstCaribbean International Bank over Tax Evasion," *The Guardian* (London), May 27, 2013.

209 Jones, *British Multinational Banking, 1830–1990*, 266–68; Kaufman, "The Internationalization of Canadian Bank Capital," 72; Baum, *The Banks of Canada in the Commonwealth Caribbean*, 23.

210 In 1988, the Bahamian government bought the institution back and renamed it the Bank of The Bahamas International (*bahamaslocal.com*).

211 Naylor, *Hot Money*, 300.

212 Vernay, *Les paradis fiscaux*, 169 [our translation].

213 Ralph Deans, "History and Success – Financial Services Evolution."

214 The Bank of Nova Scotia International, BNS (Colombia) Holdings, Scotiabank Caribbean Treasury, The Bank of Nova Scotia Trust Company, Scotiabank (Bahamas), and Scotia International ("Canadian Banks Operate Offshore: Big 5 Financial Institutions Have Branches in Locales from Switzerland to Singapore," interactive map, CBC News, June 24, 2013).

215 RBC Royal Bank of Canada, Royal Bank of Canada Trust Company (Bahamas), the Finance Corporation of Bahamas Limited (RBC FINCO), and RBC Dominion Securities (Global) ("RBC Caribbean Banking: The Bahamas," RBC).

216 CIBC Trust Company and The Bahamas FirstCaribbean International Bank ("Canadian Banks Operate Offshore").

217 According to its official website, "The Bahamas International Securities Exchange Limited (BISX) was incorporated in September 1999. In May 2000 BISX successfully launched its domestic market for the listing and trading of local public companies" ("About BISX," BISX website).

218 Naylor, *Hot Money*, 165 and 280; R. T. Naylor, *Wages of Crime: Black Markets, Illegal Finance, and the Underworld Economy* (Montreal: McGill-Queens UP, 2004 [2002]), 7.

219 Meyzonnier, *Trafics et crimes en Amérique centrale et dans les Caraïbes*, 89.

220 Ibid., 90.

221 Ibid. [our translation].

222 Ibid.

223 Ibid. [our translation].

224 Marie-Christine Dupuis-Danon, *Finance criminelle. Comment le crime organisé blanchit l'argent sale*, 2nd ed. (Paris: Presses universitaires de France, 2004 [1998]), 225–26.

225 Jason Magder and Paul Cherry, "Arrest Made in Cinar/Norshield Fraud Scandal," *Montreal Gazette*, March 3, 2011, *canadianhedwatch.com*; Rhéal Séguin, "Police Arrest Suspected Mastermind Behind Alleged Cinar Fraud," *Globe and Mail* (Toronto), March 15, 2011.

226 Rhéal Séguin, "Police Arrest Suspected Mastermind Behind Alleged Cinar Fraud."

227 "Animator Claude Robinson Wins Copyright Battle over Cinar. Cartoonist Wins 20-Year Battle over Robinson Sucroe Show," CBC News, December 23, 2013.

228 Francis Vailles, "Affaire Norshield: les comptables des Bahamas travaillaient à Saint-Léonard," *La Presse* (Montreal), February 13, 2010.

229 Carl Renaud, "Le financier Martin Tremblay à nouveau dans de beaux draps," *Canoë.ca* (Montreal), May 27, 2011.

230 Francis Vailles, "La même banque pour Tremblay, Norshield, et Cinar," *La Presse* (Montreal), January 26, 2007 [our translation]. See also Bruce Livesey, "The Offshore Banking Nightmare," *Canadian Lawyer* (Toronto), February 6, 2012.

231 Francis Vailles, "La même banque pour Tremblay, Norshield, et Cinar" [our translation]. A few years later, Canadians learned that the agency regulating derivatives markets in the United States was accusing the Royal Bank of orchestrating a "multi-hundred million dollar wash sale scheme" designed "to realize lucrative Canadian tax benefits from holding certain public companies' securities in its Canadian and offshore trading accounts" (U.S. Commodity Futures Trading Commission, "CFTC Charges Royal Bank of Canada with Multi-Hundred Million Dollar Wash Sale Scheme," news release, April 2, 2012. See also Reuters, "U.S. Futures Regulator Accuses RBC of Trading Scheme," *Chicago Tribune*, April 2, 2012; Gérard Bérubé, "La Banque Royale se défend d'avoir réalisé des transactions fictives aux États-Unis," *Le Devoir* [Montreal], April 3, 2012). In 2013, the Royal Bank chose to leave Uruguay after a raid carried out on its offices at the request of Argentinian judge Norberto Oyarbide, as part of an investigation of money-laundering activities involving soccer players. No charges were laid ("RBC quitte l'Uruguay après une saisie dans ses bureaux," Radio-Canada, September 4, 2013; "Anti-Money Laundering Measures Rattle S. America," UPI, August 21, 2013).

232 Canadian Press, "Montreal Lawyer Alleges Another Ponzi Scheme," CBC News, July 31, 2009; "Une autre combine à la Ponzi," *Le Devoir* (Montreal), August 1, 2009.

233 Jean-François Cloutier, "Revenu Canada a le bras long avec le roi du t-shirt," *Le Journal de Montréal*, December 19, 2013.

234 "Présentation des Bahamas," *France Diplomatie* (Paris), December 3, 2012.

235 Vernay, *Les paradis fiscaux*, 174.

236 Ibid., 177 [our translation].

237 Ibid. [our translation].

238 Naylor, *Hot Money*, 299.

239 Ibid., 305.

240 "The Bahamas: A Little Bit Independent," *Time* magazine, January 24, 1964.

▉ CAYMAN ISLANDS

1 Jean de Maillard and Pierre-Xavier Grezaud, *Un monde sans loi. La criminalité financière en images* (Paris: Stock, 1998), 16ff.

2 Ibid., 26.

3 Nicholas Shaxson, *Treasure Islands: Tax Havens and the Men Who Stole the World* (London: The Bodley Head, 2011), 80.

4 Jean de Maillard and Pierre-Xavier Grezaud, *Un monde sans loi*, 39 [our translation].

5 R. T. Naylor, *Hot Money and the Politics of Debt* (Montreal: McGill-Queen's UP, 2004 [1987]), 31.

6 Sebastian Mallaby, "Soros versus Soros," in *More Money than God: Hedge Funds and the Making of a New Elite* (New York: Penguin, 2010), 193–219.

7 Shaxson, *Treasure Islands*, 252ff. See also Ismail Ertürk, Julie Froud, Sukhdev Johal, Adam Leaver, Michael Moran, and Karel Williams, *City State Against National Settlement: U.K. Economic Policy and Politics after the Financial Crisis* (working paper no. 101, Manchester, UK: Centre for Research on Socio-Cultural Change [CRESC], June 2011); and the documentary film by Mathieu Verboud, *La City, la finance en eaux troubles* (France: France Télévisions/Zadig Productions, 2011), 52 minutes.

8 Shaxson, *Treasure Islands*, 84–85.

9 Christian Chavagneux and Ronen Palan, *Les paradis fiscaux* (Paris: La Découverte, 2012), 45.

10 William M. Clarke, *The City in the World Economy* (Harmondsworth, Middlesex: Penguin, 1967 [1965]), 21.

11 Shaxson, *Treasure Islands*, 90 and 92.

12 Ibid.

13 Youssef Cassis, *Les capitales du capital. Histoire des places financières internationales, 1780–2005* (Paris: Honoré Champion Éditeur, 2008), 305–6.

14 Ibid.

15 Shaxson, *Treasure Islands*, 91.

16 Gary Burn, "The State, the City, and the Euromarket," *Review of International Political Economy* 6, no. 2 (1999): 225–61.

17 R. P. T. Davenport-Hines, "Sir George Lewis French Bolton," in David J. Jeremy (ed.), *Dictionary of Business Biography* (London: Butterworth, 1984), 1:364–69.

18 Geoffrey Jones, *British Multinational Banking, 1830–1990* (Oxford: Clarendon, 1993), 266–68; Michael Kaufman, "The Internationalization of Canadian Bank Capital (with a Look at Bank Activity in the Caribbean and Central America)," *Journal of Canadian Studies* 19, no. 4 (Winter 1984–85): 72; Daniel Jay Baum, *The Banks of Canada in the Commonwealth Caribbean: Economic Nationalism and Multinational Enterprises of a Medium Power* (New York: Praeger, 1974), 23. The Bank of Montreal provided a third of the capital while BOLSA contributed a network of branches in Latin America.

19 He sat on the boards of both the Canadian Pacific Railway and Sun Life Assurance of Canada (Davenport-Hines, "Sir George Lewis French Bolton," 1:364–69).

20 Jones, *British Multinational Banking*, 265.

21 Burn, "The State, the City, and the Euromarket," 235.

22 Euromarkets were viewed as "new, uncertain, and risky," in the words of Youssef Cassis, leading banks to proceed with caution. An initiative of the Midland Bank led the Toronto Dominion to participate, with other Commonwealth institutions,

in the creation of the Midland and International Bank. In 1970, RBC also joined a banking consortium to deal with this new market (Cassis, *Les capitales du capital,* 123–24 [our translation]).

23 Shaxson, *Treasure Islands,* 90.

24 Ibid., 103.

25 Baum, *The Banks of Canada in the Commonwealth Caribbean,* 9.

26 "Population totale, Îles Caïmans," *Perspective monde* (Université de Sherbrooke) website.

27 William Brittain-Catlin, *Offshore: The Dark Side of the Black Economy* (New York: Farrar, Straus, and Giroux, 2005), 15–16.

28 Timothy Ridley, "What Makes the Cayman Islands a Successful International Financial Services Centre?" (background paper by chairman of CIMA, given at Euromoney Caribbean Investment Forum, Montego Bay [Jamaica], June 12 and 13, 2007], *bis.org.*

29 Naylor, *Hot Money,* 302.

30 Ibid., 302–4.

31 Martin Keeley, "The Tax Haven That Jim Macdonald Built," *Canadian Business* 52, no. 10 (October 1979): 67.

32 "James David Macdonald," City of Calgary website.

33 Mario Possamai, *Money on the Run: Canada and How the World's Dirty Profits Are Laundered* (Toronto: Viking, 1992), 106.

34 The State of Delaware was established as a tax haven within the United States in March 1927 (A. A. Berle, Jr., "Investors and the Revised Delaware Corporation Act," *Columbia Law Review* 29, no. 5 [May 1929]: 563–81; Alain Deneault, "Delaware, USA: The Domestic Haven," in *Offshore: Tax Havens and the Rule of Global Crime,* tr. from the French by George Holoch [New York: New Press, 2011 (2010)], 81–101).

35 Keeley, "The Tax Haven That Jim Macdonald Built," 68.

36 Ibid., 70.

37 Alan Markoff, "Cayman Develops as an Offshore Centre, Part 1: The Early Years – 1960s: The Cayman Islands: From Obscurity to Offshore Giant," *Cayman Financial Review,* January 5, 2009; Shaxson, *Treasure Islands,* 106.

38 Keeley, "The Tax Haven That Jim Macdonald Built," 68.

39 Brittain-Catlin, *Offshore,* 151.

40 Keeley, "The Tax Haven That Jim Macdonald Built," 67.

41 Ibid.

42 Michael Klein, "Transitions for Long Time Cayman Financial Services Firm," *The Cayman Islands Journal* (George Town), November 2, 2011.

43 Brian Salgado, "Butler Development Group," *Construction Today* (Chicago), n.d. (after 2008).

44 RBC, 1964 annual report, 20; Markoff, "Cayman Develops as an Offshore Centre, Part 1: The Early Years." The Bank of Nova Scotia's subsidiary was called the Bank of Nova Scotia Trust Company (Cayman Islands). The fourth bank was the British Barclays, established at a distance on Cayman Brac island.

45 Keeley, "The Tax Haven That Jim Macdonald Built," 67.

46 André Beauchamp, *Guide mondial des paradis fiscaux* (Ville Mont-Royal, QC: Éditions Le Nordais, 1982 [Paris: Grasset et Fasquelle, 1981]), 325 [our translation].

47 Bank of Nova Scotia, 1968 annual report, 20–21.

48 Ibid., 21. Like mushrooms, new bank branches sprang up in the Bahamas, Barbados, Belize, the Cayman Islands, Guyana, St. Lucia, and Trinidad, among other places (ibid., 24). Canada having signed an agreement with the United States in 1968 limiting transfers of money from the United States to third countries via Canada, the Bank of Nova Scotia turned to Euromarkets on the sidelines of "the more traditional segments of our international business" (ibid., 21).

49 Ibid., 13, and Bank of Nova Scotia, 1969 annual report, 18.

50 Keeley, "The Tax Haven That Jim Macdonald Built," 70.

51 Carol Winker, "3 Men Built Maples Foundation," *CayCompass.com* (Grand Cayman), October 7, 2010; "Maples and Calder's Co-Founding Partner Passes," MaplesFS website, June 12, 2012.

52 Markoff, "Cayman Develops as an Offshore Centre, Part 1: The Early Years."

53 Ibid.

54 Thierry Godefroy and Pierre Lascoumes, *Le capitalisme clandestin. L'illusoire régulation des places offshore* (Paris: La Découverte, 2004), 105–6 [our translation].

55 Grégoire Duhamel, *Les paradis fiscaux* (Paris: Éditions Grancher, 2006), 459.

56 Godefroy and Lascoumes, *Le capitalisme clandestin*, 108 [our translation].

57 "Cayman Islands Exempt Company," in "Cayman Islands: Offshore Legal and Tax Regime," *LowTax.net* (Kingston upon Thames).

58 Brittain-Catlin, *Offshore*, 31.

59 Ibid., 14; Mélanie Delattre, "L'argent caché des paradis fiscaux," *Le Point* (Paris), February 26, 2009, 59; Marc Roche, *Le capitalisme hors la loi* (Paris: Albin Michel, 2011), 22.

60 Brittain-Catlin, *Offshore*, 11.

61 Ibid., 31–32.

62 Ibid., 31.

63 Godefroy and Lascoumes, *Le capitalisme clandestin*, 109; Roche, *Le capitalisme hors la loi*, 26.

64 Godefroy and Lascoumes, *Le capitalisme clandestin*, 104 [our translation].

65 William Brittain-Catlin accurately sums it up: "In fundamental terms, the Cayman company is a cover or front for real flesh-and-blood individuals elsewhere, who have no connection to Cayman as an actual country, but who nonetheless 'inhabit' Cayman exclusively for the purpose of doing business *outside* Cayman" (Brittain-Catlin, *Offshore*, 24 [emphasis in the original]).

66 Ibid., 15.

67 Ibid., 22.

68 Quoted in ibid., 41.

69 Keeley, "The Tax Haven That Jim Macdonald Built," 70.

70 Marie-Christine Dupuis-Danon, *Finance criminelle. Comment le crime organisé blanchit l'argent sale*, 2nd ed. (Paris: Presses universitaires de France, 2004 [1998]), 42 [our translation].

71 Ibid.

72 Shaxson, *Treasure Islands*, 105–7.

73 Ibid., 120.

74 See "First Impressions of the Cayman Islands," correspondence from the Governor of the Cayman Islands to the Secretary of State for Commonwealth Affairs, George Town, January 26, 1972, quoted in ibid., 110.

75   Ibid., 107.

76   Ibid., 108.

77   U.S. House Committee on Banking and Currency, "Bank Records and Foreign Transactions," report 91-975 (1970), 12–13, quoted in *California Bankers Ass'n v. Shultz*, 416 U.S. 21, 28, 94 S. Ct. 1494, 39 L. Ed. 2d 812 (1974).

78   Shaxson, *Treasure Islands*, 151.

79   Beauchamp, *Guide mondial des paradis fiscaux*, 319; Édouard Chambost, *Guide mondial des secrets bancaires* (Paris: Seuil, 1980), 229.

80   Chambost, *Guide mondial des secrets bancaires*, 111 and 229.

81   This case – *United States v. Field*, 532 F.2d 404 (5th district) – created an authoritative precedent. It has been widely described, notably by Shaxson, *Treasure Islands*, 120; Chambost, *Guide mondial des secrets bancaires*, 111; Beauchamp, *Guide mondial des paradis fiscaux*, 319; Brittain-Catlin, *Offshore*, 32–38; "Cayman Islands," *Offshore Manual*.

82   Alan Block, *Masters of Paradise: Organized Crime and the Internal Revenue Service in The Bahamas* (New Brunswick, NJ: Transaction, 1991), 161ff.

83   Ibid., 16; Brittain-Catlin, *Offshore*, 33.

84   Brittain-Catlin, *Offshore*, 35.

85   Musical Group Investment Cases, "Deposition Summary of Norman L. Casper," quoted in Block, *Masters of Paradise*, 176 and 183n66. For more details on the connection between the Castle Bank and the CIBC, see our concluding chapter, "Under Siege."

86   Chambost, *Guide mondial des secrets bancaires*, 111; Naylor, *Hot Money*, 303.

87   Chambost, *Guide mondial des secrets bancaires*, 111 [our translation].

88   Ibid. [our translation].

89   Ibid., 112 [our translation].

90   "Cayman Financial Services Have Become Woven into the Fabric of the Global Economy," in "The Cayman Islands: Special Report," *Washington Times*, December 22, 2008, 1 and 3.

91   Chambost, *Guide mondial des secrets bancaires*, 229 [our translation].

92   Ibid.

93   Shaxson, *Treasure Islands*, 121.

94   "Offshore Company Formation Cayman Islands," Kaizen Corporate Services (Hong Kong) website.

95   Brittain-Catlin, *Offshore*, 37.

96   Ibid., 34.

97   Ibid., 26–27.

98   Ibid., 34.

99   Chambost, *Guide mondial des secrets bancaires*, 230.

100   Ibid., 229 [our translation].

101   Ibid., 230 [our translation].

102   Ridley, "What Makes the Cayman Islands a Successful International Financial Services Centre?" (2007), 1.

103   Chambost, *Guide mondial des secrets bancaires*, 230–31 [our translation].

104   Naylor, *Hot Money*, 302.

105 Jean-François Couvrat and Nicolas Pless, *La face cachée de l'économie mondiale* (Paris: Hatier, 1988), 168.

106 Ibid. .

107 Naylor, *Hot Money*, 303.

108 Ibid., 303 and 495n24.

109 Howard Zinn, "Robber Barons and Rebels," chapter 11 of *A People's History of the United States, 1492 – Present* (New York: HarperPerennial, 2005 [1980]).

110 Brittain-Catlin, *Offshore*, 35.

111 Timothy Ridley, "What Makes the Cayman Islands a Successful International Financial Services Centre?" (background paper by chairman of the CIMA, Port of Spain, Trinidad and Tobago, Euromoney Caribbean Investment Forum, June 11 and 12, 2008, *cimoney.com.ky*).

112 Chambost, *Guide mondial des secrets bancaires*, 228.

113 Timothy Ridley, "What Makes the Cayman Islands a Successful International Financial Services Centre?" (background paper by chairman of CIMA, given at Euromoney Caribbean Investment Forum, Port of Spain [Trinidad and Tobago], June 11 and 12, 2008, *cimoney.com.ky*; "Cayman Financial Services Have Become Woven into the Fabric of the Global Economy," *Washington Times*, 3).

114 "Insurance Statistics and Regulated Entities," CIMA (Grand Cayman) website.

115 Brittain-Catlin, *Offshore*, 12.

116 Ibid. A "captive" insurance company is one that is owned by the company that it insures (Robert E. Bertuccelli, "The Benefits of Captive Insurance Companies," *Journal of Accountancy*, March 1, 2013).

117 Naylor, *Hot Money*, 302.

118 Damien Millet and Éric Toussaint, *60 questions, 60 réponses. Sur la dette, le FMI et la Banque mondiale* (Liège and Paris: Comité pour l'annulation de la dette du Tiers-Monde [CADTM] and Syllepse, 2008).

119 Naylor, *Hot Money*, 306.

120 Brittain-Catlin, *Offshore*, 174.

121 Ibid., 174–75.

122 Naylor, *Hot Money*, 304.

123 Brittain-Catlin, *Offshore*, 174–75.

124 Naylor, *Hot Money*, 304.

125 Alan Markoff, "Cayman Develops as an Offshore Centre, Part 2: The Freewheeling 1970s," *Cayman Financial Review*, April 17, 2009.

126 Ibid.; Brittain-Catlin, *Offshore*, 155.

127 Markoff, "Cayman Develops as an Offshore Centre, Part 2: The Freewheeling 1970s."

128 Brittain-Catlin, *Offshore*, 154.

129 Markoff, "Cayman Develops as an Offshore Centre, Part 2: The Freewheeling 1970s." .

130 *L'Appel de Genève*, a document signed by a group of European judges in 1996, emphasizes the importance of information technology in the acceleration of exchanges involving tax havens. "In an era of computerized networks, Internet, modem and fax, money from fraudulent activities can circulate at great speed from one account to another and one tax haven to another, protected by anonymous offshore corporations that are supervised by respectable and generously paid trustees. The money is then deposited or invested beyond the reach of any audit. Swindlers today can be almost sure of going unpunished.

The legal system of each European country will need years to track down the money, unless the task should prove impossible under the current legal framework inherited from a period when frontiers still had a meaning for people, goods, and capital." The document is signed by Bernard Bertossa, Edmondo Bruti Liberati, Gherardo Colombo, Benoît Dejemeppe, Baltasar Garzon Real, Carlos Jimenez Villarejo, and Renaud Van Ruymbeke (available at *ge.ch/justice*) [our translation].

131 Markoff, "Cayman Develops as an Offshore Centre, Part 2: The Freewheeling 1970s."

132 Ibid.

133 Brittain-Catlin, *Offshore*, 154.

134 Markoff, "Cayman Develops as an Offshore Centre, Part 2: The Freewheeling 1970s."

135 Brittain-Catlin, *Offshore*, 155–56.

136 Quoted in Markoff, "Cayman Develops as an Offshore Centre, Part 2: The Freewheeling 1970s."

137 Ibid.

138 Winker, "3 Men Built Maples Foundation."

139 Stuart Fieldhouse, "Maples and Calder: The Leading Offshore Law Firm," *Hedgefund Journal* (London), April 2011, 1.

140 Ibid.

141 The firm's initial growth took place in the Cayman and British Virgin Islands. It then opened an office in Jersey, where in 2004 it acquired a management fund, Gartmore Fund Managers International Limited. Two years later it made a breakthrough in a European tax haven, Ireland, where in 2008 it attracted two "leading Irish lawyers," Barry McGrath and Nollaig Murphy. Maples is also found in Hong Kong and Dubai. This range of jurisdictions favours the development of new types of funds, compared to European competitors who stick to instruments from Luxembourg. The high-risk investment fund, as developed in tax havens, is designed as a "conduit" – one that is as direct and light as possible – bringing the investment directly to its object. Released from social, ecosystemic, political, and anthropological questions, finance in these mysterious legal zones is no longer subject to any disturbance as it experiences the pure materialization of its fantasy: to transform money into more money in a state of radical ignorance of what it costs to construct such operations (Fieldhouse, "Maples and Calder: The Leading Offshore Law Firm"; "Maples Finance Acquires Gartmore's Jersey Fund Administration Division," *Global Investor*, June 10, 2004; Maples FS, "Leading Irish Lawyers Join Maples and Calder," news release, July 2, 2008, quoted in *businesswire.com*).

142 Fieldhouse, "Maples and Calder: The Leading Offshore Law Firm," 2.

143 Keeley, "The Tax Haven That Jim Macdonald Built," 70.

144 Fieldhouse, "Maples and Calder: The Leading Offshore Law Firm," 2.

145 "Cayman Islands Hedge Funds Group," MapleFS website; Warren de Rajewicz, *Guide des nouveaux paradis fiscaux à l'usage des sociétés et des particuliers. Non, les paradis fiscaux ne sont pas morts!* (Lausanne: Favre, 2010), 126.

146 Quoted in "Offshore Bank Accounts," *The Current*, CBC Radio, August 16, 2012.

147 MaplesFS, "Maples and Calder Announces New Head of Cayman Funds," news release, February 17, 2010.

148 Shaxson, *Treasure Islands*, 22.

149 Guillaume Monarcha and Jérôme Teïletche, *Les hedge funds* (Paris: La Découverte, 2009; revised edition 2013), 8 [our translation].

150 Frédéric Lelièvre and François Pilet, *Krach Machine. Comment les traders à haute fréquence menacent de faire sauter la bourse* (Paris: Calmann-Lévy, 2013); [Anonymous], 6 (Brussels: Zones Sensibles, 2013).

151 Jean de Maillard, *L'arnaque. La finance au-dessus des lois et des règles* (Paris: Gallimard, 2010), 68 [our translation].

152 Ibid.

153 Déclaration de Berne (ed.), *Swiss trading SA. La Suisse, le négoce et la malédiction des matières premières* (Lausanne : Les Éditions d'en bas, 2011), 95–128; Roche, *Le capitalisme hors la loi*, 207.

154 Roche, *Le capitalisme hors la loi*, 174 [our translation].

155 Ibid.

156 François Morin, *Un monde sans Wall Street*, 47 and 48n [our translation].

157 Ibid., 48n [our translation].

158 Guillaume Monarcha and Jérôme Teïletche, *Les hedge funds*, 11.

159 Fieldhouse, "Maples and Calder: The Leading Offshore Law Firm," 1.

160 Ibid., 1.

161 Ibid.

162 Linda McQuaig and Neil Brooks, *The Trouble with Billionaires: How the Super-Rich Hijacked the World (and How We Can Take It Back)* (London: Oneworld Publications, 2013 [2011]; published in the U.S. under the title *Billionaires' Ball: Gluttony and Hubris in an Age of Epic Inequality*), 6. According to McClatchy's, a media organization that investigated the Abacus affair, Goldman Sachs (a powerful commercial bank) had made 148 deals of this kind in the Cayman Islands over a period of seven years (Shaxson, *Treasure Islands*, 187). The U.S. Securities and Exchange Commission, which regulates stock market activity in the United States, investigated Cayman Islands financial products that Goldman Sachs was selling at the same time as it was speculating on their downward movement: the bank eventually had to pay $550 million to compensate clients who had been swindled in this way (François Morin, *Un monde sans Wall Street*, 31).

163 Fieldhouse, "Maples and Calder: The Leading Offshore Law Firm," 1.

164 Saskia Scholtes and Vanessa Houlder, "Ugland House: Home to 18,857," *Financial Times* (London), May 4, 2009.

165 Nick Davis, "Tax Spotlight Worries Cayman Islands," BBC News, March 31, 2009.

166 Mélanie Delattre, "L'argent caché des paradis fiscaux," 60 [our translation].

167 Jean-François Couvrat and Nicolas Pless, *La face cachée de l'économie mondiale*, 149.

168 Fieldhouse, "Maples and Calder: The Leading Offshore Law Firm," 1.

169 Ridley, "What Makes the Cayman Islands a Successful International Financial Services Centre?" (2007).

170 Fieldhouse, "Maples and Calder: The Leading Offshore Law Firm," 1.

171 Ibid.

172 Ibid., 2.

173 Shaxson, *Treasure Islands*, 122.

174 Ibid., 188.

175 Timothy Ridley, chairman of CIMA, gave talks on this topic to the Caribbean Investment Forum in Jamaica in 2007 and to the Euromoney Caribbean Investment Forum in Trinidad and Tobago in 2008.

176 Grant Stein, "Cayman's Compliance with the OECD Standards on Tax Co-operation," *Hedgeweek* (St. Helier, Jersey), December 1, 2010, 2.

177 OECD-CFA, *Towards Global Tax Co-operation* (Paris: OECD, 2000); FATF, *Report on Non-Co-operative Countries and Territories* (Paris: FATF, 2000); FATF, *Review to Identify Non-Co-operative Countries and Territories: Increasing the Worldwide Effectiveness of Money-Laundering Efforts* (Paris: FATF, 2000); FSF, *Financial Stability Forum Releases Grouping of Offshore Financial Centres (OFCs) to Assist in Setting Priorities for Assessment* (Basel: FSF, 2000).

178 Bernard Bertossa (with Agathe Duparc), *La justice, les affaires, la corruption* (Paris: Fayard, 2009), 135–36 [our translation].

179 Jane G. Gravelle, *Tax Havens: International Tax Avoidance and Evasion* (Washington, DC: Congressional Research Service, 2013), 3.

180 Gilles Favarel-Garrigues, Thierry Godefroy, and Pierre Lascoumes, *Les sentinelles de l'argent sale. Les banques aux prises avec l'antiblanchiment* (Paris: La Découverte, 2009).

181 However, you can never be too careful. Warren de Rajewicz, a pro-tax haven tax specialist, now advises his clients not to create a trust in the Caymans, "since the impact of various measures to 'open' the islands in the area of communication of information to other states is not yet known" (Warren de Rajewicz, *Guide des nouveaux paradis fiscaux à l'usage des sociétés et des particuliers*, 129 [our translation]).

182 Roche, *Le capitalisme hors la loi*, 41; see also 24 and 27. See also the account given by Rudolf Elmer, an accountant who worked for a Swiss bank in the Cayman Islands, in Shaxson, *Treasure Islands*, 188.

183 Chambost, *Guide mondial des secrets bancaires*, 228 [our translation].

184 Shaxson, *Treasure Islands*, 122.

185 Dupuis-Danon, *Finance criminelle*, 42 [our translation].

186 Morin, *Un monde sans Wall Street*, 31; Roche, *Le capitalisme hors la loi*, 44 and 256.

187 Shaxson, *Treasure Islands*, 188.

188 Marc Roche gives this analysis of the collapse of the Lehman Brothers bank (*Le capitalisme hors la loi*, 44 and 256).

189 Before its spectacular collapse, Enron was a dedicated user of Cayman Island Special Purpose Vehicles. In the late 1990s Enron's chief financial officer, Andrew Fastow, worked to conceal the company's gigantic debts and deficits in its financial statements. The company achieved extraordinary success in financial markets by including anticipated long-term profits in its yearly balance sheets. Earnings in the range of $2 billion were declared in this way between 1996 and 2000. The firm at the time was not producing anything except long-term, fixed-price agreements between suppliers and customers (Brittain-Catlin, *Offshore*, 59). The Special Purpose Vehicle (SPV) invented in the Cayman Islands in the 1990s was the tool that enabled the company to include anticipated profits in its accounts. The SPV is a commercial entity reduced to its simplest expression: a single transaction is enough to constitute a company. Also known as an LP (for Cayman Island Limited Partnership), the SPV "has all the benefits of a Cayman offshore company – tax exemption, secrecy, minimal registration and filing requirements – but it is quite different in one respect … the LP reduces to a transaction in itself" (Brittain-Catlin, *Offshore*, 64). The partners of the transaction may eventually change, but

the transaction that is the basis of the entity remains the same. And as usual, this offshore inventiveness tends to one main goal: complete elimination of the partners' responsibility. No consequence of the commercial operation belongs to them: this commercial operation literally does not entail responsibility for anyone, including banks, major firms, or other investors. When Fastow created the LJM Special Purpose Vehicle in the Caymans (an SPV consisting of a transaction between Enron and Fastow), he paid himself a management fee equivalent to the amount of his investment (Kurt Eichenwald, *Conspiracy of Fools: A True Story* [New York: Random House, 2005], 261). This incestuous operation also involved Crédit Suisse First Boston and a British bank, NatWest. Fastow and his partners promised to buy from Enron, at an inflated price, Enron's shares in a fragile company called Rhythms. As compensation for taking this "risk," Enron provided its partners with 3.4 million of its own shares (Bethany McLean and Peter Elkind, *The Smartest Guys in the Room: The Amazing Rise and Scandalous Fall of Enron* [New York: Penguin, 2003], 191). In short, on the basis of its own stock market value, Enron was able to guarantee that someone would pick up its shaky investments; this ensured it was able to produce pristine financial statements, and this in turn meant that its stock market value would rise. The conflict of interest was tremendous, and so were the financial acrobatics involved in recording as a gain an operation that threatened to collapse at any moment – acrobatics based on the anticipated value of shares that the company owned and whose price would continue to rise because of its acrobatics. More than ever, the "pure capitalism" enabled by the Cayman Islands regime was so ethereal that it could truly be said to be based on nothing. The put-up job by which a company created its own business partner out of nothing was consigned to the secrecy that tax havens are so good at protecting.

Incestuous manoeuvres of this kind were to proliferate. "Enron was motivated by a will to override reality, so it set in motion the construction of ever more elaborate offshore structures that would cause the company to implode" (Brittain-Catlin, *Offshore*, 66). A Canadian bank, CIBC, invested tens of millions of dollars in operations of this kind (McLean and Elkind, *The Smartest Guys in the Room*, 293–94). In all, by the early years of the twenty-first century, Enron had created thousands of SPVs, including the LJM, developed thanks to Maples (Brittain-Catlin, *Offshore*, 71). One of Maples's lawyers, Henry Harford, "has said he was told very little about about the purpose of LJM Cayman" (ibid., 65). It would seem that the purposes of Special Purpose Vehicles are so special that the people framing them don't want to ask what they are. The most Maples did was to make sure Enron was aware of the fact that its own chief financial officer was managing "what was supposed to be an independent partnership" (ibid.).

There was general consternation when Enron declared enormous losses ($618 million) in November 2001 and went into bankruptcy a few weeks later. At the time it collapsed, Enron had somewhere between 692 and 800 subsidiaries in the Caymans (Brittain-Catlin, *Offshore*, 55; McLean and Elkind, *The Smartest Guys in the Room*, 310). This was in addition to its 119 subsidiaries in the Turks and Caicos Islands and dozens more in other jurisdictions (Brittain-Catlin, *Offshore*, 55).

Maples also developed entities for another multinational corporation whose bankruptcy caused great astonishment – Parmalat. Parmalat's mutual fund, Epicurum, bizarrely specializing in the leisure industry ("La Consob s'inquiète des placements de Parmalat," *Le Monde* [Paris], November 13, 2003), and its Bonlat subsidiary were fantasy entities enabling money to vanish offshore while still appearing in accounting reports (Brittain-Catlin, *Offshore*, 164–65). The "incredible opacity" of the company, which continued to post an artificially positive cashflow, was due to "dozens, or even hundreds, of subsidiaries located in the Cayman

Islands" (Marie-Noëlle Terisse, "L'affaire Parmalat ébranle le capitalisme italien," *Le Monde* [Paris], December 23, 2003 [our translation]). Eventually, it became known that the corporation had been concealing losses in tax havens for years, for a total of some 18 billion euros. And "whether they knew it or not, Maples and Calder, Cayman's largest law firm... had registered all the critical entities in Parmalat's Cayman portfolio" (Brittain-Catlin, *Offshore*, 161).

190 Jean-François Couvrat and Nicolas Pless, *La face cachée de l'économie mondiale*, 156.

191 Mélanie Delattre, "L'argent caché des paradis fiscaux," 60 [our translation].

192 Ibid.

193 Warren de Rajewicz, *Guide des nouveaux paradis fiscaux à l'usage des sociétés et des particuliers*, 36 [our translation].

194 Christian Chavagneux, "Îles Caïmans: pas seulement un paradis 'fiscal'," *L'économie politique* (blog of the *Alternatives économiques* periodical), April 4, 2013 [our translation].

195 Édouard Chambost, *Guide Chambost des paradis fiscaux*, 8th ed. (Lausanne: Favre, 2005 [1980]), 414n [our translation]. See also on this topic Bruce Livesey, *Thieves of Bay Street* (Toronto: Vintage Canada, 2012), especially 93–94.

196 Chambost, *Guide Chambost des paradis fiscaux*, 414n.

197 Ontario Securities Commission, *OSC Annual Summary Report for Dealers, Advisers, and Investment Fund Managers*, 2013; François Desjardins, "Valeurs mobilières : l'industrie de la finance n'est toujours pas irréprochable. La Commission des valeurs mobilières de l'Ontario fait la recension des tendances negatives," *Le Devoir* (Montreal), November 13, 2013.

198 Stephanie Kirchgaessne, "Fraud Charge in Man-UBS case," *Financial Times* (London), November 10, 2007; Livesey, *Thieves of Bay Street*, 152–54. See also U.S. Commodity Futures Trading Commission, "Hedge Fund Trader Paul Eustace and Philadelphia Alternative Asset Management Co. Ordered to Pay More Than $279 Million to Defrauded Customers and More than $20 Million in Civil Monetary Penalties in CFTC Action," news release pr5531-08, August 19, 2008.

199 James Ball, "IRS Targets FirstCaribbean International Bank over Tax Evasion," *The Guardian* (London), May 27, 2013; James Ball, "U.S. Tax Authorities Target Caribbean Bank," ICIJ (Washington), May 28, 2013.

200 Godefroy and Lascoumes, *Le capitalisme clandestin*, 45 [our translation].

201 Shaxson, *Treasure Islands*, 121–22.

202 Ibid.

203 Ridley, "What Makes the Cayman Islands a Successful International Financial Services Centre?" (2007), 1–2; Naylor, *Hot Money*, 304.

204 Ridley, "What Makes the Cayman Islands a Successful International Financial Services Centre?" (2007), 2.

205 OECD-CFA, *Towards Global Tax Co-operation* (Paris: OECD, 2000); FATF, *Report on Non-Co-operative Countries and Territories*; FATF, *Review to Identify Non-Co-operative Countries and Territories: Increasing the Worldwide Effectiveness of Money-Laundering Efforts*; FSF, *Financial Stability Forum Releases Grouping of Offshore Financial Centres (OFCs) to Assist in Setting Priorities for Assessment*.

206 Ibid.; Stein, "Cayman's Compliance with the OECD Standards on Tax Co-operation."

207 David Servenay, "Bertossa: 'La France n'est plus une démocratie parlementaire'," *Rue89* (Paris), May 31, 2009. The result of this moral laundering of offshore jurisdictions is apparent in the "peer review process" established by the OECD

and in which Canada obligingly participates (Global Forum on Transparency and Exchange of Information for Tax Purposes, *Tax Transparency 2014, Report on Progress* [Paris: OECD, 2014], 20).

208 *Mutual Evaluation / Detailed Assessment Report: Anti-Money Laundering and Combating the Financing of Terrorism – Cayman Islands, Ministerial Report* (Port of Spain, Trinidad and Tobago: Caribbean Financial Action Task Force [CFATF], 2007).

209 Jean-Claude Grimal, *Drogue : l'autre mondialisation* (Paris: Gallimard, 2000).

210 Patrice Meyzonnier, *Trafics et crimes en Amérique centrale et dans les Caraïbes* (Paris: Presses universitaires de France, 1999), 94.

211 Ibid. [our translation].

212 Chambost, *Guide Chambost des paradis fiscaux*, 384 and 410.

213 Bertossa (with Duparc), *La justice, les affaires, la corruption*, 137.

214 Ridley, "What Makes the Cayman Islands a Successful International Financial Services Centre?" (2007).

215 Ibid.

216 Mélanie Delattre, "L'argent caché des paradis fiscaux," 59.

217 "Cayman Islands: Offshore Legal and Tax Regimes," *LowTax.net*.

218 PricewaterhouseCoopers Canada, "Canada's TIEAs: Status at June 8, 2011," *Tax Memo: Canadian Tax Updates*, June 8, 2011.

219 "Cayman Islands Signs Tax Information Exchange Agreement with Canada," MaplesFS update, August 10, 2010.

220 "North America," MaplesFS website.

221 "John Dykstra," MaplesFS website.

222 "Cayman Islands Signs Tax Information Exchange Agreement with Canada," MaplesFS website.

223 Brittain-Catlin, *Offshore*, 16 and 30.

224 RBC Caribbean Investments, Investment Holdings (Cayman), and the Royal Bank of Canada Trust Company (Cayman) ("Canadian Banks Operate Offshore: Big 5 Financial Institutions Have Branches in Locales from Switzerland to Singapore," interactive map, CBC News, June 24, 2013).

225 Scotiabank & Trust (Cayman) ("Canadian Banks Operate Offshore").

226 CIBC Holdings (Cayman), CIBC Investments (Cayman), CIBC Bank and Trust Company (Cayman), and FirstCaribbean International Bank (Cayman) ("Canadian Banks Operate Offshore").

227 National Commercial Bank of Jamaica, "Our History"; Manulife, "Manulife Signs Agreement with AIC Limited to Acquire AIC Canadian Retail Investment Funds," news release, August 12, 2009.

228 "Canadian Banks – Jamaica, Barbados, Cayman Islands, Turks and Caicos Islands," Canadian Trade Commissioner Service website, April 22, 2015.

229 Canadian Press, "Maples and Calder s'installe à Montréal," *Les Affaires.com*, May 3, 2009 [our translation].

230 "Malaise sur la colline," Radio-Canada, July 8, 2009 [our translation].

231 Ibid. [our translation].

232 Ibid. [our translation].

233 "Home" and "About Us," MaplesFS website.

1   Figure for 2012: "Foreign Direct Investment, 2012" and "Foreign Direct Investment Positions at Year-End," Statistics Canada, May 9, 2013; figure for 2007: "Foreign Direct Investment Positions at Year-End," Statistics Canada, April 19, 2012. The population figure is from the CIA World Factbook.

2   OECD-CFA, Towards Global Tax Co-operation (Paris: OECD, 2000); FATF, *Report on Non-Co-operative Countries and Territories* (Paris: FATF, 2000); FATF, *Review to Identify Non-Co-operative Countries and Territories: Increasing the Worldwide Effectiveness of Money-Laundering Efforts* (Paris: FATF, 2000); FSF, *Financial Stability Forum Releases Grouping of Offshore Financial Centres (OFCs) to Assist in Setting Priorities for Assessment* (Basel: FSF, 2000).

3   Daniel Jay Baum, *The Banks of Canada in the Commonwealth Caribbean: Economic Nationalism and Multinational Enterprises of a Medium Power* (New York: Praeger, 1974), 32–40. Barbados did not have a central bank in 1974 at the time Baum's book was published, but had announced its intention of establishing one in 1972 (ibid., 37). Canada's ties with Barbados go back a long way and were strengthened after the American Revolution when, according to Maurice Burac, "Canada was more and more involved in providing for the inhabitants' needs," especially since sugar cane harvests, which were crucially important for the island, were often damaged by late nineteenth-century weather conditions (Maurice Burac, *Les mutations récentes d'une île sucrière* [Bordeaux-Talence: Centre de recherche des espaces tropicaux de l'Université Michel de Montaigne (Bordeaux III) et Centre d'études de géographie tropicale, 1993], 32–33 [our translation]). See also the entry on Barbados on the *LowTax.net* website: "The Companies Act 1982 legislates companies in Barbados. It was modelled on the Canadian Business Corporation Act. Company forms available under the Act are limited liability companies, companies without share capital (for non-profit purposes) and mutual insurance companies" ("Barbados: Types of Company," *LowTax.net* (Kingston upon Thames), May 2013).

4   Pedro L. V. Welch, "Structuring Independence: Foreign Relations Policy of the Barbados Government, 1966–1986," in Serge Mam Lam Fouck, Juan Gonzales Mendoza, and Jacques Adélaïde-Merlande (ed.), *Regards sur l'histoire de la Caraïbe. Des Guyanes aux Grandes Antilles* (Cayenne: Association des historiens de la Caraïbe, 2001), 361 and 367. Barbados's attempts to use tax incentives to stimulate its agricultural economy began in 1951. The island abolished duties on imports of raw materials and machines and granted corporate tax holidays, initially for a period of seven years; then, beginning in 1963, for ten years (Maurice Burac, *Les mutations récentes d'une île sucrière*, 128). The seeds of the future tax haven were being sown. Barbados also developed an industrial form of tourism that targeted Canadian customers (among others).

5   Bank of Nova Scotia, 1967 annual report, 20.

6   Bank of Nova Scotia, 1968 annual report, 24.

7   Maurice Burac, *Les mutations récentes d'une île sucrière*, 129.

8   Ibid., 128–29.

9   Ibid., 136.

10 Ibid., 136–37.

11 "Industrial Estates: Overview," The Barbados Investment and Development Corporation (BIDC) website.

12 "Fiscal Incentives," Fiscal Incentives Act, Laws of Barbados, 2001, chapter 71A.

13 Ibid., 10.

14 "Minimum Wage Is Now $250," *CaribbeanTrakker.com*, March 14, 2012.

15 "Employee Rights," *Bermudas Business*. An exception is made for shop assistants, whose minimum wage could conceivably serve as a general reference point for employers.

16 Maurice Burac, *Les mutations récentes d'une île sucrière*, 156.

17 "Canada-Barbados Relations," Canadian High Commission in Barbados website, September 2013.

18 "Temporary Foreign Worker Program," Employment and Social Development Canada website. (Note: This website has changed considerably since January 2012 in response to a public call to reform the TFWP and "put Canadians first." The Web posting mentioned has since been taken down.)

19 André Beauchamp, *Guide mondial des paradis fiscaux* (Ville Mont-Royal, QC: Éditions Le Nordais, 1982 [Paris: Grasset et Fasquelle, 1981]), 149.

20 Pedro L. V. Welch, "Structuring Independence," 361. The government's economic policy was most likely shaped by foreigners. "A cadre of foreign service officers had been developed, who would oversee the technical details of foreign policy by drafting policy papers and so on. While there is no evidence of a unit staffed by professional economists within the Foreign Service at this time, the establishment of the Central Bank of Barbados and the continuous hiring of a competent group of career economists in the Ministry of Finance meant that the necessary skills were available to foreign policy makers" (ibid., 366). Who were these "foreign policy makers"? They probably did not belong to the Marxist reading groups at the University of the West Indies accused, at the time, of putting regional security in danger (ibid., 368).

21 Maurice Burac, *Les mutations récentes d'une île sucrière*, 135 [our translation].

22 *Agreement Between Canada and Barbados for the Avoidance of Double Taxation and the Prevention of Fiscal Evasion with Respect to Taxes on Income and on Capital*, CRA website, January 22, 1980. (Note: As of December 26, 2014, the Web page is no longer active, but you can access the document by going to the French page and clicking on "English" in the upper left-hand corner.)

23 Two sources among many: "Barbados: Offshore Legal and Tax Regimes," *LowTax. net*; "Tax Haven Barbados," *TaxHaven.biz*.

24 Quebec's former minister of finance and premier Jacques Parizeau was wrong when he wrote that, at the time the tax agreement was reached in 1980, tax rates in Barbados and Canada "were about the same" (Jacques Parizeau, "Les sources d'injustice: les paradis fiscaux," in *La souveraineté du Québec. Hier, aujourd'hui et demain* [Montreal: Michel Brûlé, 2009], 222 [our translation]).

25 "Barbados: Double Tax Treaties," *LowTax.net* (Kingston upon Thames).

26 Maurice Burac, *Les mutations récentes d'une île sucrière*, 136 [our translation].

27 Paul Martin and Canada Steamship Lines are discussed in Alain Deneault, *Paul Martin & Companies: Sixty Theses on the Alegal Nature of Tax Havens* (Vancouver: Talonbooks, 2006).

28 "For example, Statistics Canada reports that Canadian direct investment in Barbados has increased from $628 million in 1988 to $23.3 billion in 2001 – over a 3,600 percent increase" (Sheila Fraser, *Report of the Auditor General of Canada* [Ottawa: Office of the Auditor General, December 2002], chapter 11, section 11.96; Hélène Buzzetti, "En 1994, Paul Martin a apporté des changements à la loi de l'impôt. La famille Martin au paradis," *Le Devoir* [Montreal], February 14, 2004).

29 Ramesh Chaitoo and Ann Weston, "Canada and the Caribbean Community: Prospects for an Enhanced Trade Arrangement" (paper given at the *Conference*

on *Canada, Latin America and the Caribbean: Defining Re-Engagement*, Ottawa, March 13 and 14, 2008), 19.

30 Édouard Chambost, *Guide Chambost des paradis fiscaux*, 8th ed. (Lausanne: Favre, 2005 [1980]), 542 [our translation].

31 Ibid. [our translation].

32 Jean-Pierre Vidal, "La concurrence fiscale favorise-t-elle les planifications fiscales internationales agressives?," in Jean-Luc Rossignol (ed.), *La gouvernance juridique et fiscale des organisations* (Paris: Éditions Tec et Doc – Lavoisier, 2010), 183 [our translation].

33 Ibid., 190 [our translation].

34 "Foreign Direct Investment, 2012," Statistics Canada website, May 9, 2013.

35 Jean-Pierre Vidal, "La concurrence fiscale favorise-t-elle les planifications fiscales internationales agressives?," 191 [our translation].

36 Ibid., 190 [our translation].

37 Brian J. Arnold, "Reforming Canada's International Tax System: Toward Coherence and Simplicity," *Canadian Tax Paper* (Toronto), no. 111 (2009): 14 and 48–61; Donald J. S. Brean, "International Issues in Taxation: The Canadian Perspective," *Canadian Tax Paper* (Toronto), no. 75 (1984): 11.

38 Brian J. Arnold, "Reforming Canada's International Tax System," 12, 143–46.

39 Ibid., 90ff and 153.

40 Ibid., 27–28.

41 Ibid., 28.

42 Ibid., 14.

43 Caroline Maxwell, "Outward Investment from Canada: The Offshore Perspective," *LowTax.net* (Kingston upon Thames).

44 The laws of Barbados, and the connection between Barbados and Canada, make it the ideal candidate for corporate tax avoidance. Even today, among the jurisdictions to which Canadian corporations can relocate funds, "for the specific purpose of establishing an active subsidiary, only Barbados and (to a lesser extent now) Cyprus are really suitable in terms of infrastructure, legislation and corporate taxation regimes," according to Caroline Maxwell (ibid.).

45 Sheila Fraser, *Report of the Auditor General of Canada 2002*, chapter 11; also quoted in Jean-Pierre Vidal, "La concurrence fiscale favorise-t-elle les planifications fiscales internationales agressives?," 192.

46 "New Canada Revenue Agency Position on Barbados Exempt Insurance Companies," *Osler.com*, November 12, 2010.

47 Maurice Burac, *Les mutations récentes d'une île sucrière*, 136.

48 Ibid.

49 The Royal Bank of Canada Insurance Company, RBC (Barbados) Funding, Royal Bank of Canada (Caribbean) Corporation, RBC Capital Markets (Japan) Ltd., RBC Holdings (Barbados), Royal Bank of Canada Financial Corporation ("Canadian Banks Operate Offshore: Big 5 Financial Institutions Have Branches in Locales from Switzerland to Singapore," interactive map, CBC News, June 24, 2013).

50 FirstCaribbean International Wealth Management Bank (Barbados), CIBC International (Barbados), CIBC Offshore Banking Services Corporation, CIBC Reinsurance Company Limited, FirstCaribbean International Bank, FirstCaribbean International Bank (Barbados) ("Canadian Banks Operate Offshore").

51 BNS International (Barbados) and Scotia Insurance (Barbados) ("Canadian Banks Operate Offshore").

52 Canada Trustco International, TD Reinsurance (Barbados), Toronto Dominion International ("Canadian Banks Operate Offshore").

53 The Barbados institution is the Bank of Montreal (Barbados) Ltd. ("Bank of Montreal (Barbados) Ltd.," *AAAdir.com*).

54 The Barbados institution is a branch of the National Bank of Canada (Global) Ltd. ("Barbados Banks," *Financial-Portal.com*).

55 Formerly known as Barrick International Bank Corp, it is now Barrick International (Barbados) Corp (Barrick Gold Corp, *FORM 40-F Annual Report [foreign private issuer]*, form produced March 28, 2012, 130).

56 Éric Bocquet interviewed by Dominique Albertini, "Paradis fiscaux: 'Un monde parallèle hyper-complexe'," *Libération* (Paris), July 18, 2012 [our translation].

57 Dale Hill, Jamal Hejazi and Mark Kirkey, *Transfer Pricing – Are You Prepared?*, Gowlings Lafleur Henderson LLP, n.d. [the report contains no references later than 2010].

58 François Vincent, *Transfer Pricing in Canada* (Toronto: Carswell [Thomson Reuters], 2009), 136. (François Vincent works for KPMG.)

59 Brean, "International issues in Taxation," 114 and 117, and also iii.

60 Arnold, "Reforming Canada's International Tax System," 15–16; Brean, "International Issues in Taxation," 47.

61 Arnold, "Reforming Canada's International Tax System," 41, 51–52, 65, and 73; Brean, "International Issues in Taxation," 10–17.

62 Arnold, "Reforming Canada's International Tax System," 73; Income Tax Act, RSC, 1985, c. 1 (5th Supp.).

63 Arnold, "Reforming Canada's International Tax System," 157–58.

64 See chart in Marie Vastel, "Budget Flaherty, Un ultimatum lancé aux provinces," *Le Devoir* (Montreal), February 12, 2014.

65 Stéphanie Grammond, "Le Canada, paradis fiscal des enterprises," *La Presse* (Montreal), July 29, 2008.

66 Fraser, *Report of the Auditor General of Canada 2002*, chapter 11.

67 Ibid., chapter 11, section 86.

68 Francis Vailles, "Paradis fiscaux: Ottawa abandonne une bataille" and "Comment fonctionne le stratagème des paradis fiscaux," *La Presse* (Montreal), February 5, 2009 [our translation].

69 "Canada's New Government Improves Tax Fairness with Anti-Tax-Haven Initiative," Department of Finance Canada website, May 14, 2007.

70 Arthur J. Cockfield, "Tax Competitiveness Program. Finding Silver Linings in the Storm: An Evaluation of Recent Canada-U.S. Crossborder Tax Developments" (Toronto: C.D. Howe Institute, no. 272, September 2008), 10; Arnaud Mary, *Canada v. Recours aux paradis fiscaux/bancaires : dans quelle mesure la politique de lutte du Canada peut-elle être améliorée* (M.A. thesis, Québec, Université Laval, Faculté de droit, 2011), 65.

71 Arnaud Mary, *Canada v. Recours aux paradis fiscaux/bancaires*, 66; Lyne Gaulin, "Cross-Border Tax: Canadian Multinationals Allowed to Double-Dip" (tax note prepared for Miller Thomson Lawyers [Toronto], March 2010).

72 Lyne Gaulin, "Cross-Border Tax: Canadian Multinationals Allowed to Double-Dip"; see also Duanjie Chen and Jack M. Mintz, "Taxation of Canadian Inbound and

Outbound Investments" (research report for Advisory Panel on Canada's System of International Taxation, December 2008), 18.

73 Maria E. de Boyrie, Simon J. Pak, John S. Zdanowicz, "Estimating the Magnitude of Capital Flight Due to Abnormal Pricing in International Trade: The Russia-USA Case," *Accounting Forum* (Elsevier) no. 29 (2005): 249–70.

74 Kerrie Sadiq, "Taxation of Multinational Financial Institutions, Using Formulary Apportionment to Reflect Economic Reality" (seminar on *Transfer Pricing: Alternative Methods of Taxation of Multinationals*, Helsinki, June 2012). By the same author: "Arm's Length Pricing and Multinational Banks: An Old-Fashioned Approach in a Modern World," *Tax Justice Focus – The Newsletter of the Tax Justice Network* (London) 7, no. 3 (2012): 5.

75 Tatiana Falcão, "Giving Developing Countries a Say in International Transfer Pricing Allocations," *Tax Justice Focus – The Newsletter of the Tax Justice Network* (London) 7, no. 3 (2012): 3.

76 OECD *Transfer Pricing Guidelines for Multinational Enterprises and Tax Administrations* (Paris: OECD, 1995).

77 Income Tax Act, section 247.2. This law is a sequel to the tinkering undertaken in the 1990s by the Technical Committee on Business Taxation, which revised some elements of the law, in particular those related to transfer pricing (Brian J. Arnold, "Reforming Canada's International Tax System," 14). New clauses were introduced in 1984 to counteract some effects of tax havens, but were notoriously ineffective according to the 1998 Technical Committee on Business Taxation (ibid., 171 and 172). Dale Hill, Jamal Hejazi, and Mark Kirkey explain how companies take advantage of the weakness of the law in their report, *Transfer Pricing – Are You Prepared?*

78 Jeff Gray, "Supreme Court Backs Glaxo in Transfer-Pricing Dispute," *Globe and Mail* (Toronto), October 18, 2012, referring to *Canada v. GlaxoSmithKline Inc.*, 2012 SCC 52.

79 Christopher Slade and Alan Kenigsberg, "Determining an Arm's Length Transfer Price: SCC Renders Decision in GlaxoSmithKline Inc.," Stikeman Elliott, December 4, 2012.

80 A court case brought by Revenue Canada against Indalex in the 1980s [*Indalex Ltd. v. The Queen*, [1986] 1 CTC 219 (FCTD), aff'd. [1988] 1 CTC 60 (FCA)] illustrates the difficulties involved in finding a standard to determine what an "objective" market price might be (Lorraine Eden, "Transfer Pricing and the Tax Courts," in *Taxing Multinationals: Transfer Pricing and Corporate Income Taxation in North America* [Toronto: University of Toronto Press, 1998], 537–38, 544).

81 IRS, "IRS Accepts Settlement Offer in Largest Transfer Pricing Dispute," news release IR-2006-142, September 11, 2006.

82 Philippe Dominati (president) and Éric Bocquet (rapporteur), *L'évasion fiscale internationale, et si on arrêtait?*, Rapport d'information, Commission d'enquête sur l'évasion des capitaux et des actifs hors de France et ses incidences fiscales, no. 673, 2 vols. (Paris: Sénat, July 2012).

83 Christian Chavagneux, quoted in ibid., 1:67 [our translation].

84 Jesse Drucker, "Google 2.4% Rate Shows How $60 Billion Lost to Tax Loopholes," *Bloomberg.com* (New York), October 21, 2010; Jesse Drucker, "Google Revenues Sheltered in No-Tax Bermuda Soar to $10 Billion," *Bloomberg.com* (New York), December 10, 2012.

85 "Apple de nouveau montré du doigt pour détournement d'impôts," *Le Monde* (Paris), July 1, 2013 [our translation].

86 Xavier Harel, *La grande évasion. Le vrai scandale des paradis fiscaux* (Arles: Actes Sud, 2012 [Paris: Les liens qui libèrent, 2010]).

87 Agence France-Presse, "Le fisc américain privé de 92 milliards," *Le Devoir* (Montreal), June 4, 2013.

88 Serge Truffaut, "Rapport de l'OCDE sur l'impôt: l'aversion," *Le Devoir* (Montreal), February 15, 2013.

89 Éric Desrosiers, "Outrés," *Le Devoir* (Montreal), May 27, 2013 [our translation].

90 *White Paper on Transfer Pricing Documentation* (Paris: OECD, July 30, 2013).

91 "Treaty Shopping – The Problem and Possible Solutions," Department of Finance Canada website, 2013.

92 *Velcro Canada Inc. v. The Queen*, 2012 TCC 57; *Canada v. Prévost Car Inc.*, 2009 FCA 57; *MIL (Investments) SA v. The Queen*, 2006 TCC 460; aff'd. 2007 FCA 236.

93 "Treaty Shopping – The Problem and Possible Solutions," Department of Finance Canada website, 2013.

94 Jennifer Smith, "Offshore Trusts Under Attack," *CA Magazine* (Montreal), January–February 2010.

95 "Supreme Court of Canada Rules on Trust Residence – St. Michael Trust Corp. v. The Queen (Garron Family Trust)," *Tax Memo*, PricewaterhouseCoopers, May 2012, referring to [*St. Michael Trust Corp. as Trustee of the Fundy Settlement*] *Fundy Settlement v. Canada*, 2012 SCC 14.

96 "Under Canadian tax rules, Canadian residents are taxed on their worldwide income. Taxpayers who use foreign bank accounts – which are not illegal *per se* – generally get around these rules in two ways: first, they often do not declare the income that was deposited abroad as the account's initial capital; second, they do not declare the investment income generated by the account over the years" (Paul Ryan, *Quand le fisc attaque: Acharnement ou nécessité?* [Montreal: Éditions La Presse, 2012], 176 [our translation]).

97 Diane Francis, *Who Owns Canada Now: Old Money, New Money, and the Future of Canadian Business* (Toronto: HarperCollins, 2008), 439.

98 Sylvain Fleury, "Abusive Tax Planning: The Problem and the Canadian Context," publication no. 2010-22-E (International Affairs, Trade and Finance Division, Parliamentary Information and Research Service, Library of Parliament, 2010), 5.

99 Laura Figazzolo and Bob Harris, *Global Corporate Taxation and Resources for Quality Public Services* (Brussels: Education International Research Institute for the Council of Global Unions, December 2011), 11, 18.

100 Brean, "International Issues in Taxation," 1.

101 Sadiq, "Taxation of Multinational Financial Institutions, Using Formulary Apportionment to Reflect Economic Reality," and "Arm's Length Pricing and Multinational Banks: An Old-Fashioned Approach in a Modern World."

102 Jomo Kwame Sundaram, "Transfer Pricing Is a Financing for Development Issue" (Berlin: Friedrich-Ebert Stiftung, February 2012).

103 "U.K., U.S., OECD Oppose Developing Country Interests on Tax," Tax Justice Network (London) website, March 7, 2011.

104 "RBC Wealth Management and Taxchambers Cordially Invite You to an Exclusive Seminar on Transfer Pricing and Tax Planning for Barbados Subsidiaries of Canadian Parent Companies with the Distinguished Canadian Tax Lawyer Jonathan Garbutt."

105 "Analyst – Transfer Pricing, New Graduate, Full Time," Deloitte (Calgary) website, 2011.

106 Steve Hurowitz and Shawn Brade, "Barbados 2012 Budget Cuts Corporate Tax Rate," *Global Tax Adviser* (KPMG Calgary and Toronto), July 10, 2012.

107 Ibid.

108 Dominique Sicot, "Mais que fait une filiale de PSA à la Barbade?," *L'Humanité Dimanche* (Paris), October 18–24, 2012. Barbados has constantly worked to improve its offshore offer, as Grégoire Duhamel explains in the fact sheet on the country included in *Les paradis fiscaux* (Paris: Éditions Grancher, 2006), 400ff.

109 "Canada-Barbados Relations," Canadian High Commission in Barbados website, January 2012. This sentence was removed from the website in September 2013.

110 Philippe Dominati and Éric Bocquet, *L'évasion fiscale internationale, et si on arrêtait?*, 12 [our translation].

111 Ibid., 17 [our translation].

112 The technical distinction between (normally legal) tax flight and (illegal) tax evasion remains relevant to the extent that there is a need to define the practical means of containing this double phenomenon. "This difference must not be ignored: it has effects on the specific form of policies to be established" (ibid. [our translation]).

113 Philippe Dominati and Éric Boquet, *L'évasion fiscale internationale, et si on arrêtait?*, 21 [our translation]; see also 16 and 18.

114 Ibid., 15 [our translation].

115 Ibid., 17 [our translation].

116 Ibid., 18 [our translation].

117 Ibid., 28 [our translation].

118 Ibid., 19 [our translation].

119 Ibid., 28 [our translation].

120 Ibid., 23.

121 Ibid., 23–24.

122 Anne Michel, "La fraude fiscale coûte 2000 milliards d'euros par an à l'Europe," *Le Monde* (Paris), October 9, 2013.

123 Collectif d'associations Échec aux paradis fiscaux, "Lancement de la campagne Levez le voile sur les paradis fiscaux!," news release, April 29, 2013.

124 Philippe Dominati and Éric Bocquet, *L'évasion fiscale internationale, et si on arrêtait?*, 28 [our translation].

125 Ibid., 29 [our translation].

126 Ibid., 28 [our translation].

127 "Société Offshore au Canada," *France-Offshore.fr* (Paris).

128 "Plateforme Paradis fiscaux et judiciaires, Que font les plus grandes banques françaises dans les paradis fiscaux?," *ccfd-terresolidaire.org* (Paris), November 13, 2013.

129 Mojca Kleva Kekuš and Eva Joly (rapporteurs), "Report on Fight against Tax Fraud, Tax Evasion, and Tax Havens" (2013/2060[INI], Committee on Economic and Monetary Affairs, Parliament of the European Union, May 2, 2013).

130 Jean-François Couvrat and Nicolas Pless, *La face cachée de l'économie mondiale* (Paris: Hatier, 1988), 29.

131 Ibid.

132 *Agreement Between Canada and Barbados for the Avoidance of Double Taxation and the Prevention of Fiscal Evasion with Respect to Taxes on Income and on Capital.*

133 Jean-François Couvrat and Nicolas Pless, *La face cachée de l'économie mondiale*, 32 [our translation].

134 André Noël, "La compagnie de Paul Martin confie la gestion de ses bateaux à une société des Bermudes," *La Presse* (Montreal), September 24, 1999.

135 Deneault, *Paul Martin & Companies.*

136 "Defining FOCs and the Problems They Pose," International Transport Workers' Federation (London) website, 2015.

137 Jean-François Couvrat and Nicolas Pless, *La face cachée de l'économie mondiale*, 41.

138 Ibid., 22 [our translation].

139 Alex Doulis, *My Blue Haven* (Etobicoke, ON: Uphill, 1997 [2001]), 112.

140 Ibid., 109.

141 Jean-Pierre Vidal, "La concurrence fiscale favorise-t-elle les planifications fiscales internationales agressives?," 191 [our translation].

142 Bruce Livesey, *Thieves of Bay Street* (Toronto: Random House Canada, 2012), 161.

143 "Improving Tax Information Exchange," in "International Taxation," in "Business Income Tax Measures," Annex 5 of the *2007 Budget*, Department of Finance Canada website, March 19, 2007. This measure ensures consistency with Regulation 5900 of Canada's Income Tax Act, RSC, 1985, c. 1 (5th Supp.) ("Part LIX: Foreign Affiliates").

144 "Tax Information Exchange Agreements," Department of Finance Canada website, August 29, 2009.

145 Quoted in Shaxson, *Treasure Islands*, 26.

146 Vincent Peillon, *Les milliards noirs du blanchiment* (Paris: Hachette, 2004), 55–56 [our translation].

147 Canada-Switzerland treaty, Article 25, quoted in Gilles Larin and Alexandra Diebel, "The Swiss Twist: The Exchange-of-Information Provisions of the Canada-Switzerland Protocol," *Canadian Tax Journal* (Toronto) 60, no. 1 (2012), 28–29.

148 Gilles Larin and Alexandra Diebel, "Protocole Canada-Suisse du 22 octobre 2010 : le secret bancaire est-il menacé, eu égard aux recettes fiscales canadiennes" (working paper prepared for Chaire de recherche en fiscalité et en finances publiques de l'Université de Sherbrooke, 2010), 20 [our translation].

149 Colin Le Bachelet, "Confidentiality vs. Secrecy – What's the Difference?" (tax update prepared for RBC Trustees [Guernsey] Limited, August 2011), 2.

150 "RC4507 Using Tax Havens to Avoid Paying Taxes: Worth the Risk?," CRA website, April 1, 2010.

151 "Barbados Budget Lowers Minimum Tax for Investors," *Trinidad and Tobago Guardian* (Port of Spain), July 9, 2012.

TURKS AND CAICOS ISLANDS

1 R. T. Naylor, *Hot Money and the Politics of Debt* (Montreal: McGill-Queen's UP, 2004 [1987]), 306.

2 Ivelaw L. Griffith, "Illicit Arms Trafficking, Corruption, and Governance in the Caribbean," *Dickinson Journal of International Law* 15, no. 3 (Spring 1997): 495–96.

3 According to the CIA World Factbook, the estimated population in July 2014 was 49,070.

4   Peter Goldring, "Turks and Caicos Update," no. 73 (March 2009): 1.

5   "Max Saltsman," Hall of Fame Members, Cambridge Archives and Records Centre, City of Cambridge (Ontario) website.

6   Gord Henderson, "Letting the Turks and Caicos Islands Slip Away," *Windsor Star*, April 6, 2013. Xenophobic responses of this kind surface whenever annexation is discussed (Andrew Steele, "The Eleventh Province?," *Globe and Mail* [Toronto], August 19, 2009).

7   Édouard Chambost, *Guide Chambost des paradis fiscaux* (Lausanne: Favre, 1980), 440 [our translation].

8   Peter Goldring, "Turks and Caicos Update," no. 73 (March 2009): 2.

9   Steve Rennie, "A Place in the Sun? A Formal Association Between the Turks & Caicos and Canada Could Be Possible," *Times of the Islands* (Providenciales, Turks and Caicos), Summer 2004.

10   Peter Goldring, "Turks and Caicos Update," no. 73 (March 2009): 2. 11 Peter Goldring, "Turks and Caicos Update," no. 111 (September 2011): 1–2.

12   Steve Rennie, "A Place in the Sun?"

13   Dan McKenzie, *Report on Practical Measures Which Might Be Taken to Increase Trade, Investment, and Economic Cooperation Between Canada and the Turks* (Ottawa: Department of External Affairs, 1989).

14   "Heaven Can Wait," *The Fifth Estate*, CBC Television.

15   This former military police officer was forced to withdraw from the Conservative caucus from 2011 to 2013 when he was accused of refusing to give a breath sample at the request of Edmonton police officers. A strange ruling from Judge Larry Anderson of the Alberta Provincial Court recognized that Goldring had refused to comply with the request, yet also found him innocent – while stating that the "decision does not set a precedent" and that "it would be wrong for people to think the best defence is to ask the police a lot of questions when pulled over" ("Harper Welcomes MP Goldring Back into Caucus After Acquittal," CBC News, June 6, 2013; "Read the Peter Goldring Decision by Judge Larry Anderson," *Edmonton Journal*, June 7, 2013). The controversial Goldring also accumulated errors and historical omissions when he sent out a brochure accusing Louis Riel of having stood in the way of Canadian Confederation, claiming that Riel had "blood on his hands" (Chinta Puxley, "Calling Louis Riel a 'Villain' Lands Conservative MP in Hot Water," *Globe and Mail* [Toronto], February 19, 2010).

16   Peter Goldring, "Turks and Caicos Update," no. 73 (March 2009): 2.

17   Ibid., 1.

18   Ibid.

19   Peter Goldring, "Turks and Caicos Update," no. 5 (February 2004): 1; Peter Goldring, Motion 474, "Private Members' Business," Order Paper and Notice Paper (no. 128B), Parliament of Canada, November 12, 2003 [published November 17, 2003]).

20   "N.S. Votes to Invite Turks and Caicos to Join It," CBC News, April 22, 2004.

21   Ibid.

22   Luc Fortin, "Young Liberals of Canada (Quebec) Annual Symposium," *Young Liberals of Canada Newsletter*, October 2005 (*collectionscanada.gc.ca*).

23   Brad Sigouin, Robert Chaput, and Leah Gregoire, "Our Wealth Management Process," RBC Dominion Securities Inc. website.

24   Ibid.

25 Amanda Banks, "Idea of a Canadian Place in the Sun Remains Alive," *Tax-News.com* (London), March 24, 2004.

26 Chris Morris, "Business Leaders and Politicians Resurrect Idea of Canadian, Caribbean Union," Canadian Press, March 15, 2004; "Indepth: Turks and Caicos, Canada's Caribbean Ambition," CBC News, April 16, 2004.

27 Peter Goldring, "Turks and Caicos Update," no. 39 (May 2005): 1.

28 Jean-Michel Demetz, "Ma cabane sous les tropiques," *L'Express international* (Paris), week of August 16–20, 2004.

29 Matt Sandy, "Michael Misick: Turks and Caicos Premier Facing Extradition from Brazil," *Telegraph* (London), April 28, 2013.

30 Peter Goldring, "Turks and Caicos Update," no. 111 (September 2011): 1; Massimo Pacetti, Motion 409, "Private Members' Business," Order Paper and Notice Paper (no. 128B), Parliament of Canada, September 15, 2009.

31 Peter Goldring, "Turks and Caicos Update," no. 111 (September 2011): 1.

32 Damien McElroy, "Turks and Caicos: Britain Suspends Government in Overseas Territory," *Telegraph* (London), August 14, 2009.

33 Peter Goldring, "Turks and Caicos Update," no. 111 (September 2011): 1.

34 "Welcome to FortisTCI," *fortistci.com* (Providenciales).

35 "Turks and Caicos Islands Projects," *InterHealthCanada.com* (Toronto).

36 "Caribbean Cops Want Mounties Removed," QMI Agency, *Canoë.ca* (Montreal), November 28, 2011.

37 Gord Henderson, "Letting the Turks and Caicos Islands Slip Away."

38 Peter Kuitenbrouwer, "Islanders Irked by RCMP Raid on Tropical Tax Haven – Paradise Threatened," *National Post* (Toronto), April 3, 1999.

39 Sinclair Stewart and Paul Waldie, "Portus Looks to Lawyer," *Globe and Mail* (Toronto), June 21, 2005. The earlier quotation from *Le Figaro* (Paris) is our translation.

40 Bruce Livesey, "The Offshore Banking Nightmare," *Canadian Lawyer* (Toronto) February 2012.

41 Grégoire Duhamel, *Les paradis fiscaux* (Paris: Éditions Grancher, 2006), 560 [our translation].

42 "Turks & Caicos," *Can-Offshore.org*.

43 Duhamel, *Les paradis fiscaux,* 559 [our translation].

44 Chambost, *Guide Chambost des paradis fiscaux,* 447 [our translation].

45 Thierry Godefroy and Pierre Lascoumes, *Le capitalisme clandestin. L'illusoire régulation des places offshore* (Paris: La Découverte, 2004), 104 [our translation]. See also "Turks & Caicos," *Can-Offshore.org*.

46 Godefroy and Lascoumes, *Le capitalisme clandestin*.

47 Patrice Meyzonnier, *Trafics et crimes en Amérique centrale et dans les Caraïbes* (Paris: Presses universitaires de France, 1999), 93 [our translation].

48 Chambost, *Guide Chambost des paradis fiscaux,* 445 [our translation].

49 "Insurance Sector Captivating the Financial Services Industry," *Turks and Caicos Free Press* (Providenciales), November 12, 2012.

50 "Captives : une solution souple et efficace pour le financement de vos risques," *Aon.fr* [our translation].

51 "Captives d'assurance et de réassurance," in "Guide des paradis fiscaux," *Slate.fr*, April 8, 2013 [our translation]. For the jurisdiction's low rating because of drug smuggling from Colombia, see Duhamel, *Les paradis fiscaux,* 559.

52 "Ceded Reinsurance Leverage," *InvestorWords.com* (Fairfax, VA)

53 "The ECB participated in the work of the FSF, which reviewed, *inter alia*, the adoption of international standards by offshore financial centres, progress with regard to its recommendations related to highly leveraged institutions, and transparency practices in the reinsurance industry" (European Central Bank, 2002 annual report, 109).

54 "Why Domicile Your Captive in the Turks and Caicos Islands?," *Captive.com* (Dallas, TX).

55 Peter Goldring, "Turks and Caicos Update," no. 39 (May 2005): 3.

56 Duhamel, *Les paradis fiscaux*, 555 [our translation].

57 Peter Goldring, "Turks and Caicos Update," no. 73 (March 2009): 3.

58 Peter Goldring, "Turks and Caicos Update," no. 39 (May 2005): 3.

59 Steve Rennie, "A Place in the Sun?"

60 Ibid.

61 "Delaware, USA: The Domestic Haven," in Alain Deneault, *Offshore Tax Havens and the Rule of Global Crime* (New York: Free Press, 2011).

62 "I do advocate an economic partnership, of one form or another, being negotiated between Canada and The Turks and Caicos Islands. This could mean partnering with the islands by establishing a free trade association with them, or perhaps establishing some sort of customs union" (Peter Goldring, "Turks and Caicos Update," no. 73 [March 2009]: 3).

63 Kuitenbrouwer, "Islanders Irked by RCMP Raid on Tropical Tax Haven – Paradise Threatened."

ALBERTA

1 See sections 92 (5) and 92A of the Canadian Constitution of 1867 (The Constitution Act, 1867, 30 & 31 Vict, c. 3).

2 "Title to Alberta's oil and gas reserves has generally not been sold or otherwise transferred to individuals and companies. In the case of oil sands, for example, approximately 97 percent of the bitumen reserves are still owned by all Albertans (current and future generations), with the provincial government acting as their agent in transactions with producers (Alberta Department of Energy 2006). Since the early 1990s, Alberta has relied on lease auctions to allocate production rights to oil sands developers. The one-time bonus bids collected from these auctions are one of the four key types of payments through which the Government of Alberta secures a direct return to ownership from the exploitation of bitumen reserves. The province also collects annual rental fees on land (an almost negligible source of payments in Alberta) and royalties on production" (Andre Plourde, "Oil Sands Royalties and Taxes in Alberta: An Assessment of Key Developments since the Mid-1990s," *Energy Journal* 30:1 [2009]: 130).

3 "In Canada, more than 80 percent of petroleum is found on Crownland, so federal and provincial gornments have always shad a direct interest in the industry as the owner of the resource" (Robert D. Bott, "Petroleum Industries," *The Canadian Encyclopedia*, 2009–2015).

4 "Petro-state" as defined in *Collins Canadian Dictionary* (2011).

5 This section draws heavily on Bruce Campbell, "A Tale of Two Petro-States (Part I of III): Norway Manages Its Oil Wealth Way Better Than Canada Does," CCPA

website, November 1, 2012; Andrew Nikiforuk, *Tar Sands: Dirty Oil and the Future of the Continent* (Vancouver: Greystone, 2010); *Who Benefits? An Investigation of Foreign Investment in the Tar Sands* (briefing paper prepared for Forest Ethics, 2012); Michael Burt, Todd Crawford, and Alan Arcand, *Fuel for Thought: The Economic Benefits of Oil Sands Investment for Canada's Regions* (report prepared for the Conference Board of Canada, October 2012).

6   Geneviève Normand, "Budget de l'Alberta 2015," Radio-Canada, March 26, 2015.

7   Bruce Campbell, *The Petro-Path Not Taken: Comparing Norway with Canada and Alberta's Management of Petroleum Wealth* (report prepared for the CCPA, January 2013), 12.

8   *Alberta Exports in 2011*, document from Alberta International and Intergovernmental Relations website, 2011.

9   "Facts and Statistics," Alberta Energy website, 2014.

10   *Consolidated Financial Statements of the Government of Alberta*, 2011–2012 annual report, 2012.

11   Geneviève Normand, "Budget de l'Alberta 2015," Radio-Canada, March 26, 2015.

12   "Facts and Statistics," Alberta Department of Energy website, n.d. (circa January 2014).

13   Nikiforuk, *Tar Sands*, chapter 11.

14   Campbell, *The Petro-Path Not Taken*, 5–6, 22, 44; Nikiforuk, *Tar Sands*, 158.

15   Peter Lougheed, "Sounding an Alarm for Alberta," interview, *Policy Options* (September 2006).

16   Campbell, *The Petro-Path Not Taken*, 23.

17   Ibid., 24.

18   Ralph Klein was elected as a member of the legislative assembly under the Getty administration in 1989, when he was assigned the role of minister of the environment, after which he took over the party leader and premier's seats in 1992 and became the majority elected government in the 1993 elections.

19   Robert Mitchell, Brad Anderson, Marty Kaga, and Stephen Eliot, *Alberta's Oil Sands: Update on the Generic Royalty Regime*, Alberta Department of Energy website, October 27–31, 1998.

20   Richard Masson and Bryan Remillard, *Alberta's New Oil Sands Royalty System* (report prepared for Royalty and Tenure Branch, Policy Division, Alberta Department of Energy, May 2, 1996), 5.

21   Campbell, *The Petro-Path Not Taken*, 44–45.

22   Ibid.

23   Ibid.

24   Andrew Nikiforuk, "Alberta – Just Another Petro State? Alberta and the Curse of the Petro-State," Alberta Surface Rights website, April 22, 2011.

25   "Royalty Information Briefing 3: Royalties – History and Description," Alberta Royalty Review Royalty Information Series, Alberta Department of Energy website, 2007.

26   "Stelmach's Royalty Steamroller," *National Post*, n.d. (circa 2007).

27   "Alberta Losing Billions on Energy Royalties: Auditor General," CBC News, October 1, 2007; "Le vérificateur blâme le gouvernement," Radio-Canada, October 1, 2007.

28   PricewaterhouseCoopers, *Oil and Gas Taxation in Canada: Framework for Investment in the Canadian Oil and Gas Sector* (2012), 6.

29 See Alain Deneault and William Sacher, "A Case Study: Quebec Colonial Ltd.," in *Imperial Canada Inc.* (Vancouver: Talonbooks, 2012), 127–77; "Redevances minières : l'Ontario se fait-il avoir?," Radio-Canada, May 11, 2015.

30 "Quebec Colonial Ltd.," in Deneault and Sacher, *Imperial Canada Inc.*

31 Campbell, *The Petro-Path Not Taken*, 6, 28–29; Nikiforuk, *Tar Sands*, 168–69.

32 Daniel Tencer, "Norway's Oil Fund Heads For $1 Trillion; So Where Is Alberta's Pot of Gold?" *Huffington Post*, January 11, 2014.

33 Campbell, *The Petro-Path Not Taken*, 5.

34 Ibid., 31; Michael A. Levi et al., *The Canadian Oil Sands: Energy Security vs. Climate Change*, special report prepared for the Council on Foreign Relations, May 2009.

35 Campbell, *The Petro-Path Not Taken*, 57.

36 "The Conservative government has gutted Environment Canada's staff and regulatory capacity. Its 2012 budget and omnibus legislation – Bills C-38 and C-45 – implemented sweeping measures to accelerate the pace of resources exploitation in the oil sands by dramatically weakening Canada's environmental laws. It cancelled almost 3,000 environmental reviews, including 678 involving fossil fuels and 248 dealing with pipelines. It limited the length of reviews and who is eligible to participate, and gave Cabinet the power to approve projects, overturning decisions of third-party tribunals. Finally, it offloaded responsibility for fisheries and inland waters protection – a clear federal jurisdiction – to the provinces. It has done so without consulting First Nations, and in breach of its constitutional obligations to protect First Nations' fishing and hunting rights" (Campbell, *The Petro-Path Not Taken*, 58).

37 In the post-1995 land rush to secure oil sands leases, many First Nations quickly found their treaty land fenced in by tar sands mining operations. As Ian Urquhart of the University of Alberta writes, "In a very real sense, First Nations were presented with a *fait accompli* by the state – these lands, lands that may have mattered in order to pursue traditional practices, became nothing more than oil sands leases" (Ian Urquhart, *Between the Sands and a Hard Place? Aboriginal Peoples and the Oil Sands*, working paper prepared for Buffett Center for International and Comparative Studies [Working Paper No. 10-005: Energy Series, Department of Political Science, University of Alberta, November 2010], 26, quoted in Michelle Mech, *A Comprehensive Guide to the Alberta Oil Sands: Understanding the Environmental and Human Impacts, Export Implications, and Political, Economic, and Industry Influences* [report prepared for the Green Party, May 2011], 29).

38 Nikiforuk, 2010, 101.

39 Lorne Stockman, with David Turnbull and Stephen Kretzmann, *Petroleum Coke: The Coal Hiding in the Tar Sands* (report prepared for Oil Change International, January 2013).

40 Ibid.

41 Marty Klinkenberg, "Oil Sands Pollution Linked to Higher Cancer Rates in Fort Chipewyan for First Time: Study," *National Post*, July 8, 2014.

42 Émilien Pelletier, "Les risques des produits pétroliers en milieu aquatique," in Ianik Marcil (ed.), *Sortir le Québec du pétrole* (Montreal: Éditions Somme toute, 2015), 158 [our translation].

43 Melina Laboucan-Massimo, "Oil on Lubicon Land: A Photo Essay," YouTube.

44 Kim Cornelissen, "La Norvège : De l'État-providence à l'État-pétrolier ?," in Ianik Marcil (ed.), *Sortir le Québec du pétrole*, 100 [our transation].

45 "Overview of CEPA 1999," Environment Canada website, September 15, 2014.

46 "A Guide to Understanding the Canadian Environmental Protection Act, 1999," Environment Canada website, July 18, 2013.

47 Alain Deneault and Catherine Anne Morin, "Le crime écologique est-il encore un 'crime'? Considérations théoriques autour des lois canadiennes en matière d'environnement" [forthcoming], 2015.

48 "Mens Rea / Actus Reus," Ontario Justice Education Network website, 2011.

49 Ibid.

50 Report of the Commissioner of the Environment and Sustainable Development, Office of the Auditor General of Canada website, December 2011, section 3.64; see also section 3.22.

51 Revised Statutes of Alberta 2000, chapter E-12; Ariane Gagnon-Rocque, La peine en droit de l'environnement canadien : de la sanction dissuasive à une approche centrée sur la réparation de l'atteinte (M.A. thesis, Faculty of Law, Université Laval, 2011), 71.

52 Kelly Cryderman, "The Dispute the Entire Oil Industry Is Watching," Globe and Mail (Toronto), December 14, 2013.

53 Jeff Langlois and Claire Truesdale, "Fort McKay First Nation v. Alberta Energy Regulator: Alberta's Top Court to Rule on Regulator's Jurisdiction to Decide Constitutional Questions," Eco-Bulletin (newsletter of the CBA National Environmental, Energy, and Resources Law Section, Canadian Bar Association).

54 Fort McKay First Nation v. Alberta Energy Regulator, 2013 ABCA 396.

55 Nikiforuk, "Alberta and the Curse of the Petro-State."

56 Alberta Minister of Environment Diana McQueen, as quoted in David Dufresne, Fort McMoney, documentary film (Montreal: National Film Board of Canada, 2014), 52 minutes.

57 Nikiforuk, Tar Sands, 177–78.

58 Ibid.

59 Ibid.

60 Ibid.

61 The three incidents saw over four million litres of oil leaking into the Rainbow Lake watershed, Red Deer River, which provides drinking water for many Albertan communities, and the Elk Lake watershed. All three incidents happened within a few weeks (Mitchell et al., Alberta's Oil Sands: Update on the Generic Royalty Regime).

62 "Alberta Pledges Pipeline Safety Review," CBC News, July 20, 2012.

63 "Documents Reveal Alberta Colludes with Industry in Tar Sands Pipeline Review," National Energy Board News and Information, Canadian Association of Energy and Pipeline Landowners Association website.

64 Ibid.

65 Ibid.

66 Environmental Assessment (Mandatory and Exempted Activities) Regulation, Alberta Regulation 111/1993 as amendment by Alberta Regulation 62/2008.

67 Alberta Chief Electoral Office, "Political Party Annual Financial Statement 2011; Progressive Conservative Association of Alberta," Elections Alberta website.

68 "Oil Companies Donate $600,000 to Alberta's Progressive Conservative Party" (research paper prepared for Public Records Research, University of King's College, Halifax, August 1, 2013).

69 "Big Oil's Relentless Lobby," Polaris Institute website, December 4, 2009.

70 Ian Urquhart, "Petrostate? Our Overdeveloped Sense of Prosperity May Be the Cause of Our Underdeveloped Sense of Democracy," *Alberta Views* 13, no. 8 (October 2010): 26–32.

71 Anthony M. Sayers and David K. Stewart, *Is This the End of the Tory Dynasty? The Wildrose Alliance in Alberta Politics* (research paper prepared for University of Calgary School of Public Policy, May 2011), 18.

72 Ian Urquhart, "Petrostate?"

73 David Dufresne, "Les corbeaux (Trois hivers à Fort McMoney)," in David Dufresne, Nancy Huston, Naomi Klein, Melina Laboucan-Massimo, and Rudy Wiebe, *Brut: La ruée vers l'or noir* (Montreal: Lux Éditeur, 2015) [our translation].

74 "Alberta Votes: Voters Think Alberta Depends Too Much on Oil and Gas," CBC News, April 15, 2015; "Alberta Election 2015 Results: NDP Wave Sweeps across Province in Historic Win," CBC News, May 5, 2015.

75 Campbell, *The Petro-Path Not Taken*, 6, 22–23.

76 Tony Clarke et al., *The Bitumen Cliff* (reported prepared for the CCPA, February 2013), 58. "Moving to tar sands, one of the dirtiest, most carbon-intensive fuels on the planet, is a step in exactly the opposite direction, indicating either that governments don't understand the situation or that they just don't give a damn" (David Biello, "How Much Will Tar Sands Oil Add to Global Warming? To constrain climate change, such conventional oil use needs to be stopped, according to scientists," *Scientific American*, January 23, 2013, quoted in Mel Hurtig, *The Arrogant Autocrat: Stephen Harper's Takeover of Canada* [Vancouver: Mel Hurtig Publishing, 2015], 27).

ONTARIO

1 Thierry Michel, *Katanga Business*, documentary film (Brussels: Les Films de la Passerelle, Les Films d'Ici, and RTBF, 2009), 120 minutes [our translation].

2 Canada's relation to the international mining industry is discussed at length in Alain Deneault and William Sacher, *Imperial Canada Inc.* (Vancouver: Talonbooks, 2012).

3 "A Capital Opportunity – Mining," TSX website, 2012. This document is no longer available online, and the TSX has also withdrawn more recent versions.

4 Deneault and Sacher, *Imperial Canada Inc.*; Alain Deneault, Delphine Abadie, and William Sacher, *Noir Canada. Pillage, corruption, et criminalité en Afrique* (Montreal: Écosociété, 2008); Alain Deneault and William Sacher, *Paradis sous terre. Comment le Canada est devenu la plaque tournante de l'industrie minière mondiale* (Montreal and Paris: Écosociété and Rue de l'Échiquier, 2012); Alain Deneault and William Sacher, "L'industrie minière reine du Canada. La Bourse de Toronto séduit les sociétés de prospection et d'extraction," *Le Monde diplomatique* (Paris), September 2013.

5 *Building the Canadian Advantage: A Corporate Social Responsibility (CSR) Strategy for the Canadian International Extractive Sector* (policy paper prepared for Foreign Affairs, Trade, and Development Canada, March 2009).

6 Lou Schizas, "Buying This Junior Miner's Stock Is Speculating, Not Investing," *Globe and Mail* (Toronto), January 12, 2015.

7 Deneault and Sacher, *Imperial Canada Inc.*, 87–125; Alain Deneault and William Sacher, "Prolégomènes," *Paradis sous terre*, 29–53 (Écosociété) and 33–61 (Rue de l'Échiquier).

8 Christopher Armstrong, *Moose Pastures and Mergers: The Ontario Securities Commission and the Regulation of Share Markets in Canada, 1940–1980* (Toronto: University of Toronto Press, 2001), chapter 6.

9 Deneault and Sacher, *Imperial Canada Inc.*, 118 and 122.

10 Peter Koven, "UraMin Assets a Nearly $2 Billion Drag on Areva," *Financial Post* (Toronto), December 12, 2011.

11 The Dodge, Jackson, and Flaherty comments are from Bruce Livesey, *Thieves of Bay Street* (Toronto: Vintage Canada, 2012), 226.

12 "Ontario Teachers' Pension Plan Boss Rails Against Handling of White-Collar Crime," CBC News, September 11, 2007; "Les crimes financiers sont ignorés au Canada. Claude Lamoureux estime que ce type de délit est traité avec légèreté," *Le Devoir* (Montreal), September 12, 2007.

13 William J. McNally and Brian F. Smith, "Do Insiders Play by the Rules?," *Canadian Public Policies – Analyses de politiques* 29, no. 2 (2003): 129, 137.

14 François Desjardins, "Régler sans avouer : La CVMO devra être prudente dans l'application de sa nouvelle politique, dit Fair Canada," *Le Devoir* (Montreal), October 25, 2011.

15 Livesey, *Thieves of Bay Street*, 233.

16 In a March 2014 interview on CBC's *The Sunday Edition*, Dennis Howlett, executive director of Canadians for Tax Fairness, stated that according to *Bloomberg*, few multinationals pay even that low rate. Of the TSX 60 – the top 60 companies trading on the TSX – only four paid 25 percent tax or more between 2007 and 2011 (*Huffington Post*, March 15, 2014).

17 "Kinross Gold and Katanga Mining: Part of the Pillage of the Democratic Republic of Congo?," Mining Watch (Ottawa), April 8, 2006.

18 Christophe Lutundula (chair), *Commission spéciale chargée de l'examen de la validité des conventions à caractère économique et financier conclues pendant les guerres de 1996–97 et de 1998* (report for Parliament of the Democratic Republic of Congo, Kinshasa, made available on the Internet in 2006), section identified within the document as "page 150," *Congoonline.com*.

19 Amnesty International, *Democratic Republic of Congo: Arming the East* (London: AI Index: AFR 62/006/2005, July 5, 2005), 41.

20 Gilles Labarthe with François-Xavier Verschave, *L'Or africain: Pillage, trafics, et commerce international* (Marseille: Agone, 2007), 56. See also *Golden Profits on Ghana's Expense* (Copenhagen: DanWatch and Concord Danmark, May 2010), 9, *ida.dk* (Copenhagen).

21 Christophe Lutundula (chair). *Commission spéciale chargée de l'examen de la validité des conventions à caractère économique et financier conclues pendant les guerres de 1996–97 et de 1998*, 122.

22 Raymond W. Baker, *Capitalism's Achilles Heel: Dirty Money and How to Renew the Free-Market System* (Hoboken, NJ: Wiley, 2005), 165, 172.

23 Ibid., 252.

24 "How Big Is the Problem, and What Is Its Nature?" (report for Globalisation for the Common Good Initiative [Oxford], August 8, 2012, based on data from the Tax Justice Network [London]). See also "The top Tax Havens in the world – USA is #1" (graphic presentation published in *National Geographic*, May 2010, reproduced in *DemocraticUnderground.com*). Also of interest: *Stolen Asset Recovery (StAR) Initiative: Challenges, Opportunities, and Action Plan* (New York: United Nations Office on Drugs and Crime and Washington, World Bank, June 2007).

25 Oxfam International, "Tax Haven Crackdown Could Deliver $120bn a Year to Fight Poverty," news release, March 13, 2009.

26 OECD, Working Group on Bribery, "Canada" in 2011 annual report, 52–54; OECD, Working Group on Bribery, *Phase 3 Report on Implementing the OECD Anti-Bribery Convention in Canada*, March 2011, 9; Julian Sher, "OECD Slams Canada's Lack of Prosecution of Bribery Offences," *Globe and Mail* (Toronto), March 28, 2011.

27 OECD, Working Group on Bribery, *Phase 3 Report on Implementing the OECD Anti-Bribery Convention in Canada*, 9.

28 United Nations, *Report of the Panel of Experts on the Illegal Exploitation of Natural Resources and Other Forms of Wealth of the Democratic Republic of the Congo*, S/2001/357, Annex I, April 12, 2001; *Final Report of the Panel of Experts on the Illegal Exploitation of Natural Resources and Other Forms of Wealth of the Democratic Republic of the Congo*, S/2002/1146, Annex III, October 16, 2002.

29 *Final Report of the Panel of Experts on the Illegal Exploitation of Natural Resources and Other Forms of Wealth of the Democratic Republic of the Congo*, 31.

30 *Building the Canadian Advantage* (Foreign Affairs, Trade, and Development Canada).

31 See Canadian Securities Administrators' Continuous Disclosure Obligations, National Instrument 51-102, quoted in Claire Woodside, *Lifting the Veil: Exploring the Transparency of Canadian Companies* (Ottawa: Publish What You Pay – Canada, 2009), 14.

32 Oxford Pro Bono Publico, "Obstacles to Justice and Redress for Victims of Corporate Human Rights Abuse" (comparative submission prepared for Professor John Ruggie, UN Secretary-General's Special Representative on Business and Human Rights, November 3, 2008).

33 Bertrand Marotte, "Guatemalan Mine Claims Against HudBay Can Be Tried in Canada, Judge Says," *Globe and Mail* (Toronto), July 23, 2013; "Choc v. Hud-Bay Minerals Inc. & Caal v. HudBay Minerals Inc.: Lawsuits against Canadian Company HudBay Minerals Inc. over Human Rights Abuse in Guatemala," *chocversushudbay.com* (Toronto); Drew Hasselback, "Canadian Mining Companies Face Lawsuits over Foreign Activities," *Financial Post*, December 10, 2014.

34 World Bank, "Commodity Annex," *Global Economic Prospects*, January 2012, 6.

35 Stephen Kerr and Kelly Holloway, "Bulyanhulu: Special Investigative Report. The Men Who Moil for Gold," *The Varsity* (Toronto) and *The Atkinsonian* (Toronto), April 15, 2002. See also Deneault and Sacher, *Imperial Canada Inc.*, 70–77; Deneault and Sacher, *Paradis sous terre*, chapter 6.

36 Colin Freeze and Stephanie Nolen, "Charges That Canada Spied on Brazil Unveil CSEC's Inner Workings," *Globe and Mail* (Toronto), October 7, 2013.

37 Finance and Taxation Issue Group, *Final Report* (Whitehorse Mining Initiative, October 1994), 1 [emphasis in the original].

38 "A Capital Opportunity – Mining," TSX website.

39 For more on this topic see Alain Deneault, *"Gouvernance": le management totalitaire* (Montreal: Lux, 2013).

40 Finance and Taxation Issue Group, *Final Report*, iii.

41 "Whitehorse Mining Initiative," Natural Resources Canada website, November 16, 2013.

42 Ibid.

43 Forest Peoples Programme, Philippine Indigenous Peoples Links, and World Rainforest Movement, *Undermining the Forests. The Need to Control Transnational*

Mining Companies: A Canadian Case Study (Moreton-in-Marsh, UK: Forest Peoples Programme, January 2000), 18.

44   *The Northern Miner* (Toronto), September 26, 1994, quoted in ibid., 18 and 88n136.

45   Testimony to House of Commons Standing Committee on Environment and Sustainable Development, Parliament of Canada, 35th Parliament, 1st Session, November 28, 1995.

46   "Whitehorse Mining Initiative."

47   Testimony to House of Commons Standing Committee on Environment and Sustainable Development, Parliament of Canada, 35th Parliament, 1st Session, November 28, 1995.

48   "Flow-Through Shares," CRA website, April 28, 2008; House of Commons Standing Committee on Environment and Sustainable Development, Parliament of Canada, 35th Parliament, 1st Session, November 28, 1995.

49   Under this system, an investor who buys $50,000 worth of shares in a Canadian mining company can deduct the full amount from his or her annual taxable income, as well as an extra 15 percent of this amount at the federal level (15 percent × $50,000 = $7,500) and another percentage at the provincial level (for example, in Saskatchewan, 10 percent: 10 percent × $50,000 = $5,000). In the example, the investor can deduct a total of $62,500, for a $50,000 investment.

50   David Ndubuzor, Katelyn Johnson, and Jan Pavel, "Using Flow-Through Shares to Stimulate Innovation Companies in Canada" (project presented to Greater Saskatoon Chamber of Commerce, December 2009), 13.

51   Guy Taillefer, "Barrick Gold – Liste noire," *Le Devoir* (Montreal), February 5, 2009; Jean-François Barbe, "Desjardins bénéficie de la popularité des fonds de fonds et de l'ISR," *Finance et investissement*, September 5, 2013.

52   For an example of companies in the energy sector making use of trusts in this way, see Keith Schaefer, "Energy Income Trusts: A Comeback in the Making," *Oil and Gas Investment Bulletin*, 2011.

53   In Canada, uranium mines have been operating for decades in Saskatchewan, Ontario, and the Northwest Territories (Alain Deneault and William Sacher, *Imperial Canada Inc.: Legal Haven of Choice for the World's Mining Industries* [Vancouver: Talonbooks, 2012], 170–77).

▨ CANADA

1   Sylvain Fleury, *Abusive Tax Planning: The Problem and the Canadian Context*, publication no. 2010-22-E (Ottawa: International Affairs, Trade and Finance Division, Parliamentary Information and Research Service, Library of Parliament, 2010), 1.

2   "International Tax Avoidance and 'Tax Havens,'" Department of Finance Canada website, news release backgrounder, May 14, 2007.

3   Sylvain Fleury, *Abusive Tax Planning*, 8.

4   "International Tax Avoidance and 'Tax Havens.'"

5   Ibid.

6   CRA, Planning and Annual Reporting Division Corporate Planning, Governance and Measurement Directorate, *Annual Report to Parliament 2007–2008*, 19.

7   Sylvain Fleury, *Abusive Tax Planning*, 1.

8 James Rajotte, *Tax Evasion and the Use of Tax Havens* (report for House of Commons Standing Committee on Finance, Parliament of Canada, 41st Parliament, First Session, May 2013).

9 Rejecting the committee's official conclusions, opposition parties appended their own analysis ("Supplementary Opinion of the New Democratic Party" and "Supplementary Opinion of the Liberal Party of Canada," in Rajotte, *Tax Evasion and the Use of Tax Havens*, 43–51).

10 In response to a question from Senator Downe, in Rajotte, *Tax Evasion and the Use of Tax Havens*, 48.

11 Statistics Canada, "Foreign Direct Investment, 2012," *The Daily*, May 9, 2013; Canadians for Tax Fairness, "Canadian Money in Tax Havens at an All-Time High," news release, May 10, 2013.

12 Alain Deneault made this argument when he appeared before the committee in June 2013 (House of Commons Standing Committee on Finance, Evidence, Parliament of Canada, June 17, 2013).

13 Rajotte, *Tax Evasion and the Use of Tax Havens*, 43–44.

14 Ibid., 32.

15 $15 million was added to the CRA's operating budget to improve the analysis of international electronic fund transfers of $10,000 or more, and another $15 million (already included in the CRA budget) was to be reallocated to provide "new audit and compliance resources dedicated exclusively to international compliance issues and revenue collection" (CRA, "Harper Government Announces New Measures to Crack Down on International Tax Evasion and Aggressive Tax Avoidance," news release, May 8, 2013).

16 Marco Fortier, "Paradis fiscaux: Ottawa défend son offensive," *Le Devoir* (Montreal), April 6, 2013; Denis-Martin Chabot, "Évasion fiscale: Ottawa ferme son centre montréalais de divulgation volontaire," Radio-Canada, April 5, 2013.

17 Countries were ranked as follows in 2014, from most to least competitive in terms of taxes: (1) Canada, (2) United Kingdom, (3) Mexico, (4) Netherlands, (5) United States, (6) Australia, (7) Germany, (8) Japan, (9) Italy, (10) France (KPMG, *Competitive Alternatives 2014. Special Report: Focus on Tax*, 2014).

18 The *Total Tax Index* (TTI) combines national and local taxes; it includes corporate income tax, property taxes, capital taxes, sales taxes, other municipal and provincial corporate taxes, and statutory labour costs.

19 PricewaterhouseCoopers with the World Bank, *Paying Taxes 2015: The Canadian Summary* (PricewaterhouseCoopers, 2014).

20 Claude-André Mayrand, "Laval intéresse les Chinois: un centre de commerce mondial et un 'Chinatown' de luxe dans l'ancien ciné-parc," *Le Journal de Montréal*, November 27, 2013.

21 Jeff Gray, "Inside the Takeover of Tim Hortons," *Globe and Mail* (Toronto), August 27, 2015; Gérald Fillion, "Un trio avec une baisse de taxes SVP!," Radio-Canada, August 25, 2014; "Burger King et Tim Hortons fusionnent pour créer un géant," Radio-Canada and Reuters, August 26, 2014. In December 2014, the Canadian government approved 3G Capital's purchase of Tim Hortons for $12.5 billion, and the subsequent merger of Burger King with Tim Hortons into a restaurant chain renamed in the deal as Restaurant Brands International ("Tim Hortons Confirms Layoffs at Headquarters, Regional Offices," CBC News, January 27, 2015).

22 Éric Yvan Lemay and Jean-François Cloutier, "Paradis fiscal à Laval," *Le Journal de Montréal*, August 27, 2014.

23 Ibid.

24 "Valeant Expects $200 million in Savings in 2012," *Globe and Mail* (Toronto), January 6, 2012.

25 Lemay and Cloutier, "Paradis fiscal à Laval."

26 PricewaterhouseCoopers with the World Bank, *Paying Taxes 2015: Overall Ranking and Data Tables* (Washington, DC: PricewaterhouseCoopers, 2014).

27 Ibid.

28 "Société Offshore au Canada," *France-Offshore.fr* (Paris), 2012 [our translation]; "Ouvrir un compte bancaire au Canada," *Company-Creation.com* [our translation]. (Note: This website no longer exists.) France Offshore was a somewhat unsavoury outfit that helped clients set up offshore companies; in 2012, it was charged with conspiring to conceal tax fraud and placed under court supervision ("Un patron d'un site offshore en examen," *Le Figaro* (Paris), December 19, 2012).

29 "Canada," *France-Offshore.fr* [our translation]. (As noted above, this website no longer exists.)

30 *Wealthy individuals* are not simply the 1 percent of the Canadian population that has an annual income of more than $250,000. The term refers to those whose wealth is derived from capital gains, returns on investment, or stock options, as well as speculation involving the stock market, real estate, currency, etc. When someone's income is not subject to payroll deductions, as is the case for wage earners, it is much easier for that person to practise tax avoidance.

31 Frédéric Rogenmoser, Martine Lauzon, and Léo-Paul Lauzon, *Le réel taux d'imposition de grandes entreprises canadiennes : du mythe à la réalité. Analyse socio-économique de 2009 à 2011 des plus grandes entreprises* (report for Laboratoire d'études socio-économiques, UQAM, October 2012), 8–10.

32 According to statements reported by QMI Agency in "Ces riches qui ne paient toujours pas d'impôts," *Canoë.ca* (Montreal), February 11, 2011 [our translation].

33 "Budget 2006: Focusing on Priorities," Department of Finance Canada website, 2006.

34 Securitization of debt is a strategy that involves fragmenting debts, then reselling them on financial markets. Among other things, it frees the lender from any risk that loans will not be reimbursed.

35 Kathleen Penny, "Canadian Securitization Update – Capital Tax Elimination – Implications for Cross-Border Securitization" (Toronto: Blake, Cassels & Graydon LLP, 2006), posted on *docstoc.com*.

36 Gordon Isfelt, "Canadian Corporate Cash Hoard Rises to $630 Billion in First Quarter," *Financial Post* (Toronto), June 19, 2014.

37 Éric Pineault, "Baisse d'impôt aux entreprises. Une baisse d'impôt pour des milliards qui dorment," *Le Devoir* (Montreal), April 14, 2011 [our translation].

38 Jim Stanford, "The Failure of Corporate Tax Cuts to Stimulate Business Investment Spending," in Richard Swift (ed.), *The Great Revenue Robbery: How to Stop the Tax Cut Scam and Save Canada* (Toronto: Between the Lines, 2013), 67.

39 Léo-Paul Lauzon, *Le recel des gains de capitaux* (report for Chaire d'études socio-économiques, UQAM, 2011), 7.

40 Ibid., 8 [our translation].

41 Marc-André Séguin, "Shell Companies: Blinders On," *National* (Canadian Bar Association, Ottawa), June 2013.

42 Jason C. Sharman, Michael Findley, and Daniel Nielson, *Global Shell Games: Experiments in Transnational Relations* (Cambridge: Cambridge UP, 2013).

43 Timothy Sawa, "Tax Evasion: Sophisticated Scam Revealed by CBC Hidden Camera," CBC News, September 30, 2013; "Évasion fiscale : les pratiques douteuses de professionnels canadiens," based on a story by Marie-Maude Denis and Timothy Sawa, Radio-Canada, October 2, 2013.

44 Heather Gardiner, "SCC to Hear Lawyers' Privilege Argument over Money Laundering Law," *Canadian Lawyer* (Toronto), October 10, 2013.

45 Chantal Cutajar et al., *L'avocat face au blanchiment d'argent* (Paris: Éditions Francis Lefebvre, 2013).

46 *Canada's Tax and Duty Advantages: Enjoy the Benefits of Foreign Trade Zones… Anywhere in Canada!* (Ottawa: Transport Canada, 2009).

47 Ibid., 1.

48 "Canada," *France-Offshore.fr* [our translation].

49 Ulysse Bergeron and Jean-François Nadeau, "Au Canada, une industrie comme chez elle," *Le Monde diplomatique* (Paris), December 2013.

50 Brigitte Alepin, *Ces riches qui ne paient pas d'impôts* (Montreal: Éditions du Méridien, 2004), 207.

51 Léo-Paul Lauzon, *44 milliards de dollars d'impôts reportés par vingt entreprises canadiennes en 2005* (report for Chaire d'études socio-économiques, UQAM, 2008), 8 [our translation].

52 Ibid., 4 [our translation].

53 Michel Bernard, Léo-Paul Lauzon, and Martin Poirier, *La désinvolture des gouvernements face à l'évitement des impôts par les compagnies* (report for the Département des sciences comptables, UQAM, 1995).

54 In the 1990s, a craze for new Internet companies such as Yahoo and AltaVista led to the equivalent of a gold rush on the stock market. The dot-com firms raked in speculators' investments, and the price of their shares rose to dizzying heights. These shares provided investors with rates of return that were impressive, or, to be absolutely accurate, incredible. As with any bubble, when it burst, the shares took a spectacular nosedive. Investors who withdrew from the dot-coms were looking for other investments that would be equally profitable, and income trusts appeared as a solution.

55 Peter Beck and Simon Romano, *Canadian Income Funds: Your Complete Guide to Income Trusts, Royalty Trusts, and Real Estate Investment Trusts* (Mississauga, ON: Wiley Canada, 2004), 6.

56 "Flaherty Imposes New Tax on Income Trusts," CBC News, October 31, 2006.

57 "Corporation Tax Rates," CRA website, March 3, 2014.

58 Keith Schaefer, "Energy Income Trusts: A Comeback in the Making," *Oil and Gas Investment Bulletin* (North Vancouver, BC), 2011.

59 Ibid., 2.

60 The 2010 Flaherty budget eliminated "the need for tax reporting under section 116 of the Income Tax Act for many investments by narrowing the definition of taxable Canadian property" (Department of Finance Canada, "Minister of Finance Deposits the *Jobs and Economic Growth Act*," news release, March 29, 2010).

61 Brigitte Alepin, presentation to the House of Commons Standing Committee on Finance, Parliament of Canada, February 1, 2011.

62   A limited liability company incorporated in Switzerland can issue bearer shares. These differ from ordinary shares in that the name of the real owner of the shares is not found in any official registry; thus, he or she remains anonymous. The shares are given to the investor in the form of a proof of purchase, of which he or she becomes the bearer. The company functioning under this system may then appoint a president who becomes the only public face of an otherwise completely anonymous entity.

63   According to François Lavoie of Statistics Canada, "an investor who owns at least 10% of the voting equity of a company is in a direct investment relationship" (Lavoie, "Canadian Direct Investment in 'Offshore Financial Centres,'" *Analysis in Brief*, catalogue no. 11-621-MIE2005021 [Ottawa: Statistics Canada, 2005]).

64   Ibid., 1.

65   Ibid., 3.

66   Carole Graveline, "L'évasion fiscale canadienne augmente," Radio-Canada, October 15, 2009.

67   François Lavoie, "Canadian Direct Investment in 'Offshore Financial Centres,'" 2.

68   Statistics Canada, "Foreign Direct Investment, 2012"; Canadians for Tax Fairness, "Canadian Money in Tax Havens at an All-Time High."

69   Jean-Pierre Vidal, "La concurrence fiscale favorise-t-elle les planifications fiscales internationales agressives?," in Jean-Luc Rossignol (ed.), *La gouvernance juridique et fiscale des organisations* (Paris: Éditions Tec et Doc – Lavoisier, 2010), 190 [our translation].

70   Walid Hejazi, "Dispelling Canadian Myths about Foreign Direct Investment," IRPP Study, no. 1, January 2010, 17.

71   François Lavoie, "Canadian Direct Investment in 'Offshore Financial Centres,'" 6.

72   Léo-Paul Lauzon and Marc Hasbani, *Les banques canadiennes et l'évasion fiscale dans les paradis fiscaux : 16 milliards de dollars d'impôts éludés* (report for the Chaire d'études socio-économiques, UQAM, 2008).

73   Ibid., 18 [our translation].

74   Ibid., 11 [our translation].

75   Ibid., 5 [our translation].

76   Nicole Reinert and Zach Dubinsky, "How Canada's Banks Help Money Move In and Out of Tax Havens," CBC News, June 25, 2013.

77   See earlier chapters on Barbados and on Turks and Caicos Islands.

78   OECD Global Forum Working Group on Effective Exchange of Information, *Model Agreement on Exchange of Information on Tax Matters* (Paris: OECD, 2002).

79   In the January 2009 federal budget, the government cites the work of the Advisory Panel on Canada's System of International Taxation, which stresses the importance of tax agreements and TIEAs for Canadian fiscal competitiveness. The panel's report asserts that "a dividend from active business income earned by a foreign affiliate is exempt from Canadian tax if the affiliate is resident and carries on its business in a country with which Canada has a tax treaty…Under recently enacted changes for taxation years beginning after 2008, the same treatment applies to dividends from active business income earned by a foreign affiliate in a country with which Canada has a comprehensive Tax Information Exchange Agreement or TIEA" (Advisory Panel on Canada's System of International Taxation, *Final Report: Enhancing Canada's International Tax Advantage* [Department of Finance Canada website, December 2008], 22, section 4.12).

80 Advisory Panel on Canada's System of International Taxation, *Final Report: Enhancing Canada's International Tax Advantage*, 25, section 4.29.

81 Ibid., 28, section 4.41.

82 The panel consisted of the following members: Peter C. Godsoe, former chairman of Scotiabank, corporate director of Barrick Gold, Ingersoll-Rand, Lonmin PLC, Onex Corporation, and Rogers Communications; Kevin J. Dancey, president and CEO of the Canadian Institute of Chartered Accountants; James Barton Love of the Toronto law firm Love & Whalen; Nick Pantaleo, international tax specialist with PricewaterhouseCoopers LLP; Finn Poschmann, director of research at the C.D. Howe Institute; Guy Saint-Pierre, former chairman of the RBC board and former president and CEO of SNC-Lavalin Group; Cathy Williams, former chief financial officer of Shell Canada and member of the board of directors of Enbridge (Advisory Panel on Canada's System of International Taxation, "Appendix D – Biographical Notes," in *Final Report: Enhancing Canada's International Tax Advantage*, 112–15).

83 "Status of Tax Treaty Negotiations: Notices of Tax Treaty Developments," Department of Finance Canada website, 2012.

84 "Tax Information Exchange Agreements: Notices of Developments," Department of Finance Canada website, July 9, 2014.

85 Francis Vailles, "Budget Flaherty : les échappatoires des riches colmatées," *La Presse* (Montreal), April 4, 2013.

86 Brian J. Arnold, "Reforming Canada's International Tax System: Toward Coherence and Simplicity," *Canadian Tax Paper* (Toronto), no. 111 (2009): 14 and 48–61; Donald J. S. Brean, "International Issues in Taxation: The Canadian Perspective," *Canadian Tax Paper* (Toronto), no. 75 (1984): 74.

87 Sylvain Fleury, *Abusive Tax Planning*, 4.

88 Ibid., 4.

89 Ibid., 3.

90 In Quebec, since 2009, a provincial version of the GAAR states that tax evaders will pay back 125 percent of the amount of the tax fraud. However, there is a maximum penalty of $100,000, which is a relatively small amount for private companies and wealthy individuals.

91 André Lareau, "L'amnistie fiscale à la rescousse des tricheurs," *Le Devoir* (Montreal), May 26, 2009 [our translation].

92 "Treaty Shopping – The Problem and Possible Solutions," Department of Finance Canada website, 2013.

93 Dennis Howlett, presentation to the House of Commons Standing Committee on Finance, Parliament of Canada, June 17, 2013.

94 "Lough Erne Declaration," Foreign Affairs, Trade, and Development Canada website, June 18, 2013.

▨ HALIFAX

1 "Population density is 1,100 inhabitants per square kilometre… It is very difficult to obtain right of residence on the basis of employment" (Grégoire Duhamel, *Les paradis fiscaux* [Paris: Éditions Grancher, 2006], 433 [our translation]).

2 "About Us," NSBI website.

3 *More Than Ever*, 2008–2009 annual report, NSBI website, 2009, 2.

4 "Janice Stairs," McInnes Cooper LLP (Halifax) website.

5   "Stairs New Chairwoman of Nova Scotia Business Inc.," *Chronicle Herald* (Halifax), October 5, 2012.

6   "How Payroll Rebates Work," NSBI website.

7   "Venture Capital," NSBI website.

8   "Incentives," NSBI website.

9   "How Payroll Rebates Work," NSBI website.

10   "Programs and Services," NSBI website.

11   "Eligible expenditures [for the Scientific Research and Experimental Development Program] include salaries, consumable goods, external research fees, overhead costs, etc. Some expenditures abroad are also eligible" ("Le crédit d'impôt recherche canadien," *Lettre d'information* [Montreal, F. Iniciativas], no. 35 [July 2009] [our translation]).

12   "Incentives," NSBI website.

13   "Locate Your Business in Nova Scotia," NSBI website.

14   NSBI, "Financial Services Sector in Halifax Adds Due Diligence," news release, March 22, 2010, quoted in *NovaScotia.ca.*

15   Government of Nova Scotia, "Halifax Welcomes International Investment Management Firm Nova Scotia Business Inc.," news release, December 6, 2005, quoted in *NovaScotia.ca.*

16   "West End Capital Management (Bermuda) Ltd., Global Hedge Fund Looking to Hire Fixed Income Analysts and Financial Software Professionals," *CareerAge.com*, August 30, 2005.

17   "Mr. Patrick Boisvert," *Zoominfo.com* (Waltham, MA).

18   "Warren Buffett-Linked Bermuda Firm Taps First Marketer," *InstitutionalInvestorsAlpha.com* (New York), February 13, 2004; Niki Natarajan, "West End Capital Beefs Up Team," *Financial News* (London), October 1, 2001.

19   Ben Stein, "In Class Warfare, Guess Which Class Is Winning," *New York Times*, November 26, 2006.

20   NSBI, "Halifax Welcomes International Investment Management Firm Nova Scotia Business Inc.," news release, December 6, 2005.

21   Ibid.

22   Ibid.

23   *Halifax's Finance and Insurance Industry: Our Opportunity* (Halifax: Shift Central and Greater Halifax Partnership, June 2007), 5; Grant Surridge, "Hedge Funds to Set Up Shop in Halifax," *Financial Post* (Toronto), November 29, 2006, quoted in *CanadianHedgeWatch.com.*

24   NSBI, 2006–2007 annual report, 7.

25   Butterfield Fund, "Butterfield Fund Services to Open in Halifax, Canada," news release, November 16, 2006, quoted in *CanadianHedgeWatch.com.*

26   "Company Overview of Butterfield Fund Services (Bermuda) Ltd.," *Bloomberg.com* (New York). (Note: The Butterfield group changed its name to MUFG Fund Services in September 2013.)

27   Simon Gray, "Hedge Fund Industry Gathers Momentum as Canada Booms," in "Toronto Hedge Fund Services 2007," *Hedgeweek Special Report* (Saint Helier, Jersey), May 2007, 3.

28   Butterfield Fund, "Butterfield Fund Services to Open in Halifax, Canada."

29   Ibid.

30 "Hedge Fund Linked to Olympus Accounting Scandal," *Finalternatives.com* (New York), November 16, 2011.

31 NSBI, "Halifax Welcomes Hedge Fund Administration Company," news release, November 21, 2006, quoted in *NovaScotia.ca*.

32 Tim Kelly and Kevin Gray, "Exclusive: Olympus Accounting Tricks Queried Back in 1990s," Reuters, November 15, 2011.

33 "Hedge Fund Linked to Olympus Accounting Scandal," *Finalternatives.com*. This kind of manoeuvre is not unusual in Bermuda.

34 "Halifax Welcomes Hedge Fund Administration Company," NSBI website.

35 "Nova Scotia Financial Services Sector – Timeline," NSBI website.

36 "Meridian Fund Services," *MeridianFundServices.com* (Hamilton, Bermuda).

37 Ibid.

38 Ibid.

39 Grant Surridge, "Hedge Funds to Set up Shop in Halifax."

40 "Nova Scotia Financial Services Sector – Timeline," NSBI website.

41 "Admiral International Locations," *Admiraladmin.com* (Georgetown, Cayman Islands), May 2012.

42 Bill Power, "Flagstone Sale to Put 90 Out of Work," *Chronicle Herald* (Halifax), November 15, 2012.

43 Tim Bousquet, "Nova Scotia Business, Inc. Drops $800,000 into Intelivote – What Do We Get for Our $2.8 Million Investment in Internet Voting Firm?," *The Coast* (Halifax), July 6, 2012.

44 Grant Surridge, "Hedge Funds to Set Up Shop in Halifax"; Marc Roche, "La controverse sur les impôts des grands groupes oblige Dublin à revoir sa fiscalité," *Le Monde* (Paris), May 25, 2013.

45 "Nova Scotia Financial Services Sector – Timeline," NSBI website.

46 Ibid.

47 Ibid.

48 Peter Moreira, "Halifax, a Centre for International Finance? It's No Fish Tale," *Globe and Mail* (Toronto), November 16, 2006.

49 "Living and Working in Canada," *Hamilton-Recruitment.com* (London).

50 "Incentives," NSBI website.

51 Ibid.

52 Ibid.

53 Ibid.

54 Quoted in Suchita Nayar, "Canadian Managers Strive to Repair Hedge Funds' Reputation," in "Toronto Hedge Fund Services 2007," *Hedgeweek Special Report* (Saint Helier, Jersey), May 2007, 17–18.

55 "CMA Regional Office for Nova Scotia and the Caribbean," Certified Management Accountants of Nova Scotia (Halifax) website.

56 "Welcome, CMA Caribbean," Certified Management Accountants of Nova Scotia, Bermuda, and the Caribbean (Halifax) website; "How to Become a Certified Management Accountant in the Caribbean," University of the West Indies (Kingston) website.

57 "We See Opportunities at Every Stage of Your Career," Certified Management Accountants Regional Office for Nova Scotia, Bermuda, and the Caribbean, September 2012.

58 Diane Francis, "Tax Avoidance Becoming Bigger Than the U.S. Economy," *Financial Post* (Toronto), April 5, 2013.

59 Keith Archibald Forbes, "Bermuda's Connections With and Ties to Canada: Business, Commerce, Culture, Education, History, Military, and More," *Bermuda-online. org* (Pembroke, Bermuda). In 2009, a quarrel among Irving heirs had an impact on the family's offshore structures (Jacques Poitras, *Irving vs. Irving. Canada's Feuding Billionaires and the Stories They Won't Tell* [Toronto: Viking Canada, 2014]). (An excerpt from this book was published in the *Globe and Mail* [Toronto] on November 2, 2014, under the title "The Disintegration of the Irving Family.")

60 Brigitte Unger, Greg Rawlings, Melissa Siegel, Joras Ferwerda, Wouter de Kruijf, Madalina Busuioic, and Kristen Wokke, *The Amounts and the Effects of Money Laundering: Report for the Ministry of Finance* (Netherlands, February 16, 2006). The authors adapted the model developed by criminologist John Walker to analyze money laundering on the basis of factors such as the ratio between the GDP and the number of inhabitants, the degree of opacity of bank secrecy, the size of bank deposits, and the attitude of the government to corruption issues (John Walker, "How Big Is Global Money Laundering?," *Journal of Money Laundering Control* 3, no. 1 (1999): 25–37).

61 Brigitte Unger and Gregory Rawlings, "Competing for Criminal Money," *Global Business and Economics Review* (Cambridge, UK) 10, no. 3 (2008): 349.

62 Thierry Fabre, "La colonie britannique devient un vrai centre financier international. Bermudes : le plus fréquentable des paradis fiscaux," *L'Express* (Paris), November 20, 1997.

63 Marc Roche, *Le capitalisme hors la loi* (Paris: Albin Michel, 2011), 44 and 256.

64 "Assurances en Suisse," *Miralux.ch* (Lugano, Switzerland) [our translation]. See also "Comptes bancaires," *Firstbalticbancorp* (Geneva).

65 The purpose of reinsurance "is to insure insurance companies against losses from their primary holdings, allowing them to write more policies than they have capital in the bank...Companies set up reinsurance companies as a hedge against losses. They are the insurance version of credit default swaps [CDSs], where companies find other companies to buy their risk. You pay a premium to investors who are responsible for your losses. Many companies don't like the idea of paying another company premiums, so they set up their own reinsurance company, and pay themselves a premium to manage risk across their subsidiaries. Unlike CDSs, reinsurance is subject to regulation. Individual states have specific cash reserves limits you're required to hold to sell insurance. Locating your company in Bermuda, you can exceed the insurance limits of your cash reserves because you're not bound by those state laws" ("Understanding Reinsurance in Bermuda's Tax Haven," *24thstate* [Missouri], May 7, 2009).

66 Rod McQueen, *The Moneyspinners: An Intimate Portrait of the Men Who Run Canada's Banks* (Toronto: Macmillan of Canada, 1983), 169.

67 Ibid.

68 Jesse Drucker, "Google Revenues Sheltered in No-Tax Bermuda Soar to $10 Billion," *Bloomberg.com* (New York), December 10, 2012.

69 Ibid.; see also François Desjardins, "Deux milliards d'impôts éludés par Google en 2011," *Le Devoir* (Montreal), December 11, 2012.

70 Jesse Drucker, "Google 2.4% Rate Shows How $60 Billion Lost to Tax Loopholes," *Bloomberg.com* (New York), October 21, 2010.

71 Ibid.

72 "Lexapro's Long, Strange Trip," *BloombergBusinessweek* (New York), May 17–23, 2010; Jesse Drucker, "Forest Laboratories' Globe-Trotting Profits," *Bloomberg-Businessweek* (New York), May 17–23, 2010.

73 Ibid.

74 Jemima Kiss, "Google, Amazon, and Starbucks Face Questions on Tax Avoidance from MPs – Campaigners, MPs, and Taxpayers' Alliance Agree Large Companies Are Exploiting Loopholes in International Tax Regimes," *The Guardian* (London), November 12, 2012.

75 Philippe Dominati (president) and Éric Boquet (rapporteur), *L'évasion fiscale internationale, et si on arrêtait?*, Rapport d'information, Commission d'enquête sur l'évasion des capitaux et des actifs hors de France et ses incidences fiscales, no. 673, 2 vols. (Paris: Sénat, July 2012).

76 Connie Guglielmo, "Apple, Called a U.S. Tax Dodger, Says It's Paid 'Every Single Dollar' of Taxes Owed," *Forbes*, May 21, 2013; "Apple de nouveau montré du doigt pour détournement d'impôts," *Le Monde* (Paris), July 1, 2013.

77 Department of Finance Canada "Minister of Finance Promotes Investment, Trade, and Tax Fairness During Visit to Bermuda," news release, April 11, 2013.

78 "Foreign Direct Investment Positions at Year-End" (Ottawa: Statistics Canada, April 19, 2012).

79 Mario Possamai, *Money on the Run: Canada and How the World's Dirty Profits Are Laundered* (Toronto: Viking, 1992), 132.

80 Diane Francis, *Who Owns Canada Now? Old Money, New Money, and the Future of Canadian Business* (Toronto: HarperCollins, 2008), 362.

81 "Lutte contre l'évasion fiscale: les Bermudes expriment leurs 'réserves,'" *Paradis fiscaux et judiciaires* website, June 13, 2013.

82 Sophie Cousineau, "Le Canada, nouveau paradis bancaire?," *La Presse* (Montreal), June 22, 2010 [our translation].

83 TSX, "TMX Group Makes Investment in the Bermuda Stock Exchange. BSX and TMX Group to Open Trading Today at Toronto Stock Exchange," news release, December 21, 2011.

84 Ibid.

85 Duhamel, *Les paradis fiscaux*, 437 [our translation].

CANADA, THE BAHAMAS, BARBADOS, BELIZE, ST. KITTS AND NEVIS, ETC.

1 ATTAC (France), *Les paradis fiscaux* (Paris: Mille et une nuits, 2000); Global Witness, *All the President's Men* (London and Washington: Global Witness, December 1999); Oxfam GB, *Tax Havens: Releasing the Hidden Billions for Poverty Eradication* (Oxford: Oxfam International, 2000).

2 In French, François-Xavier Verschave, *Noir silence* (Paris: Les Arènes, 2000); Alain Labrousse and Michel Koutouzis, *Géopolitique et géostratégies des drogues* (Paris: Économica, 1996); Denis Robert and Ernest Backes, *Révélation$* (Paris: Les Arènes, 2001). In English, the first edition of R. T. Naylor's *Wages of Crime: Black Markets, Illegal Finance, and the Underworld Economy* was published in 2002 (Montreal:

McGill-Queen's UP [rev. ed. 2004]); Ronen Palan's *The Offshore World* appeared in 2003 (Ithaca, NY: Cornell UP); William Brittain-Catlin's *Offshore: The Dark Side of the Global Economy* was published in 2005 (New York: Farrar, Straus, and Giroux).

3   OECD-CFA, *Towards Global Tax Co-operation* (Paris: OECD, 2000); FATF, *Report on Non-Co-operative Countries and Territories* (Paris: FATF, 2000); FATF, *Review to Identify Non-Co-operative Countries and Territories: Increasing the Worldwide Effectiveness of Money-Laundering Efforts* (Paris: FATF, 2000); FSF, *Financial Stability Forum Releases Grouping of Offshore Financial Centres (OFCs) to Assist in Setting Priorities for Assessment* (Basel: FSF, 2000).

4   OECD-CFA, *Improving Access to Bank Information for Tax Purposes*, 2000.

5   *IMF Board Reviews Issues Surrounding Work on Offshore Financial Centers*, IMF (Washington, DC), July 26, 2000.

6   Thierry Godefroy and Pierre Lascoumes, *Le capitalisme clandestin. L'illusoire régulation des places offshore* (Paris: La Découverte, 2004), 156ff.

7   "FATF Issues New Mechanism to Strengthen Money Laundering and Terrorist Financing Compliance" (FATF Recommendation, February 22, 2013).

8   Alain Deneault, "'The Comedy of the 'Fight Against Tax Havens': Who's Afraid of the Rule of Law," in *Offshore: Tax Havens and the Rule of Global Crime*, tr. from the French by George Holoch (New York: New Press, 2011 [2010]), 106–7.

9   Grégoire Duhamel, *Les paradis fiscaux* (Paris: Éditions Grancher, 2006), 558 [our translation].

10   Warren de Rajewicz, *Guide des nouveaux paradis fiscaux à l'usage des sociétés et des particuliers. Non, les paradis fiscaux ne sont pas morts!* (Lausanne: Favre, 2010), 15.

11   Gilles Favarel-Garrigues, Thierry Godefroy, and Pierre Lascoumes, *Les sentinelles de l'argent sale. Les banques aux prises avec l'antiblanchiment* (Paris: La Découverte, 2009).

12   "Panama Bank Secrecy," *Panama Offshore Worldwide* website [emphasis in the original].

13   In early April 2009, the OECD published a list of tax havens as part of "efforts agreed at the G20 summit to clamp down on non-cooperative tax havens" (BBC News). This document had only four countries on its blacklist (Costa Rica, Malaysia, the Philippines, and Uruguay). A week later, all four were removed from the most stigmatized category as it was claimed they were now willing to comply with international standards (OECD, "A Progress Report on the Jurisdictions Surveyed by the OECD Global Forum in Implementing the Internationally Agreed Tax Standard: Progress Made as at 2 April 2009" [report for OECD, Centre for Tax Policy and Administration, April 2009]; "OECD Removes Tax Havens from List," BBC News, April 7, 2009).

14   Christian Chavagneux and Ronen Palan, *Les paradis fiscaux* (Paris: La Découverte, 2006), 91.

15   Sylvain Besson, *L'argent secret des paradis fiscaux* (Paris: Seuil, 2002), 229 and 250–55.

16   Godefroy and Lascoumes, *Le capitalisme clandestin*, 145; Selçuk Altindag, *La concurrence fiscale dommageable: la coopération des états membres et des autorités communautaires* (Paris: L'Harmattan, 2009), 45; Besson, *L'argent secret des paradis fiscaux*, 251–52. The ITIO includes the following countries: Anguilla, Antigua and Barbuda, the Bahamas, Barbados, Belize, the British Virgin Islands, the Cayman Islands, the Cook Islands, Malaysia, St. Kitts and Nevis, St. Lucia, the Turks and Caicos Islands, and Vanuatu.

17 Christian Chavagneux and Ronen Palan, *Les paradis fiscaux*, 90.

18 Special Purpose Vehicles (SPVs) were invented in the Cayman Islands in the 1990s to enable a company to include anticipated profits in its accounts. Also known as an LP (for Cayman Island Limited Partnership), the SPV "has all the benefits of a Cayman offshore company – tax exemption, secrecy, minimal registration, and filing requirements – but it is quite different in one respect...the LP reduces to a transaction in itself" (Brittain-Catlin, *Offshore*, 64).

19 Godefroy and Lascoumes, *Le capitalisme clandestin*, 145 [our translation].

20 "Barbados Rejects Sarkozy Tax Haven Charge," *Stabroek News* (Georgetown, Guyana), November 14, 2011.

21 *Report on Operations under the Bretton Woods and Related Agreements Act* (report for Department of Finance Canada, April 29, 2008); "Office of the Executive Director – Antigua and Barbuda, The Bahamas, Barbados, Belize, Canada, Dominica, Grenada, Guyana, Ireland, Jamaica, St. Kitts and Nevis, St. Lucia, and St. Vincent and the Grenadines," now "Office of the Executive Director for Canada, Ireland, and the Caribbean – EDS07," World Bank Group (Washington, DC) website. It should be noted that Canada represents Guyana at the World Bank, but not at the IMF.

22 "Samy H. Watson," *StrategyInterface.com*; "Biography of Samy," *Katagogi.com*.

23 "The Canadian Executive Director is supported in his functions by an Alternate Executive Director from one of the Caribbean members of the constituency" ("Caribbean Ambassadors Meet Over Election of World Bank President," *Bahamas Spectator*, April 6, 2012).

24 Lightbourne allegedly was involved in a financial scandal in Nigeria in which individuals lost $1.4 million. In an unlikely affair involving email fraud around a mining project in Ghana, Lightbourne is said to have transferred this amount to a mysterious diplomat known as Mustapha (real name: Igwe Godwin Madu); Lightbourne later claimed to have been defrauded by Mustapha (Tony Udemba, "My 419 Story," *Online Nigeria*, May 11, 2008; "Retrial of Ishmael Light-Bourne vs. Igwe Godwin Madu 419 Scam Case: A Test Case for Government's Foreign Direct Investment Drive," *TheNigerianVoice.com*, January 1, 2012). In another affair, investors in the Bahamas, believing they had been defrauded of $40 to $70 million, took legal action against the M. J. Select Global firm of which Lightbourne was the designated liquidator before Bahamian and U.S. courts (*LegalMetric.com*).

25 Department of Finance Canada, "Minister of Finance Announces Nominations to the International Monetary Fund and the World Bank," news release, August 11, 2006. Canada's representative today at the World Bank is Alister Smith, a former vice-president of the CIBC (Department of Finance Canada, "Minister Flaherty Welcomes Canada's New Executive Director at the World Bank," news release, November 26, 2013), while Serge Dupont plays the same role at the IMF (*Canada at the IMF and World Bank Group 2013–2014* [report for Department of Finance Canada, 2014], 39).

26 "Economic Crisis and Offshore," Tax Justice Network USA website.

27 Ibid.

28 "Identifying Tax Havens and Offshore Finance Centres" (briefing paper prepared for Tax Justice Network [London], July 2007).

29 *Canada at the IMF and World Bank: Report on Operations Under the Bretton Woods and Related Acts 2009* (report for Department of Finance Canada, 2009), 84.

30 Ronald Sanders, "'Tax Haven' Jurisdictions – Sitting Ducks and Scapegoats," *Kaieteur News* (Georgetown, Guyana), March 8, 2009.

31 Nicholas Shaxson, *Treasure Islands: Tax Havens and the Men Who Stole the World* (London: The Bodley Head, 2011), 22–23.

32 "G20 Leaders Statement: The Pittsburgh Summit" (Pittsburgh, September 24–25, 2009), *G20.org*.

33 Gideon Rachman, "Sarkozy, Obama, and Hatoyama: A Study in Contrasts," *Financial Times* (London), blog, September 26, 2009.

34 "The G20 Toronto Summit Declaration" (Toronto, June 26–27, 2010), *G20.org*.

35 "We are committed to protect our public finances and the global financial system from the risks posed by tax havens and non cooperative jurisdictions. The damage caused is particularly important for the least developed countries" ("Cannes G20 Final Declaration" [Cannes, November 3–4, 2011], section 35, *G20.org*.

36 "Lough Erne Declaration," Foreign Affairs, Trade, and Development Canada website, June 18, 2013.

37 In preparing for the summit, the British prime minister, David Cameron, "was meeting continued resistance from his Canadian counterpart, Stephen Harper, over critical plans to require countries to reveal the true beneficial owners of shell companies and trusts. The measure is vital to combatting money laundering, fighting tax evasion, and turning tax information exchange into something meaningful. Cameron laid on the diplomatic red carpet for Harper, giving him the rare honour of speaking to both houses of parliament, a visit to the Queen and a lengthy bilateral meeting at Downing Street. But Harper is worried about exposing private Canadian tax affairs and fears complications arising from Canada's federal structure" (Patrick Wintour, "G8: David Cameron Faces 11th-Hour Battle over Objectives," *The Guardian* [London], June 13, 2013).

38 Duhamel, *Les paradis fiscaux*, 349 [our translation].

39 Clifford Krauss, "Antigua's Leader Vows Cooperation with U.S. in Investigation of Its Banks," *New York Times*, February 23, 2009.

40 Ibid.; Clifford Krauss, Julie Creswell, and Charlie Savage, "Fraud Case Shakes a Billionaire's Caribbean Realm," *New York Times*, February 20, 2009.

41 Drew Hasselback, "Canadian Lawyer Sues U.S. Government over Allen Stanford Ponzi Scheme," *National Post* (Toronto), May 7, 2013.

42 "Offshore Banks in Antigua & Barbuda," *OffshoreBankingIndex.com*; "Antigua and Barbuda Offshore Bank Accounts," *OffshoreIndex.com*.

43 David Santerre, "La nouvelle vie de Jean Lafleur," *Le Journal de Montréal*, September 16, 2008.

44 Brian Myles, "Le trésor convoité de Jean Lafleur. La Couronne demande cinq ans de pénitencier contre le fraudeur," *Le Devoir* (Montreal), June 2, 2007 [our translation].

45 Duhamel, *Les paradis fiscaux*, 418–19.

46 "Belize Offshore Company," Worldwide Incorporation Services website.

47 "Banking," *Ambergriscaye.com* (Ambergris Caye, Belize).

48 Édouard Chambost, *Guide Chambost des paradis fiscaux*, 8th ed. (Lausanne: Favre, 2005 [1980]), 521 [our translation].

49 Quoted in Marie-Christine Dupuis-Danon, *Finance criminelle. Comment le crime organisé blanchit l'argent sale* (Paris: Presses universitaires de France, 2nd ed., 2004 [1998]), 137–38 [our translation].

50 "Banks in Dominica. Offshore Accounts in Dominica," *ICG-Offshore.com.*

51 Chambost, *Guide Chambost des paradis fiscaux*, 556 [our translation].

52 "Is Grenada's Offshore Banking Industry Re-Emerging? Grenada's Offshore Banking Industry Was Rocked by Catastrophic Scandal. Can It Now Rebuild and Re-Emerge?," *ShelterOffshore.com.*

53 "Scotiabank in Grenada," Scotiabank website; "Grenada FirstCaribbean International Bank (Barbados) Ltd.," CIBC FirstCaribbean International Bank website.

54 Andrew Theen, "Four Sentenced in Bank of Grenada Ponzi Scheme," Oregon Public Broadcasting (*OPB.org*), August 27, 2007.

55 "The Michael Creft Testimony," *Grenada Today* (St. George's), October 13, 2007.

56 "Anti-Money Laundering Bill," *Guyana Times* (Georgetown), May 24, 2013.

57 Groundstar Resources (Calgary), "Groundstar Resources Provides Update on the Apoteri K-2 Exploration Well in Guyana," news release, March 7, 2011; "Groundstar Resources Announces Extension to Petroleum Prospecting Licence in Guyana," *OilVoice.com* (Milton Keynes, England), August 24, 2012.

58 "Positioned for Success in the Guyana Atlantic Basin," CGX Energy Inc. website.

59 "Guyana Needs More Prepping for Oil Find – Devine," *Guyana Times* (Georgetown), May 1, 2013.

60 "Locations," Scotiabank (Georgetown) website.

61 Duhamel, *Les paradis fiscaux*, 536 [our translation].

62 Justin M. Rao and David H. Reiley, "The Economics of Spam," *Journal of Economic Perspectives* 26 no. 3 (2012): 87–110.

63 "St. Kitts: Offshore Business Sectors," *LowTax.net* (Kingston upon Thames).

64 *2006 Economic and Social Review* (Ministry of Economic Affairs, Economic Planning, and National Development, Government of St. Lucia, 2006); Pierre Lascoumes and Thierry Godefroy, "Émergence du problème des 'places offshore' et mobilisation internationale" (Mission de recherche Droit et Justice and Commission of the European Communities, 2002); "International Financial Services," Invest Saint-Lucia website.

65 François Taglioni, *Géopolitique des Petites Antilles. Influences européenne et nord-américaine* (Paris: Karthala, 1995).

66 R. O. Orisatoki and O. O. Oguntibeju, "Knowledge and Attitudes of Students at a Caribbean Offshore Medical School Towards Sexually Transmitted Infections and Use of Condoms," *West Indian Medical Journal* 59, no. 2 (2010): 171–76.

67 CIBC has four branches on the island, managed from Barbados (CIBC First-Caribbean International Bank website).

68 RBC was present on the island from 1920 to 1932 before opening offices again in 1980 ("About St. Lucia," RBC Caribbean Banking website).

69 "Contact Us," Scotiabank website.

70 "Les banques de Sainte-Lucie. Comptes à l'étranger à Sainte-Lucie," *ICG-Offshore.com.*

71 "Scandals," *InvestorVoice.ca.*

72 "St. Vincent and the Grenadines: Types of Company," *LowTax.net* (Kingston upon Thames), January 2013.

73 "Activities Relating to the Acquisition, Disposal, Licence, Sub-Licence, and Exploitation Generally of Intellectual Property Rights," *LowTax.net* (Kingston upon Thames).

74 *Canada at the IMF and World Bank Group 2013–2014* (report for Department of Finance Canada, 2014), 39; *Canada at the IMF and World Bank 2007: Report on Operations on the Bretton Woods and Related Agreements Act* (report for Department of Finance Canada, 2008), 54.

75 Patrice Meyzonnier, *Trafics et crimes en Amérique centrale et dans les Caraïbes* (Paris: Presses universitaires de France, 1999), 18.

76 "The Colombian Cartels" (background information for *Frontline* TV documentary), pbs.org (Arlington, VA).

77 Meyzonnier, *Trafics et crimes en Amérique centrale et dans les Caraïbes*, 6 [our translation].

78 Ibid., 84 [our translation].

79 Ibid., 89 [our translation].

80 Ibid., 96 [our translation].

81 Ibid., 98 [our translation].

82 Ibid., 99 [our translation].

83 Ibid., 100 [our translation].

84 Marie-Christine Dupuis-Danon, *Finance criminelle*, 215 [our translation].

85 Greg McArthur, "Bad Dream. The Casinos, the Mob, and the Missing Millions," *Globe and Mail* (Toronto), January 23, 2015.

86 German Gutierrez, *Sociétés sous influence*, documentary (National Film Board of Canada, 1997), 52 minutes 17 seconds.

87 "CARICOM-Canada Free Trade Agreement," Trinidad and Tobago Coalition of Services Industries (Port of Spain); Foreign Affairs, Trade, and Development Canada, "Canada-Caribbean Community (CARICOM) Trade Agreement Negotiations," June 2014.

88 Ramesh Chaitoo and Ann Weston, "Canada and the Caribbean Community: Prospects for an Enhanced Trade Arrangement," *Canadian Foreign Policy Journal* 14, no. 3 (2008): 9.

89 Ibid., 4.

90 "Notes for an Address of the Right Honourable Stephen Harper, Prime Minister of Canada, to the Parliament of Jamaica," Prime Minister's Office (Ottawa), April 20, 2009.

91 Jeff Gray, "U.S. Firm to Launch NAFTA Challenge to Quebec Fracking Ban," *Globe and Mail* (Toronto), November 15, 2012; Council of Canadians, "Lone Pine Resources Files Outrageous NAFTA Lawsuit Against Fracking Ban," news release, October 3, 2013; Ilana Solomon, "No Fracking Way: How Companies Sue Canada to Get More Resources," *Huffington Post*, October 3, 2013.

92 Gary Rivlin, "Gambling Dispute with a Tiny Country Puts U.S. in a Bind," *New York Times*, August 23, 2007.

93 Doug Palmer, "U.S. Warns Antigua Against 'Government-Authorized Piracy,'" Reuters, January 28, 2013. The United States has refused to pay any compensation, despite the fact that on many other occasions it has presented itself as the WTO police force, ready to enforce its decisions (Larry Josephson, "Inside Straight: Gaming Industry News Update," *Covers*, February 14, 2011).

94 Norman Girvan, "The CARICOM-Canada FTA: What's the Hurry?," *Caribbean Political Economy* (blog), March 23, 2009.

95 Chaitoo and Weston, "Canada and the Caribbean Community," 19n.

96   Girvan, "The CARICOM-Canada FTA: What's the Hurry?," 2.

97   "Canada – Trinidad and Tobago Relations," High Commission of Canada in Trinidad and Tobago website.

98   Kyle De Lima, "Can T&T Survive Extreme Extraction?," *EarthWise Limited* (Trinidad), (blog) April 22, 2012, reproduced in *oilsandstruth.org*.

99   "T&T Is a Tax Haven," *Trinidad and Tobago Guardian* (Port of Spain), November 12, 2011.

100 "H. E. Philip Buxo, High Commissioner Remarks at Reception in Honour of Prime Minister's Visit to Canada, April 24, 2013," High Commission for the Republic of Trinidad and Tobago website, April 24, 2013.

101 "High Commission, Ottawa," High Commission for the Republic of Trinidad and Tobago website, April 25, 2013.

102 Afra Raymond, "An Overview of the Uff Report," Real Estate, Property Matters website (*raymondandpierre.com*), April 8, 2010.

103 Ewart S. Williams, "Anti-Money Laundering and Combating the Financing of Terrorism," Governor of the Central Bank of Trinidad and Tobago (paper presented at 6th Annual Compliance Conference on Anti-Money Laundering and Combating the Financing of Terrorism, Port of Spain, January 14, 2010); Asha Javeed, "$1b in Suspicious Transaction Reports," *Trinidad Express* (Port of Spain), April 3, 2012.

104 Al Edwards, "Trinidad & Tobago Plants Its Flag in Corporate Jamaica," *Jamaica Observer* (Kingston), January 15, 2010; "Is Trinidad the Hegemonist of the Caribbean?," *Barbados Underground*, June 18, 2007; "T&T 2006–2010 Exports to Jamaica: $23 Billion," *Trinidad and Tobago Guardian* (Port of Spain), January 12, 2012; John Blackman, "Straight to the Point: Trinidad – Benefiting from CARICOM," *The Barbados Advocate*, January 7, 2012; "Guyana Looking to Trinidad to Help Develop Its Oilfields," *The Gleaner* (Kingston, Jamaica), January 19, 2011.

105 "Scandalous Wheeling and Dealing at CL Financial," *Trinidad and Tobago News* (Port of Spain), September 21, 2011; "CLICO: Trinidad Politicians Before Policy Holders?," *Keltruthblog.com* (Miami, FL), July 8, 2009; Afra Raymond, "CL Financial Bailout," *AfraRaymond.com* (blog), series of texts from 2009 to 2013.

106 "Canada – Trinidad and Tobago Relations," High Commission of Canada in Trinidad and Tobago website.

107 Ron Fanfair, "C'dn Scholarships Open to Caribbean Students," *Sharenews.com*, April 20, 2010.

108 Kejan Haynes, "Canada, T&T Join Forces in Health, Security," *Trinidad Express* (Port of Spain), May 1, 2012; Governor General of Canada, "Governor General Underlines 50 Years of Bilateral Relations with Trinidad and Tobago," news release, May 2, 2012.

109 Ibid.

110 Radhica Sookraj, "Roodal: Govt Can Veto Penal Hospital Contract," *Trinidad and Tobago Guardian* (Port of Spain), July 2, 2013; Radhica Sookraj, "SNC-Lavalin Gets $2.2m to Design Hospital in Penal ... Despite Ten-Year World Bank Ban," *Trinidad and Tobago Guardian* (Port of Spain), July 10, 2013.

111 "Canadians Leave Top Police Posts in Trinidad and Tobago," CBC News, July 31, 2012; Brian Kemp, "Canadian Leads Gang Crackdown in Trinidad and Tobago. Former Edmonton Police Officer Running Country's Police Force in State of Emergency," CBC News, September 20, 2011.

112 Charlotte Ingham, "Crime and Punishment: State of Emergency in Trinidad and Tobago," The Inkerman Group website, November 17, 2011.

113 Robert Weissman, "Playing with Numbers: The IMF's Fraud in Trinidad and Tobago," *The Multinational Monitor* 11, no. 6 (June 1990).

114 "Canada – Trinidad and Tobago Relations," High Commission of Canada in Trinidad and Tobago website.

115 According to the Canadian government, "In the last decade alone, Canada has spent over CAD$1 million to send over 60 officers from Trinidad and Tobago on training," ibid.

116 Ibid.

117 Ibid.

118 The minister responsible for UDeCOTT in 2006, Camille Robinson-Regis, became her country's High Commissioner to Canada a year before the beginning of the commission of inquiry.

119 Afra Raymond, "Learning the Lessons of the UDeCOTT Fiasco: Part 2," *Afra-Raymond.com* (blog), April 22, 2010.

120 Andrew McIntosh and Kinia Adamczyk, "Enquête Genivar: 'Je n'ai rien fait de mal,'" QMI Agency, quoted in *Canoë.ca* (Montreal), September 13, 2012; "Chamber Supports AG," *Trinidad Express* (Port of Spain), May 4, 2012.

121 Afra Raymond, "Property Matters – Spending and Savings," *AfraRaymond.com* (blog), September 29, 2011.

122 Nalinee Seelal, "Sunway Director Is Mrs Hart's Brother," *Trinidad and Tobago Newsday* (Port of Spain), May 8, 2012.

123 Afra Raymond, "End-Notes on the Uff Commission," *AfraRaymond.com* (blog), December 17, 2009.

124 Afra Raymond is a committed Trinidadian citizen and journalist whose illuminating description of the state of corruption prevailing in Trinidad and Tobago and throughout the Caribbean can be heard in "Afra Raymond: Three Myths About Corruption," *TED.com*, February 2013.

125 Afra Raymond, "Learning the Lessons of the UDeCOTT Fiasco: Part 2."

126 "Budget Statement 2011: Turning the Economy Around, Partnering with All Our People, Facing the Issues," Ministry of Finance and the Economy, Government of the Republic of Trinidad and Tobago, 2010.

127 "About Calder Hart," *Calderhart.com*.

128 Afra Raymond, "End-Notes on the Uff Commission."

129 Having benefited from many contracts with UDeCOTT, Genivar eventually sued its former partner for interrupting a number of projects and finally got $20 million through an out-of-court settlement (Derek Achong, "UDeCOTT Must Pay Can $20M," *Trinidad and Tobago Guardian* [Port of Spain], November 30, 2013; Anika Gumbs-Sandiford, "UDeCOTT Quashes Genivar/DCAL Contract," *Trinidad and Tobago Guardian* [Port of Spain], May 6, 2012; Andre Bagoo, "Possible UDeCOTT/Genivar Link," *Trinidad and Tobago Newsday* [Port of Spain], April 8, 2010; Andrew McIntosh and Kinia Adamczyk, "Enquête Genivar: 'Je n'ai rien fait de mal'"; Andre Bagoo, "Genivar Sues UDeCOTT for $122M," *Trinidad and Tobago Newsday* [Port of Spain], December 2, 2012).

130 Another Canadian firm, IBI-MAAK, also developed water treatment projects in Trinidad and Tobago ("What's in a Name?," *Nasty Little Truths* [Port of Spain], May 26, 2008).

131 "AICQ's Leonard Prize Goes to Genivar for Remote Energy Project," April 9, 2009. (Despite the title of this article, the prize awarded to Genivar and UDeCOTT was not the Leonard prize but a prize in the "project and construction management" category for "revitalization of seafront at Port of Spain.") See also "Canadians – Can There Be Any More? (Updated)," *Nasty Little Truths* (Port of Spain), April 9, 2009; Afra Raymond, "Reforming UDeCOTT," Real Estate, Property Matters website (*raymondandpierre.com*), February 24, 2011; "UDeCOTT: Robinson-Regis Pleased with Progress of Waterfront," UDeCOTT Corporate Communications website, June 22, 2007.

132 They were active in the oil sector in the early twentieth century ("The First Oil Well in the World," The Caribbean History Archives, August 18, 2011), and in 1900 in electricity (Christopher Armstrong and H. V. Nelles, *Southern Exposure: Canadian Promoters in Latin America and the Caribbean 1896–1930* [Toronto: University of Toronto Press, 1998]).

133 "Methanex in Trinidad and Tobago," *Methanex.com* (Vancouver), January 4, 2013.

134 "RBTT: Deal or No Deal?," *Trinidad Express* (Port of Spain), March 3, 2008. The Royal Bank had put an end to the chief part of its operations in Trinidad and Tobago in 1988, selling its assets to a Trinidadian bank (Hugues Létourneau and Pablo Heidrich, "Canadian Banks Abroad: Expansion and Exposure to the 2008–2009 Financial Crisis," *North-South Institute* (Ottawa), May 2010, 6).

135 Sean Ng Wai, "Why Do Banks Disappear? A History of Bank Failures and Acquisitions in Trinidad, 1836–1992," *Journal of Business, Finance, and Economics in Emerging Economies* 5, no. 1 (2010).

136 Examples include companies such as Atlas Methanol, Cleghorn & Associates, and EnEco Industries ("Canada – Trinidad and Tobago Relations," High Commission of Canada in Trinidad and Tobago website).

137 Ministry of Natural Resources and the Environment, Government of Guyana, "Large Audience for Guyana Day Forum at the PDAC 2013 in Toronto, Canada," news release, March 4, 2013.

138 Andrew P. Rasiulis, "The Military Training Assistance Program (MTAP): An Instrument of Military Diplomacy," *Canadian Military Journal* (Autumn 2001): 63–64.

139 "Canada – Trinidad and Tobago Joint Statement," Prime Minister's Office (Ottawa), April 25, 2013.

140 Ibid.

141 "Canada – Antigua and Barbuda Relations," Canadian High Commission in Barbados website, July 2013.

142 "Canada – Barbados Relations," Canadian High Commission in Barbados website, January 2012. (Note: The website no longer includes the passage quoted.)

143 Andrew P. Rasiulis, "The Military Training Assistance Program (MTAP)."

144 "Money Laundering and Financial Irregularity," Antigua Investment Authority website, 2008.

145 Yves Engler, *The Black Book on Canadian Foreign Policy* (Black Point, NS, and Vancouver: Fernwood and RED, 2009), 13–16.

146 John Grisham, *The Firm* (New York: Doubleday, 1991), 193, 285, 300.

147 Courtney Tower and C. Alexander Brown, "O, Canada, He Stands on Guard for Thee," *Maclean's* (Toronto), July 1970.

148 Sumiko Ogawa, Joonkyu Park, Diva Singh, and Nita Thacker, "Financial Interconnectedness and Financial Sector Reforms in the Caribbean" (IMF Working Paper, Western Hemisphere Department, July 2013), 5.

149 "Storm Survivors," *The Economist*, February 16, 2013.

150 Hugues Létourneau and Pablo Heidrich, "Canadian Banks Abroad," 15.

151 Except in Cuba when the regime changed (ibid.).

152 Ibid.

153 RBC, 1965 annual report, 21. The Royal Bank in 2013 had 116 branches, 6,000 employees, and 1 million customers in the 19 Caribbean countries in which it operated.

154 "Le MEDAC s'en prend aux filiales des banques dans les paradis fiscaux," *Le Devoir* (Montreal), November 26, 2010; "Paradis fiscaux: quel parti politique mettra fin au scandale?," *L'aut'journal* (Montreal), April 8, 2011.

155 "The Canadian Connection: Providing Banking, Business, and Policemen," *The Economist*, May 27, 2008.

156 "Our History (1990s)," Barbados Light and Power Company website; "Canadian Utility Acquires Stake in St. Lucia Electricity Company," *CaribbeanNetNews.com* (Germany), January 17, 2007; Fortis Turks and Caicos, "Fortis Inc., Through a Wholly Owned Subsidiary, Acquired All of the Outstanding Shares of P.P.C. Limited ('PPC') and Atlantic Equipment and Power (Turks and Caicos) Limited ('Atlantic')," news release, August 28, 2006.

157 Shaxson, *Treasure Islands*, 25–26.

158 Stuart Fieldhouse, "Maples and Calder, the Leading Offshore Law Firm," *Hedgefund Journal* (London), April 2011, 2.

159 Ibid.

160 Ibid.

◼ PANAMA

1 The Canada-Panama Free Trade Agreement and parallel agreements on labour co-operation and the environment were signed on May 14, 2010, and came into force April 1, 2013, "further locking in and expanding access for Canadian investors and their investments," according to Foreign Affairs, Trade, and Development Canada, "Canada-Panama Free Trade Agreement," news release, April 1, 2013.

2 "Panama Banks – Complete List," Panama Forum (discussion forum). According to the Colon Free Trade Zone agency, there are over 120 banks in Panama's International Financial District ("Colon Free Zone: The Colon Free Trade Zone, Panama, Republic of Panama," Colon Free Trade Zone website).

3 "List of Informal Finance Companies in Panama Grows. The Number of Companies or Individuals Raising Money from Investors Without Authorization from the Superintendency of Banks Now Totals 73," *Central America Data* website, January 17, 2013.

4 "Banks, Banks, and More Banks in Obarrio, Panama," *Panama Bank List* website, April 30, 2009.

5 Michel Planque et al., *Panama: L'essentiel d'un marché* (Paris: Éditions UbiFrance, 2010), 39.

6 "The Panamanian government does not have any monopolies in the banking industry (and there is no central bank in Panama), but it does own a 100% interest in certain 'official' banks, such as the Banco Nacional de Panamá and the Caja de Ahorros" (*lexmundi.com*).

7 Swiss Federal Act on Banks and Banking, SR 952, enacted November 8, 1934.

8 Ibid.

9 Édouard Chambost, *Guide Chambost des paradis fiscaux*, 8th ed. (Lausanne: Favre, 2005 [1980]), 359.

10 Ibid. [our translation].

11 Grégoire Duhamel, *Les paradis fiscaux* (Paris: Éditions Grancher, 2006), 523; Ernst and Young, *Worldwide Corporate Tax Guide 2014*, EYG no. DL0917, 1034, *ey.com*.

12 Chambost, *Guide Chambost des paradis fiscaux*, 358 [our translation].

13 Duhamel, *Les paradis fiscaux*, 527 [our translation].

14 "Panama Bank Secrecy," *Panama Offshore* website.

15 "International Banking Centre," *Business Panama* website.

16 Planque et al., *Panama*, 78 [our translation].

17 "The Colon Free Trade Zone," Colon Free Trade Zone website.

18 Duhamel, *Les paradis fiscaux*, 514 [our translation].

19 Ibid., 526 [our translation].

20 Planque et al., *Panama*, 78 [our translation].

21 Ibid., 192 [our translation].

22 Patrice Meyzonnier, *Trafics et crimes en Amérique centrale et dans les Caraïbes* (Paris: Presses universitaires de France, 2000), 56 [our translation].

23 Ibid. [our translation].

24 Alain Delpirou and Eduardo Mackenzie, *Les cartels criminels. Cocaïnes et héroïne : une industrie lourde en Amérique latine* (Paris: Presses universitaires de France, 2000), 112. See also Thierry Cretin, *Mafias du monde. Organisations criminelles transnationales. Actualités et perspectives*, 3rd ed. (Paris: Presses universitaires de France, 2002 [1997]). The author, a former investigating magistrate in France, wrote this book when he was seconded to the European Commission's European Anti-Fraud Office. He also discusses the presence of the Russian mafia in Canada (53–54 and 56), as well as the Jamaican mafia (220). Patrice Meyzonnier emphasizes the presence in Canada of the Guyana mafia (*Trafics et crimes en Amérique centrale et dans les Caraïbes*, 120) and the Sicilian mafia (ibid., 177).

25 Criminal Intelligence Service Canada (CISC), *Report on Organized Crime 2010* (Ottawa: Government of Canada, 2010); Cretin, *Mafias du monde*, 48.

26 Antonio Nicaso, quoted in "Canada Mob Haven – Experts," *Halifax Daily News*, November 9, 1994.

27 "The Colon Free Trade Zone," Colon Free Trade Zone (Houston, TX) website.

28 "Companies Established in the Area," Zona libre de Colón; *Mundo Zona Libre.com*.

29 Planque et al., *Panama*, 81.

30 Ibid., 167.

31 Duhamel, *Les paradis fiscaux*, 525.

32 "Why So Many Shipowners Find Panama's Flag Convenient," BBC News, August 4, 2014.

33 Duhamel, *Les paradis fiscaux*, 525 [our translation].

34 Meyzonnier, *Trafics et crimes en Amérique centrale et dans les Caraïbes*, 58.

35 Ibid., 56 [our translation]. Canada is doubly exposed to Colombian trafficking and money laundering since it also signed a free-trade agreement with Colombia in 2008. This treaty came into force in 2011 (Étienne Roy Grégoire, "Le traité de libre-échange Canada-Colombie et les droits de la personne: les défis de la cohérence

dans la politique étrangère canadienne" [Centre d'études sur l'intégration et la mondialisation, UQAM, June 2009]).

36 Planque et al., *Panama*, 26.

37 Ibid., 81.

38 Ibid., 27, 33–38, 60, 64, and 81.

39 Meyzonnier, *Trafics et crimes en Amérique centrale et dans les Caraïbes*, 57.

40 Planque et al., *Panama*, 81. The figure for 2008 was US$18.6 billion (ibid., 30).

41 Ibid., 33 and 81. Planque's book provides two different figures.

42 Ibid., 33.

43 Ibid., 33 [our translation].

44 Ibid., 41 [our translation].

45 Quoted in Marie-Christine Dupuis-Danon, *Finance criminelle. Comment le crime organisé blanchit l'argent sale*, 2nd ed. (Paris: Presses universitaires de France, 2004 [1998]), 80.

46 Meyzonnier, *Trafics et crimes en Amérique centrale et dans les Caraïbes*, 57 [our translation].

47 Marie-Christine Dupuis-Danon, *Stupéfiants, prix, profits* (Paris: Gallimard, 1996), 111 [our translation].

48 Dupuis-Danon, *Finance criminelle*, 77 [our translation].

49 Ibid., 89.

50 Ibid., 202.

51 Jean-Claude Grimal, *Drogue : l'autre mondialisation* (Paris: Gallimard, 2000), 165.

52 Marie-Christine Dupuis-Danon, *Finance criminelle*, 84.

53 Jean-Claude Grimal, *Drogue : l'autre mondialisation*, 168 [our translation].

54 Ibid., 173 [our translation].

55 Marie-Christine Dupuis-Danon, *Finance criminelle*, 122.

56 Ibid., 140.

57 R. T. Naylor, *Hot Money and the Politics of Debt* (Montreal: McGill-Queen's UP, 2004 [1987]), 194.

58 Jean-Claude Grimal, *Drogue : l'autre mondialisation*, 186.

59 Ibid. [our translation].

60 Jean de Maillard, "La criminalité financière. Face noire de la mondialisation," in Dominique Plihon (ed.), *Les désordres de la finance. Crises boursières, corruption, mondialisation* (Paris: Encyclopædia Universalis, 2004), 186.

61 A case of money laundering in the real estate sector in Panama, involving the city of Laval, Quebec, was covered in the media (Andrew McIntosh and Annie-Laure Favereaux, "Une revente très payante. Une société enregistrée au Panama fait 190 000 $ en une journée sur des lots de la ville," *Le Journal de Montréal*, January 15, 2013).

62 Bill C-24, An Act to Implement the Free Trade Agreement between Canada and the Republic of Panama, Statutes of Canada 2012, chapter 26, section 7.

63 Dupuis-Danon, *Stupéfiants, prix, profits*, 112 [our translation]. Alain Delpirou and Eduardo Mackenzie make a similar point (*Les cartels criminels*, 149).

64 Dupuis-Danon, *Stupéfiants, prix, profits*, 56 [our translation].

65 Delpirou and Mackenzie, *Les cartels criminels*, 148 [our translation].

66 Ibid. [our translation].

67 Planque et al., *Panama*, 42 [our translation].

68 Grimal, *Drogue : l'autre mondialisation*, 10–11 [our translation].

69 Planque et al., *Panama*, 43.

70 Jamie Kneen, "Alert to Investors Re: Petaquilla Minerals and the Molejón Gold Mine in Panama," Mining Watch (Ottawa), news release, November 28, 2008.

71 Proceedings of the House of Commons Standing Committee on International Trade, Evidence, Parliament of Canada, 40th Parliament, 3rd Session, November 17, 2010.

72 Proceedings of the Standing Senate Committee on Foreign Affairs and International Trade, Evidence, meeting of December 6, 2012.

73 See earlier chapter on Canada, the Bahamas, Barbados, Belize, St. Kitts and Nevis (note 91).

74 Duhamel, *Les paradis fiscaux*, 520 [our translation].

75 Simon Black, "5 Factors to Consider Before Moving to Panama," *Business Insider*, March 13, 2012.

CONCLUSION

1 "Tax Evasion in Quebec: Its Sources and Extent," special issue of *Economic, Fiscal and Budget Studies* (Ministère des Finances du Québec) 1, no. 1 (April 22, 2005).

2 For example, the bibliography of "Tax Evasion in Quebec: Its Sources and Extent," includes the following works: Seymour Berger, "The Unrecorded Economy: Concepts, Approach, and Preliminary Estimates for Canada, 1981," *Canadian Statistical Review* (Ottawa: Statistics Canada, CANSIM Division), 61, no. 4 (April 1986); Don Drummond, Mireille Éthier, Maxime Fougère, Brian Girard, and Jeremy Rudin, "The Underground Economy: Moving the Myth Closer to Reality," *Canadian Business Economics* (Ottawa: Canadian Association for Business Economics, Summer 1994, the authors of which were employed by the Department of Finance Canada); Bernard Fortin, Gaétan Garneau, Guy Lacroix, Thomas Lemieux, and Claude Montmarquette, *L'économie souterraine au Québec. Mythes et réalité* (Quebec City: Presses de l'Université Laval, 1996); Gylliane Gervais, *The Size of the Underground Economy in Canada* (Ottawa: Statistics Canada, June 1994); David E. A. Giles and Lindsay Tedds, "Taxes and the Canadian Underground Economy," *Canadian Tax Paper* (Toronto), no. 106; Rolf Mirus, Roger S. Smith, and Vladimir Karoleff, "Canada's Underground Economy Revisited: Update and Critique," *Canadian Public Policy* 20, no. 3 (1994); Dominique Pinard, *Un regard sur la taille de l'économie souterraine: une méthode d'estimation pour le Québec* (M.A. thesis under the supervision of Bernard Fortin, economics department, Université Laval, 2005); Friedrich Schneider and Dominik H. Enste, "Shadow Economies: Size, Causes, and Consequences," *Journal of Economic Literature* (Pittsburgh), 38, no. 1 (2000); Peter S. Spiro, "Estimating the Underground Economy: A Critical Evaluation of the Monetary Approach," *Canadian Tax Journal* (Toronto) 42, no. 4 (1994).

3 As noted by the authors of *L'économie souterraine au Québec*, a well-researched volume cited by the Quebec ministry, the term "underground economy" is limited both as a concept and in the methods it implies. "There is a great deal of confusion around concepts such as the underground economy, non-market activities, criminal activities and tax fraud," and in fact the first concept, "underground economy," excludes all the others. Unlike tax fraud or misdeeds related to tax avoidance, it is strictly "a component of the market economy" (Fortin et al., *L'économie souterraine au Québec*, 6–7 [our translation]).

4 Ibid., 7.

5 Berger, "The Unrecorded Economy," ix.

6 Gervais, *The Size of the Underground Economy in Canada*, 1.

7 Ibid., 2 [emphasis in the original].

8 Ibid., 4 [emphasis in the original].

9 The GDP method involves an attempt to estimate the size of the unrecorded economy by measuring the gap between market transactions recorded as part of the GDP and those that should have been recorded but went unobserved. The gap appears, initially, as a discrepancy between data from various sources that ought to support each other: for instance, revenue generated in the production sector, the sum of amounts involved in the sales sector, and the gross value of production in each sector of activity. The method also requires consideration of transactions that cannot be recorded because they are related to illegal activities such as smuggling, drug trafficking, or prostitution. Gylliane Gervais's concern is to determine whether amounts missing from GDP estimates because of one form of bias may not be indirectly recorded in some other way through subsequent transactions involving the same funds. Money laundering, for example, is the incorporation into the real economy, on a false basis, of the proceeds of transactions that had not previously been recorded because they were part of the shadow economy; these proceeds do ultimately appear in GDP data (Gervais, *The Size of the Underground Economy in Canada*, 4–5).

10 Ibid., 2. The author also notes that transactions such as inheritances, real estate transactions, and interest on loans between individuals are left out of GDP calculations.

11 Ibid., 40.

12 Ibid., 3.

13 Ibid., 11.

14 "The focus of the System of National Accounts is economic production. This is why, with respect to measurement, the primary concern is with underground production rather than with untaxed transactions." This approach necessarily emphasizes domestic market transactions and related issues such as the avoidance of consumer taxes by merchants (Gervais, *The Size of the Underground Economy in Canada*, 1 and 4; Mirus et al., "Canada's Underground Economy Revisited," 237).

15 Gervais, *The Size of the Underground Economy in Canada*, 4. Friedrich Schneider and Dominik H. Enste also mention the gap between tax evasion and the shadow economy ("Shadow Economies: Size, Causes, and Consequences," 79).

16 David E. A. Giles and Lindsay Tedds deplore the fact that the GDP data approach omits several variables such as capital gains and inheritances, not to mention criminal production, which Statistics Canada would be likely to underestimate (Giles and Tedds, "Taxes and the Canadian Underground Economy," 92). Peter Spiro finds it unfortunate that Statistics Canada, unlike the United States IRS, does not use scientific random-sampling methods to gain a better understanding of non-compliant taxpayers. According to him, the agency's methodology does not make it possible to identify an upper limit for the underground economy. The problem remains so ill-understood that "there is a risk of seriously understating the problem of tax evasion" (Spiro, "Estimating the Underground Economy," 1073–75).

17 Social profiling leads to surprising statements from the authorities: the president of Quebec's revenue agency, for instance, when he commented that "taxpayers must be educated," was referring essentially to people with low incomes (Patrice Bergeron, "Le Québec n'est pas la Grèce, mais...," *Le Devoir* (Montreal), April 17, 2012 [our translation]).

18 According to formulas often repeated in treatises on the underground economy, tax authorities' number one enemies are "small contractors and independent artisans" or "small retail shops and restaurants." Seymour Berger, one of the authorities quoted by the Quebec ministry, states that the unrecorded economy can be detected only to the extent that those participating in it can be detected (Berger, "The Unrecorded Economy," vi and xv). This type of argument is also used by Gylliane Gervais in *The Size of the Underground Economy in Canada*, 41, for example.

19 Giles and Tedds, "Taxes and the Canadian Underground Economy," 36. According to Gylliane Gervais, "there is a very strong presumption that most corporations, certainly the large ones, are not involved in underground activity" (*The Size of the Underground Economy in Canada*, 42).

20 Giles and Tedds, "Taxes and the Canadian Underground Economy," 36.

21 Gervais, *The Size of the Underground Economy in Canada*, 41.

22 In Fortin et al., *L'économie souterraine au Québec*, 18, it is acknowledged that companies are able wrongfully to conceal profits, but this fact is then simply excluded from the object under study. The authors explicitly state that their survey method of assessment ignores the avoidance tactics used by corporations: "The unreported profits of companies should also be included: this is a component that is not very well measured by a household survey." In a note, it is suggested that the exclusion of large corporations is actually part of the basic hypothesis: "Following the hypothesis that the underground economy is non-existent in the financial sector and in large corporations, the value of underground production would then be the sum of unreported wages and the unreported profits of small businesses" (ibid., 18n [our translation]).

23 Gervais, *The Size of the Underground Economy in Canada*, 19.

24 Ibid., 20.

25 Ibid.

26 "Tax Evasion in Quebec: Its Sources and Extent," 3.

27 Ibid.

28 Alberta economists Rolf Mirus, Roger S. Smith, and Vladimir Karoleff, also quoted by the Quebec ministry, confirm the importance of extraterritorial investments as criteria to assess tax evasion. (They base this claim on a report published by the IMF.) "Additionally, integration of the global economy created opportunities for underground economy activities, as data collection struggles to keep up with international financial flows. The IMF, for example, found that '... reported portfolio investment income is the fastest growing, and now the largest, of all individual discrepancies'. In other words, interest and dividends reported by companies as paid abroad are much larger than the amount reported as income by the recipients." In 1991, the amounts involved in these transfers were already thought to reach $90 billion worldwide. It is implicitly understood that the beneficiaries who are concealing these dividends from tax authorities are not only individuals; they also include investors that may easily be recognized as "corporate bodies," for example, banks or institutional investors. The authors' conclusion also focuses on international issues: "There is a growing need for greater international co-operation in tax enforcement. Canadians derive increasing amounts of investment incomes from foreign holdings, yet Revenue Canada cannot keep track of the investments held by Canadians in the U.S. or other countries." We are faced here with a sudden shift in vocabulary. No longer are we dealing with petty crooks; we are now talking about "foreign holdings" that handle "investment incomes" belonging

to Canadians. And these are Canadians about whom, at this point, we don't dare say anything more. The authors have no more to offer than this evasive stance (Mirus et al., "Canada's Underground Economy Revisited," 237 and 248). (The IMF document quoted in Mirus et al. is *Report on the World Current Account Discrepancy*, IMF [Washington, DC], September 1987.)

29 Ministère des Finances du Québec, "Fighting Aggressive Tax Planning," *Information Bulletin*, no. 5 (October 15, 2009); Ministère des Finances du Québec, "Aggressive Tax Planning: Easing Related to Certain Confidentiality Undertakings," *Information Bulletin*, no. 4 (February 26, 2010).

30 Ministère des Finances du Québec, *Aggressive Tax Planning: Working Paper* (January 30, 2009), 3.

31 Ibid., 9.

32 Ibid.

33 Ibid., 7.

34 Even today, only 50 percent of capital gains are taxed. According to Léo-Paul Lauzon, in 2003, this explained why "executives receive over 60 percent of their annual earnings in the form of shares: tax evasion, pure and simple" (Léo-Paul Lauzon, "Le scandale des gains de capitaux," *Comptes et contes*, July 2003 [our translation]).

35 Ministère des Finances du Québec, *Aggressive Tax Planning: Working Paper*, 21.

36 "Section F – The Fight Against Tax Evasion," in *Budget Plan, Budget 2013–2014* (Québec : Ministère de l'Économie et des Finances, 2013), F-5.

37 Jocelyne Richer, "La lutte contre l'évasion fiscale progresse à petits pas," *Le Devoir* (Montreal), March 7, 2012.

38 Jean-Luc Lavallée, "3,5 G$ de plus dans les coffres," *Le Journal de Montréal*, September 6, 2013.

39 Ministère des Finances du Québec, *Aggressive Tax Planning: Working Paper*, 6.

40 Department of Finance Canada, "Canada's New Government Strengthens the Income Tax System," news release, November 9, 2006; "Flaherty Imposes New Tax on Income Trusts," CBC News, October 31, 2006.

41 Revenu Québec, "Évasion fiscale – Revenu Québec lance le deuxième volet de sa campagne de sensibilisation sur la lutte contre l'évasion fiscale," news release, March 29, 2013; Alain Deneault, "Que penser de la campagne publicitaire de l'Agence du revenu du Québec contre les paradis fiscaux?," Tax Justice Network (Montreal), interview, October 13, 2013.

42 Jean-François Cloutier, "Six familles ciblées par le fisc," *Le Journal de Montréal*, September 24, 2013; Andrew McIntosh and Adamczyk Kinia, "Enquête sur un client douteux," *Le Journal de Montréal*, January 4, 2011.

43 Cloutier, "Un premier Québécois rattrapé par le fisc," *Le Journal de Montréal*, October 4, 2013.

44 Mirus et al., "Canada's Underground Economy Revisited: Update and Critique," 247.

45 Ibid.

46 Friedrich Schneider and Dominik H. Enste, "Shadow Economies: Size, Causes, and Consequences," 77.

47 Ibid.

48 Ibid., 86ff.

49 Ibid., 78.

50 Ibid., 91.

51 Drummond et al., "The Underground Economy: Moving the Myth Closer to Reality," 7.

52 Ministère des Finances du Québec, *The Underground Economy: Unreported Work and Tax Evasion* (Sainte-Foy: Publications du Québec, 1996). This document cites a number of studies already used in the ministry's 2005 publication, "Tax Evasion in Quebec: Its Sources and Extent."

53 Ministère des Finances du Québec, *The Underground Economy: Unreported Work and Tax Evasion*, 17–22.

54 Ibid., iv.

55 Ibid., 28–29.

56 Ibid., 1.

57 Ibid., 23–24.

58 Ibid., 24.

59 Ibid., 23.

60 Ibid., 24.

61 Ibid., 25; see also v.

62 Ibid., 25.

63 We may legitimately ask whether officials demonstrating these mental restrictions are not, in fact, under the sway of wrongful influences. They are certainly not incorruptible, and corruption is known to exist at the Canada Revenue Agency. As mentionned below, in the early 2010s, the CRA carried out an internal investigation focusing on civil servants who had been bribed to drop, or at least soft-pedal, inquiries into specific cases of tax fraud. In thinking about this issue, we need to avoid conspiracy theories that are too simplistic, yet we must also avoid the irresponsibility of ignoring them completely.

64 Brigitte Alepin, *Ces riches qui ne paient pas d'impôts. Des faits vécus impliquant des gens du milieu des affaires, de la politique, du spectacle, des sociétés publiques et même des Églises* (Montreal: Éditions du Méridien, 2004).

65 Alepin's book was presumably too heretical in tone and content to be included in an official bibliography. However, no other unorthodox thinker is even mentioned in passing in the ministry's 2005 document, not even the internationally known criminologist R. T. Naylor, who teaches at McGill University (R. T. Naylor, *Wages of Crime: Black Markets, Illegal Finance, and the Underworld Economy* [Montreal: McGill-Queen's UP, 2004 (2002)]).

66 Brigitte Alepin, *Ces riches qui ne paient pas d'impôts*, 30.

67 Ibid., 38.

68 Ibid., 65.

69 Ibid., 152.

70 In 2012, for instance, "Montreal printing giant Transcontinental sent a legal warning to a UQAM professor of accounting, Léo-Paul Lauzon, who in a blog entry on the *Journal de Montréal* website questioned a tax regulation" (Lauzon's article was critical of a tax strategy that allows businesses to reduce their tax payments by declaring the losses of a subsidiary). "Transcontinental also asked Québec solidaire MNA Amir Khadir to withdraw comments made during a news briefing earlier this week" (Jean-François Cloutier, "Amir Khadir et le prof Lauzon visés par Transcontinental," *Canal Argent, Canoë.ca* [Montreal], May 18, 2012 [our translation]).

71 Naylor, *Wages of Crime*.

72 Published in English as Alain Deneault, *Paul Martin & Companies: Sixty Theses on the Alegal Nature of Tax Havens* (Vancouver: Talonbooks, 2006 [2004]).

73 "Revenu Canada: corruption de fonctionnaires?," QMI Agency, *Canoë.ca* (Montreal), November 4, 2011; Daniel Leblanc, "RCMP Widens Canada Revenue Agency Probe After New Allegations," *Globe and Mail* (Toronto), November 3, 2011; Daniel Leblanc and Sean Gordon, "Canada Revenue Agency Workers Accused of Helping Firms Avoid Taxes," *Globe and Mail* (Toronto), August 12, 2010.

74 "Enquête administrative sur neuf employés," Radio-Canada, December 10, 2010; "L'Agence du revenu du Canada suspend quatre fonctionnaires," Radio-Canada, April 8, 2009; Daniel Leblanc, "Canada Revenue Agency Fires Six, Suspends Three in Montreal Office," *Globe and Mail* (Toronto), December 10, 2010; "Canada Revenue Agency Employees Arrested in Corruption Probe," CBC News, April 8, 2009.

75 "Infiltration mafieuse à 'L'Agence du revenu du Canada?," based on an investigation by Alain Gravel, Radio-Canada, September 26, 2013; Daniel Leblanc, "CRA Says It 'Incorrectly' Issued $382,000 Cheque to Mafia Boss," *Globe and Mail* (Toronto), September 26, 2013. The CRA eventually concluded that "there was no fraud, collusion or corruption on the part of its employees in the issuing of a refund cheque" (Daniel Leblanc, "Six-Figure Tax Refund to Mafia Boss Was Done in Error, CRA Investigation Finds," *Globe and Mail* [Toronto], December 13, 2013).

76 Brian Myles, "Allégations de corruption à l'Agence du revenu du Canada : BT Céramique a fait des travaux à la résidence du vérificateur Nick Iammarrone," *Le Devoir* (Montreal), April 28, 2011; Daniel Leblanc, "New Links Found Between Tax Auditors and Montreal's Construction Industry," *Globe and Mail* (Toronto), September 20, 2011.

77 Daniel Leblanc, "Three Former Tax-Agency Workers Charged in Alleged Bribery Schemes," *Globe and Mail* (Toronto), May 1, 2012.

78 Canadian Press, "CRA Says 44 Tax Cheats Convicted in Canada since 2006," *Financial Post* (Toronto), May 10, 2013.

79 Caroline Touzin, "Revenu Québec renvoie Benoît Roberge," *La Presse* (Montreal), October 10, 2013; Ingrid Peritz and Tu Thanh Ha, "Former Montreal Police Officer Arrested in Connection with Leaks to Hells Angels," *Globe and Mail* (Toronto), October 7, 2013.

80 André Dubuc, "Un ex-policier devient directeur des enquêtes à Revenu Québec," *La Presse* (Montreal), October 12, 2011.

81 "M. Florent Gagné, président du conseil d'administration," Agence du revenu du Québec, June 8, 2011.

82 Caroline d'Astous, "De vives tensions chez Revenu Québec, dénonce le syndicat des employés," *Huffington Post*, September 13, 2012.

83 Caroline d'Astous, "Après les bonis, des compressions de postes chez Revenu Québec," *Huffington Post*, September 24, 2012.

84 Léo-Paul Lauzon, "Les banques donnent le ton et mènent le bal," *L'aut'journal* (Montreal), December 2010 – January 2011 [our translation].

85 Ibid.

86 As noted earlier in the chapter on Canada as a tax haven, the panel consists of corporate executives, tax lawyers, and tax accountants (note 82).

87 Francis Vailles, "Paradis fiscaux: Ottawa abandonne une bataille," *La Presse* (Montreal), February 5, 2009; Brian J. Arnold, "Critique of the Report of the Advisory Panel on Canada's International Tax System," *IBFD – Bulletin for International Taxation* 63, no. 9 (August 2009): 348–56, quoted in Mary Arnaud, *Canada v.*

Recours aux paradis fiscaux/bancaires: dans quelle mesure la politique de lutte du Canada peut-elle être améliorée (M.A. thesis, Law Faculty, Université Laval, Quebec, 2011), 66–67.

88   R. T. Naylor, *Hot Money and the Politics of Debt* (Montreal: McGill-Queen's UP, 2004 [1987]), 304.

89   Bank of Nova Scotia, 1956 annual report, 6.

90   Ministère des Finances du Québec, "Création d'un centre d'expertise dans la lutte contre la criminalité financière: une importante avancée, selon le ministre Alain Paquet," news release, March 23, 2012.

91   Université de Sherbrooke, "L'Université de Sherbrooke crée un centre d'expertise en lutte contre la criminalité financière," news release, March 22, 2012.

92   Thierry Godefroy and Pierre Lascoumes, *Le capitalisme clandestin: l'illusoire régulation des places offshore* (Paris: La Découverte, 2004), 64n19.

93   François-Xavier Verschave, *L'envers de la dette. Criminalité politique et économique au Congo-Brazza et en Angola* (Marseille: Agone, 2001).

94   *La lettre du continent*, Africa Intelligence, September 15, 1994, November 10, 1994, May 6, 1995, and July 11, 1996, quoted in François-Xavier Verschave, *L'envers de la dette.*

95   Godefroy and Lascoumes, *Le capitalisme clandestin*, 64n19.

96   Alan Block, *Masters of Paradise: Organized Crime and the Internal Revenue Service in The Bahamas* (New Brunswick, NJ: Transaction, 1991), 176.

97   Ibid., 13, 166, and 173.

98   Ibid., 175.

99   Ibid., 176. In 1977, the Castle Bank shut down its Cayman and Bahamas operations to find an even safer haven in Panama (Naylor, *Hot Money*, 315).

100 Block, *Masters of Paradise*, 287.

101 Ibid., 289.

102 Ibid.

103 Jim Drinkhall, "IRS vs. CIA: Big Tax Investigation Was Quietly Scuttled by Intelligence Agency," *Wall Street Journal*, April 18, 1980, quoted in Peter Dale Scott, "Deep Events and the CIA's Global Drug Connection," Global Research (Montreal), September 6, 2008. See also Naylor, *Hot Money*, 315.

104 "Charles Sirois cautionne l'utilisation de filiales étrangères," TVA Nouvelles (Montreal), May 28, 2012.

105 Université de Sherbrooke, "L'Université de Sherbrooke crée un Centre d'expertise en lutte contre la criminalité financière" [our translation].

106 "Quatrième colloque annuel de la prévention de la fraude," March 23, 2012, Faculty of Administration, Université de Sherbrooke. This event illustrates the incestuous relationships that prevail in today's universities in the name of the "knowledge economy." It was a peculiar type of colloquium chiefly attended by its sponsors: two professors from the Université de Sherbrooke's program on financial crime and official representatives of Quebec's financial regulatory agency (Autorité des marches financiers), the Canadian Institute of Chartered Accountants, the Quebec order of chartered accountants (Ordre des comptables agrees du Québec), and the Quebec Construction Commission (Commission de la construction du Québec). In other words, it was an academic colloquium without academics. Participants self-indulgently took their turn at the podium to laud their institution and show their website. There was no question period. The goal of the event was not research

but marketing: it was an opportunity for program managers to attract the target clientele for their newly created "graduate degree in fighting financial crime." The day-long "annual colloquium" also provided a political platform as the minister of finance, Alain Paquet, inaugurated the event with a public announcement that the Quebec Ministry of Finance would provide $350,000 to fund the Université de Sherbrooke's new Centre of Expertise in Fighting Financial Crime. This took place in the middle of a student strike designed to challenge the university's loss of bearings – of which the colloquium was a perfect illustration.

107 *Analys6.com* (Bromont, QC).

108 Montreal criminologist R. T. Naylor also says that offshore financial flows often come back to their starting point; however, this does not lead him to conceal the many problematic ways in which the money may also be mobilized in tax havens (Naylor, *Wages of Crime*, 192–95).

109 Éric Pineault, "Baisse d'impôt aux entreprises: une baisse d'impôt pour des milliards qui dorment?," *Le Devoir* (Montreal), April 14, 2011.

110 Gordon Isfelt, "Canadian Corporate Cash Hoard Rises to $630 Billion in First Quarter," *Financial Post* (Toronto), June 19, 2014.

111 Professor Abda made these comments during an exchange with us at a workshop on tax havens ("Paradis fiscaux: une injustice fiscale," Mòntreal, February 18, 2012).

112 Paul Ryan, *Quand le fisc attaque. Acharnement ou nécessité?* (Montréal: Éditions La Presse, 2012).

113 Ibid., 162 and 164 [our translation].

114 Jim Stanford, "The Failure of Corporate Tax Cuts to Stimulate Business Investment Spending," in Richard Swift (ed.), *The Great Revenue Robbery: How to Stop the Tax Cut Scam and Save Canada* (Toronto: Between the Lines, 2013), 72–73.

115 Luc Godbout, Pierre Fortin, and Suzie Saint-Cerny, *La défiscalisation des entreprises au Québec est un mythe. Pour aller au-delà de la croyance populaire* (report for Chaire de recherche en fiscalité et en finances publiques, Université de Sherbrooke, October 5, 2006).

116 Marco Van Hess, *Les riches aussi ont le droit de payer des impôts* (Brussels: Éditions Aden, 2013).

117 Ibid., 119 [our translation].

118 Gérard Bérubé, "Imposer les riches," *Le Devoir* (Montreal), August 30, 2012 [our translation].

119 Léo-Paul Lauzon, "La propagande fiscale patronale expliquée aux nuls," *L'aut'journal* (Montreal), February 25, 2013.

120 "Taxing Times," *Fiscal Monitor*, IMF (Washington, DC), October 2013, quoted in Éric Desrosiers, "Taxez les riches, dit le FMI," *Le Devoir* (Montreal), October 10, 2013.

121 Jean-François Cloutier, "Marceau surpris qu'il soit si facile d'ouvrir un compte offshore," *Le Journal de Montréal*, November 22, 2013.

122 "IBC Belize Benefits," *Canada-Offshore*.

123 Bruce Livesey, *Thieves of Bay Street* (Toronto: Vintage Canada, 2012), 151.

124 "Consultation Paper on Treaty Shopping – The Problem and Possible Solutions," Department of Finance Canada website, 2013.

125 Ibid.

126 All three quotations, ibid.

127 Osler, Hoskin & Harcourt, "Update: Canada Considers a New Anti-Treaty Shopping Rule," August 14, 2013, 1.

128 Patrick McCay, "Treaty Shopping: An Update," McCarthy Tétrault LLP website, August 28, 2009.

129 In the eyes of Waffle members, Canada had been subject to colonial domination by the United States since the end of the Second World War. See their manifesto *For an Independent Socialist Canada*, 1969 (*socialisthistory.ca*).

130 Kari Levitt, *Silent Surrender: The Multinational Corporation in Canada* (Montreal: McGill-Queen's UP, 2002 [1970]).

131 Ibid., 29–32. Kari Levitt's work was well received in Quebec nationalist and pro-independence circles. Translated into French by André d'Allemagne, a major figure in the history of the pro-independence movement, it was published with a preface by Jacques Parizeau. In his preface, the future premier of Quebec took a position different from Levitt's, arguing that the transformation of Canada into a "branch economy" and the country's political fragmentation created an opportunity for Quebec to negotiate directly with American multinationals as to the terms of their presence and investments in Quebec (ibid., xi; Jacques Parizeau, "Preface," in Kari Levitt, *La capitulation tranquille. La mainmise américaine sur le Canada* [Montreal: Réédition-Québec, 1972]).

132 Levitt acted as adviser to the Trinidad and Tobago government again in 1987 when the IMF brought up statistical irregularities and made its aid conditional on their being corrected. She spoke in favour of some of the adjustments required by the IMF (Kari Levitt, *Reclaiming Development: Independent Thought and Caribbean Community* [Kingston: Ian Randle, 2005], xvii).

133 Kari Levitt, *The Great Financialization* (acceptance speech for the John Kenneth Galbraith Prize awarded by the Progressive Economics Forum [Canada], 2008).

134 The models are actually a series of four stages that are supposed to mark the evolution by which Caribbean countries, traditionally exporters of resources and dependent on foreign investments and markets, might take back control of their resources, the goods they produce, and the use of national wealth. The first stage is the "pure plantation economy" based on slavery: under a mercantilist regime, a merchant protected by a monarch carried out overseas trade. In the second stage, exclusivist mercantilist trading systems dissolved and local agricultural protoproduction appeared, along with small-scale crafts and the production of new staples for export (such as cocoa or bananas). There was no definitive break between the first stage and the second, and this facilitated the eventual emergence, in the mid-twentieth century, of the third stage: the "New Mercantilism of transnational corporations." The fourth stage, hoped for by the authors, implied a level of national evolution and sovereignty that would enable the country to exploit its resources not for the profit of foreign companies, but for the benefit of its population (Levitt, "The Plantation Economy Models: My Collaboration with Lloyd Best," in *Reclaiming Development*, 36–39).

135 Levitt, "'Capitalism and Slavery': Institutional Foundations of Caribbean Economy," in *Reclaiming Development*, 9.

136 *For an Independent Socialist Canada*, sections 5 to 11 (*socialisthistory.ca*).

137 Levitt, "The Plantation Economy Models," in *Reclaiming Development*, 41. While never explicitly asserting the resemblances, Levitt has given some indication that her analysis of the Caribbean stems directly from the one she developed for Canada. Thus, an initial collection dealing with the "plantation economy" (actually a preliminary report on a vast research program that she planned to carry out with Lloyd Best) consisted of seven articles of Kari Levitt, which she had written three (ibid., 41). As Levitt herself acknowledged, for this analysis she adapted to the Caribbean the architecture and some of the data of the analysis

she was then developing for Canada. The titles of her three chapters – "The New Mercantilism," "Hinterland Economy," and "The Metropolitan Balance of Payments" – reappear, in almost identical form, in *Silent Surrender*. Levitt was clearly convinced that her analyses of Canada's economic dependency were relevant to anticolonial circles in the Caribbean, since she published in a Caribbean journal, the *New World Quarterly*, the article that was soon to be expanded and published as *Silent Surrender* (Levitt, *Silent Surrender*, xlv).

138 Levitt, "The Plantation Economy Models," 54. According to the staples theory developed by Harold Innis in the 1920s, Canada's economic history is based on the massive export of cheap natural resources or staples (that is, in successive order, fur, timber, grain, and oil), a mode of development that has Canada in a state of dependency on purchasing countries and explains, at least to some degree, its political problems. This specifically Canadian school of economic theory directly influenced the theses that Levitt was to develop fifty years later with regard to multinationals (Levitt, *Silent Surrender*, xlvi).

139 The first chapter of *Silent Surrender* deals with "The Recolonization of Canada" by American multinationals, a term Levitt would later use to describe the same phenomenon in the Caribbean (Levitt, "'Capitalism and Slavery': Institutional Foundations of Caribbean Economy," 7). Radical economists of the 1960s, with Mel Watkins in the forefront, thought that this model could help explain the economic development of other countries such as Australia (Mel Watkins, "Staple Thesis," *The Canadian Encyclopedia*).

140 For Levitt, the fact that Canada is much better off economically than the Caribbean does not invalidate the comparison. On the contrary, as the first beneficiary of American direct investment, Canada is the archetype of an economy subservient to American multinationals (see the quantitative data in the appendix to *Silent Surrender*). In an interview given in 2012, Levitt insists on the persistence of American domination, noting that 50 percent of Canada's manufacturing industry is in the hands of American and foreign corporations ("Interview with Kari Levitt – 'Bring the State Back In!'," *Revue Interventions économiques / Papers in Political Economy*, no. 45 [2012]).

141 Levitt, "'Capitalism and Slavery': Institutional Foundations of Caribbean Economy," 5, 31–32.

142 Levitt deserves credit for having criticized, often in the heat of the moment, the nature and impact of these plans in the Caribbean, especially in Jamaica and Trinidad and Tobago, while supporting the counter-example of a country such as Barbados that had refused IMF aid. She was rapidly able to demonstrate that societies had been "savaged" by the IMF's structural adjustment programs, whose effects included growing inequalities and exclusion, the erosion of social cohesiveness, and greater class tensions (Levitt, "The Origins and Consequences of Jamaica's Debt Crisis, 1970–1990," 132–80; "Debt, Adjustment, and Development: A Perspective on the 1990s," in *Reclaiming Development*; "'Capitalism and Slavery': Institutional Foundations of Caribbean Economy," 26–27, 32 [the word *savaged* is from this last page]).

143 Levitt, "'Capitalism and Slavery': Institutional Foundations of Caribbean Economy," 7.

144 Levitt writes: "The policy mix of de-regulation, privatisation, trade liberalisation, 'flexible' labour markets, and the dismantling of social welfare measures has also been called the 'Washington Consensus'. The term is appropriate because the United States is the epicentre of the diffusion of the 'globalisation' agenda" (ibid., 5).

145 The structural adjustment programs were rooted in the American reversal with regard to debt repayment. This reversal was caused by the oil shocks of the 1970s, themselves triggered by the U.S. decision in the early 1970s to end the convertibility of the dollar to gold (Levitt, "'Capitalism and Slavery': Institutional Foundations of Caribbean Economy," 95–97).

146 Levitt, "Debt, Adjustment, and Development: A Perspective on the 1990s," 183–85.

147 Ibid., 182.

148 Levitt, "The Origins and Consequences of Jamaica's Debt Crisis, 1970–1990," 110.

149 "Interview with Kari Levitt – 'Bring the State Back In!'"

150 Daniel Jay Baum, *The Banks of Canada in the Commonwealth Caribbean: Economic Nationalism and Multinational Enterprises of a Medium Power* (New York: Praeger, 1974).

151 For Levitt, Canadian multinationals in the Caribbean, including those in the mining sector, are small, do not exert any kind of control over the conditions in which natural resources are sold, and remain marginal. As a consequence, they conform to positions taken by large American corporations (Levitt, *Silent Surrender*, 103–4).

152 See, among others, Jean-Pierre Vidal of HEC Montréal, quoted in Stéphane Desjardins, "Des institutions québécoises investissent massivement dans un paradis fiscal," *Québec inc.* (Montreal), May 2005, or Franck Jovanovic of TELUQ (Télé-Université de l'Université du Québec), who prefers to speak with delicacy of "extraterritorial financial centres" related to issues of "development" in poor countries (Professor Jovanovic's CV at *benhur.teluq.uquebec.ca* for his "work in progress" on "Paradis fiscaux, centres financiers extraterritoriaux et développement économique local").

153 See Nicholas Shaxson and John Christensen, *The Finance Curse: How Oversized Financial Centres Attack Democracy and Corrupt Economies* (London: Tax Justice Network, 2013). See also on this topic: Nicolas Ressler, "Le Belize: la 'Grèce des Caraïbes,'" in Alexis Bautzmann, *Atlas géopolitique mondial* (Paris: Éditions Argos, 2013), 124; Olivier Cyran, "Chronique des jours ordinaires à Jersey. La tourmente financière vue d'un paradis fiscal," *Le Monde diplomatique* (Paris), December 2008; Alain Vernay, *Les paradis fiscaux* (Paris: Seuil, 1968), 262–67, 283; Fred Celimène and François Velas, *La Caraïbe et la Martinique* (Paris: Economica, 1990); William Brittain-Catlin, *Offshore: The Dark Side of the Black Economy* (New York: Farrar, Straus, and Giroux, 2005), 19.

154 Quoted in Stéphane Desjardins, "Des institutions québécoises investissent massivement dans un paradis fiscal," *Québec inc.* (Montreal), May 2005 [our translation].

155 Brian J. Arnold, "Reforming Canada's International Tax System: Toward Coherence and Simplicity," *Canadian Tax Paper* (Toronto), no. 111 (2009): 371.

156 Brian J. Arnold, "Unlinking Tax Treaties and the Foreign Affiliate Rules: A Modest Proposal," *Canadian Tax Journal* (Toronto) 50, no. 2 (2002): 607.

157 Brian J. Arnold, "Reforming Canada's International Tax System," 73–74.

158 Ibid., 374. Arnold's conclusion is not entirely convincing, given the federal government's frenzied approach to signing fiscal agreements with tax havens.

159 Ibid., 71.

160 Ibid., 72. Tax lawyer Paul Ryan also wonders why the Quebec government did not imitate the federal government when the latter, in 1998, required taxpayers to declare foreign assets valued at more than $100,000 and established penalties for undeclared income (Ryan, *Quand le fisc attaque*, 177).

161 Donald J. S. Brean, "International Issues in Taxation: The Canadian Perspective," *Canadian Tax Paper* (Toronto), no. 75 (1984): 118.

162 Ibid.

163 Ibid., 111.

164 Ibid.

165 Ibid., 117, 119, and 121.

166 Ibid., 122.

167 Georges Lebel, "La loi Forget inc.," *Relations* (Montreal), no. 739 (March 2010) [our translation].

168 André Lareau, "Réflexions sur la passivité du législateur en matière de fiscalité internationale," *Les Cahiers de droit* 41, no. 3 (September 2000): 614, quoted in Arnaud Mary, *Canada v. Recours aux paradis fiscaux/bancaires*, 115 [our translation].

169 Jean-Pierre Vidal, "La concurrence fiscale favorise-t-elle les planifications fiscales agressives?," in Jean-Luc Rossignol (ed.), *La gouvernance juridique et fiscale des organisations* (Paris: Éditions Tec et Doc – Lavoisier, 2010).

170 Ibid., 172 [our translation].

171 Vidal seems unable, however, to pursue his criticism to its logical end – as if he had to stop for no reason in the middle of a thought to avoid reaching the point where he would be forced to question the ultra-liberal and competitive system that is the root cause of tax havens. "The only logical comment on this situation is that the investments of pension funds in tax havens are scandalous. In practice, this is not perfectly clear." Obviously it's more complicated than that, always more complicated, so complicated that no conclusion can be reached – even if simplistic arguments must be employed to justify this philosophical suspension of judgment. A prime example is the accepted stereotype that poor countries can develop thanks to their tax haven status. "In the struggle to obtain capital, tax resources, and the jobs that come with them, every country has its own formula. Rich countries offer gifts of electricity, income tax credits, five-year municipal tax exemptions, and other benefits. No one sees anything wrong with this. But when poor countries brandish the only advantage they have compared with developed countries – a more generous tax system – suddenly this is immoral…" (quoted in Stéphane Desjardins, "Des institutions québécoises investissent massivement dans un paradis fiscal" [our translation]). This stereotype is entirely unfounded.

172 Gilles Larin and Robert Duong, "Effective Responses to Aggressive Tax Planning: What Canada Can Learn from Other Jurisdictions," *Canadian Tax Paper* (Toronto), no. 112 (2009). However, Larin and Duong do locate desirable policies in a context of short-term competition with other tax regimes throughout the world, particularly the United States.

173 Brigitte Alepin, *Bill Gates, Pay Your Fair Share of Taxes… Like We Do!* (Toronto: Lorimer, 2012 [2011]), 85–123.

174 Stephen Kibsey, vice-president of equity risk management at the Caisse de dépôt et placement du Québec, even claims that tax evasion may be justified if a business "does good things for the community" (Colloque québécois sur l'investissement responsable, Table ronde no 1: Stephen Kibsey, Claude Normandin, Rosalie Vendette, February 19, 2013, 38th to 41st minute [our translation]).

175 Diane Francis, *Who Owns Canada Now? Old Money, New Money, and the Future of Canadian Business* (Toronto: HarperCollins, 2008), 362.

176 Diane Francis, *Controlling Interest: Who Owns Canada?* (Toronto: Macmillan, 1986), 269.

177 Diane Francis, *Who Owns Canada Now?*, 257.

178 Ibid., 326.

179 Ibid., 305.

180 Ibid., 334.

181 Ibid., 349.

182 Ibid., 193.

183 "Switzerland is the most successful country in the world even though it has no natural resources," quoted in ibid., 196.

184 W. Earle McLaughlin, "Address of the Chairman and President," RBC, 1963 annual report, 14.

185 Ibid.

186 Ibid.

187 Ibid.

188 Diane Francis, *Who Owns Canada Now?* 436–37.

189 Diane Francis, *Controlling Interest*, 268–69.

190 Marco Bélair-Cirino, "Le Québec sera encore plus généreux avec les entreprises du multi-média," *Le Devoir* (Montreal), October 1, 2013; Canadian Press, "Lassonde investit 19 millions dans ses installations de Rougemont," *Le Devoir* (Montreal), October 12, 2013; Canadian Press, "Les gens d'affaires entendent (enfin) parler d'économie," *Le Devoir* (Montreal), October 8, 2013.

191 Jean de Maillard, "La criminalité financière. Face noire de la mondialisation," in Dominique Plihon (ed.), *Les désordres de la finance. Crises boursières, corruption, mondialisation* (Paris: Éditions Universalis, 2004), 88 [our translation].

192 François Desjardins, "L'impôt joue-t-il bien son rôle?," *Le Devoir* (Montreal), April 28 and 29, 2012.

193 See the TV documentary by Valentine Oberti and Wandrille Lanos, "Ces milliards de l'évasion fiscale," broadcast on the France 2 network as part of the *Cash Investigation* program, June 11, 2013, as well as Doreen Carjaval and Raphael Minder, "A Whistle-Blower Who Can Name Names of Swiss Bank Account Holders," *New York Times*, August 8, 2013.

194 Mike Esterl, Glenn R. Simpson, and David Crawford, "Stolen Data Spur Tax Probes," *Wall Street Journal*, February 18, 2008, A4; "The Liechtenstein Affair: German Banks Suspected of Helping Clients Evade Taxes," *Spiegel Online International*, February 21, 2008.

195 Benoît Aubin, "Enfin: congé de taxes!," *Le Journal de Montréal*, June 17, 2013.

■ GLOSSARY

Abusive or aggressive tax planning   Euphemism used to describe accounting strategies designed to avoid tax payments through the abusive interpretation of technical terms and provisions included in tax laws.

Accommodating jurisdiction   Generic term for territories and states that knowingly provide a highly permissive environment for corporations and wealthy individuals subject to laws, regulations, or tax rules in other countries. Accommodating jurisdictions include tax havens, banking havens (international financial centres), regulatory havens, free ports, and free zones.

Banking haven   See *International financial centre*

Bank secrecy   A set of laws and regulations adopted by an accommodating jurisdiction to prevent or discourage investigations initiated by foreign powers (tax investigators, investigating magistrates, and so on).

Call loan   Loan that a creditor may call in – or a borrower pay back – at any moment.

Captive bank   Managed directly by the company that owns it in order to finance the parent company and its customers and suppliers.

Captive insurance corporation   Managed directly by the company that owns it in order to cover the risks to which the parent company is exposed.

Chartered bank   Canadian financial institution whose existence is authorized by the federal Department of Finance under the Bank Act, S.C. 1991, c. 46.

Double taxation agreement or tax treaty   Treaty by which two jurisdictions agree to coordinate their tax systems so that a taxpayer who is economically active in both will pay taxes only once on declared earnings.

Eurodollars   American dollars deposited in banks outside the United States (initially in Europe) by someone who is not a resident of the country in which the bank is located.

Exempted company   A company, established by a corporation or capital holder in an accommodating jurisdiction, that is in a position to flout tax laws and laws in general.

Flag of convenience   See *Free port*

Flow-through shares   Special type of common share, issued only in Canada by oil and gas or mineral exploration companies, that allow these companies to provide shareholders with tax deductions for expenses that the companies themselves cannot claim.

Foundation   Private non-profit corporation created by a company or an individual, theoretically in order to carry out a project that will benefit many, but often used for other purposes in accommodating jurisdictions.

Free port   Regulatory haven allowing registry of ships (pleasure craft, freighters, oil tankers, and so on), which then acquire a "flag of convenience," as well as offshore drilling rigs, enabling them to function independently of normal regulations regarding ship maintenance, maritime waste disposal, health and safety at work, labour standards, and taxes.

Free zone   Specific area created by a regulatory haven in which factories do not have to comply with labour laws or environmental standards, or are governed by permissive standards and regulations.

Hedge fund   Speculative investment fund, usually registered in an accommodating jurisdiction in order to bypass the financial regulations that prevail elsewhere.

Holding company   Corporation responsible for managing one or several companies in which it owns shares.

International financial centre or *offshore financial centre* or *banking haven*   Traditional jurisdiction that authorizes non-resident financial corporations to register under rules – such as bank secrecy – that are similar to those of tax havens.

Offshorization   The process of moving capital to offshore accounts, or relocating business to a foreign country to take advantage of lower costs or less stringent regulation.

Petro-states   State whose wealth depends on the sale of oil and whose laws are shaped by the desires of the oil industry. The citizens of this state have very little control over the government, since it is controlled by oil companies.

Regulatory haven   Jurisdiction authorizing laissez-faire for a given type of activity.

Reinsurance company   Insures insurance companies and as a result spreads the risk associated with selling insurance and minimizes the danger of one large monetary loss. When these companies are registered offshore, they provide insurance companies with a way of eluding some of the constraints the insurance companies face on their home turf.

Shell company   Company, registered in a tax haven, that serves as an alibi enabling a corporation or capital holder to bypass the laws, regulations, and tax systems of the jurisdictions in which it or he or she operates.

Special Purpose Vehicle   Structure created in an accommodating jurisdiction, often focusing on a single operation and designed to reduce the liabilities on a corporation's balance sheet.

Tax avoidance   An accounting and financial operations strategy designed to reduce the amount of taxes that will be paid, without using illegal means.

Tax evasion   An accounting and financial operations strategy designed to reduce the amount of taxes that will be paid, using illegal means.

Tax haven   Jurisdiction providing bank secrecy and a null or almost null tax rate on earnings declared by certain types of company or entity.

Tax treaty   See *Double taxation agreement*

Transfer pricing   Financial operation by which a subsidiary established in a tax haven charges its parent company for various goods and services, on an imaginary basis, in order to concentrate as much capital as possible in accounts opened where the subsidiary is registered – often a tax haven or an offshore financial centre in which the tax rate is null or almost null.

Trust   Tax avoidance tool, formerly used only by families but now also available to corporations, that makes it possible to isolate profits as an independent stream of earnings and distribute them among beneficiaries. The trustee who manages the trust is responsible for the assets assigned to it by the founder (the trustor) for the benefit of a third party (the beneficiary). All three parties remain anonymous thanks to the bank secrecy that prevails in accommodating jurisdictions.

■ THE RESEARCH TEAM

These researchers and writers, many associated with Réseau pour la justice fiscale, contributed to this book.

AARON BARCANT is studying for a B.A. at Concordia University in the interdisciplinary geography program. For this book, he did research on Trinidad and Tobago and on CARICOM.

CATHERINE BROWNE has a degree in history from the Université de Provence and has taken sociology courses at the M.A. level at Université du Québec à Montréal. She is currently employed as a translator and is also a researcher and tour guide for a non-profit educational organization called Montréal Explorations. She contributed to the chapter on the Dominion of Canada. She also translated this book into English.

PIERRE-ANTOINE CARDINAL holds a law degree (LL.L./J.D.) and a B.A. in social sciences from the University of Ottawa. He is currently working toward a master's in law (LL.M) at McGill University and is doing research in postcolonial theory with a focus on Islam and international law. For this book, he researched the Alberta government's policies in relation to the oil industry.

MATHIEU DENIS has a Ph.D. in history from Humboldt University in Berlin and is the senior science officer at the International Social Science Council. His contribution to this book concerns the history of Canadian institutions in the British Caribbean and the analysis of Canadian intellectuals' uncritical attitude to Canadian involvement in the Caribbean.

NORMAND DOUTRE is a retired union activist in the health care (auxiliary services) sector. He participated in struggles for workers' rights for forty years. For this book, he did documentary research on the role of Canadian politicians, bankers, and lawyers in the development of the Bahamas and the Cayman Islands.

GABRIEL MONETTE has an M.A. in philosophy from the Université du Québec à Montréal and is working toward a Master's in Public Administration at the École nationale d'administration publique. For this book, he did research on hedge funds and the Cayman Islands.

STÉPHANE PLOURDE has a Ph.D. in contemporary history from the Université de la Sorbonne (Paris-I) and is interested in North-South relations. He has written about the structural adjustment program imposed on Côte d'Ivoire by the Bretton Woods institutions. For this book, he did documentary research on the Bahamas.

GHISLAINE RAYMOND holds an M.A. in political science from the Université du Québec à Montréal and is a retired labour activist from a teachers' union. She is the author of Le *"partenariat social": Sommet socio-économique de 1996, syndicats et groupes populaires* (Montreal: Éditions M, 2012). Focusing on the issues of globalization, social justice, and tax havens, she is currently active as a member of Réseau pour la justice fiscale. For this book, she did documentary research on financial institutions in various tax havens in the British Caribbean.

PIERRE ROY, accounting assistant, did research on the Cayman Islands and the Turks and Caicos Islands.

WILLIAM SACHER has a Ph.D. in atmospheric and ocean sciences from McGill University and is currently working toward a Ph.D. in development economics from the Facultad Latinoamericana de Ciencias Sociales. He is the co-author of *Imperial Canada Inc.: Legal Haven of Choice for the World's Mining Industries* (Vancouver: Talonbooks, 2012) and contributed to *Noir Canada: Pillage, corruption et criminalité en Afrique* (Montreal: Écosociété, 2008). In this book, he contributed to the chapter on Ontario and the world mining industry.

ALEXANDRE SHELDON is a filmmaker, researcher, and journalist. He has a master's degree in international political economy from McMaster University and has made several short films dealing with sustainable urban planning and economic and regional issues. He has published articles in *L'Inter*, the *Journal Ensemble*, and the *Quebec Chronicle-Telegraph*. In this book, he participated in research and writing for the chapter on Canada as a tax haven.

ALINE TREMBLAY has done graduate work in cognitive development and personal and organizational psychosynthesis. After a career teaching physical education at the college level, she became an adviser for the Centrale des syndicats du Québec (CSQ), a Quebec labour confederation. Now retired, she has worked to promote fair trade for OXFAM-Québec's Équita and is a co-founder of the Réseau pour la justice fiscale. In this book, among other things, she participated in research and writing for the chapter on Canada as a tax haven.

INDEX

▨ GEOGRAPHICAL LOCATIONS

Burger King 173–74
Butler, Brian 80
Butler, Don 80
Butterfield Fund Services (Bermuda)
  Limited 195–96

Cahan, Charles 29
Calder, Douglas 91
Caledonian 80
Cali (cartel) 238
Camaguey Company 31
Canada Steamship Lines
  (CSL) 108, 124, 133
Canada-Offshore (website) 257
Canadian Advantage 163
Canadian Bank of Commerce.
  See Canadian Imperial Bank
  of Commerce
Canadian Breweries 69
Canadian Club 80
Canadian Commercial
  Corporation 224, 227
Canadian Imperial Bank of Commerce
  (CIBC) 13, 16–17, 19–20, 22, 27, 29,
  35, 63, 70, 80, 86, 99, 102, 111, 187,
  215–17, 226, 228, 251–53
Canadian International Power 229
Canadian Oil Sands Limited 177
Canadian Pacific Railway 21, 177
Capone, Al 55
Carrington, John 167
Castle Bank 85–86, 88, 252–53
Castle Hall Alternatives 194
Cayman Island Stock Exchange (CSX) 101
CDO (Collateralized Debt
  Obligations) 94–95
CDS (Credit Default Swaps) 95
Certified Management Accountants of
  Canada (CMA Canada) 199–200
CGX Energy 217
Chagnon (family foundation) 249
Chamandy, Glenn 72
Chartered Institute of Management
  Accountants (CIMA) 86, 88, 96–97
Chase Manhattan Bank 20
Chesler, Louis Arthur 53
Chiquita 117

CIBC. See Canadian Imperial
  of Commerce
Cinar 71, 249
Citco Group 195
Citicorp 88
Citigroup 117, 203
CLICO 223
Collins, Enos 19
Colonial Bank. See Barclays Bank
Columbus Communications 270
Columbus Trust 57
Cornfeld, Bernie 99
Cott Corporation 177
Credit Suisse 251
Creft, Michael 216
Cuba Company 21–22
Cusson, Georgette 52

Damji, Salim 254
Danzer 117
Davies, Bryn 42–43
Davis, Carlton E. 45
DeGroote, Mike 270
Deloitte 120
Demerara Electric Company 29
Dole 117
Dominion Investment 71
Dominion Stores 69
Double Irish (money transfer) 202
Doucet, Jean 59, 89
Dow Chemical 83
Dunlop, Roy 80
Dutch Sandwich (money transfer) 202
Duvalier (family) 7, 25
Dykstra, John 102

Eagle Energy Trust (EGL.UN) 183
Eisenhauer, Jim 193
Emaxon 161
Emera Inc. 177
Enbridge 177
Enron 98, 201, 254
European Central Bank (BCE) 137
Eustace, Paul 99
ExxonMobil 117

Facebook 117
Fastow, Andrew 201
Field, Anthony 85
First International Bank of Grenada 216
First National City Bank 35

■ PUBLIC DOMAIN

ALAIN DENEAULT is the co-author of *Imperial Canada Inc.: Legal Haven of Choice for the World's Mining Industries* (Talonbooks, 2012), *Offshore: Tax Havens and the Rule of Global Crime* (New Press, 2012), and other books. He teaches critical theory at the University of Montreal, writes a column for the arts and political journal *Liberté*, and is a Tax Justice Network researcher. Deneault's research and writing practices are diverse and often collaborative, focusing on how international financial and legal agreements increasingly foster the interests of "stateless" transnational corporations over those of nation states and the interests of their human communities.

PHOTO: Étienne Boilard